THE CAMBRIDGE COMPANION TO
IRISH MODERNISM

The story of Irish modernism constitutes a remarkable chapter in the movement's history. This volume serves as an incisive and accessible overview of that brilliant period in which Irish artists not only helped create a distinctive national literature but also changed the face of European and Anglophone culture. This *Companion* surveys developments in modernist poetry, drama, fiction, and the visual arts. Early innovators, such as Oscar Wilde, George Bernard Shaw, Jack B. Yeats, and James Joyce, as well as late modernists, including Elizabeth Bowen, Samuel Beckett, Flann O'Brien, Máirtín Ó Cadhain, and Francis Bacon, all appear here. But this volume ranges beyond such iconic figures to open new ground with chapters on Irish women modernists, Irish American modernism, Irish-language modernism, and the critical reception of modernism in Ireland.

Joe Cleary is a Professor of English at the National University of Ireland, Maynooth, and a Visiting Professor of English at Yale University. He is the author of *Literature, Partition and the Nation-State: Culture and Conflict in Ireland, Israel and Palestine* (Cambridge University Press, 2002) and *Outrageous Fortune: Capital and Culture in Modern Ireland* (2007). He has also co-edited (with Claire Connolly) *The Cambridge Companion to Modern Irish Culture* (Cambridge University Press, 2005) and (with Michael de Nie) a special issue of *Éire-Ireland* on empire studies. He has previously served as director of the Notre Dame Irish Seminar in Dublin and was a visiting professor at Notre Dame in 2000. His articles have appeared in *Textual Practice, South Atlantic Quarterly, Boundary 2, Modern Language Quarterly, Field Day Review, Éire-Ireland,* and other journals. He is currently working on books on modernism, empire and world literature and on a study of twentieth-century Irish cultural criticism.

A complete list of books in the series is at the back of this book.

THE CAMBRIDGE
COMPANION TO
IRISH MODERNISM

EDITED BY
JOE CLEARY
National University of Ireland, Maynooth

CAMBRIDGE
UNIVERSITY PRESS

32 Avenue of the Americas, New York, NY 10013-2473, USA

Cambridge University Press is part of the University of Cambridge.

It furthers the University's mission by disseminating knowledge in the pursuit of education, learning, and research at the highest international levels of excellence.

www.cambridge.org
Information on this title: www.cambridge.org/9781107655812

First published 2014

Printed in the United States of America

A catalog record for this publication is available from the British Library.

Library of Congress Cataloging in Publication data
The Cambridge Companion to Irish Modernism / edited by Joe Cleary.
pages cm. – (Cambridge Companions to Literature)
Includes bibliographical references and index.
ISBN 978-1-107-03141-8 (hardback) – ISBN 978-1-107-65581-2 (paperback)
1. Modernism (Literature) – Ireland. 2. English literature – Irish authors – History and criticism. I. Cleary, Joe (Joseph N.) editor of compilation.
PR8755.C36 2014
820.9'11209417–dc23 2014002502

ISBN 978-1-107-03141-8 Hardback
ISBN 978-1-107-65581-2 Paperback

Cambridge University Press has no responsibility for the persistence or accuracy of URLs for external or third-party Internet Web sites referred to in this publication and does not guarantee that any content on such Web sites is, or will remain, accurate or appropriate.

CONTENTS

Notes on Contributors   *page* vii

Acknowledegments   ix

Developments in Irish Modernism – Chronology, 1845–1969   xi

Introduction   I
JOE CLEARY

PART I   FORMATIONS

1. Intellectual and Aesthetic Influences   21
    JEAN-MICHEL RABATÉ

2. European, American, and Imperial Conjunctures   35
    JOE CLEARY

3. The Irish Revival and Modernism   51
    RÓNÁN MCDONALD

4. Style and Idiom   63
    BARRY MCCREA

PART II   GENRES AND FORMS

5. W. B. Yeats and Modernist Poetry   77
    LAURA O'CONNOR

6. James Joyce and the Mutations of the Modernist Novel   95
    EMER NOLAN

7. Modernist Experiments in Irish Theatre   III
    BEN LEVITAS

CONTENTS

8. Visual Modernisms   128
   LUKE GIBBONS

        PART III   CONSTITUENCIES

9. Women and Modernism   147
   ANNE FOGARTY

10. Irish Language Modernisms   161
    LOUIS DE PAOR

11. Irish American Modernisms   174
    JOE CLEARY

   PART IV   DOMESTIC RECEPTIONS, WORLD IMAGINATIONS

12. Critical Receptions of Literary Modernism   195
    ENDA DUFFY

13. Irish Modernist Imaginaries   206
    MICHAEL VALDEZ MOSES

    Further Reading   221
    Index   229

NOTES ON CONTRIBUTORS

JOE CLEARY is Professor of English at the National University of Ireland, Maynooth, and Visiting Professor of English at Yale University. His previous publications include *Literature, Partition and the Nation-State: Culture and Conflict in Ireland, Israel and Palestine* (2002); *The Cambridge Companion to Modern Irish Culture*, co-edited with Claire Connolly (2005); and *Outrageous Fortune: Capital and Culture in Modern Ireland* (2007).

LOUIS DE PAOR is Director of the Centre for Irish Studies at the National University of Ireland, Galway. Previous publications include *Faoin mBlaoisc Bheag Sin: An Aigneolaíocht i Scéalta Mháirtín Uí Chadhain* (1991), *An Paróiste Míorúilteach/ The Miraculous Parish: Rogha Dánta/Selected Poems, Máire Mhac an tSaoi* (editor, 2011), and *Míorúilt an Chleite Chaoin: Rogha Dánta Liam S. Gógan* (editor, 2012).

ENDA DUFFY is Professor of English at the University of California, Santa Barbara. He is the author of *The Subaltern Ulysses* (1994) and *The Speed Handbook: Velocity, Pleasure, Modernism* (2009), which won the Modernist Studies Prize for Best Book in 2010. With Maurizia Boscagli, he is a co-editor of *Joyce, Benjamin and Magical Urbanism* (2010).

ANNE FOGARTY is Professor of James Joyce Studies at University College, Dublin, and founder with Luca Crispi of the *Dublin James Joyce Journal*. She is a co-editor, with Timothy Martin, of *Joyce on the Threshold* (2005); with Morris Beja of *Bloomsday 100: Essays on "Ulysses"* (2009); with Éilís Ní Dhuibhne and Eibhear Walshe of *Imagination in the Classroom: Teaching and Learning Creative Writing in Ireland* (2013); and with Fran O'Rourke of *James Joyce: Multidisciplinary Perspectives* (2014).

LUKE GIBBONS is Professor of Irish Literary and Cultural Studies at the National University of Ireland, Maynooth. His publications include *Cinema and Ireland*, co-authored with Kevin Rockett and John Hill (1988); *Transformations in Irish Culture* (1996); *The Quiet Man* (2002); *Edmund Burke and Ireland: Aesthetics, Politics and the Colonial Sublime* (2003); and *Gaelic Gothic: Race, Colonialism and Irish Culture* (2004).

BEN LEVITAS is Reader in Theatre History at Goldsmiths, University of London. His previous publications include *The Theatre of Nation: Irish Drama and Cultural Nationalism 1890–1916* (2002), *Irish Theatre in England* (2008, co-edited with Richard Cave), and *W. B. Yeats in Context* (2009, co-edited with David Holdeman).

BARRY MCCREA is Professor of English and Comparative Literature and Keough Family College Chair of Irish Studies at the University of Notre Dame. He is the author of a novel, *The First Verse* (2005), as well as *In the Company of Strangers: Family and Narrative in Dickens, Conan Doyle, Joyce, and Proust* (2011) and *Languages of the Night: Minor Languages and the Literary Imagination in 20th-Century Ireland and Europe* (2014).

RÓNÁN MCDONALD holds the Australian Ireland Fund Chair in Modern Irish Studies at the University of New South Wales, Sydney, where he is Director of the Global Irish Studies Centre. His publications include *Tragedy and Irish Literature* (2002), *The Cambridge Introduction to Samuel Beckett* (2007), and *The Death of the Critic* (2008). He is President of the Irish Studies Association of Australia and New Zealand.

MICHAEL VALDEZ MOSES is Associate Professor of English and an Affiliated Member of the faculty in the Literature Program at Duke University. He is the author of *The Novel and the Globalization of Culture* (1994), editor of *The Writings of J. M. Coetzee* (1993), and co-editor with Richard Begam of *Modernism and Colonialism: British and Irish Literature, 1899–1939* (2007). He is co-editor of the journal *Modernist Cultures*.

EMER NOLAN is Senior Lecturer in English at the National University of Ireland, Maynooth. She is the author of *James Joyce and Nationalism* (1995) and *Catholic Emancipations: Irish Fiction from Thomas Moore to James Joyce* (2007).

LAURA O'CONNOR is Associate Professor at the University of California, Irvine. She is the author of *Haunted English: The Celtic Fringe, the British Empire, and De-Anglicization* (2006), and she has published widely on modern Irish poetry in English and Irish, and on bilingualism and translation.

JEAN-MICHEL RABATÉ is Professor of English and Comparative Literature at the University of Pennsylvania since 1992, a curator of the Slought Foundation, an editor of the *Journal of Modern Literature*, and a Fellow of the American Academy of Arts and Sciences. He has authored or edited more than thirty books on modernism, psychoanalysis, and philosophy.

ACKNOWLEDGEMENTS

My first thanks go to all of the contributors to this volume; I would like to acknowledge their hard work and scholarly care in bringing this *Companion* to completion. I want to express special gratitude to those who went an extra mile to offer comradely critical commentary on the chapters of fellow contributors working on cognate topics in the volume. I also greatly appreciate the support of Ray Ryan, Literature Editor at Cambridge University Press, who commissioned the study and who offered sound advice along the way. Thanks, too, to Louis Gulino and Caitlin Gallagher at the Press for their courteous assistance as the project developed. Cormac Deane was a fastidious copy editor who sharpened the work of all involved. Among the many colleagues or friends who offered timely encouragement or welcome second readings when they were most needed I would especially like to mention Jed Esty, Luke Gibbons, Kevin Honan, Colleen Lye, Breandán MacSuibhne, Catherine Morris, and Kevin Whelan. Emer Nolan in Maynooth and Barry McCrea, then at Yale, acted as sage counsellors or wry commentators at vexed moments. For ongoing stimulus and support more generally I must also thank my colleagues in the English departments at NUI Maynooth and Yale University. While preparing this volume, I was fortunate to be able to teach seminars on Irish and Anglophone modernisms to students at both of the aforementioned institutions. I learned a great deal in the process from all involved, but would like to thank Jordan Brower, Julia Chan, Niamh Cunningham, Margaret Deli, Bridget English, Paul Franz, Seo Hee Im, Edward King, Fidelma Mahon, Chris McGowan, Tess McNulty, Michelle Taylor, and Tomas Ungar for particularly memorable responses. Gemma Murphy and Conor Cleary were conscripts to this volume, but their steady encouragement and good humour were absolutely essential to its completion.

A project such as this is ultimately made possible not only by the immediate contributors but also by the many generations of critics and writers who have helped to crack at least some of the conundrums of Irish modernism. It would be pleasant to think that this study, completed on the one hundredth anniversaries of the publication of James Joyce's *Dubliners* and W. B. Yeats's *Responsibilities*, might be taken as a small salute to acknowledge that longer history of intrepid scholarship and sometimes brilliantly disputatious critical activity. The subjects and views represented in this collection are inevitably partial and cannot be representative of such a diversity of critical activity, but one's sense of appreciation of all those who have written so well on Irish modernists or Irish modernism may nonetheless be recorded here.

My interest in Irish and European modernisms was first whetted by Fr. Peter Connolly's trenchantly erudite lectures at what is now NUI Maynooth, and then later reanimated by Edward Said's elegantly illuminating seminars at Columbia University. To these two exceptionally intelligent and impassioned teachers I would like to pay a personal tribute.

DEVELOPMENTS IN IRISH MODERNISM – CHRONOLOGY, 1845–1969

Date	Irish Historical Events	Irish Modernist Works and Related Cultural Events	International Cultural and Intellectual Events	International Historical Events
1845	The Great Famine (–1852) commences; leaves 1 million people dead and compels 1 million to emigrate		Friedrich Engels, *The Condition of the Working Class in England*; Richard Wagner, *Tannhäuser*	First British-Sikh War in India; Maori uprising in New Zealand; the United States annexes Texas
1848	Young Irelander rebellion		Karl Marx and Friedrich Engels, *The Communist Manifesto*; J. S. Mill, *Principles of Political Economy*; Charles Dickens, *Dombey and Son*	Revolutions across Europe; California Gold Rush; first settlers arrive at Dunedin, New Zealand
1858	Irish Republican Brotherhood (IRB) founded; its American counterpart – the Fenian Brotherhood (The Fenians) – founded in the United States			Government of India Act places sovereignty over India in hands of British monarch, beginning of British Raj
1867	Fenian Rising		Karl Marx, *Das Kapital* I; Matthew Arnold, *On the Study of Celtic Literature*; Henrik Ibsen, *Peer Gynt* published	British North American Act establishes the Dominion of Canada

(continued)

Date	Irish Historical Events	Irish Modernist Works and Related Cultural Events	International Cultural and Intellectual Events	International Historical Events
1869	Disestablishment of the Church of Ireland; Ladies National Association for the Repeal of the Contagious Disease Act formed in London (branches later opened in Ireland by 1871)		Leo Tolstoy, *War and Peace*; Gustave Flaubert, *A Sentimental Education*	First Vatican Council (–1870); Mahatma Gandhi born (d. 1948)
1870	Home Rule movement launched in Dublin; Gladstone's First Land Act; first public suffrage meeting in Dublin; Married Women's Property Act		J. S. Mill, *Chapters and Speeches on the Irish Land Question*; Charles Dickens, *The Mystery of Edwin Drood*; *Revue Celtique* founded	Franco-Prussian War
1876	Dublin Women's Suffrage Association founded		Henrik Ibsen, *Peer Gynt* premieres in Christiania	Queen Victoria proclaimed Empress of India; Battle of the Little Bighorn
1879	Irish National Land League founded in Mayo; campaign to extend Royal University Act to women		Henrik Ibsen, *A Doll's House* premieres in Copenhagen; Henry James, *Daisy Miller*	The British–Zulu War; *La Marseillaise* becomes French national anthem; First telephone exchanges established in London

1884	Gaelic Athletic Association founded; Fenian dynamite campaign in Great Britain		Joris-Karl Huysmans, *A rebours*; Mark Twain, *Huckleberry Finn*	Berlin Conference on Africa (–1885)
1886	Gladstone presents Home Rule Bill to House of Commons, rejected by House of Lords; Contagious Diseases Act repealed	George Moore, *A Drama in Muslin*; Standish O'Grady, *Toryism and the Tory Democracy*	Friedrich Nietzsche, *Beyond Good and Evil*; Jean Moréas, *Symbolist Manifesto*; Stéphane Mallarmé, *Poésies*; Henry James, *The Bostonians* and *The Princess Casamassima*	Britain annexes Upper Burma; First meeting of Indian National Congress; Opening of Statue of Liberty in New York
1889	Pigott forgeries attempting to damage Charles Stewart Parnell exposed	W. B. Yeats, *The Wanderings of Oisin*		Cecil Rhodes launches the British South Africa Company; Eiffel Tower completed
1890	Fall of Parnell, split in the Irish Parliamentary Party	Belfast City Art Gallery opened; National Library and of Science and Art Museum opened	J. G. Frazer, *The Golden Bough*; Henrik Ibsen, *Hedda Gabler* published; Emily Dickinson, *Poems*; William Morris, *News From Nowhere*; Peter Tchaikovsky, *Queen of Spades*	The dismissal of Bismarck; Eritrea becomes Italian colony; U.S. Bureau of Census declares the American frontier closed
1891	Death of Parnell; John Redmond becomes leader of the Parnellites	Oscar Wilde, *The Picture of Dorian Gray* and *The Soul of Man under Socialism*; George Bernard Shaw, *The Quintessence of Ibsenism*	Henrik Ibsen, *Hedda Gabler* premieres in Munich; Émile Zola, *Money*; Thomas Hardy, *Tess of the d'Urbervilles*; José Martí, "Our America"; Paul Gauguin goes to live in Tahiti	Franco-Russian Entente

(continued)

Date	Irish Historical Events	Irish Modernist Works and Related Cultural Events	International Cultural and Intellectual Events	International Historical Events
1892	Ulster Convention in Belfast; Belfast Labour Party (first Irish labour party) formed	National Literary Society founded; W. B. Yeats and Lady Gregory, *Countess Cathleen* published; W. B. Yeats, *The Rose*; W. E. H. Lecky, *A History of Ireland in the Eighteenth Century*; Douglas Hyde, "On the Necessity for De-Anglicising the Irish People"	Peter Tchaikovsky, *The Nutcracker Suite*; Rudyard Kipling, *Barrack-Room Ballads* (second part 1896)	Keir Hardie becomes first British Labour M.P.; Pan-Slav conference held at Cracow
1893	Gladstone introduces Second Home Rule Bill; Disturbances in Belfast; Home Rule Bill passes in House of Commons; Trades Union Congress meets in Belfast	Gaelic League founded; Oscar Wilde, *Salomé* published; George Egerton, *Keynotes*; W. B. Yeats, *The Celtic Twilight*; George Moore, *Modern Painting*	William Morris, *Socialism: Its Growth and Outcome*	World Exhibition in Chicago; Lumière Brothers invent the cinematograph; Natal granted responsible self-government; Swaziland annexed by the Transvaal
1894	Horace Plunkett founds Irish Agricultural Organisation Society; first Irish Trade Union Congress meeting	George Egerton, *Discords*; W. B. Yeats, *The Land of Heart's Desire* premieres in London	Kate Chopin, *Bayou Folk*; Claude Debussy, *Prélude à l'après-midi d'un faune*	Conviction of Dreyfus for treason; Alfred Webb, M.P. for Waterford West, elected president of Indian National Congress
1895	Trial of Oscar Wilde in London	Oscar Wilde, *The Importance of Being Ernest and An Ideal Husband* premiere in London	First film projection by the Lumière Brothers; Thomas Hardy, *Jude the Obscure*; H. G. Wells, *The Time Machine*; Gustav Mahler, *Resurrection Symphony*	The Jameson Raid into the Transvaal Republic; Wilhelm Röntgen's discovery of X-rays

1896	Irish Socialist Republican Party founded, secretary James Connolly	Oscar Wilde, *Salomé* premieres in Paris; Kuno Meyer founds *Zeitschrift für celtische Philologie*	Anton Chekhov, *The Seagull* premieres in St. Petersburg; first commercial motion picture exhibition given in New York	Guglielmo Marconi files the world's first patent application for a system of telegraphy using Hertzian waves; first modern Olympiad held in Athens
1897		Establishment of the Irish Literary Theatre	Stéphane Mallarmé, *Divagations*; Rudyard Kipling, "Recessional"; Henry James, *What Maisie Knew*	Queen Victoria's Diamond Jubilee; widespread famine in India; First Zionist Congress launches the Basel Programme to resettle Jewish people in Palestine
1898	Local government vote granted to women	Oscar Wilde, *The Ballad of Reading Gaol*; G. B. Shaw, *The Perfect Wagnerite* and *Mrs Warren's Profession* published; John Eglinton, W. B. Yeats, et al., *Literary Ideals in Ireland*	National Gallery of British Art (Tate Gallery) opened in London; Émile Zola, "J'Accuse"; Thomas Hardy, *Wessex Poems*; Henry James, *The Turn of the Screw*; H. G. Wells, *The War of the Worlds*	United States declares war on Spain over Cuba; the Fashoda Incident; Boxer uprising in China; the Curies discover radium and plutonium; first Zeppelin airship built
1899	Michael Davitt withdraws from Westminster in protest at the Anglo-Boer War; John MacBride raises Irish Transvaal Brigade to aid the Boers	W. B. Yeats, *The Wind Among the Reeds*	Joseph Conrad, *Heart of Darkness*; Arthur Symonds, *The Symbolist Movement in Literature*; Kate Chopin, *The Awakening*; Rudyard Kipling, "The White Man's Burden"; Anton Chekhov, *Uncle Vanya* premieres in Moscow; Leo Tolstoy, *Resurrection*; Thorstein Veblen, *Theory of the Leisure Class*	Outbreak of the Anglo-Boer War (–1902)

(continued)

Date	Irish Historical Events	Irish Modernist Works and Related Cultural Events	International Cultural and Intellectual Events	International Historical Events
1900	Cumann na nGaedheal founded (later becomes Sinn Féin); first meeting of Inghinidhe na hÉireann; Queen Victoria visits Dublin	First number of D. P. Moran's *The Leader*; Alice Milligan, *The Last of the Fianna*; death of Oscar Wilde	Joseph Conrad, *Lord Jim*; Henrik Ibsen, *When We Dead Awaken* premieres in London; Sigmund Freud, *The Interpretation of Dreams*; Giacomo Puccini, *Tosca*; José Enrique Rodó, *Ariel*	International Ladies' Garment Workers Union formed; Boxer rebellion crushed in China; First Pan-African Conference in London
1901	Queen Victoria succeeded by Edward II	Ulster Literary Theatre founded; Alice Milligan, *The Deliverance of Hugh O'Neill*	Nobel Prize in Literature established; Anton Chekhov, *Three Sisters* premieres in Moscow; Thomas Mann, *Buddenbrooks*; Rudyard Kipling, *Kim*	Australian Federation established; Nigeria becomes British Protectorate
1902		Emergence of Ulster branch of Irish Literary Theatre; W. B. Yeats and Augusta Gregory, *Cathleen ni Houlihan* premieres in Dublin; Lady Gregory, *Cuchulain of Muirthemne* published; G. B. Shaw, *Mrs Warren's Profession* premieres in London; John B. Yeats, *George Moore*	André Gide, *The Immoralist*; V. I. Lenin, *What is to be Done?*; J. A. Hobson, *Imperialism*; Euclides da Cunha, *Rebellion in the Backlands*; William James, *Varieties of Religious Experience*	The South African War ends; death of Cecil Rhodes; first meeting of the Committee of Imperial Defence

1903	Wyndham Land Purchase Act passed in House of Commons; University of Dublin (Trinity College) announces that it is to award degrees to women	Irish National Theatre Society founded; An Túr Gloine founded; W. B. Yeats, *In the Seven Woods*; J. M. Synge, *In the Shadow of the Glen* premieres in Dublin; George Moore, *The Untilled Field*; Jack B. Yeats, *The County of Mayo*	W. E. B. Du Bois, *The Souls of the Black Folk*; Henry James, *The Ambassadors*; Edwin S. Porter, *The Great Train Robbery*; E. D. Morel, *The Congo Slave Trade*; Georg Simmel, *The Metropolis and Mental Life*	Emily Pankhurst founds the Women's Social and Political Union; first airborne flight by the Wright Brothers; British complete conquest of Northern Nigeria
1904	Construction of Government Buildings in Merrion Square, Dublin starts (–1922); Limerick pogrom against Jews	Abbey Theatre opens; W. B. Yeats, *In the Seven Woods*; W. B. Yeats, *On Baile's Strand* premieres in Dublin; J. M. Synge, *Riders to the Sea* opens in Dublin; G. B. Shaw, *John Bull's Other Island* premieres in London; Mary Swanzy, *The Infant*; Michael Davitt, *The Fall of Feudalism in Ireland*; Arthur Griffith, *The Resurrection of Hungary: A Parallel for Ireland*	Joseph Conrad, *Nostromo*; Anton Chekhov, *The Cherry Orchard* premieres in Moscow; Giacomo Puccini, *Madame Butterfly*; Henry James, *The Golden Bowl*	Beginning of Russo-Japanese War; second wave of Jewish immigration to Palestine; Panama Canal opens

(continued)

Date	Irish Historical Events	Irish Modernist Works and Related Cultural Events	International Cultural and Intellectual Events	International Historical Events
1905	Sinn Féin party founded	J. M. Synge, *The Well of the Saints* premieres in Dublin; W. B. Yeats, *Deirdre* premieres in Dublin; G. B. Shaw, *Man and Superman* premieres in London; Oscar Wilde's *De Profundis*; D. P. Moran, *The Philosophy of Irish Ireland*; George Moore, *The Lake*; Jack B. Yeats, *The Man from Aranmore*	Richard Strauss, *Salomé*	Revolution in Russia; George Curzon initiates partition of Bengal; Swadeshi movement formed in India
1907	Dockers and Carters strike in Belfast; Sinn Féin protest disrupts Irish Parliamentary Party meeting in Dublin	J. M. Synge, *The Playboy of the Western World* premieres in Dublin (riots at Abbey Theatre); Augusta Gregory and Douglas Hyde, *The Rising of the Moon*; James Joyce, *Chamber Music*	Cubist exhibition in Paris; Pablo Picasso, *Les Demoiselles d'Avignon*; August Strindberg, *The Ghost Sonata* premieres in Stockholm; Henri Bergson, *Creative Evolution*; Henry Adams, *The Education of Henry Adams*; *Votes for Women* newspaper founded in London	Pius X issues *Ne Temere* decree on mixed marriages; Women's Federation League founded in the United Kingdom; self-governing (white) colonies declared British Dominions
1908	Irish Transport and General Workers' Union established; Irish Women's Franchise League founded	Cuala Press founded by Elizabeth Yeats; Dublin Municipal Gallery of Modern Art founded by Hugh Lane; Katherine	Béla Bartók, *String Quartet No. 1*; Gertrude Stein, *Three Lives*; Rabindranath Tagore, *Home and the World*; Georges Sorel, *Reflections*	Young Turks revolution in Istanbul; Henry Ford produces Model T Ford; King Leopold transfers Congo from his private possession to Belgium

1909	Royal University of Ireland dissolved	Cecil Thurston, *The Fly on the Wheel*; J. M. Synge, *The Tinker's Wedding* premieres in London; Rudolf Thurneysen, *Handbuch des Altirischen*	on Violence; Women Writers Suffrage League founded; F. T. Marinetti, "The Founding and Manifesto of Futurism"; Gertrude Stein, *Three Lives*; Ezra Pound, *Personae*; Arnold Schönberg, *Five Orchestral Pieces*; Gustav Mahler, *Symphony No. 9*; H. G. Wells, *Tono-Bungay*; Mohandas J. Gandhi, *Hind Swaraj*	U.S. troops occupy Nicaragua (–1925)
1910	Death of Edward VII and accession of George V	W. B. Yeats, *The Green Helmet and Other Poems*; Katherine Cecil Thurston, *Max*; Jack B. Yeats, *The Felons of our Land*; James Connolly, *Labour in Irish History*	Igor Stravinsky, *The Firebird*; E. M. Forster, *Howards End*; Post-Impressionist Exhibition organized by Roger Fry in London; Georges Braque, *Violin and Candlestick*; Rabindranath Tagore, *Gitanjali* (English, 1912)	Mexican Revolution begins; W. E. B. Du Bois founds National Association for Advancement of Coloured People (NAACP) in the United States
1911	Home Rule Bill introduced in Westminster; Anti-Home Rule agitation in northern Ireland; Irish Vigilance Association founded; Statue of Charles Stewart Parnell by Augustus St. Gaudens unveiled in Dublin	George Moore, *Hail and Farewell* (3 vols –1914); Augusta Gregory, *Grania*; Kuno Meyer, *Selections from Ancient Irish Poetry*	Georg Lukács, *Soul and Form*; Dora Marsden founds and edits *The Freewoman* under patronage of Harriet Shaw Weaver; first complete English translation of Nietzsche published	Revolution ends imperial regime in China and establishes provisional republic; first flight across the United States; international crisis at Agadir

(continued)

Date	Irish Historical Events	Irish Modernist Works and Related Cultural Events	International Cultural and Intellectual Events	International Historical Events
1912	Ulster Volunteers formed and Ulster Solemn League and Covenant signed; sinking of the *Titanic*	G. B. Shaw, *Pygmalion* published; Augusta Gregory, *Irish Folk-History Plays*	Thomas Mann, *Death in Venice*; Arnold Schönberg, *Pierre Lunaire*; Karl Jung, *Psychology of the Unconscious*; Harriet Monroe founds *Poetry* magazine in Chicago	Formation of the South African Native National Congress (later the African National Congress); beginning of the Balkan Wars
1913	Great Lockout of unionized workers in Dublin; Irish Volunteers founded; Irish Citizen Army founded	G. B. Shaw, *Pygmalion* premieres in Vienna	Marcel Proust, À la Recherche du temps perdu (–1927); D. H. Lawrence, *Sons and Lovers*; Igor Stravinsky, *The Rite of Spring* (ballet); Alban Berg, *Three Orchestral Pieces*; Edmund Husserl, *Phenomenology*; Rabindranath Tagore wins Nobel Prize for Literature; International Exhibition of Modern Art (Armory Show) opened by John Quinn in New York; Russian Futurist Manifesto published	Violent Suffragette demonstrations in Britain; War in the Balkans; South Africa Native Lands Acts passed to deprive Africans of right to own land

1914	Third Home Rule Bill suspended at outbreak of Great War; Cumann na mBan founded; "The Curragh Incident"	James Joyce, *Dubliners*; W. B. Yeats, *Responsibilities*	Founding of *Blast*; Gertrude Stein, *Tender Buttons*; Robert Frost, *North of Boston*; Margaret Anderson founds *Little Review*; Harriet Shaw Weaver becomes editor of *The Egoist* (originally *The Freewoman*)	World War I (–1918) commences
1915	25,000 National Volunteers assemble in Phoenix Park; RMS *Lusitania* torpedoed by German submarine off coast of Kinsale	Hugh Lane, art collector, dies in sinking of the RMS *Lusitania*; Thomas MacDonagh's *Pagans* opens in Dublin; Jack B. Yeats, *The Lying-in-State of O'Donovan Rossa*	Nikolai Bukharin, *Imperialism and World Economy*; Virginia Woolf, *The Voyage Out*; D. H. Lawrence, *The Rainbow*; D. W. Griffith, *The Birth of a Nation*; Amy Lowell, ed., *Some Imagist Poets* (3 vols –1917); Mariano Azuela, *The Underdogs*	Armenian genocide begins (–1916); British conquest of Mesopotamia; U.S. troops occupy Haiti (–1934)
1916	Easter Rising	James Joyce, *A Portrait of the Artist as a Young Man*; W. B. Yeats, *At The Hawk's Well* performed in Dublin; Cuala Press publish *Certain Noble Plays of Japan*, introduced by W. B. Yeats; Jack B. Yeats, *The Double Jockey Act*; Seán Keating, *Men of the West*; Ernest Boyd, *Ireland's Literary Renaissance*	Albert Einstein, *General Theory of Relativity*; Ferdinand de Saussure, *Course in General Linguistics*; D. W. Griffith, *Intolerance*; H. D., *Sea Garden*; Henry Cowell, *Dynamic Motion*	Battle of the Somme; Great migration of African Americans from the southern U.S. begins

(continued)

Date	Irish Historical Events	Irish Modernist Works and Related Cultural Events	International Cultural and Intellectual Events	International Historical Events
1917	David Lloyd-George announces Home Rule to be passed in Ireland but six northeastern counties to be excluded for five years; Irish Convention held in Dublin	W. B. Yeats, *The Wild Swans at Coole*; John Eglinton, *Anglo-Irish Essays*	T. S. Eliot, *Prufrock and Other Observations*; V. I. Lenin, *Imperialism: The Highest Stage of Capitalism*; Sigmund Freud, *Introduction to Psychoanalysis*; Henry Cowell, *The Tides of Manaunaun*; Amy Lowell, *Tendencies in Modern American Poetry*; George Grosz, *The Funeral*	Bolshevik Revolution; United States enters World War I; Balfour Declaration confirms British support for a Jewish national home in Palestine
1918	Sweeping Sinn Féin victory in General Election; Franchise granted to women over 30 in Britain and Ireland; Countess Markievicz elected first woman to British Parliament but does not take her seat	James Joyce, *Exiles*; *Ulysses* begins serialization in *Little Review*	Tristan Tzara, "Dada Manifesto"; Gerard Manley Hopkins, *Poems*; Lytton Strachey, *Eminent Victorians*; Lu Hsun, "A Madman's Diary"; Willa Cather, *My Ántonia*	The Allies and Germany sign Armistice on November 11; start of Russian Civil War (–1920)
1919	Dáil Éireann established and Irish War of Independence commences (–1921)	W. B. Yeats, *The Wild Swans at Coole*; Dublin Drama League founded	Bauhaus founded at Weimar by Walter Gropius; Pablo Picasso, *Pierrot and Harlequin*; Thomas Hardy, *Collected Poems*; Ezra Pound, *Hugh Selwyn Mauberley*;	Peace Conference in Versailles creates the League of Nations; Amritsar Massacre; division of the Austro-Hungarian Empire; establishment of Third International Congress

1920	First enrolments of "Black and Tans" to suppress IRA; "Bloody Sunday"; Government of Ireland Act passed to provide Northern and Southern Ireland with separate parliaments; anti-Catholic riots in Belfast	G. B. Shaw, *Heartbreak House* premieres in New York	J. M. Keynes, *The Economic Consequences of the Peace*; Sigmund Freud, *Beyond the Pleasure Principle*; Georg Lukács, *Theory of the Novel*; D. H. Lawrence, *Women in Love*; Eugene O'Neill, *The Emperor Jones* premieres in New York; Edith Wharton, *The Age of Innocence*; Katherine Mansfield, *Bliss and Other Stories*; Paul Klee, *Angelus Novus*	(Comintern); First Pan-African Congress meets in Paris Women in the United States achieve the vote; Britain given Mandate over Iraq, Transjordan, Palestine; Chinese Communist Party founded; Kemal Atatürk abolishes Ottoman sultanate
1921	Anglo-Irish Treaty; Northern Ireland Parliament opened by George V	W. B. Yeats, *Michael Robartes and the Dancer* and *Four Plays for Dancers* published; George Moore, *Heloise and Abelard*; Mainie Jellett, *Girl in Blue* and *The Three Graces*	Luigi Pirandello, *Six Characters in Search of an Author* premieres in Rome; Pablo Picasso, *Three Musicians*; Edvard Munch, *The Scream*; Marianne Moore, *Poems*; Eugene O'Neill, *Anna Christie* premieres in New York.	Non-Cooperation Movement begins in India led by Gandhi (–1922); New Economic Policy in the USSR

(continued)

Date	Irish Historical Events	Irish Modernist Works and Related Cultural Events	International Cultural and Intellectual Events	International Historical Events
1922	Anglo-Irish Treaty approved in Dáil Éireann; establishment of Irish Free State confirms partition; Irish Civil War begins (–1923); Northern Ireland Parliament opened by George V	James Joyce, *Ulysses*; W. B. Yeats, *Later Poems*; G. B. Shaw, *Back to Methuselah* premieres in New York; Dorothy Macardle, *Earth-Bound*; Mainie Jellett, *Standing Female Nude*	T. S. Eliot, *The Waste Land*; F. Scott Fitzgerald, *The Beautiful and the Damned*; Virginia Woolf, *Jacob's Room*; Bertolt Brecht, *Drums in the Night* premieres in Moscow; Ludwig Wittgenstein, *Tractatus Logico-Philosophicus*; T. S. Eliot founds and edits *The Criterion* (–1939); British Broadcasting Company (BBC) founded; Eugene O'Neill wins Pulitzer Prize for *Anna Christie*	Benito Mussolini becomes Italian Prime Minister; Britain recognizes "independence" of the Kingdom of Egypt but maintains control of foreign policy
1923	Irish Free State joins League of Nations; Cumann na nGaedheal party founded; Censorship of Films Act introduced	W. B. Yeats receives the Nobel Prize; Seán O'Casey, *The Shadow of a Gunman* premieres in Dublin; G. B. Shaw, *Saint Joan* premieres in New York; Jack B. Yeats, *A Lake Regatta*; Mainie Jellett and Evie Hone exhibitions in Dublin	Georg Lukács; *History and Class Consciousness*; Bertolt Brecht, *Baal* premieres in Leipzig; Le Corbusier, *Towards a New Architecture*; Bertrand Russell, *The Prospects of Industrial Civilisation*; Jean Toomer, *Cane*	Escalation of postwar inflation and collapse of German currency

1924	First meeting, in London, of Irish Boundary Commission to determine partition boundary between Free State and Northern Ireland	Seán O'Casey, *Juno and the Paycock* premieres in Dublin; Daniel Corkery, *The Hidden Ireland*	Thomas Mann, *The Magic Mountain*; E. M. Forster, *A Passage to India*; André Breton, "The Surrealist Manifesto"; Eugene O'Neill's *All God's Chillun Got Wings* premieres (with Paul Robeson) in New York; Pablo Neruda, *Twenty Love Poems and a Song of Despair*	Zinoviev letter published; first minority Labour government in Britain; Gandhi fasts against Hindu-Muslim riots; death of V. I. Lenin
1925	Boundary Commission powers revoked	G. B. Shaw receives the Nobel Prize; W. B. Yeats, *A Vision*; Seán Keating, *An Allegory*	Adolf Hitler, *Mein Kampf*; Pablo Picasso, *Three Dancers*; Franz Kafka, *The Trial*; F. Scott Fitzgerald, *The Great Gatsby*; Alain Locke, *The New Negro*; Virginia Woolf, *Mrs. Dalloway*; Gertrude Stein, *The Making of Americans*; Alban Berg, *Wozzeck*; Henry Cowell, *The Banshee*; Sergei Eisenstein, *Battleship Potemkin*	Locarno Conference; John Logie Baird transmits first televised image
1926	Fianna Fáil party founded by Éamon de Valera; Radio Éireann begins broadcasting	Seán O'Casey, *The Plough and the Stars* premieres in Dublin, riots ensue in Abbey Theatre	H. D., *Palimpsest*; D. H. Lawrence, *The Plumed Serpent*; Ernest Hemingway, *The Sun Also Rises*; Lewis Mumford, *The Golden Day*; T. E. Lawrence, *Seven Pillars of Wisdom*; Ho Chi Minh, *Colonization on Trial*	Imperial Conference defines Dominion status and allows Dominions to opt out of treaties signed by the United Kingdom

(*continued*)

Date	Irish Historical Events	Irish Modernist Works and Related Cultural Events	International Cultural and Intellectual Events	International Historical Events
1927	Kevin O'Higgins assassinated	James Joyce, *Pomes Penyeach*	Academy of Motion Pictures Arts and Sciences founded in the United States; Virginia Woolf, *To The Lighthouse*; Marcel Proust, *Le temps retrouvé* (posthumous); Walter Benjamin begins *The Arcades Project*; Martin Heidegger, *Being and Time*; Wyndham Lewis, *Time and Western Man*; Laura Riding and Robert Graves, eds., *A Survey of Modernist Poetry*; James Weldon Johnson, *God's Trombones: Seven Negro Sermons in Verse*	League against Imperialism and Colonial Oppression holds international conference in Brussels
1928	Foundation stone laid for new Northern Ireland Parliament Building at Stormont	W. B. Yeats, *The Tower*; Seán O'Casey, *The Silver Tassie* rejected by Abbey Theatre; James Joyce, *Anna Livia Plurabelle*; Jack B. Yeats, *Dinner Hour on the Docks*; Mainie Jellett, *Religious Composition*; first production by the Gate Theatre: *Peer Gynt*; Oscar Wilde, *Salomé* staged in Dublin	Bertolt Brecht and Kurt Weill, *The Threepenny Opera* premieres in Berlin; Sergei Eisenstein, *October*; D. H. Lawrence, *Lady Chatterley's Lover*; Radcliffe Hall, *The Well of Loneliness*; Federico García Lorca, *The Gypsy Ballads*; Claude McKay, *Home in Harlem*; André Gide, *Voyage to the Congo*; André Breton, *Nadja*; Eugene	Start of First Soviet Five Year Plan; Antonio Gramsci sentenced to 20 years by Italian Special Tribunal

1929	Censorship of Publications Act passed in the Irish Free State; Proportional representation abolished for parliamentary elections in Northern Ireland; Shannon Hydro-Electric scheme begins	Elizabeth Bowen, *The Last September*; W. B. Yeats, *A Packet for Ezra Pound*; Seán O'Casey, *The Silver Tassie* premieres in London; G. B. Shaw, *The Apple Cart* premieres in Warsaw; Denis Johnston, *The Old Lady Says "No"!* premieres in Dublin; Louis MacNeice, *Blind Fireworks*; Jack B. Yeats, *Going to Wolfe Tone's Grave*	O'Neill wins Pulitzer Prize for *Strange Interlude* (premieres in New York); Academy of Motion Pictures Awards (Oscars) established; Museum of Modern Art (MoMA) opened in New York; Second Surrealist Manifesto; William Faulkner, *The Sound and the Fury*; Ernest Hemingway, *A Farewell to Arms*; Claude McKay, *Banjo*; Virginia Woolf, *A Room of One's Own*; Alfred Döblin, *Berlin Alexanderplatz*; Rómulo Gallegos, *Doña Barbara*; M. M. Bakhtin, *Problems of Dostoevsky's Poetics*	Wall Street Crash heralds start of world economic crisis and the Great Depression
1930	Irish Free State elected to the Council of the League of Nations; First Free State censorship board appointed	Samuel Beckett, *Whoroscope*; W. B. Yeats, *Words upon the Window Pane* premieres in Dublin; Brian Coffey and Denis Devlin, *Poems*; Jack B. Yeats, *Power Station*; Gate Theatre moves to buildings at Rotunda Hospital; Irish Folklore Institute founded	Sigmund Freud, *Civilisation and Its Discontents*; Max Weber, *The Protestant Ethic and the Spirit of Capitalism*; Robert Musil, *The Man Without Qualities* (–1943); T. S. Eliot, *Ash Wednesday*; William Faulkner, *As I Lay Dying*; James Weldon Johnson, *Black Manhattan*; F. R. Leavis, *Mass Civilisation and Minority Culture*	Launch of Negritude movement in Paris by Francophone intellectuals; Amy Johnson flies from London to Australia

(continued)

Date	Irish Historical Events	Irish Modernist Works and Related Cultural Events	International Cultural and Intellectual Events	International Historical Events
1931	First number of *Irish Press* issued	Samuel Beckett, *Proust*; W. B. Yeats, *The Dreaming of the Bones* premieres in Dublin; Daniel Corkery, *Synge and Anglo-Irish Literature*; Thomas MacGreevy, *T. S. Eliot: A Study*	Eugene O'Neill, *Mourning Becomes Electra* premieres in New York; Hermann Broch, *The Sleepwalkers*; Henri Matisse, *The Dance*; Virginia Woolf, *The Waves*; Vita Sackville-West, *The Edwardians*; Edmund Wilson, *Axel's Castle*; Salvador Dalí, *The Persistence of Memory*	Japan invades Manchuria; Britain abandons the gold standard; Statute of Westminster recognizes constitutional equality of the Dominions with Britain
1932	Ten years of Cumann na nGaedheal government ends and first Fianna Fáil government under Éamon de Valera formed; International Eucharistic Congress; Army Comrades Association (Blueshirts) founded; Northern Ireland parliament buildings at Stormont formally open	G. B. Shaw and W. B. Yeats with other writers found Academy of Irish Letters; Elizabeth Bowen, *To the North*; Death of Augusta Gregory	Joseph Roth, *The Radetzky March*; Aldous Huxley, *Brave New World*; Bertolt Brecht, *The Mother* premieres in Berlin; William Faulkner, *Light in August*; Louis-Ferdinand Céline, *Journey to the End of the Night*	Indian National Congress declared illegal and Gandhi arrested; Iraq becomes independent; the atom is split at Cambridge University

1933	Vote to remove the Oath of Allegiance to the British Crown passed in Dáil Éireann	W. B. Yeats, *The Winding Stair and Collected Poems*; Blanaid Salkeld, *Hello, Eternity!*	T. S. Eliot, *The Use of Poetry and the Use of Criticism*; Gertrude Stein, *The Autobiography of Alice B. Toklas*; André Malraux, *The Human Condition*; Mulk Raj Anand, *The Untouchable*; Claude McKay, *Banana Bottom*	Hitler becomes Chancellor of Germany
1934	Anglo-Irish "cattle and coal" agreement	Samuel Beckett, *More Pricks than Kicks* and (alias "Andrew Belis") "Recent Irish Poetry"; Robert Flaherty, *Man of Aran*; Kate O'Brien, *The Ante-Room*; W. B. Yeats, *The Resurrection* premieres in Dublin; Thomas MacGreevy, *Poems*	T. S. Eliot, *After Strange Gods*; Wyndham Lewis, *Men Without Art*; Ezra Pound, *The A. B. C. of Reading*; Jean Rhys, *Voyage in the Dark*; Nancy Cunard, ed., *The Negro Anthology*	Hitler becomes "Führer"; Chinese Communists' "Long March" begins
1935	The Dance Halls Act, designed to regulate Irish dance by clergy, police and judiciary	Elizabeth Bowen, *The House in Paris*; Samuel Beckett, *Echo's Bones*; Louis MacNeice, *Poems*; Kate O'Brien, *Mary Lavelle*; Jack B. Yeats, *A Morning*; John Eglinton, *Irish Literary Portraits*	T. S. Eliot, *Murder in the Cathedral* premieres in Canterbury Cathedral; Elias Canetti, *Auto-da-Fé*; Dmitri Shostakovich, *Symphony No. 1*; Dorothy Richardson, *Clear Horizon*; Marianne Moore, *Selected Poems*; Zora Neale Hurston, *Mules and Men*	Italian invasion of Abyssinia; Nuremberg Laws passed in Germany

(continued)

Date	Irish Historical Events	Irish Modernist Works and Related Cultural Events	International Cultural and Intellectual Events	International Historical Events
1936	Left-wing Irish unit under Frank Ryan joins republican government forces in Spain	W. B. Yeats edits *The Oxford Book of Modern Verse, 1892–1935*	International Surrealist Exhibition held in London; William Faulkner, *Absalom, Absalom*; Djuna Barnes, *Nightwood*; Dylan Thomas, *Twenty-five Poems*; Charles Chaplin, *Modern Times*; Piet Mondrian, *Composition in Red and Blue*	Spanish Civil War breaks out (–1939); Great Arab Revolt breaks out against British rule in Palestine
1937	Éamon de Valera introduces new Constitution of Ireland	W. B. Yeats, *A Vision*, revised version; Jack B. Yeats, *A Race in Hy Brasil* and *In Memory of Boucicault and Bianconi*; Louis MacNeice (with W. H. Auden), *Letters from Iceland*; Denis Devlin, *Intercessions*	David Jones, *In Parenthesis*; Wyndham Lewis, *Blasting and Bombardiering: Autobiography (1914–26)*; Virginia Woolf, *The Years*; Zora Neale Hurston, *Their Eyes Were Watching God*	Shanghai falls to Japanese forces, Mao Zedong calls for "National Salvation Progam" to create united front against Japanese invasion
1938	Douglas Hyde, founder of the Gaelic League, becomes first President of Ireland	W. B. Yeats, *New Poems*; W. B. Yeats, *Purgatory* premieres in Dublin; Samuel Beckett, *Murphy*; Elizabeth Bowen, *The Death of the Heart*; Brian Coffey, *Third Person*	Jean-Paul Sartre, *Nausea*; Béla Bartók, *Violin Concerto*; Sergei Eisenstein, *Alexander Nevsky*; C. L. R. James, *The Black Jacobins*; George Antonius, *The Arab Awakening*; Jomo Kenyatta, *Facing Mount Kenya*	Munich crisis over German claims to the Sudetenland; Franco begins Catalonian offensive in Spanish Civil War; Lázaro Cárdenas nationalizes the oil business in Mexico

1939	Emergency Powers Act comes into force in Irish Free State as war is declared in Europe	James Joyce, *Finnegans Wake*; Flann O' Brien, *At Swim-Two-Birds*; Seán O'Casey, first volume of *Autobiographies* (-1954): Louis MacNeice, *Autumn Journal*; Death of W. B. Yeats	Eugene O'Neill, *Long Day's Journey Into Night* (written); Thomas Mann, *Lotte in Weimar*; T. S. Eliot, *The Family Reunion* opens in London; John Steinbeck, *The Grapes of Wrath*; Aimé Césaire, "Notebook of a Return to the Native Land"; David Alfaro Siqueiros, *Portrait of the Bourgeoisie*	World War II (-1945) begins with Nazi occupation of Poland
1940	Éamon de Valera refuses to hand over Irish ports for British wartime use	W. B. Yeats, *Last Poems*; Seán O'Casey, *The Star Turns Red* premieres in London; *The Bell* (-1954) founded by Seán Ó Faoláin; Ulster Group Theatre formed	Ernest Hemingway, *For Whom the Bell Tolls*; W. H. Auden, *Another Time*	Fall of Paris to German occupation
1941	Bread rationing; German bombings in Belfast and Dublin; Announcement that British conscription will not be applied to Northern Ireland	Flann O'Brien, *An Béal Bocht*; Kate O'Brien, *The Land of Spices*; Louis MacNeice, *Plant and Phantom* and *The Poetry of W. B. Yeats*; death of James Joyce	F. Scott Fitzgerald's *The Last Tycoon* edited and published by Edmund Wilson; Bertolt Brecht, *Mother Courage and Her Children* premieres in Zurich; W. H. Auden, *New Year Letters*; Virginia Woolf, *Between the Acts*	Japan bombs Pearl Harbor and the United States enters World War II; Japanese troops invade Cambodia, Vietnam, Thailand, Hong Kong, and Malaya; Leon Trotsky assassinated in Mexico

(continued)

Date	Irish Historical Events	Irish Modernist Works and Related Cultural Events	International Cultural and Intellectual Events	International Historical Events
1942		Patrick Kavanagh, *The Great Hunger*; Máirtín Ó Direáin, *Coinnle Geala*; Elizabeth Bowen, *Bowenscourt*; Jack B. Yeats, *The Two Travellers*; Joseph Hone, *W. B. Yeats, 1865–1939*	Walter Benjamin, *Theses on the Philosophy of History*; Albert Camus, *The Stranger* and *The Myth of Sisyphus*; T. S. Eliot, *Little Gidding*	Enrico Fermi splits the atom in the United States; Quit India movement leads to violent confrontation between Indian National Congress and the British Raj
1943	Central Bank of Ireland established	Irish Exhibition of Living Art; National Film Institute founded in Free State; Arts Council established in Northern Ireland; Seán O'Casey, *Red Roses for Me* staged in Dublin; Máirtín Ó Direáin, *Dánta Aniar*; Jack B. Yeats, *This Grand Conversation was under the Rose*	Jean-Paul Sartre, *Being and Nothingness*; Bertolt Brecht, *The Life of Galileo* premieres in Zurich	Famine in Bengal (–1944) kills almost 4 million people; Battle of Stalingrad
1944	The United States condemns Irish neutrality; British government bans all travel between Great Britain and Ireland	Francis Bacon, *Three Studies for Figures at the Base of a Crucifixion*; Mainie Jellett, *Achill Horses*; Mary Swanzy, *The Mêlée*; Louis MacNeice, *Springboard*	Jean Anouilh, *Antigone* premieres in Paris; Marianne Moore, *Nevertheless*	Famine in Vietnam kills 2 million; Bretton Woods conference and foundation of World Bank and International Monetary Fund (IMF)

1945	Congress of Irish Trade Unions formed; Sean T. O'Kelly succeeds Douglas Hyde as President of Éire; Éamon de Valera expresses sympathy to German Ambassador on death of Hitler and responds by radio broadcast to Winston Churchill	Elizabeth Bowen, *The Demon Lover and Other Stories*; Jack B. Yeats, *No Flowers*; Thomas MacGreevy, *Jack B. Yeats*	Hermann Broch, *The Death of Virgil*; Gertrude Stein, *Wars I Have Seen*; H. D., *Tribute to Angels*; George Orwell, *Animal Farm*; Frida Kahlo, *Without Hope*	Unconditional surrender of German High Command and atomic bombs drop on Hiroshima and Nagasaki
1946	Clann na Poblachta party formed	Denis Devlin, *Lough Derg and Other Poems*; Jack B. Yeats, *Above the Fair* and *Men of Destiny*; Francis Bacon, *Painting*; G. B. Shaw made freeman of Dublin	Eugene O'Neill's *The Iceman Cometh* premieres in New York; Miguel Ángel Asturias, *El Señor Presidente*; Erich Auerbach, *Mimesis*	United Nations convenes for first time; Vietnamese resist reimposition of French colonial rule after the war
1947	Roman Catholic bishops express disapproval of the clauses in the Health Act having to do with mother and child services		Theodor Adorno and Max Horkheimer, *Dialectic of Enlightenment*; Malcolm Lowry, *Under the Volcano*; Thomas Mann, *Doctor Faustus*; Eugene O'Neill, *A Moon for the Misbegotten* premieres in Columbus, Ohio	Partition of India; Independence of India and Pakistan

(continued)

Date	Irish Historical Events	Irish Modernist Works and Related Cultural Events	International Cultural and Intellectual Events	International Historical Events
1948	Republic of Ireland Bill passed	Mairtín Ó Cadhain, *Cré na Cille*; Francis Stuart, *The Pillar of Cloud*; Francis Bacon, *Head VI*; Jack B. Yeats, *The Last Dawn But One and Many Ferries*; Louis le Brocquy, *Irish Tinkers*; Music Association of Ireland set up to promote classical music; Richard Ellmann, *Yeats, The Man and the Masks*	Jean-Paul Sartre, "Black Orpheus"; T. S. Eliot *Notes Towards the Definition of Culture*; Georg Lukács, Thomas Mann; F. R. Leavis, *The Great Tradition*	European Recovery Program (Marshall Plan) launched (–1951); Partition of Palestine and the creation of the state of Israel; Ceylon achieves independence; Gandhi assassinated
1949	Éire formally becomes a Republic and leaves the British Commonwealth	Mairtín Ó Direáin, *Rogha Dánta*; Louis MacNeice, *Collected Poems*; Elizabeth Bowen, *The Heat of the Day*; Francis Stuart, *Redemption*; Seán O'Casey, *Cock-a-Doodle Dandy* premieres in Newcastle upon Tyne; Jack B. Yeats, *The Singing Horseman and Confidence*; Francis Bacon, *Head II*; A. N. Jeffares, *W. B. Yeats: Man and Poet*	Simone de Beauvoir, *The Second Sex*; Theodor Adorno, *Philosophy of New Music*; Georges Bataille, *The Accursed Share*; Naguib Mahfouz, *The Beginning and the End*; Miguel Angel Asturias, *Men of Maize*; Alejo Carpentier, *The Kingdom of this World*; Jorge Luis Borges, *The Aleph and Other Stories*	People's Republic of China declared; National Government in South Africa implements apartheid

1950	Dr. Noel Browne resigns as Minister of Health over "mother and child scheme"	Arts Council founded in the Irish Republic; Lyric Players Theatre founded in Belfast; Francis Stuart, *The Flowering Cross*; T. R. Henn, *The Lonely Tower*; death of G. B. Shaw	Pablo Neruda, *Canto General*; Eugene Ionesco, *The Bald Soprano* premieres in Paris; Jackson Pollock, *No 5. 1948*; Octavio Paz, *The Labyrinth of Solitude*; Lionel Trilling, *The Liberal Imagination*; E. H. Gombrich, *The Story of Art*	Outbreak of Korean War (–1953); Chinese invasion of Tibet; Jordan annexes West Bank in Palestine
1951		Samuel Beckett, *Molloy* (English 1955); *Malone Dies* (English 1958); Jack B. Yeats, *Grief and For the Road*; Arts Council founded in the Irish Republic; Lyric Players Theatre founded in Belfast	Marguerite Yourcenar, *Memoirs of Hadrian*; Tennessee Williams's *The Rose Tattoo* premieres in New York	Libya gains independence; Iran nationalizes oil industry; guerrilla war against British forces in Suez Canal zone
1952		Samuel Beckett, *Waiting for Godot* published; Seán Ó Ríordáin, *Eireaball Spideoige*	Flannery O'Connor, *Wise Blood*; David Jones, *The Anathemata*; Ralph Ellison, *Invisible Man*; Frantz Fanon, *Black Skins, White Masks*	Mau Mau emergency begins in Kenya

(continued)

Date	Irish Historical Events	Irish Modernist Works and Related Cultural Events	International Cultural and Intellectual Events	International Historical Events
1953	Protests by civil servants and unemployed in Dublin	Samuel Beckett, *En attendant Godot* premieres in Paris; *The Unnamable* (English 1960) and *Watt* published; Francis Bacon, *Study after Velásquez's Portrait of Pope Innocent X*; Pike Theatre established; Chester Beatty Library opens	Alejo Carpentier, *The Lost Steps*; James Baldwin, *Go Tell It on the Mountain*; Roland Barthes, *Writing Degree Zero*	CIA-backed coup deposes Mohammad Mosaddegh in Iran; uprising against British colonialism in British Guiana; Egyptian republic proclaimed
1954		First public celebration of Bloomsday in Dublin; Brendan Behan, *The Quare Fellow* premieres in Dublin; Richard Ellmann, *The Identity of Yeats*		Vietnamese army defeats French colonial army at Dien Bien Phu; Algerian War begins (−1962)
1955	Republic of Ireland joins United Nations	Samuel Beckett, *Molloy*; English language premiers of *Waiting for Godot* in Dublin and London; Elizabeth Bowen, *A World of Love*; Francis Bacon, *Figure with Meat*	Flannery O'Connor, *A Good Man is Hard to Find*; Vladimir Nabokov, *Lolita*; Claude Lévi-Strauss, *Tristes Tropiques*	Bandung Conference; Messina conference plans creation of European Economic Community
1956		Thomas Kinsella, *Poems*; Seán Ó Faoláin, *The Vanishing Hero*	Eugene O'Neill, *Long Day's Journey into Night* premieres in Stockholm; Albert Camus, *The Fall*; Naguib Mahfouz,	Suez Crisis; Hungarian uprising crushed by Soviet troops; Fidel Castro lands in Cuba to overthrow the Batista

Year				
			Cairo Trilogy (–1957); Tennessee Williams, *Cat on a Hot Tin Roof* premieres in New York; Allen Ginsberg, *Howl*	dictatorship; Independence of Sudan
1957	IRA launches border campaign	Samuel Beckett, *Endgame* published in French and premieres in London, and *All That Fall* broadcast on BBC; Máirtín Ó Direáin, *Ó Mórna agus Dánta Eile*; Louis le Brocquy, *Young Woman (Anne)*; Stanislaus Joyce, *My Brother's Keeper*	Jack Kerouac, *On the Road*; Albert Memmi, *The Colonizer and the Colonized*	Founding of the Common Market; Independence of Malaya and Ghana; Battle of Algiers
1958		Samuel Beckett, *Krapp's Last Tape* premieres in London; Thomas Kinsella, *Another September*; Brendan Behan, *The Hostage* premieres in London; Mary (and Padraic) Colum, *Our Friend, James Joyce*	Chinua Achebe, *Things Fall Apart*; Giuseppe Tomasi di Lampedusa, *The Leopard*; Harold Pinter, *The Birthday Party*; Raymond Williams, *Culture and Society*	Chairman Mao launches "Great Leap Forward"; United Arab Republic founded by merger of Syria and Egypt
1959	Inaugural congress of Irish Congress of Trades Unions	Seán Ó Riada composes score for *Mise Éire*; Seán O'Casey, *The Drums of Father Ned*; Richard Ellmann, *James Joyce*	Günter Grass, *The Tin Drum*; Robert Lowell, *Life Studies*; Jean Genet, *The Blacks* premieres in Paris	Famine in China kills 40 million; Fidel Castro assumes power in Cuba

(continued)

Date	Irish Historical Events	Irish Modernist Works and Related Cultural Events	International Cultural and Intellectual Events	International Historical Events
1960			Flannery O'Connor, *The Violent Bear it Away and Everything that Rises Must Converge*; Harold Pinter, *The Caretaker* premieres in London; George Lamming, *The Pleasures of Exile*	Independence of Nigeria and Cyprus; Harold Macmillan's "wind of change" speech in Cape Town; Sharpeville masscare; ANC and Pan-African Congress banned
1961	Republic of Ireland applies for membership of EEC; Telefís Éireann (RTÉ) begins transmission	Samuel Beckett, *The Beckett Trilogy*	Musée d'Art Moderne de la Ville de Paris opened; Frantz Fanon, *The Wretched of the Earth*; Jean Genet's *The Screens* premieres in Berlin; V. S. Naipaul, *A House for Mr Biswas*; Marshall McLuhan, *The Gutenberg Galaxy*	Bay of Pigs invasion; Cuban Missile Crisis; Berlin Wall erected; Yuri Gagarin first man in space
1962	IRA calls off border campaign	Thomas Kinsella, *Downstream*; Máirtín Ó Direáin, *Ár Ré Dhearóil*; Vivian Mercier, *The Irish Comic Tradition*	Andy Warhol, *32 Campbell's Soup Cans*; Carlos Fuentes, *The Death of Artemio Cruz*; William Carlos Williams, *Pictures from Brueghel and Other Poems* (posthumous); Lawrence Durrell, *The Alexandria Quartet*	Second Vatican Council; Cuban Missile Crisis; Independence of Algeria, Jamaica, Trinidad, and Uganda
1963	President John F. Kennedy visits	Seán Ó Riada, *Nomos. No. 2*; Louis MacNeice, *The Burning Perch*	Ghassan Kanafani, *Men in the Sun*; Thomas Pynchon, *V*; Julio Cortázar, *Hopscotch*; E. P. Thompson, *The Making of the English Working Class*	Martin Luther King, "I have a dream" speech; Assassination of J. F. Kennedy; Kenya gains independence

1964	Seán Ó Riordáin, *Brosna*; Flann O'Brien, *The Dalkey Archive*; Patrick Kavanagh, *Collected Poems*; Denis Devlin, *Collected Poems*	Jean-Paul Sartre refuses Nobel Prize for Literature; Michel Foucault, *Madness and Civilization*; Peter Weiss, *Marat/Sade* premieres in Berlin; Philip Larkin, *The Whitsun Weddings*	States of Tanzania and Zambia established; PLO established
1965	Taoiseach Seán Lemass visits Northern Prime Minister Terence O'Neill in Belfast	Francis Bacon, *Crucifixion*; Louis le Brocquy, *Evoked Head of an Irish Rebel Hero*; Conor Cruise O'Brien, "Passion and Cunning: An Essay on the Politics of W. B. Yeats"	Sylvia Plath, *Ariel*; Harold Pinter, *The Homecoming* premieres in London; Guillermo Cabrera Infante, *Three Trapped Tigers*	U.S.–Vietnam War begins (–1975) when President Lyndon Johnson commits U.S. forces to the defense of Southern Vietnam
1966	Easter Rising 50th anniversary commemorations; UVF founded; Admiral Nelson's Pillar destroyed in Dublin	New Abbey Theatre opens; Francis Bacon, *Study for the Head of George Dyer*	Claude Lévi-Strauss, *The Savage Mind*; Jacques Lacan, *Écrits*; Hans Blumenberg, *The Legitimacy of the Modern Age*; Thomas Pynchon, *The Crying of Lot 49*; Marguerite Duras, *The Vice-Consul*	Guyana, Lesotho, Botswana, and Barbados gain independence
1967	Taoiseach Jack Lynch holds talks with Charles de Gaulle on European Community	Denis Devlin, *The Heavenly Foreigner*; Flann O'Brien, *The Third Policeman* (written 1939–40) published in London; New Writers Press founded by Michael Smith and Trevor Joyce to promote avant-garde poetry	Gabriel García Márquez, *One Hundred Years of Solitude*; Ngugi Wa Thiong'o, *A Grain of Wheat*; V. S. Naipaul, *The Mimic Men*; Jacques Derrida, *Of Grammatology*	Six-Day Arab–Israeli War; British withdrawal from Aden

(*continued*)

Date	Irish Historical Events	Irish Modernist Works and Related Cultural Events	International Cultural and Intellectual Events	International Historical Events
1968	People's Democracy march from Belfast to Derry ambushed by militant Protestants; British troops move into Derry	Lyric Theatre opened in Belfast; Elizabeth Bowen, *Eva Trout*; Thomas Kinsella, *Nightwalker and Other Poems*; Derek Mahon, *Night Crossing*		Student insurrections across the world; "Prague Spring" uprising crushed by Soviet troops; Martin Luther King assassinated in the United States; "Tet Offensive" and My Lai massacre in Vietnam; Paul VI issues *Humanae vitae* condemning artificial contraception
1969	Major rioting in Belfast; Battle of the Bogside in Derry; British troops deployed to Northern Ireland; Irish Republic receives its first World Bank loan; Terence O'Neill resigns as Prime Minister in Northern Ireland; IRA splits into Official and Provisional wings	Samuel Beckett receives the Nobel Prize; abolition of income tax for writers and artists on their income from the arts in Irish Republic; Francis Stuart, *Black List, Section H*; Thomas Kinsella, *The Táin* (translation) and *Nightwalker and Other Poems*; Maeve Brennan, *In and Out of Never-Never Land*	John Berryman, *The Dream Songs*; Ursula Le Guin, *The Left Hand of Darkness*; Tayib Salih, *Season of Migration from the North*; Mario Vargas Llosa, *Conversation in the Cathedral*	Apollo 11 moon landing; United States bombs Cambodia; first U.S. troop withdrawals from Vietnam; Yasser Arafat elected leader of PLO; border clashes between the Soviet Union and China; Stonewall Riots in New York mark start of U.S. Gay Rights movement

JOE CLEARY

Introduction

I

The story of Irish modernism constitutes one of the more remarkable chapters in the eventful history of European modernism. The names of William Butler Yeats, James Joyce, and Samuel Beckett are now so familiar that it is difficult for us to recapture any sense of how unlikely it would have seemed in 1900 that a small island more famed for its economic backwardness and calamitous history than for anything that might be considered "modern" should have produced three figures as significant to the development of modernism as any of the major writers to emerge in England, France, Germany, Russia, or the United States in the same era. Nineteenth-century Ireland had produced outstanding political leaders in Daniel O'Connell and Charles Stewart Parnell and charismatic political writers such as Thomas Davis, James Fintan Lalor, John Mitchel, and Michael Davitt. It had also won a reputation in Europe and beyond for its "Celtic" spirituality and imagination, a reputation burnished in the writings of Johann Gottfried Herder, Matthew Arnold, and Ernest Renan. Nevertheless, nineteenth-century Irish artists had generally languished on the outer edges of the great traditions of English and French romanticism and realism or on those of German or Italian classical music, and even those who won metropolitan recognition in the period exerted little of the transformative effect on English and European high culture that Yeats, Joyce, and Beckett were to do after World War I. Modernism today is part of a receding history, but works such as *Ulysses* (1922), *A Vision* (1925, revised edition 1937), *The Tower* (1928), *Finnegans Wake* (1939), *The Unnameable* (1953), or *Endgame* (1957) retain a capacity to compel that time seems to increase rather than diminish.

However, it is arguable that precisely because they were so remarkable, the achievements of Yeats, Joyce, and Beckett have ultimately contributed to an attenuated conception of the history and achievements of Irish modernism more broadly. Such is the distinction of these luminaries that they have not only been separated from the mainstream of modern Irish literature more generally to be treated as honorific British, European, or "world" figures, but they are also often detached from any more extensive consideration of Irish modernism as such. Thus, there are now great stacks of books and a constant round of scholarly events devoted to the appreciation of Yeats, Joyce, and Beckett, and there is a smaller but steadily growing body of work on some of their other compatriots such as Jack B. Yeats, Elizabeth Bowen, Flann O'Brien, or Francis Bacon. Nevertheless, despite the attention these individuals command, there are scarcely any broad-ranging studies of Irish modernism and it has always been easier for scholars to accept that twentieth-century Ireland produced a small handful of émigré modernists than that it generated a more extended modernism in its own right, one that flowered most spectacularly in literature and drama, but that also saw notable developments in the visual arts, architecture, music, cinema, and design.

Were it not so dominated by the iconic figures of Yeats, Joyce, and Beckett, how might we reconfigure our sense of Irish modernism? The achievements of these outstanding writers are deservedly admired and will remain at the centre of this volume, but, as the chapters by Laura O'Connor, Emer Nolan, Ben Levitas, and Luke Gibbons variously remind us, they are also part of a tapestry of modernist artistic achievement that encompasses several media, and that was created in several locations in the period roughly between 1890 and 1960. To consider Irish modernism in this expanded frame even in the literary field is to push out the customary boundaries and to acknowledge the importance of figures such as George Moore, George Egerton, Oscar Wilde, or George Bernard Shaw, all more conventionally treated as minor precursors to Yeats, Joyce, and Beckett rather than as serious contributors to modernism in their own right. Nevertheless, these earlier figures – who, like Yeats, came of age professionally in fin de siècle England and made their reputations there before World War I – had all been notable enthusiasts of the earliest continental European avant gardes: Moore championed in turn French impressionism, naturalism, and aestheticism; Egerton was the first writer in English to reference Friedrich Nietzsche and to translate Knut Hamsun; Wilde was the most flamboyant English-language practitioner of European decadence; Shaw was a committed advocate of Henrik Ibsen at a time when the Norwegian's work provoked scandal or incomprehension in British theatrical circles. After Yeats and Joyce were widely feted as major writers in the high modernist decade of the 1920s, Ireland went on to produce not only another major late modernist in Beckett but also a considerable company of experimental dramatists, poets, and novelists – such as Sean O'Casey, Louis MacNeice, Elizabeth Bowen, Flann O'Brien, Máirtín

Ó Cadhain, Thomas MacGreevy, Denis Devlin, Brian Coffey, and Seán Ó Ríordáin – who made their own estimable contributions to modernism in Ireland. Beckett's accomplishments normally dominate any discussion of this later period, but if his work is viewed in terms of some of his other Irish contemporaries in various disciplines the lineaments of a remarkable but still scarcely conceptualized late Irish modernism begin to appear.

Beyond the literary field there was also from the outset a considerable body of Irish visual artists, many of them women, attentive to new developments in European painting, sculpture, and design and finding in the continental avant gardes the inspiration and resources to get beyond the academicist conventions that regulated the production of painting and the plastic arts in Britain and Ireland. Like their literary contemporaries, many of these artists plied their careers between Dublin, London, and Paris; like the writers, some sidestepped the Irish Revival in favour of more abstract European avant-garde currents, whereas others attempted (as Yeats or Joyce in their respective ways were to do) to tap both revivalist and modernist energies. Scholarship on the Irish visual arts has advanced significantly in recent decades, but even now treatments of Irish modernism that deal with May Guinness, Mary Swanzy, Mainie Jellett, Eileen Gray, Jack B. Yeats, Seán Keating, Francis Bacon, Louis le Brocquy, Patrick Scott, or Sean Scully (to mention only some of the figures involved) are relatively few, and, given the disciplinary specialisms involved, the capacity of cultural historians to make compelling connections between Irish literary and visual media modernisms remains limited. Though there have been significant advances in recent times in these fields too, scholarship on Irish musical, architectural, and cinematic modernisms is only in its pioneering phase; thus, in many ways the history of Irish modernism in the wider sense is still, for all the attention devoted to Yeats, Joyce, and Beckett, in its early stage and tentative.[1]

The object of this *Companion* is to consolidate contemporary scholarship on Irish modernism with a view also to expanding its scope and ambition. This volume aims to (1) present accessible but wide-ranging and critically challenging overviews of the sociohistorical, intellectual, and aesthetic forces that contributed to the emergence of an Irish modernism; and (2) chart some of the contours of that modernism as it evolved in a variety of media such as poetry, the novel, theatre, and the visual arts. The *Companion* surveys these subjects over a period of more than half a century and tracks them across an international terrain that includes not only Ireland but also England, France, and the United States. It attends to the particular ambitions and constraints that shaped the modernist literatures produced by Irish women, Irish-language writers, and Irish American modernists. These pages dwell primarily on literature and the visual arts, but because this *Companion* focuses on a spectrum of modernist achievement in several media, it aims to make a significant contribution to a larger revaluation of modernism in Ireland more generally.

II

As will already perhaps be clear, the term "Irish modernism" provokes knotty questions of definition. Should it refer to a modernism produced by Irish artists? And what exactly would the term "Irish" encompass in an era during which Ireland underwent a radical and continuous process of political and cultural redefinition as a territory that had historically been part of the United Kingdom of Great Britain and Ireland was contested by Irish nationalists and unionists, and was divided shortly after World War I into two states, the Irish Free State and Northern Ireland, each of which retaining constitutionally contested and emotionally fraught links with Great Britain? Or should the term refer to the modernism produced by Irish artists and those of Irish extraction working either in Ireland itself or beyond its shores? "Modernism" too has always presented its own difficulties as a term because it refers to changes of very discrepant kinds to the conception and function of a whole variety of arts. This *Companion* leans generally towards the more capacious conceptions of "Irish modernism" because, however defined, it was from the outset a decidedly transnational phenomenon. Several of the most canonical figures associated with modernism spent substantial parts of their careers outside of Ireland: Yeats lived some of his formative childhood years in London before returning to Dublin; Joyce left Ireland at the age of twenty-three for Trieste and never lived permanently in Ireland thereafter; and Beckett abandoned an academic post at Trinity College Dublin in 1931 to develop his artistic career in Paris. Paris is obviously crucial to any history of Irish modernism as it was there that George Moore first came into contact with French naturalism and impressionism, that Wilde's *Salomé* (1896) premiered, that *Ulysses* (1922), *Waiting for Godot* (1953), and *Endgame* (1957) first appeared, and that so many Irish visual artists such as Mainie Jellett or Mary Swanzy or Eileen Gray came into contact with modernist movements or mentors that influenced their own experimental works. Likewise, the careers of George Moore, George Bernard Shaw, Elizabeth Bowen, Sean O'Casey, or Francis Bacon were based largely in London and therefore their works belong in that sense as much to the story of English as to Irish modernism. There has been a determined and valuable attempt in Irish Studies in recent decades to reclaim most of these figures for Irish culture and to critically evaluate the extent to which their works are informed by Irish social and cultural history.[2] This *Companion* is indebted to this work of reclamation, and in some degree continues that project, but it also recognizes that to stress the "Irish" at the expense of the "international" dimension of the works considered, or indeed vice versa, is historically and conceptually unproductive. Because of the peculiarities of nineteenth-century Irish colonial history, there were very good reasons, social and cultural, why Irish artistic production generally and Irish modernism more specifically should have developed in several different sites, many of them beyond Ireland.

The case of music offers a useful entry point here. Nineteenth-century Ireland may have been more commonly identified abroad with music than with either painting or literature. Thomas Moore's *Irish Melodies* (1806–7) won fame across early-nineteenth-century Europe and captured the imagination of the late Romantic era in a manner that recalled the spectacular success that the Scottish James Macpherson's *The Works of Ossian* (1765) had enjoyed several decades earlier among German romantics such as Herder, Friedrich Klopstock, and Johann Wolfgang von Goethe. In other countries, such as Russia, Bulgaria, Hungary, Germany, Spain, and the United States, popular folk idioms and modernist aesthetic experiment were integrated in the new music in fascinating ways. Yet despite its wealth of folk culture, folk music, and popular song, all of which were so influential on the literature and theatre of the Irish Revival, as indeed were Moore's songs on Joyce's imagination, this integration of high art music and popular music was not managed to any really distinguished effect in Ireland and even the most talented Irish-based exponents of Irish modernist art music such as Frederick May, Brian Boydell, and Aloys Fleischmann never attained a prominence equal to that of their contemporaries in other modernist media. Musicologists continue to debate the reasons for this: some claim that the precedence accorded by Irish cultural nationalism to ethnic folk music stymied the emergence of a European art music, whether in its classical or modernist forms; others, more persuasively, argue that because it was a backward province of the United Kingdom that had itself become separated from the more advanced currents in European art music, Ireland lacked the developed infrastructure necessary to produce a strong musical modernism.[3]

It may therefore be the case, as Axel Klein has proposed, that the most significant contributor with Irish associations to modernist music before the Cold War was Henry Cowell, born in California in 1897 to an Irish Protestant immigrant father, Harry Cowell, and an American Midwestern mother, Clarissa Dixon, a writer and editor of the anarchist paper, *The Beacon*.[4] Growing up in this bohemian milieu, and thus obviously well outside of Ireland and its domestic music establishment, Cowell became an early explorer of techniques such as atonality and polytonality and he was also interested in Asian classical music. But through his father and his friend, the Dublin-born poet and theosophist John Varian, who prior to his emigration to the United States in 1894 had been a member of the Theosophical Society and friend of George Russell (AE) in Dublin, Cowell nevertheless developed an interest in Irish music and mythology. His early experiments in tone cluster combined these high art and Irish interests, as is evident in the titles of some of his early avant-garde compositions: *The Tides of Mananaun* (1917), *The Trumpet of Angus Og* (1918–24), and *The Banshee* (1925). When he toured Europe in the 1920s, Cowell's tone cluster technique captured the interest of the Hungarian composer Béla Bartók, who asked his permission to adopt it into his own work. Cowell later became one of a distinguished group of ultra-modernist American composers and was mentor to George Gershwin, Lou Harrison, and John Cage. However, he retained his interest in folk and non-Western music; he taught a course on "Music of the World's Peoples" at the New School for Social Research in New York in the late 1920s and in 1928 founded the Pan-American Association of Composers to promote the music of the Americas generally and to build a transnational sense of musical community.

By background, Cowell derived on his Irish side from the same Anglo-Irish Protestant milieu to which composers Boydell and May also belonged, and the mix of theosophical, oriental, Irish folk, and mythological influences that Cowell absorbed into his early compositions have some remarkable similarities to that which, in various ways, stimulated Yeats, Augusta Gregory, AE, Standish O'Grady, James Cousins, and other Protestant revivalists, including the Irish Revival-influenced English composer Arnold Bax. But culturally, Cowell is closer perhaps to Irish American literary and theatrical modernists such as Eugene O'Neill, born in 1888, and F. Scott Fitzgerald, born in 1896, and thus a year Cowell's senior. Like these and older Irish American modernists, such as the architect Louis Henry Sullivan or the art collector John Quinn, Cowell made his career at a time when the influence of the Irish Revival on American and European culture was at its height and when the United States was also beginning to develop its own forms of modernist expression. In this late-nineteenth- and early-twentieth-century period, when Irish revivalism and modernism were both still in their fledgling and most protean phases, they did not seem as antithetical to each other as they would later appear to many after each had assumed more programmatic definition from the 1920s or 1930s onwards. Cowell, O'Neill, Fitzgerald, Sullivan, and others are now, properly, claimed for American modernism, but they were all conscious of the achievements of the Irish Revival and indeed of Irish émigré figures such as Wilde and Shaw in London and later of Joyce in Paris, and to this extent at least there are ways in which Ireland and Irish culture were significant to the wider history of European and American modernisms even before these modernisms made their impact on twentieth-century Ireland. Because writers, painters, and designers – such as Moore, Joyce, and Beckett or Swanzy, Guinness, and Gray – resided in Paris, and Wilde, Shaw, O'Casey, Bowen, and Bacon made their careers in London, it has been conventional to think of Irish modernism almost exclusively in terms of an Irish-European axis. But the United States also has its place in any serious account of Irish modernist history, and, as I argue in Chapter 11, several leading figures in American modernism were shaped by the wider cultural history of the post-Famine Irish diaspora in the United States.

It is also worth noting in this context that the production of what we now retrospectively call "modernism" was never solely the labour of its immediate creators. Many other kinds of cultural mediation were always involved, including the work of publishers and translators, actors and stage-designers, editors and cultural magazines, patrons and impresarios, and critics and curators of various kinds. At this level, too, the story of Irish modernism is constitutively both national and transnational in its dimensions. Some major patrons of modernism in its early stages were Irish. Hugh Lane is one example; Lane's aunt, Augusta Gregory, a generous patron of Yeats as well as co-founder of and playwright for the Abbey Theatre, is another. Other patrons, such as Harriet Shaw Weaver and Nancy Cunard, were radicalized members of the English upper class: Weaver was a financial supporter of *The Freewoman*, later re-titled *The Egoist*, as well as a generous supporter of Joyce; Cunard founded and financed the Hours Press, which published, among many other notable works, *The Negro Anthology* (1934) and Beckett's first book, *Whoroscope* (1930). Several other patrons, collectors, and curators were Irish American. John Quinn was not only a major collector of French post-impressionist and Irish Revivalist art, but also the attorney who defended the *Little Review* when it was prosecuted for obscenity for serializing *Ulysses*; James Johnson Sweeney, whose family emigrated to United States from Co. Donegal, contributed a defence of modern painting to AE's *Irish Statesman* before going on to write an incisive book on modernist art, *Plastic Redirections in 20th-Century Painting* (1934), and to become an associate editor of *Transition*, in which position he helped Joyce to correct what became *Finnegans Wake* as it was serialized in that journal. When he became Visiting Lecturer at New York's Institute of Fine Arts (1934–40), Sweeney was confirmed as one of the leading American experts on twentieth-century avant-garde art and he held important curatorial positions or directorships at the Museum of Modern Art and the Solomon R. Guggenheim Museum in New York.

As even these slight cameos may suggest, the histories of Irish modernism and of Irish exile and emigration are, and in a manner that includes but also goes well beyond the famous instances of Joyce's or Beckett's residences in Paris, complexly connected. The vast majority of those born in Ireland associated with the development of modernist experiment in all media, and especially in its initial stages, were middle- or upper-class Anglo-Irish Protestants. As a consequence of a colonial history dating back to the sixteenth- and seventeenth-century plantations, Protestants had dominated nearly all of the higher professions – commercial, professional, educational, artistic – in Ireland and would continue to do so into the twentieth century. It was because of this colonial context, too, that so many Irish literary and visual artists especially had consistently gravitated towards London, the great imperial metropole that remained the cultural capital of the Anglophone world throughout the modernist period, although this role was increasingly appropriated by New York as the United States replaced Great Britain as the world's leading capitalist state. And it was in turn because of the overwhelming dominance of London over the wider Anglophone world that so many Irish writers and painters reactively gravitated to Paris in the late nineteenth and early twentieth centuries. In Paris, the Irish émigrés discovered not only what Pascale Casanova has called "the capital of Art in the purest sense" but also a cosmopolitan crucible of avant-garde activity and a means to reduce longstanding Irish cultural dependency on London.[5] Parisian consecration, moreover, conferred on the consecrated a "universality" of recognition more prestigious than anything London could offer in this period.

But if a colonial history can explain why so many Irish talents ended up in London or Paris, it was the political tribulations and economic destitution occasioned by this same colonial history that also impelled Irish people of lower social classes to emigrate to the United States. In the seventeenth and eighteenth centuries, this emigration had been mainly from the northern counties of Ireland and was comprised largely of Dissenting Protestants escaping Anglican domination; after the Great Famine, the tide of emigration was predominantly Catholic. By the beginning of the twentieth century, this Irish-American Catholic community was becoming increasingly economically powerful and politically assertive, and the enthusiasm of some of its more talented literary and intellectual figures – such as O'Neill, Fitzgerald, Sweeney, and others – for the higher arts was almost certainly connected to their desire to shake off their nineteenth-century Irish predecessors' association with low-brow mass culture. In the circumstances, the metropolitan nature of Irish modernism – the fact that so much of it was to be produced in Paris, London, and New York – and its colonial origins are not, as sometimes thought, contradictory; they are, rather, dialectically connected.

These colonial origins are probably responsible not only for Irish modernism's characteristic oscillation between "vernacular" and "cosmopolitan" imaginaries – the subject of Michael Valdez Moses's final chapter in this volume – but also for its combinations of restless formal experiment and its tendency in many instances to be sceptical of liberal notions of historical progress. For most cultural historians, the defining watershed catastrophe of the modernist epoch is World War I: a climacteric that left millions dead, collapsed old dynasties across Europe, and loosened the mortar of relatively settled class and gender hierarchies; as the prewar social order disintegrated, it released both radical new social movements aiming to revolutionize the world and fiercely reactionary restorationist forces fighting under the banners of national purity and tradition. However, the Great Famine of 1845–50, which left more than a million dead because of hunger and disease, and precipitated the emigration of a million more, arguably represented in the Irish case a pulverization of society at least as drastic and as consequential in effect as World War I was later to be for other European countries. This is not to say that the Famine was Ireland's earlier Victorian version of World War I, but that when Irish society experienced the Great War, and the local responses to that wider turmoil – which included the arming of the Ulster and Irish Volunteers, Easter 1916, and the War of Independence – this turmoil unfolded within relatively recent memory of the preceding domestic calamity. Hence, the cultural and political shocks still reverberating from one great catastrophe were sharpened by a second, and aggravated soon afterwards again by a third if we include the events of the late 1920s and 1930s that ultimately issued in World War II.

A traumatic sense of modernity-as-catastrophe nurtured by Irish history had already found memorable literary expression in the writings of figures as various as Seathrún Céitinn (Geoffrey Keating), Jonathan Swift, John Mitchel, James Clarence Mangan, Michael Davitt, or Standish O'Grady, and in modes of Irish writing as different as Gaelic *aisling* or Anglo-Irish Gothic. Drawing on this acrimonious history and unsettled literary inheritance, Joyce produced in *Ulysses* an epic humorously receptive to the small graces that a single day may bring but vibrant also with the nightmarish quality of modern history and with a corresponding wariness of what Stephen Dedalus calls "those big words which make us so unhappy."[6] From similar resources, Yeats created a poetry in which a well-brewed Anglo-Irish colonial contempt for the Catholic middle class is nearly always straining at the leash, but that is at the same time more responsive than the work of any of his contemporaries to the intellectual and visionary drama of the

Irish revolutionary struggle. Beckett can seem the most wilfully apolitical of writers given the political savagery of Europe at the time when he made his reputation, yet he created a theatre that registers even more profoundly perhaps than that of Bertolt Brecht the wretchedness of a world brought to such a pass that the very idea of hopefulness seems the ultimate mockery. And in the works of several of Beckett's contemporaries, whether a writer like Ó Cadhain or a painter like Francis Bacon, the spiritual debacle of the Irish and international twentieth century find unforgettable expression. Irish colonial history had conferred on these and other Irish modernists, whatever their gender, denomination, or politics, a sense of the collapsibility of all social and cultural systems, whether "traditional" or "modern," and from that domestic inheritance, and from the madly careering whirligig of the arts in their own times, they made a strange (sometimes downright eccentric) art, formally inventive, provocatively and perversely erudite, and – for the most part – politically more vexed than anything else. Like other modernisms, Irish modernism has its sinister dimensions, these most obviously manifest in the authoritarian and sometimes fascist leanings of Yeats or in the work of Francis Stuart, who actually collaborated with Nazi Germany. However, to single out Yeats and Stuart for specific condemnation can sometimes lead to a very facile evaluation of the politics of Irish modernism. Given the complex ways in which modernism as a whole is related to the wider history of European colonialism and imperialism (and anti-imperialism), and given too its connections to left- and right-wing authoritarianisms in the period from World War I through the Cold War, not to mention the abiding complexities of its class, sexual, and gender politics, there are good reasons to resist the notion that progressive and reactionary versions of modernism can easily be separated from each other.

But if a colonial history scattered Irish modernists across Britain, Europe, and the United States and charged the work they produced with an acute sense of civilizational distress that could take any number of political directions, it would be wrong to stress only the elements of collapse and disintegration. Nineteenth- and early-twentieth-century colonial history might have made the Irish artists connoisseurs of crisis, but that history had also produced a broad concatenation of elite and popular resistance movements, mostly national in focus but transnational in reach. These included Home Rule parliamentary campaigns conducted in Ireland and England, Fenian insurrectionary organizations with underground networks running from Ireland and England to the United States, syndicalist labour movements stretching across the same spaces, and a militantly international women's movement. Modernism in Europe generally flourished at a time when history seemed radically open-ended because very different social futures were imaginable, and when ideas and art assumed correspondingly urgent forms. A byword for political agitation from the Famine onwards, Ireland between the 1880s and the 1930s especially was as volatile as many places in Europe and so knew its own versions of the chronic discontent with the status quo and the rage for change that energized avant garde and modernist movements everywhere.

Culturally, the most important movement to emerge out of this late-nineteenth-century period of political agitation was the Irish Revival, a term given to a loosely affiliated set of organizations that hoped to repair the cultural devastation caused by the final meltdown of Gaelic Ireland precipitated by the Famine. Because the two developed roughly concurrently, the relationship between that Revival and Irish modernism has remained a matter of abiding controversy in Irish Studies, a topic reviewed by Rónán McDonald in Chapter 3. The most common conception of that relationship has been that the two phenomena were polar opposites: the Revival, until recently at least, has been widely conceived as a late romantic and antiquarian-minded form of cultural nationalism that encouraged an insular aesthetic traditionalism preoccupied with the Gaelic past, the peasant West of Ireland, and aristocratic or folk culture; modernism, conversely, has typically been taken to represent a broadly progressive commitment to aesthetic innovation, outward-looking internationalism, and a repudiation of the Catholic bourgeois nationalist mentalities coming to the fore as the campaign for Irish national independence gained momentum. However, in its most extreme versions at least, this view issues in a very dualistic sense of Irish cultural production in which even Yeats is dissociated from modernism and conceived only as the leading representative of the Revival, while Joyce and Beckett are set at a long remove from their Irish contemporaries to represent an exemplary cosmopolitanism that wholly transcends the nation. One of the things that this critical manicheanism misses is the degree to which the rhetorics of "revivalism" or "renaissance" and the rhetorics of what we now call "modernism" nurtured each other. In their different ways, both modernism and revivalism shared the conviction that the culture inherited from the nineteenth century was a philistine impediment to genuine artistic creation and in each case the broad impetus was similar: to reject the immediate past as almost wholly compromised; to create a new art that would find its rightful place not in the degraded present but in some renovated future of a transformed nation or new era.[7]

Here, too, the effects of a long cultural colonialism may be registered. In the nineteenth century, as cultural nationalism was on the rise almost everywhere, both Ireland and the United States felt themselves to be abjectly subordinate to English cultural tradition. But each had also produced during that century intermittent cultural "renaissances" to combat this sense of subordination, and this colonial resentment of English domination lent Irish and American discourses of renaissance and modernism their special edges. In both situations, that is, the moribund culture that was dismissed as second-rate was not simply nineteenth-century Irish or American national cultures per se, but also the English imperial culture that these inferior local versions had, the revivalists asserted, abjectly emulated. For those Irish or American artists who gave themselves primarily to the business of national revival, the emphasis was on de-anglicization and creating a more authentically grounded vernacular Irish or American national culture. For those who believed that this commitment to national revival or renaissance was merely to replace English cultural provincialism with nationalized Irish or American replicas, modernism was not a simple repudiation, but a dialectical version of revivalism, one that sought to overleap in a single motion the provincialisms of their own nations and that of the English metropolis. Irish modernism was in this sense perhaps a higher-order second-wave revivalism rather than something entirely contrary to the Irish Revival in either its Yeatsian or Gaelicist versions.

Viewed in this larger historical context, the Irish Revival might be seen less as the diametric antithesis of modernism than as its discursive sibling. Moreover, while some revivalists were certainly insular, the rhetoric of "revival" and the cultural productions of the Irish Revival were both highly mobile and may well have energized the discourse of American renaissance, the most aesthetically (if not always politically) radical versions of which in turn morphed into the rhetoric of American modernism. This idea has been advanced by Michael Soto who argues that "the influence of the Irish Renaissance can be traced along a direct line from Dublin and London to Boston, New York and Philadelphia" and that the Revival "served as the primary model for several modernist movements in the United States."[8] It is a truism of modernist studies to say, for example, that Pound helped an Irish revivalist or late Victorian Yeats to harden and modernize his poetics when the American served as the Irish poet's secretary in Stone Cottage in 1913. But it might equally be the case that it was Pound who assimilated Yeats's revivalist rhetoric to articulate his own conception of an "American Risorgimento," the subject of *Patria Mia*, a manifesto Pound drafted in 1913, and which was lost by his publisher, although its substance appeared in three articles titled "Renaissance" published in *Poetry* in 1915. As Soto has noted, Pound had studied at the University of Pennsylvania "with Cornelius Weygandt, professor of English and one of the leading boosters of the Irish Renaissance during the first two decades of the twentieth century."[9] Pound later remembered being "drunk with Celticism" at the time, an inebriation shared by F. Scott Fitzgerald and many other young literary Americans, including by some of the leading members of the Harlem Renaissance such as Alain Locke, Countee Cullen, and Claude McKay, who were also inspired by the Irish movement.[10] Later, Pound and Irish modernists such as Beckett would vehemently dismiss the Irish Revival, but for a time at least it had served as a foundational template for artistic experiment on both sides of the Atlantic.

Did the Irish and American rhetorics of revival and renaissance help to sow the seeds for a major modernist art in these countries, but – by another historical twist – simultaneously produce a Revivalist-minded cultural-nationalist criticism that left Ireland poorly equipped to make sense of its modernist achievement? As Enda Duffy points out in his chapter on "Critical Receptions of Literary Modernism" the domestic critical response to literary modernism in Ireland was by no means universally hostile, but it was often ambivalent and intellectually timorous. Works such as *Ulysses* or *A Vision* or Beckett's novels and plays have such a bizarre physiognomy that they would probably have been assimilated only tentatively into any national culture, but, as Duffy points out, the Irish intellectual world was shaped by a number of factors that inhibited a strong response. It was fractured along nationalist-unionist and Catholic-Protestant lines and the Irish literary market was so small that Irish writing and criticism were each oriented as much towards England and the United States as any domestic audience. Some Irish-based critics writing in a new state nominally committed to restoring the Irish language and to fostering a Gaelic literature struggled to find ways to fit the modernists into any kind of serviceable national canon. Conversely, the Irish language was so intrinsically associated with "tradition" that an Irish-language modernism may have seemed a logical improbability to scholars of all kinds. Equally, a more extroverted cosmopolitan-minded Irish criticism that tried to explain the emergence of a modern Irish national literature to American or English audiences found it difficult to determine with any assurance what was national and what international, as so much of it had been produced in Paris or London to begin with.

Thus, what struck a leading revivalist critic like Daniel Corkery was less the novelty of Joyce's enterprise than its continuity with a colonial history of literary expatriation that detached the writer from any rootedness in or responsiveness to the changing actualities of modern Irish social life.[11] Later Counter-Revivalist critics such as Seán Ó Faoláin or Louis McNeice rejected Corkery's conception of a national literature, but, because they were struggling to find a socially responsible relationship between writer and nation (at a time when so much modernist work seemed to have taken politically reactionary or narcissistically formalist directions), these critics too continued to have difficulties with Yeats and also with Joyce, and they mostly ignored a young Beckett still finding his own way in France.[12] There were empathetic accounts of Joyce that took the form of short essays; Duffy gives pride of place in Joyce's Irish reception to Beckett's essay "Dante ... Bruno ... Vico ... Joyce" (1929) and to Elizabeth Bowen's "James Joyce" (1941). But, he suggests, it was not until the Irish universities expanded in the 1970s and the Northern Troubles provoked a socially urgent reassessment of twentieth-century Irish society and its culture that a more vigorous domestic critical coming-to-terms with Irish modernism was advanced. Vivian Mercier's *The Irish Comic Tradition* (1962) and *Beckett/Beckett* (1977) were generally ahead of their times in their recognition of the Irishness of Irish literary modernist achievement. However, the most intellectually accomplished engagements with the works of Irish literary modernism were undertaken in the last decades of the twentieth century. Seamus Deane's *Celtic Revivals* (1985) and the many remarkable introductory essays to the key modernist writers by several major Irish critics to be found in the *Field Day Anthology of Irish Writing* (1991, 2002) and pioneering feminist studies of Irish literary modernism such as Elizabeth Butler Cullingford's *Gender and History in Yeats's Love Poetry* (1993), Emer Nolan's *James Joyce and Nationalism* (1995), and Marjorie Howes's *Yeats's Nations* (1996) are indicative of a much wider critical reexamination of modernism in this period.[13] By then, it must be said, modernism had been thoroughly canonized and institutionalized in Europe and the United States, and after a long period of post-World War II conservatism, both Northern Ireland and the Irish Republic had entered another period of acute and protracted crisis. That an artistic phenomenon that had initially flourished during a period of radical global disturbance and national redefinition should have been reclaimed during a later moment of national redefinition was perhaps not coincidental.

III

This volume would not be possible without the labours of the several generations of Irish critics mentioned in Duffy's chapter; today, at the start of a new century, the best way to honour their contributions to a domestic assessment of Irish modernism is to consolidate that work and to move matters out in new directions. An overview of Irish modernism that gives due acknowledgement of the extraordinary achievements of Yeats, Joyce, and Beckett, but which can also find room for treatments of women's modernism, Irish-language modernism, and Irish American modernism, and that might eventually encourage readers also to find a place in the story of modernism for several other artistic media and for patrons, promoters, and curators – such as Lane, Gregory, Weaver, Cunard, Quinn, and Sweeney – as well as for critics and presses and other mediators can offer its readers something better than a wider and more colourful canvas. To open out the study of Irish modernism in these directions is neither simply an opportunistic attempt to swell the narrative to make it seem grander than it already is nor merely to accommodate inclusiveness for its own sake. Instead, its proper purpose is to recognize the tangled roots from which Irish modernism grew and to acknowledge the capillary and often surprising routes along which it was later to evolve and accrue social meaning.

Some closing words on this study's structure may be useful. The first section is titled *Formations* and deals with various intellectual, international, and national contexts that contributed to the development of Irish modernism and that gave it its characteristic energies and styles. Jean-Michel Rabaté's opening chapter argues for the catalytic intellectual importance of the work of Friedrich Nietzsche, demonstrating how Joyce and Yeats absorbed Nietzsche's concept of the will to power into the contents, rhetorics, and forms of their works. Beckett, too, Rabaté suggests, draws on Nietzsche, but more deeply on Arthur Schopenhauer and Giambattisto Vico; hence the "unwill to power" that made Beckett's oeuvre quite different to that of his predecessors. My chapter on "European, American, and Imperial Conjunctures" attempts to connect successive phases of Irish modernist production to a major restructuring of the early-twentieth-century capitalist world system, a restructuring that was ultimately cultural as well as economic and political in its dimensions. Rónán McDonald's "The Irish Revival and Modernism" then focuses on the fractious critical debates, historical and contemporary, about the relationship between revivalist and modernist currents in Irish culture. Barry McCrea's "Style and Idiom" argues that the post-Famine collapse of the Irish language contributed to an acute scepticism on the part of Irish writers with regard to the ontological status of the sign, a scepticism attuned to metropolitan modernism's critique of mimesis more generally.

The second section of this volume, *Genres and Forms*, forms its spine. Laura O' Connor's "W. B. Yeats and Modernist Poetry" demonstrates how strongly the generations that came after Yeats reacted against his influence, finding in Joyce and Eliot satiric or spiritual resources to rework to their own purposes. Emer Nolan's "James Joyce and the Mutations of the Modernist Novel" proposes, in broadly parallel fashion, that the modernist novel in Ireland emerged by means of a series of experiments with French naturalism and then proceeded in its more formally adventurous versions to self-generate eccentrically largely by way of negative reactions to earlier achievements – Joyce reacting against Moore, O'Brien and Beckett against

Joyce, and so on. In "Modernist Experiment in Irish Theatre" Ben Levitas examines a dazzling arc of experimental drama running from Wilde and Shaw working at the end of the nineteenth century through Yeats, O'Casey, and Beckett and on to Tom Murphy, Stewart Parker, and Marina Carr working at end of the twentieth century. Luke Gibbons's "Visual Modernisms" covers the same historical span for the visual and architectural arts, noting how the shattered hopes for Irish art represented by the Hugh Lane Gallery controversy of 1913 would be symbolically repaired in 2001 when émigré Francis Bacon's studio was relocated from London. Individually, these chapters offer considered overviews of the long history of Irish modernism in various media; collectively, they present the most sustained reevaluation of Irish modernism now available.

The third section, *Constituencies*, surveys some of the specific communities that contributed to Irish modernism. The opening chapter by Anne Fogarty, "Women and Modernism," argues that the more experimental devices of Irish women's writing in the early part of the twentieth century were often motivated by a drive to militancy and public engagement. But by the middle of the century, Fogarty suggests, this militancy had receded to the point that the radical impulses in women's modernism found expression primarily as psychological complexity and formal self-consciousness. Louis de Paor's chapter on "Irish Language Modernism" argues, against the grain of much criticism on the subject, that this minority literature is marked less by a loss of confidence in the power of the Irish language or by a sense of the collapse of the Gaelic world as by a remarkable confidence in the capacity of Irish, despite its travails, to serve the needs of the modern writer. The pressures that impelled Irish-language experiment, he proposes, do not stem from any sense of literary penury but from a problematic plenitude. The Gaelic language offered a treasury of forms and techniques to work with, but the difficulty for the Irish writer was to harness the available resources with their strongly communal bias to the subjectivist exigencies of modern self-expression. In "Irish American Modernisms," I offer a survey of the works of Eugene O'Neill, F. Scott Fitzgerald, and Flannery O'Connor to argue the case for the contribution of the Irish diaspora to an American modernism that emerged concurrently with its Irish counterpart.

The final section, *Domestic Receptions, World Imaginations*, concludes matters with chapters by Enda Duffy and Michael Valdez Moses. As already mentioned, Duffy's chapter explores the vagaries of the Irish critical reception of literary modernism, from the works of early critics who were contemporaries of Yeats and Joyce to the beginnings of the new postcolonial criticism that emerged alongside the Field Day Theatre Company in the 1980s. Michael Valdez Moses argues in "Irish Modernist Imaginaries" that the many varieties of Irish modernism try, with acrobatic verve, to reconcile national and global imaginaries. These ingenious attempts to do so – sometimes successful, sometimes hubristic – represent, in Valdez Moses's view, Irish modernism's major contribution to the constitution of the so-called global culture that is our contemporary inheritance and dilemma.

NOTES

1 Standard texts on these arts include S. B. Kennedy, *Irish Art and Modernism* (Belfast: Institute of Irish Studies, 1991); Linda King and Elaine Sisson, eds., *Ireland, Design and Visual Culture: Negotiating Modernity, 1922–1992* (Cork: Cork University Press, 2011); Enrique Juncosa and Christina Kennedy, eds., *The Moderns: The Arts in Ireland from the 1900s to the 1970s* (Dublin: Irish Museum of Modern Art, 2011); Paul Larmour, *Free State Architecture: Modern Movement Architecture in Ireland, 1922–1949* (Oysterhaven: Gandon Editions, 2009); and Sean Rothery, *Ireland and the New Architecture 1900–1940* (Dublin: Lilliput, 1991).

2 The works of reclamation are too numerous to cite here and many are on individual artists. Some general and influential surveys include Seamus Deane, *Celtic Revivals: Essays in Modern Irish Literature, 1880–1980* (London: Faber and Faber, 1985) and *Strange Country: Modernity and Nationhood in Irish Writing Since 1790* (Oxford: Clarendon Press, 1997); David Lloyd, *Anomalous States: Irish Writing and the Postcolonial Moment* (Durham, NC: Duke University Press, 1993); Terry Eagleton, *Heathcliff and the Great Hunger: Studies in Irish Culture* (London: Verso, 1995); Declan Kiberd, *Inventing Ireland: The Literature of the Modern Nation* (London: Jonathan Cape, 1995); and Terence Brown, *The Literature of Ireland: Culture and Criticism* (Cambridge: Cambridge University Press, 2010).

3 Major texts on modern music are Harry White, *The Keeper's Recital: Music and Cultural History in Ireland, 1770–1970* (Cork: Field Day/Cork University Press, 1998) and *The Progress of Music in Ireland* (Dublin: Four Courts Press, 2005). White's views are disputed in Patrick Zuk, "Music and Nationalism" (Part 1), *Journal of Music in Ireland* 2, 2 (2002), 5–10 and "Music and Nationalism," *Journal of Music in Ireland* 2, 3 (2002), 25–30.

4 Axel Klein, "How Ireland Came to Shape Musical Modernism," Paper read to the Ninth Annual Conference of the Society of Musicology in Ireland, 25 June 2011, 1–5. For more on Cowell, see Joel Sachs, *Henry Cowell: A Man Made of Music* (Oxford: Oxford University Press, 2012).

5 Pascale Casanova, *The World Republic of Letters*, M. B. DeBevoise, trans. (Cambridge, MA: Harvard University Press, 2004), 128.

6 James Joyce, *Ulysses* (New York: Vintage Books, 1986), 26.

7 For contrasting takes on the Revival, see G. J. Watson, *Irish Identity and the Literary Revival: Synge, Yeats, Joyce and O'Casey* (London: Croom Helm, 1979); Declan Kiberd, *Inventing Ireland*; and P. J. Mathews, *Revival: The Abbey Theatre, Sinn Féin, the Gaelic League and the Co-operative Movement* (Cork: Field Day/Cork University Press, 2003). See also McDonald, Chapter 3, in this volume.

8 Michael Soto, *The Modernist Nation: Generation, Renaissance, and Twentieth-Century American Literature* (Tuscaloosa: The University of Alabama Press, 2004), 65, 12.

9 Soto, *Modernist Nation*, 65.

10 Soto, *Modernist Nation*, 65. See also Tracy Mishkin, *The Harlem and Irish Renaissances* (Gainesville: University Press of Florida, 1998). On the changing nature of Irish and African American conceptions of race in America in this period, see Matthew Guterl Pratt, "The New Race Consciousness: Race, Nation and Empire in American Culture, 1910–1925," *Journal of World History* 10, 2 (1999), 307–52 and Bruce Nelson, *Irish Nationalists and the Making of the Irish Race* (Princeton, NJ: Princeton University Press, 2012), especially Part 4.

11 Daniel Corkery, *Synge and Anglo-Irish Literature* (Cork: Cork University Press, 1931), 4–5.

12 See Louis MacNeice, *The Poetry of W. B. Yeats* (1941, reprinted London: Faber and Faber, 1967); and Seán Ó Faoláin, *The Vanishing Hero: Studies in Novelists of the 1920s* (London: Eyre and Spottiswoode, 1956).

13 Seamus Deane, *Celtic Revivals*, and Deane, general editor, *The Field Day Anthology of Irish Writing*, Vols. 1–3, (Derry: Field Day Publications, 1991); Angela Bourke et al., eds., *The Field Day Anthology of Irish Writing*, Vols. 4–5, *Irish Women's Writings and Traditions* (Cork: Field Day/Cork University Press, 2002); Elizabeth Butler Cullingford, *Gender and History in Yeats's Love Poetry* (Cambridge: Cambridge University Press, 1993); Emer Nolan, *James Joyce and Irish Nationalism* (London: Routledge, 1995); and Marjorie Howes, *Yeats's Nations: Gender, Class and Irishness* (Cambridge: Cambridge University Press, 1996).

PART I

Formations

I

JEAN-MICHEL RABATÉ

Intellectual and Aesthetic Influences

What seems best to capture Irish modernism is its Nietzschean quality, by which I refer not only to the attested influence of Nietzsche's thought on writers such as Yeats and Joyce but also to a way of describing specific features of the Irish moderns between 1902 and 1932. If I describe Irish modernism as a "Nietzschean" moment, it is because I am struck by the prevalence of a fundamental discordance in themes, groups, programs, and ideologies. My dates imply that Irish modernism started earlier than is generally assumed; because of its precocity, it quickly absorbed various and complex influences but never tried to unify them. The creativity of its main actors and authors was spurred by contrarian impulses that brought forward inner strife and not ecumenical attempts to unify its forces. What is called high modernism in the context of Anglo-American modernism manifested itself as retrospective programs bringing together different individualities under a single banner. Instead of striving toward the cohesion of a movement, Irish modernism tended to be at war against itself and against the world, especially when the world was embodied by British imperialism. Very early on, its evolution was caught up in centrifugal patterns and thrived on controversies and conflict that in turn generated fissiparous offshoots. Although they were almost impossible to contain, let alone to channel into a single goal, these anarchic tensions were productive. The two main chroniclers of the movement, George Moore and Oliver St. John Gogarty, produced books that were deemed libelous, and for good reasons. *Hail and Farewell: Ave, Salve and Vale* (1911–14) and *As I Was Going Down Sackville Street: A Phantasy in Fact* (1937) are retrospective constructions, but they keep vivid traces of the spirit of contentious mockery and ad hominem satire that pervaded interactions among the main proponents of an Irish modernism.

If the modernist impulse in Ireland was marked by intrigue and satire, in the end, inner dialogism generated dynamic change and transmuted the Irish renaissance into a modernism that became both local and global. As soon as major achievements had been accomplished in the 1920s, there was an effort at revision; the wish to smooth tensions and ease discordance came at the end. Irish modernism then entered its golden phase, producing the somewhat overblown syntheses of Yeats's *A Vision* (1925, revised 1937) or Joyce's *Finnegans Wake* (1939), both *summae poeticae* quoting each other with distant respect. Yet, the contrarian voice remained with the young Beckett's querulous admonitions to his elders, which included a critique of the Revival's parochialism in the name of an internationalism of Irish modernism. And even then, this "late style" did not avoid a certain Nietzscheism, but in a different sense: it was grounded in the irrepressible affinities of Nietzsche's thought with mythological patterns presenting universal history as a grandiose cyclical scheme, the "eternal return of the same."

To discover a degree of order in such a state of permanent cultural war, I examine the main European intellectual trends that influenced it by choosing Nietzsche as a privileged catalyst. Nietzsche is helpful to survey the debates on aesthetics and politics that conceptually shaped Irish modernism. Focusing on three main figures – Yeats, Joyce, and Beckett – I follow their attempts at becoming modern. And to simplify even more, I look at modernist reviews to grasp how those ideas were disseminated. One should begin with Yeats, who initiated his own modernization by taking Nietzsche's thought as a weapon against the vagueness and vagaries of aesthetic decadence. For Joyce, fin-de-siècle Nietzscheism was integrated into his farewell to Dublin. It worked dialogically and satirically and provided a good device to point out the limitations of earlier egotistic posturing via Stephen Hero. And for the young Beckett, Nietzsche would have to be replaced by older models, first by Nietzsche's own "educator," Arthur Schopenhauer, and then by Nietzsche's precursor, the universal historian of metaphors, Giambattista Vico.

I. Neiche Is Not Celtic[1]

Yeats had known of Nietzsche's thought as early as 1896, when *The Savoy* published a series of long articles on him by Havelock Ellis.[2] Ellis knew Nietzsche well and was the first to point out the parallels between Nietzsche and the philosophies of William Blake, which would be a recurrent theme for Yeats. *The Savoy* can be taken as a useful point of departure as it exhibited a rare mixture of decadent thought, post-Symbolist writing, and new "modernist" ideas. Its eight issues, from January to December 1896, were published by Leonard Smithers, a declared libertine and pornographer. Its intellectual content was in the charge of Arthur Symons, also a libertine who specialized in "decadence." Symons's *The Symbolist Movement in Literature* (1899) would soon leave a huge mark on English literature, and it was dedicated to Yeats. Aubrey Beardsley had chosen the name of the review, thinking a new London hotel would evoke ideas of luxury and modernity. He also provided the covers as well as numerous illustrations. The group gathered by *The Savoy* was associated with Oscar Wilde, whose recent trials (in 1895) added to the magazine's sulfurous reputation. Thus, the first accounts of Nietzsche's thought to catch the eye of Yeats were associated with decadence. Yeats knew Ellis's essays on Nietzsche because Yeats contributed regularly to *The Savoy*: his story "Rosa Alchemica" was published in the third issue, and "The Tables of the Law" was published in the seventh. He also published his essay "William Blake and His Illustrations to the Divine Comedy" in *The Savoy*.

This third essay was revised in 1924 to include a reference to Nietzsche. When discussing Blake's suspicion of government in general and his dalliance with revolutionary thought, Yeats wrote: "One is reminded of Shelley, who was the next to take up the cry, though with a less abundant philosophic faculty, but still more of Nietzsche, whose thought flows always, though with an even more violent current, in the bed Blake's thought has worn."[3] This was a later addition; the original essay in *The Savoy* had begun with a comparison between Blake and French Symbolism that sounded very much like Symons: "The recoil from scientific naturalism has created in our day the movement the French call *symboliste*, which, beginning with the memorable 'Axel' by Villiers de l'Isle Adam, has added to drama a new kind of romance, at once ecstatic and picturesque, in the works of M. Maeterlinck."[4] Thus, the Nietzsche whom Yeats discovered in 1896 was caught up in the context of a Symbolism that was still too cloyingly in thrall to the "mystery" contained in poetry and still fraught with deliberate vagueness, calculated indirection, and evocative suggestion. What remained of a Paterian-inflected aestheticism blocked Yeats's comprehension of Nietzsche's most revolutionary theses.

Propitiously, Yeats's interest in Nietzsche was reawakened by his American friend, the rich New York lawyer John Quinn. In September 1902, Quinn sent Yeats copies of *Thus Spake Zarathustra* (1883–5, all dates are for first publication in German), *The Case of Wagner* (1888), and *On the Genealogy of Morals* (1887). Soon after, Yeats mentions his own fascination in a letter to Lady Gregory: "You have a rival in Nietzsche, that strong enchanter.... Nietzsche completes Blake and has the same roots – I have not read anything with so much excitement since I got to love Morris's stories which have the same curious astringent joy."[5] Yeats also worked closely on Thomas Common's *Nietzsche as Critic, Philosopher, Poet and Prophet* (1901), a collection of passages from the main works in which he underlined or annotated passages from *Beyond Good and Evil* (1886), *On the Genealogy of*

Morals, and *Thus Spake Zarathustra*. Yeats's library also contained *The Case of Wagner*, *The Dawn of Day* (1881), *The Birth of Tragedy* (1872), and *Thoughts out of Season* (1873–6). Listing points of convergence, critics have documented Yeats's sustained immersion in Nietzsche's writings and have pointed out the importance of Yeats's marginal annotations on Common's book.[6] Yeats remained engaged in a productive, albeit critical, dialogue with his German mentor.

Above all, Yeats learned from Nietzsche a new "hardness" and a new masculinity. In his dealings with people, Yeats became more imperious and less passive and would often impose his ideas, as shown by the complex history of the founding and handling of the Abbey Theatre. The new attitude led him to change his style: the trembling of the veil was replaced by a rending of the veil, the Celtic twilight turned into a Nietzschean "Twilight of the Idols." At first, Nietzsche's philosophy appeared compatible with an older aestheticism based on Walter Pater's ideas. After all, Nietzsche wanted a renaissance, as did Pater, who in *The Renaissance* (1873) portrayed the mind as a supreme subjectivity fluctuating uncontrollably between moods and impressions that were flickering and inconstant. Yeats's first catechism had been Paterian, and now the object of the quest remained the same, but the diction and the underlying gestures had changed. It was from Nietzsche's revisions of his texts and selves that Yeats adopted the practice of self-remaking. He expressed this in 1908, stating that when he rewrote earlier versions of his poems or plays, it was "myself that I remake." "The fascination of what's difficult" deplores that the "theatre business" and the "management of men"[7] in the Abbey impinged on his free time, yet in the end he proved remarkably successful in his business transactions.

The plays written by Yeats in the first decade of the twentieth century resonate with Nietzschean echoes. In *The King's Threshold* (1903), the dying words of the poet Seanchan, who started a hunger strike the day he was expelled from King Guaire's counsel, convey defiance not only facing earthly powers but also facing the mirage of a god in heaven:

> I need no help.
> He needs no help that joy has lifted up
> Like some miraculous beast out of Ezekiel.
> The man that dies has the chief part in the story,
> And I will mock and mock that image yonder,
> That evil picture in the sky – no, no!
> I have all my strength again, I will outface it.[8]

This climax of a "joy before death," later to be sung vociferously by Georges Bataille in his Nietzschean review *Acéphale*, here conflates a metaphysical gesture of defiance with a political posture. When Yeats revised his play and gave it a tragic ending in 1922, he noted that at the time "neither suffragette nor patriot had adopted the hunger strike," hinting that he may have invented its use as a "political weapon."[9] In a similar way, the hero Cuchulain offers a perfectly Nietzschean definition of love in *On Baile's Strand* (1903). For him, love has to be considered in all its fundamental ambivalence, and the poet knows that true love ought to make room for hate:

> I never have known love but as a kiss
> In the mid-battle, and a difficult truce
> Of oil and water, candles and dark night,
> Hillside and hollow, the hot-footed sun,
> And the cold sliding, slippery-footed moon –
> A brief forgiveness between opposites
> That have been hatreds for three times the age
> Of this long-'stablished ground.[10]

Such ambivalent feelings were inspired by a frustratingly diffident but tantalizing Maud Gonne. Gonne, who had not read Nietzsche, and did not like him, had good grounds to object to his influence on "Willie." Indeed, she had a point at which she failed to see any Celtic note in what she took for the ravings of a mad Protestant. Gonne was, after all, a staunch Francophile who had adapted for Irish aims what Zeev Sternhell has called "French fascism."[11] Sternhell showed how the combination of populist Boulangisme from the late 1880s and Georges Sorel's concept of revolutionary violence produced a blueprint for Benito Mussolini's later fascist doctrine. Gonne's association with Lucien Millevoye, a notorious Boulangist, situates her in the camp of a nascent European fascism. When she announced to Yeats that she was in a French convent preparing to convert to Catholicism so that she could marry Millevoye, she wrote those famous words: "I have always told you I am the voice, the soul of the crowd."[12] Her reactionary populism could justify even a half-hearted conversion as most people in Ireland were Catholic.

What saved Yeats from the temptation of joining such a budding Irish fascism was, paradoxically, a topos that he found in Nietzsche, namely the elitism he always associated with the doctrine of Zarathustra's *Übermensch*. This explains his efforts to invent an ideal Irish peasant who would be, fundamentally, a half-converted pagan sticking to ancient beliefs in fairies and Irish goddesses, and who would ally himself naturally with a no less ideal aristocrat, who would embody the best values of what the Anglo-Irish ascendancy had to offer to the country. These constituted a "healthier" constituency of people, one that instinctively shrank from the excess and the vociferousness of a Catholic populace, which was exactly the kind of audience Gonne had chosen as her constituency. Yeats was saved, in short, by a decision to be both "timely" and "untimely" in his self-willed, aristocratic heroism; and in this he proved, like Nietzsche, that he was at least a true modernist, if not always "modern." In his 1885–6 notebook, Nietzsche had written: "If I once wrote the word 'untimely' on my books, how much youth, inexperience, peculiarity that word expressed! Today I realize it was precisely the kind of complaint, enthusiasm and dissatisfaction that made me one of the most modern of the modern."[13] This led to "Attempt at Self-Criticism," introducing a new edition of *The Birth of Tragedy* (first published in 1872). Nietzsche satirizes the "excess" of a book seen retrospectively as tainted by Schopenhauer's pessimism, a prey to "enervated" Indian Buddhism. One alternative was the positivist belief in science as a cure for all the ills of humanity; or he could try to find a balance between art, science, and life. In the end, for Nietzsche as for Yeats, the point was not to change philosophy or poetry, but to transform radically the whole of life. Nietzsche insisted that his first book was badly written; hence an injunction to write well, using Flaubertian *mots justes*, would underpin any effort at self-modernization. This entailed an imperative to reread oneself so as to erase all the remnants of juvenile enthusiasm and romantic illusions. The ultimate value would finally rest with "Life," a life freed from its shackles by the claim that "God is dead," a claim bequeathing to humans the power to create. And because humans have created God, they will also create like God, but are therefore all the more responsible for their creations. Yeats summarized this cryptically with the famous motto: "In dreams begin responsibility" (*CP*, 112). The Blake quoted by Yeats in *Last Poems* (1938–9) has absorbed Nietzsche, who, in *A Vision*, appears as a seer and a madman. Symptomatically, the first notes for *A Vision* conflate Nietzsche with Pound, the other great modernizer: "I am more interested at 12 where Neitzsche [sic] emerges & all men discover their super man, though there are also more violent among whom I would be sorry to include types like <your friend Mr Pound of whom> your enemy Mr Pound."[14] The impact of Pound on Yeats and his crucial role in forcing the older poet to become harder, sparer, and more direct have been well documented.[15] What is revealing in the first typescript of *A Vision* is the hesitation between "friend" and "enemy," a hesitation all the more telling that in the final version, Wyndham Lewis, the arch "enemy," is listed next to Pound and Joyce, just after Nietzsche.[16] Joyce is praised as having given to the "vulgarity of a single day prolonged through 700 pages" the dignity of myth, yet he also exemplifies the moment when "the intellect turns against itself."[17]

II. Sparring Partners

There have been as many accounts of the famous meeting between Joyce and Yeats in 1902 as of the encounter between Joyce and Proust. What stands out for certain is that Yeats was generous with Joyce, who indirectly owed him the contact with Pound, which in turn connected him with a powerful network leading to the publication of his major works. What paved the way for the meeting had been Joyce's critique of his elder's position in the essay "The Day of the Rabblement" (1901), in which Joyce wonders whether Yeats has genius (later he would say that Yeats incarnated poetic genius). Joyce praises *The Wind Among the Reeds* (1899) as "poetry of the highest order" and notes that the best Russian writers could have written "The Adoration of the Magi" (1897), texts that show what Yeats "can do when he breaks with the half gods."[18] The following sentence is more damaging: "But an aesthete has a floating will, and Mr. Yeats's treacherous instinct of adaptability must be blamed for his recent association with a platform from which even self-respect should have urged him to refrain."[19] These are severe words from a nineteen-year-old student, but Joyce had identified what Yeats himself saw as his own weakness: uncertain willpower, which Yeats resolved to tackle with the "masculine" virtues of constancy and direction. In 1901, Joyce saw through the regressive side of the Irish Literary Theatre that "cut itself adrift from the line of advancement" by its "surrender to the trolls."[20] This alludes ironically to Yeats's apparently unshakeable belief in fairies and other fanciful creatures from Celtic folklore. Joyce contrasts Yeats's lack of direction with the solid Truth embodied by Ibsen, whose rightful successor is not Irish but the German playwright, Gerhard Hauptmann, almost Yeats's age.

In *Ulysses* (1922), we discover a certain version of Irish modernism, mostly of the Irish Revival, and it is not flattering. Most of its actors are gathered in the library to hear Stephen lecture on *Hamlet*. The last to arrive and the most Nietzschean is Buck Mulligan, who has sounded the note of parody and irreverence at the outset. He has nicknamed Stephen "Kinch the superman"[21] (*U.* 3:496) and speaks of "hyperboreans" (*U.* 1:92), which marks him out as a disciple of Nietzsche. His reliance on parody facing religious rituals evokes the parodic tone of Zarathustra, whose gospel inverts that of Christ. Mulligan also makes fun of Yeats, Synge, and Lady Gregory and imitates Synge's fake Irish brogue several times to devastating effect. He upbraids Stephen for not having displayed "the Yeats touch," which means kowtowing to Lady Gregory and extravagantly praising her limited literary means. Meanwhile, he takes off Yeats's personal style: "He went on and down, mopping, chanting with waving graceful arms: –The most beautiful book that has come out of our country in my time. One thinks of Homer" (*U.* 9:1163–6). He adds that Shakespeare is "the chap that writes like Synge" (*U.* 9:510–11). Indeed, these were easy targets for the Dublin wits in 1904.

Stephen appears closer in spirit to Mulligan than to the others, but even if his audience soon diminishes, he faces an impressive group of intellectuals. What stands out is the fact that an Irish renaissance is happening in Dublin and that he is not welcome in it. He is not invited to the gatherings celebrating new magazines and collections. One of the three librarians, Richard Irvine Best, who had translated Arbois de Jubainville's book on Celtic mythology and was a disciple of Mallarmé, mentions new publications, and Stephen is painfully aware that he is not included. The most important critic in Ireland at the time according to Yeats, William Magee, is among the listeners. A renowned essayist who intellectually dominated the scene of the Irish Literary Revival, Magee quoted Novalis and Goethe, knew the Vedas, and had a sharply critical mind. In the episode, he staunchly resists Stephen's sophistic reasoning. In May 1904, Magee had just launched with Fred Ryan a new little review, *Dana*, which survived only one year. Joyce had submitted the eight pages of his first version of *The Portrait of the Artist as a Young Man* (eventually published in 1916), which were rejected by Magee, who found them unreadable. Yet, Stephen quotes Magee's recent collection *Pebbles from a Brook* (1901), seemingly to flatter him, but also because he defers to his opinions.

Yeats had shown the same deference. He and Magee exchanged opinions in *The Express* in the autumn of 1898, Magee accusing Yeats of distorting the Irish legends he was adapting without understanding them. On the whole, Magee's position was that of a cosmopolitan intellectual who rejected Yeats's glib and sentimental appropriation of Celtic mythologies as passing fads. He objected to the idea of the "peasant plays" that Lady Gregory and Yeats were promoting as the best subjects for a national drama. His position was therefore not far from that of Joyce, which is why their confusion in "Scylla and Charybdis" is so important. In fact, even the title of the episode appears in *Pebbles from a Brook*: "In spite of the Scylla and Charybdis of sensuality and ennui, the human soul is enamoured of the ideal."[22] It would be unfair to reduce Magee's position as a critic to this idealist thesis. More pointedly, in the library scene, Stephen is suspicious of Magee's religious leanings and mentions that he was the son of a Presbyterian minister. Magee was a solid intellectual, even if his rejection of Joyce's youthful (and, to be fair, not so comprehensible) autobiographical essay was motivated by his disapproval of the sexual confession it contained, and he had also accepted one poem by Joyce, "My Love in Light Attire,"[23] which appeared in the fourth issue of *Dana* as a simple "song." Magee never suspected that the "light attire" of the loved is "lifted up" so as to reveal an erotic posture that attracted Joyce most: the glimpse of a peeing female form.

I want to insist on the role of Magee in the creation of a different Irish modernism, taking *Dana* as representing a spirit of openness and balanced critical evaluation. In fact, at the outset, *Dana* juxtaposed two versions of modernism: the recent controversy in the Catholic Church opposing Abbé Loisy and the refusal of the hierarchy to consider the possibility of evolution, and Nietzsche's notion of the "death of God." The debate was summarized by Edouard Dujardin in his essay "The Abbé Loisy" published in the first issue of *Dana*.[24] Dujardin, author of *The Bays are Sere* (1888), the first novel written as an interior monologue, was a recent discovery of Joyce, who had read his work during his trip to Paris in 1903.[25] In his essay, Dujardin outlines the theses of the followers of Loisy, sympathizes with them, and concludes that the Church has made a deep mistake in deciding that Aristotle was a better guide than Darwin (21). Even though this meaning of "modernism" has been lost today, it reverberated in Dublin's literary circles, especially at University College with its doctrinal emphasis on neo-Thomism. The confrontation with Nietzsche appears in the sixth issue of *Dana*. Magee's essay "A Way of Understanding Nietzsche" (182–8) begins by addressing what Catholics found objectionable: the proclamation that "God is dead." Magee evinces a remarkable equanimity. Magee ironizes about bourgeois who expect to find God always there, but never worry long about His existence. Nietzsche criticized such "moral cowardice," but then often became as dogmatic as the Church. In fact, his teachings went in the opposite direction; they did not so much "kill" God as attempt to redress a worse temptation, that of pessimism or nihilism. For Magee, Nietzsche was more courageous than Schopenhauer, who took refuge in a wholesale pessimism, treating hopelessness as the fate of suffering humanity. Magee quotes Goethe's observation that "man never knows how anthropomorphic he is" (184). By contrast, Nietzsche affirmed a wholly non-anthropomorphic Life. He was an optimist, a lover of fate, or a "yea-saying man" (184). What he rejected, perhaps perversely, was "the ideal."

This is where Magee perceives a certain inconsistency: on the one hand, Nietzsche praises power when it manifests itself in history; on the other hand, he appears on the side of those who "confront the might of the world with the might of the idea" (186). How can he extol men like Cesare Borgia who terrorized crowds in the spirit of "masters," when he refuses the domination of the state (186)? If he denounces Christianity as a perversion stemming from a "slave morality," is he not also on the side of the excluded, the heretics, and the revolutionaries? Finally, he suggests that the doctrine of the Superman seems "a little crazy" (187). Why this Romantic cult of the genius?

"Nietzsche, with his insane denial of idealism and devotion to 'physiology,' came to acknowledge greatness only in such men" (188). These are serious questions, which point to a real weakness in Yeats's position as, no doubt, a lot of this exposition is aimed at his Nietzschean posturing. With Magee, we see the possibility of a milder version of modernism that will not cut all ties with religion (even if it is suspicious of Catholic dogmatism and archaic paganism). It does not postulate a radical break with the past but keeps a connection with the spirit of Romanticism.

However, Stephen Dedalus espouses a different philosophy and is more radical; he refuses both Catholic modernism, with its attempt at blending Darwinism and the Bible, and Nietzsche's joyous affirmation of a free life devoid of *ressentiment*. He opts for a "perverted" religiosity without God, and jumps uneasily between Berkeley and Blake, Aristotle and the anarchists. In matters of cultural politics, Stephen inverts the foundation of Irish modernism, its deep link with a mythified nation, when he tells Bloom late in the night "Ireland must be important because it belongs to me" (*U.* 16:1164–5). Here, quite explicitly, Stephen adopts the philosophy of the Left Hegelian Max Stirner, who is often considered to be a precursor of Nietzsche. Stirner deployed all the meanings of the concept of "ownership" – hence here "belonging" by refusing to be "owned" by God, the Spirit, the Nation, the State, or even by Love. All capitalized notions are refused: owning oneself will become the motto of a paradoxical program of self-liberation, and it will inform the modernism of the feminist writers who launched *The Egoist* in London.[26]

In *Ulysses*, the Nietzschean Buck Mulligan will be confronted and ultimately defeated by a Stirnerian Stephen, whereas both Blooms – Leopold and Molly – are somehow Spinozist. Joyce knew that the last word of his novel had to be given to Penelope, whom he presents as a *Weib* (woman) in a famous letter.[27] This amoral and indifferent woman is a more positive version of the *Frauenzimmer* (woman) evoked by Stephen in "Proteus." Nietzsche had imagined that Truth may be a woman, and described "her" both as *Weib* and *Frauenzimmer*, the latter a disparaging term that appears at the beginning of *Beyond Good and Evil*. If, for Joyce, one may say that Truth finally erupts as a woman, it is a woman who does not let herself be possessed – and here the links between Gonne and Molly Bloom should become evident. Joyce's rejection of Nietzscheism was not only a belated feminism – it lay in the direction pointed out by Magee. Joyce refused the heroic posture of the male hero who uses women for his aesthetic ends. This is why his truth is more modest, and begins *in medias res*, with Molly and Leopold Bloom engaged in dialogue as a married couple (albeit with some problems). Hence, it was logical that Vico should be for Joyce the ultimate philosophical reference. His *Scienza Nuova* (1725) demonstrated how the age of the gods would be followed by the age of the heroes and then by that of the populace: the third age's layered cacophony fills the pages of *Finnegans Wake*, whose "hero" is the aptly named "Here Comes Everybody."

This theme was developed by Beckett in his first effort at literary criticism. In his 1929 essay "Dante ... Bruno. Vico ... Joyce," he defends Joyce's method from any imputation of obscurity and shows the importance of its reliance on Vico's philosophy of language. Beckett's contribution to *Our Exagmination Round His Factification for Incamination of Work in Progress* (1929) remains the best introduction to Joyce's later work because it shows the links between language and history. Taking the example of the multiple meanings of *lex* in Latin, from a gathering of acorns to the Law, he points to a new religion of language. Vico's *religio* is understood as a collective "gathering" of knowledge. Thus Giordano Bruno's identification of contraries, Vico's poetic wisdom, and Dante's divine comedy will converge to create a new linguistic universe. This process is called "purgatorial," in a last resurgence of the cyclical: "This inner elemental vitality and corruption of expression imparts a furious restlessness to the form, which is admirably suited to the purgatorial aspect of the work. There is an endless verbal germination, maturation, putrefaction, the cyclic dynamism of the intermediate."[28] Beckett meditates on universal history conceived both as flux and evolving language. Vico anticipates Nietzsche on metaphor and language as history, as one can see from Nietzsche's take on metaphor in "On Truth and Lies in a Nonmoral Sense" (1873).

Beckett returned to Trinity College as a lecturer in 1930, but resigned in 1931 to follow Joyce's heroic example and become a true artist. His last effort at academic publication was his monograph on Proust. Published in 1931, this presents the French author as Schopenhauerian from beginning to end: *A la recherche du temps perdu* (1913–27) seems to be *The World as Will and Representation* (1818) rewritten as a novel. Its innate pessimism entails a nonmoral position reminiscent of Nietzsche. More than once, Beckett observes that Proust forces his readers to plunge into spirals of perversion and inversion. After Sodom and Gomorrah have been destroyed, no valid ethical system remains – only art can provide salvation. As Beckett writes: "Here, as always, Proust is completely detached from all moral considerations. There is no right and wrong in Proust nor in his world."[29] We know that Beckett immersed himself in Schopenhauer in the summer of 1930 to prepare for his Proust study: "I am reading Schopenhauer.... But I am not reading philosophy, nor caring whether he is right or wrong or a good or worthless metaphysician. An intellectual justification of unhappiness – the greatest that has been attempted – is worth the examination of one who is interested in Leopardi and Proust rather than in Carducci and Barrès."[30] Schopenhauer systematized a coherent pessimism for Beckett and offered an antidote to the exacerbated Romantic nationalism of Maurice Barrès, whose anti-Semitic populism was more in line with the Boulangiste doctrine already mentioned in relation to Gonne. Barrès was "tried" in 1921, two years before his death, by the Dadaists, who condemned him to forced labor for his dubious political views. They had a point, yet the mock trial itself marked the end of Dada's political gestures: no social justice could be dispensed by a Dadaist and they disbanded, leaving room for André Breton's more muscular tactics. Given this refusal to condemn, Beckett had more in common with Tristan Tzara than with Breton.

Above all, Beckett used Schopenhauer to stress a philosophy of non-action. Schopenhauer led Beckett to explore other marginal thinkers: Beckett's motto came from a recurrent maxim in Arnold Geulincx's *Ethics* (1665) – *Ubi nihil vales, ibi nihil velis* (Where you are worth nothing, you will want nothing). This addressed the question of the "will" that had so obsessed Schopenhauer and Nietzsche. Beckett would agree in the end with Heidegger who famously denounced Nietzsche's pretension to overcome metaphysics by staking his all on the "will to power."[31] Yet, Heidegger observed, because the will is the most metaphysical concept, Nietzsche unwittingly marked the culmination of metaphysics. When Beckett praises an "un-will" to power leading to radical impotence as the solution to the world's quandaries, he ushers in a different modernism, a late modernism that owes much to Irish poets and artists. But this is the beginning of another cycle, and another story.

NOTES

1 This is what Maud Gonne wrote to Yeats after her marriage to John MacBride in 1903. Quoted by R. F. Foster, *W. B. Yeats: A Life*, vol. I, *The Apprentice Mage, 1865–1914* (Oxford: Oxford University Press, 1997), 287.

2 *The Savoy* 2, April 1896, 79–94; *The Savoy* 3, July 1896, 68–81; *The Savoy* 4, August 1896, 57–63.

3 William Butler Yeats, "William Blake and His Illustrations to *The Divine Comedy*," in *The Collected Works*, vol. IV, George Bornstein and Richard J. Finneran, eds. (New York: Scribner, 2007), 97.

4 Yeats, "William Blake," 377.

5 *Letters of W. B. Yeats*. Edited by Allan Wade (Lond: Rupert Hart-Davis, 1954), 379.

6 See Richard Ellmann, *The Identity of Yeats* (New York: Oxford University Press, 1964), 91–7; David Thatcher, *Nietzsche in England, 1890–1914* (Toronto:

University of Toronto Press, 1970), 139–73; Denis Donoghue, *William Butler Yeats* (New York: Viking, 1971), 52–60; Otto Bohlmann, *Yeats and Nietzsche* (Totowa, NJ: Barnes and Noble, 1982); Frances Nesbitt Oppell, *Yeats and Nietzsche: Mask and Tragedy, 1902–1910* (Charlottesville: University Press of Virginia, 1987).

7　William Butler Yeats, *The Collected Poems* (London: Macmillan, 1965), 104. Hereafter abbreviated as *CP*.

8　*The King's Threshold*, in *The Collected Works of W. B. Yeats*, vol. II, *The Plays*, David R. Clark and Rosalind E. Clark, eds. (New York: Scribner, 2001), 148.

9　See Yeats's note in *The Collected Works*, vol. II, 686. Yeats was spurred to this revision by the hunger strike of Terence MacSwiney, Lord Mayor of Cork, in 1920. MacSwiney was a playwright himself and his courageous death inspired Nehru and Gandhi, among many others.

10　Yeats, *The Collected Works*, vol. II, 160.

11　Zeev Sternhell, with Mario Sznajder and Maia Asheri, *The Birth of Fascist Ideology* (Princeton, NJ: Princeton University Press, 1989) and Zeev Sternhell, *Neither Right nor Left: Fascist Ideology in France* (Princeton, NJ: Princeton University Press, 1995).

12　*The Gonne-Yeats Letters, 1893–1938*, Anna MacBride White and A. Norman Jeffares, eds. (New York: Norton, 1994), 166.

13　Friedrich Nietzsche, *Writings from the Late Notebooks*, Rüdiger Bittner. ed., Kate Sturge, trans. (Cambridge: Cambridge University Press, 2003), 98.

14　*Yeats's Vision Papers*, vol. 4, George Mills Harper and Mary Jane Harper, eds. (New York: Palgrave, 2001), 86. See pp. 31–2 for an earlier version in which Nietzsche figures as "always on the verge of madness."

15　See James Longenbach, *Stone Cottage: Pound, Yeats, and Modernism* (Oxford: Oxford University Press, 1988).

16　W. B. Yeats, *A Critical Edition of Yeats's A Vision*, George Mills Harper and Walter Kelly Hood, eds. (London: Macmillan, 1978), 211.

17　Yeats, *A Vision*, 211–12.

18　James Joyce, *The Day of the Rabblement* (Folcroft, PA: Folcroft Library Reprint, 1974), 17.

19　Joyce, *Day of the Rabblement*, 17.

20　Joyce, *Day of the Rabblement*, 18.

21　James Joyce, *Ulysses*, H. W. Gabler, W. Steppe, and K. Melchior, eds. (New York: Random House, 1986), chapter 3, line 496. All further references as *U*. followed by chapter and line numbers.

22　John Eglinton, *Pebbles from a Brook* (Kilkenny: O'Grady, 1901), 115. "John Eglinton" is a pseudonym used by William Magee.

23　James Joyce, *Poems and Exiles*, J. C. C. Mays, ed. (London: Penguin, 1992), 10, 270, and 275.

24　I am referring throughout to the facsimile reproduction of *Dana: An Irish Magazine of Independent Thought*, John Eglinton, ed. (Dublin: Hodges Figgis, 1904–5), provided by *The Modernist Journals Project*, an online archive hosted by Brown University and the University of Tulsa.

25　Richard Ellmann, *James Joyce* (Oxford: Oxford University Press, 1983) 126.

26　I have discussed this in *James Joyce and the Politics of Egoism* (Cambridge: Cambridge University Press, 2001).

27 James Joyce, *Selected Letters*, Richard Ellmann, ed. (London: Faber, 1975), 285.
28 Samuel Beckett, "Dante ... Bruno. Vico ... Joyce," in *Disjecta* (London: John Calder, 1983), 29.
29 Samuel Beckett, *Proust and Three Dialogues* (London: John Calder, 1965), 66.
30 Samuel Beckett, *The Letters, 1929–1940*, vol. I, Martha Fehsenfeld and Lois Overbeck, eds. (Cambridge: Cambridge University Press, 2009), 33.
31 Martin Heidegger, *Nietzsche* (Pfullingen: Guenther Neske, 1961).

2

JOE CLEARY

European, American, and Imperial Conjunctures

[British literature] was kept alive during the last century by a series of exotic injections. Swinburne read Greek and took English metric in hand: Rossetti brought in the Italian primitives; FitzGerald made the only good poem of its time that has gone to the people ... Morris translated sagas, the Irish took over the business for a few years; Henry James led, or rather preceded, the novelists, and then the Britons resigned *en bloc*; the language is now in the keeping of the Irish (Yeats and Joyce); apart from Yeats, since the death of Hardy, poetry is being written by Americans. All the developments in English verse since 1910 are due almost wholly to Americans. In fact, there is no longer any reason to call it English verse, and there is no present reason to think of England at all.
We speak a language that was English.
Ezra Pound, "How to Read," *New York Herald Tribune*, 1929.[1]

I

Irish modernism flourished at a particular conjuncture in Irish national and world history and at a transitional moment in European, American, and British imperial cultural history, and it is usefully understood in this wider context. For Ezra Pound writing in 1929 British literature had been artificially animated since the late nineteenth century by a series of "exotic injections" from the Greek classics, early Italian poetry, translations from Persian and Oriental literatures, reworkings of Scandinavian saga, and early French literature. Then the American and Irish expatriates had come to Paris and London and over two generations from Henry James and W. B. Yeats to T. S. Eliot, James Joyce, Gertrude Stein, and Pound himself had taken over from the Britons as the makers of a distinctively modern literature in English. The Irish and American interlopers did not, Pound contends, so much renovate as transmogrify the English language to create something altogether strange and new. "We speak a language that was English," he declares, as though British English was already a dead tongue and the modernists had fashioned another more cosmopolitan medium to replace it. As Pound tells it, the Irish had their chapter in this grand reverse-colonial-invasion narrative, but his is essentially a tale of American triumph and takeover ("All the developments in English verse since 1910 are due almost wholly to Americans"), as "English" is taken firmly into American custody.

To many, Pound's passage will smack of braggadocio, its swagger attained by presenting aspiration as already accomplished fact. The catastrophic turns in world history that occurred during the 1930s and led to World War II would certainly check the gallop of the earlier modernist avant gardes and high modernist coteries, and chasten the conception of total artistic and cultural renovation that had once fired them. Still, whatever its shortcomings, Pound's account of how Irish and American modernisms emerged in tandem and cumulatively helped to provincialize or decentre London, the hitherto supreme capital of the English-speaking world, is nothing if not suggestive. This chapter sketches some of the salient features of the world-historical and literary-historical contexts within which the various forms of Irish modernism were produced, and then tracks three successive stages of Irish modernist achievement from the late nineteenth century to the period immediately after World War II. The focus will be primarily on literary modernism, with occasional references to the visual and other arts also.

II

Modernism in Europe and America flourished between the breakdown of the Pax Britannica in the late nineteenth century and the Cold War consolidation of the Pax Americana. In the nineteenth century, London was the capital of the world's largest empire and the British ruling elites were able to manage the balance of power in continental Europe and to indirectly influence vast regions beyond Great Britain's imperial dominions, such as South America and China. The stability of this British-controlled system generated massive profits in the core regions of Europe, which sought returns from such profits in new investments in far-flung regions of the world, thus extending the capitalist system and intensifying inter-imperial competition for natural resources, new markets, or profitable investment sites. Meanwhile, as semi-peripheral states in this system – such as the United States, Germany, Japan, and Italy – developed their own industrial economies, Britain's earlier lead over its competitors was gradually reduced and the world system became increasingly volatile. The eventual upshot was World War I, which paved the way in the East for the Bolshevik Revolution and the establishment of the Soviet Union and in the West for the growing strength of the United States, which escaped most of the devastation of the European conflict but was able to take advantage of British and French postwar indebtedness to challenge the hegemony the latter states had hitherto enjoyed.

The settlements agreed at Versailles after World War I only aggravated the more fundamental problems that had troubled the wider system before 1914. Obvious symptoms of the deepening crisis *entre deux guerres* included the Great Depression, the rise of powerful fascist movements in Europe and Asia, the collapse of the League of Nations, and the Spanish Civil War. By 1940, the great powers of the interstate system were plunged into yet another military conflagration, one conducted this time on an even wider planetary scale. World War II represented the terminal breakdown of the old UK-centred and Western European-dominated world system; by the time that second conflict had concluded, the new global order was now firmly commanded by two continental-sized states, the United States and the USSR, on either flank of the old European core.[2]

London was the undisputed politico-financial capital of the world system under the nineteenth-century Pax Britannica, but Paris had remained Europe's leading cultural capital. As Pascale Casanova argues in *The World Republic of Letters* (1999), this Parisian distinction had been achieved over many centuries; one of its manifestations was that French became, from the early modern period onwards, the adoptive language of choice for the upper classes and the higher intellectual strata across the European continent from Madrid to Moscow. However, just as London's political and financial supremacy was eventually challenged by emerging rival powers, so too Parisian cultural capital in time provoked a series of rivalries, initially on the part of France's nearest sister nations, Britain and Germany, later from the more peripheral and "backward" literary regions of the globe. As Casanova argues, the modern literary world system was created out of a recurring series of national struggles for cultural recognition and distinction. Thus, when late-eighteenth- and nineteenth-century England and Germany had asserted themselves against French cultural supremacy in Europe, and in so doing had established themselves as major cultural centres with impressive national literatures in their own right, so too their intellectual provinces and satellites had in turn reacted against English and German cultural domination. Accordingly, the English struggle in the nineteenth century to compete with French supremacy was accompanied on its own flanks by Irish and American attempts to bolster their resistance to English cultural domination, and, in the same period, the Scandinavians and Russians also attempted to find ways to counter French and German intellectual ascendancy.[3] The efflorescence of European and American modernisms between 1890 and the end of World War II might be regarded both as a symptom of the wider breakdown of the old European bourgeois cultural order sustained under the Pax

Britannica and under Parisian cultural leadership and as a grand climax of the struggles for cultural self-assertion undertaken by the previously dominated or peripheral regions of the literary world system.

The capitals of old Europe – London, Paris, Vienna, and Moscow – were certainly crucibles of avant garde and high modernist production, but many of the most daring modernist experiments in the arts were actually undertaken by artists from the peripheries or semi-peripheries of Europe. Joyce, Stein, Franz Kafka, Alfred Döblin, and William Faulkner undermined the conventions of the realist novel; Yeats, Pound, Eliot, Wallace Stevens, Rainer Maria Rilke, Stefan George, and Federico García Lorca were some of the most distinguished practitioners of high modernist poetry; Pablo Picasso became the iconic modernist painter; American and German architecture created the high-rise modern city; the Italian, Spanish, German, Scandinavian, and Russian avant gardes pushed modernist experiment in music, theatre and the performance arts to extremes. This is not to negate the significance of the English and especially French modernists, but when critics such as Perry Anderson or Franco Moretti contend that the most hectic modernist experiments emerged in conditions of combined and uneven development on the peripheries and semi-peripheries of the European-dominated world system, it is cultural developments such as these that they have in mind.[4]

The European, American, and Irish modernisms that emerged in the extraordinarily turbulent period between 1890 and 1950 were never simply superstructural symptoms of these larger historico-cultural processes; instead, they were ambitious attempts to artistically register and interpret the crises of meaning occasioned by these processes and to find ways beyond the collapse of the old cultural dispensations. In the context of the English-speaking world at least, the two most immediate beneficiaries of these systemic crises were Ireland and the United States. After centuries of English domination, Irish nationalists took advantage of the weakening of British imperial power after World War I to establish the Irish Free State in 1922, whereas the United States, also a former British colony, would gradually displace Britain after 1918 to become a new world hegemon, although this process was not completed until after World War II when the rival claims of Germany and Japan had finally been put to rest. Ireland and the United States were able to take cultural as well as political advantage of the wider systemic crisis. Both countries had remained subordinate cultural satellites of England throughout the nineteenth century and many of the most talented figures from each society had therefore migrated to London to make their reputations: Edmund Burke, Sydney Owenson, James Barry, Thomas Moore, Washington Irving, Henry James, Bret Harte, Bram Stoker, James McNeill Whistler, Oscar Wilde, and George Bernard Shaw are exemplary instances. Others had remained at home and were commonly conceived in the literary world of the time as peripheral eccentrics or anomalies: Charles Maturin, Herman Melville, James Clarence Mangan, and Emily Dickinson meet this description. Others still – such as Maria Edgeworth, William Carleton, Nathaniel Hawthorne, Walt Whitman, and Mark Twain – were celebrated as interesting but essentially regional talents athwart the English mainstream tradition.

For those Irish and Americans born in the latter half of the nineteenth century, London and Paris were still home to the absolute arbiters of literary fashion and cultural modernity. The Irish and American modernist émigrés who made their careers in these metropoles had assimilated the standard nineteenth-century verities about the "backwardness" and "provincialism" of their own national cultures. However, the crucial difference between these émigrés and those who had migrated to the centre before them was that the later voyagers in could sense that while London and Paris remained essential to the consecration of international reputations neither capital was the self-sufficient cultural law-giver it once was. However much they might scorn the pieties of their own clamant cultural nationalisms back home, the Irish and American émigrés seem to have felt a sense of grand destiny buoyed up by the increasingly self-assertive cultural nationalisms of their natal societies and indeed by a perception – widespread in Western Europe itself and loudly proclaimed by Friedrich Nietzsche, William Thomas Stead, Oswald Spengler, Arnold Toynbee, and many others – that the old centres of European civilization were now in crisis. If the corruptions or collapse of the European imperial capitals is the subject of modernist classics such as Pound's "Hugh Selwyn Mauberley" (1920), Eliot's *The Waste Land* (1922), or Robert Musil's *The Man Without Qualities* (1930–42), the increasingly assertive notes of the peripheries are registered in works such as Stein's *The Making of Americans* (1925) and are also signified by Yeats's decision to offer himself to the world as an Irish rather than a British poet, or by Joyce's decision to settle in Paris but to set *Ulysses* (1922) and *Finnegans Wake* (1939) in his native Dublin. The flight of the Irish and American émigrés from their own countries to Paris and London attests in one way, then, to the still insuperable prestige of these metropolitan centres, but by the same token the unprecedentedly concentrated success of several generations of Irish and American parvenus in these capitals in this era is itself an index of change, a sign that an old world literary system was giving way and a new order gradually taking shape.

Writing in October 1892, Yeats observed that every time he crossed the Irish Sea he became increasingly aware that culturally Ireland and Britain "could not differ more if they were divided from each other by a half score of centuries." In England, Yeats remarks, "amongst the best minds art and poetry are becoming every day more entirely ends in themselves," whereas in Ireland there prevails the contrary belief "that literature must be the expression of conviction, and be the garb of noble emotion and not an end in itself." London's commitment to art for art's sake is attributable, Yeats says, in large degree to "[t]he influence of France," which is "every year pervading more completely English literary life." Much may be said, Yeats allows, for the art for art's sake doctrine of the French decadents and their English imitators, but it is not a doctrine he can embrace because his creed is that the very highest literature depends "upon conviction and upon heroic life." In Ireland, he continues, this sense of the heroic is a vitalizing force, and even though Irish writers had not as yet refined that heroic sensibility into the highest kinds of literature, the basic impulse was nonetheless more likely to be generative of great art than the morbid aesthetics of England and France: "We [Irish]," Yeats asserts, "have the limitations of dawn. They have the limitations of sunset."[5] Sunsets in the core states of Europe, new dawns or "renaissances" on its outer perimeters in Scandinavia, Russia, America, and Ireland: the idea that a European or English crisis might be Ireland's opportunity had been sounded in Irish letters well before the republican insurrectionists would take up that slogan for their own ends at the start of World War I.

III

If these ramifying social and political crises in the international world system conditioned the emergence of Irish modernism, how did that modernism develop over this period? Any attempt to address this question will require us to scan three or four generations of Irish-born or Irish-descended writers and artists and to keep in view at least as many literary capitals.

Wilde, Shaw, George Moore, and George Egerton (Mary Chavelita Dunne) were all born in the 1850s in the immediate aftermath of the Great Famine and all made careers in London or Paris in an era when these were the great capitals of European arts and letters. Son of a Catholic landlord and Westminster MP, Moore was born in 1852 in County Mayo and lived between 1873 and 1880 in Paris, where he became acquainted with several key Parisian Impressionists and with Émile Zola's Médan circle, also falling under the spell of Joris-Karl Huysmans's novel *À rebours* (1884), the breviary of French decadence. As a champion of French Impressionism in works such as *Confessions of a Young Man* (1888), *Impressions and Opinions* (1891), and *Modern Painting* (1893), as Zola's defender against English censorship, and as one of the earliest emulators of French aestheticism, Moore was, with his Celtic-periphery confrères, Arthur Symons and Wilde, a courageous advocate of some of the earliest European avant-garde currents in a late Victorian world generally antipathetic to such developments. Born in Dublin in 1854, Wilde holidayed as a child with his family near Moore Hall and befriended Moore in Mayo; later, like Moore, Wilde would become an enthusiast of French symbolism and decadence and his *The Picture of Dorian Gray* (1890) served as a conduit of continental aestheticism into the English novelistic tradition. But it is Wilde's *Salomé*, written in French in 1891, proscribed in London in 1892, and first staged in Paris in 1896, while its author was confined in an English prison, that has strongest claim to be regarded as the first major work of Irish modernism: it combined those traits of religious and moral provocation, deliberate stylistic excess, anti-mimeticism and Francophilia that were to become signature features of one major strand of Irish modernism. Shaw, born two years later than Wilde in Dublin in 1856, moved to London at the age of twenty, where – in his position as drama critic for Galway-born American-naturalized Frank Harris's *Saturday Review* – he became an early advocate of Henrik Ibsen and Richard Wagner (enthusiasms shared with Moore) and a brusque critic of the inherited conventions of the Victorian stage. With his Scottish friend and fellow drama-critic William Archer, Shaw campaigned vigorously for a modern English drama capable of taking on the social and philosophical issues of the new century. Egerton, born in 1859 in Australia to a Welsh Protestant mother and Irish Catholic father, was the most cosmopolitan of all this generation, having travelled as a child in Australia, New Zealand, and Chile, and then, after spending her formative years in Dublin, migrating to London, New York, and later Norway. Immersing herself in northern European modernism, particularly the works of Nietzsche, Ibsen, August Strindberg, and Knut Hamsun (and translating the latter's *Hunger* in 1899), Egerton, like Wilde and Shaw, was a flamboyant early exponent of intellectual audacity and sexual radicalism. *Keynotes* (1893) and *Discords* (1894) are briskly paced volumes of short stories that cut boldly from Norway to Ireland to England, from realism to reverie, and from complex psychology to "New Woman" protest and polemic. Thematically, Egerton explores the transports of kinetic or instinctive rather than socially sanctioned relationships with remarkable verve. The volumes created a sensation on both sides of the Atlantic, earning Egerton a place with her Irish émigré contemporaries on the radical fringes of the Anglophone literary world, and perhaps the right to be considered the first major exponent of the Irish modernist short story.

In the post-Famine decades when Moore, Wilde, Shaw and Egerton were growing up in Ireland, the parents of several distinguished Irish-American modernists were departing Ireland for further shores. Patrick Sullivan, an Irish dancing-master, left in the late 1840s for England and then Massachusetts, where he married a recent Swiss emigrant, Adrienne List. In 1874, their son Louis Henry Sullivan, who would become known as the "father of sky-scrapers" and "father of American modernism," set sail for Paris to study architecture at l'École des Beaux Arts (where Moore also studied), and then toured France and Italy before taking up a career as a draftsman in Chicago in 1875. James O'Neill, father of Eugene O'Neill, was born in Kilkenny in 1847 and emigrated to the United States in 1854, where in 1874 he married an Irish-American, Mary Ellen Quinlan, and went on to become one of the most notable commercial stage actors of his day and later a silent screen matinée idol. Born in 1888 in New York, Eugene O'Neill would eventually be as significant to the reshaping of twentieth-century American theatre as Shaw was to its twentieth-century English counterpart. Philip F. McQuillan, born in County Fermanagh, left Ireland with his family for the United States in 1843; in 1857 he moved from Illinois to St. Paul, Minnesota and became a wealthy businessman in that city. Thirty years later, his eldest daughter, Mollie, married Edward Fitzgerald, son of Maryland storekeeper Michael Fitzgerald, also of Irish Catholic background, and in 1896, the year Wilde's *Salomé* was first produced in Paris, F. Scott Fitzgerald was born in St. Paul. Kate Chopin, born Katherine O'Flaherty in St. Louis, Missouri in 1850 was the third daughter of Thomas O'Flaherty, a wealthy businessman who had emigrated from Galway and married Eliza Faris, a woman of French-Canadian descent. When Katherine married Oscar Chopin in 1870, she settled in French-speaking New Orleans, taking over her husband's business there when he died in 1882. Later, she returned to St. Louis, publishing her most famous work, *The Awakening*, which displays strong French and Ibsenite naturalist influences, in 1899. The Great Famine is now considered one of the historical triggers of the Irish revivalist and modernist enterprises, but it also had significant cultural consequences across the Atlantic as some of the sons and daughters of those Irish migrants who fled westwards were to be in the vanguard of early American modernist assertion.[6]

Separated by a generation and by the Atlantic, neither of these two groups – the mainly Protestant Irish émigrés who made their careers in London and the mainly Catholic Irish Americans whose reputations were largely made in the United States – would have identified themselves in any simple sense as "Irish." Different though their ancestral histories and career paths might be, both sets of artists nonetheless came of age in an era when the Irish were making rapid economic and political strides in the core cities of an Anglo-American world where Irishness had long served as a byword for poverty and backwardness. Moore, Wilde, Shaw, and Egerton were all well-educated, upper- or middle-class individuals who would become significant mediators between continental European and English cultures in the period leading up to World War I; Sullivan, Chopin, O'Neill, and Fitzgerald were the children of a rising Irish American Catholic middle-class that had prospered in the United States, and as such they were the first of their kind to have access to the upper tiers of American education and society. In their different ways, both groups were "arrivistes" – the one in a strongly Protestant England that regarded the Irish of all creeds as benighted or eccentric provincials, the other in a Protestant America, where the recently well-to-do Irish remained anxious to keep their distance from the more impoverished masses of their race, and where Catholicism was still a suspect creed.[7] If the London émigrés loudly disavowed their provincialism by acting as the importers to the English of things Parisian and continental European, the Irish Americans were pioneers in a different sense as they were the first generation to make the passage from American popular culture (where the Irish were associated with blackface minstrelsy, commercial song, and vaudeville) into the field of high culture.

The second and pivotal generation of Irish modernists stretches from the visual artist May Guinness, born in Dublin in 1863, and William Butler Yeats, born there in 1865, to Joyce, also born in the Irish capital in 1882. This generation includes Jack B. Yeats and John Millington Synge (both born in 1871), Eileen Gray (b. 1878), and Sean O'Casey (b. 1880). John Quinn, who was born in Ohio in 1870 to James W. and Mary Quinlaw Quinn, and who became a wealthy corporate lawyer in New York and a major patron to post-impressionist European art and to both Irish and American literary modernisms, can also be identified with this cohort. A major backer of the *Armory Show* (*The International Exhibition of Modern Art*) hosted in New York in 1913, Quinn's role as supporter to the Irish Revival and as mediator of contemporary Irish literature and art to American audiences probably ranks him second only to W. B. Yeats as one of the decisive impresarios of Irish revivalism and Irish modernism.

Like Moore, Wilde, Shaw, and Egerton before them, all of these second-generation figures eagerly absorbed continental European avant-garde influences; unlike the earlier group, none except the Yeats brothers and Eileen Gray served an artistic apprenticeship in London. After his education in Trinity College, Dublin, Synge studied music in Germany and languages in Paris before famously returning to the Aran Islands in 1896. Following in the footsteps of Moore and Synge, Joyce too left for Paris in 1903, settling in Trieste in 1905. The second generation of American émigrés – Pound, Eliot, and Stein – followed on the heels of an earlier generation of "passionate pilgrims" to Europe led by Henry James and James McNeill Whistler, but took on the received conventions of the English cultural establishment in a much more daring manner than their immediate forebears had done; so too the second generation of Irish modernists was also much less prepared to assimilate into the English literary world than were their immediate predecessors.[8] Whereas Moore, Shaw, Wilde, and Egerton were anxious to find a place in the world of English letters even as they also tried to shake it up, the succeeding generation of Irish writers had more extravagant ambitions.

Leading figures in the Irish Revival, Yeats, Gregory, and Synge deployed the Abbey Theatre, the Cuala Press, and later the Irish Academy to establish Dublin as an alternative literary capital to London, while – after the publication of *Ulysses* in 1922 and his conscription into Pound's "big brass band" of modernist mandarins – Joyce became the leading light of an exilic multinational Parisian avant garde.[9] Unlike Pound, Stein, and Eliot, who never returned permanently to America or set their major works there, the Yeats brothers, Synge, Joyce, and O'Casey all combined formal experiment with an expressly Irish subject-matter and dialect. World War I and Easter 1916 were formative watersheds for this second-generation group (except for Synge, who had died young in 1909); after this great divide the writers particularly began to subordinate much of the fin-de-siècle naturalist, symbolist, or aestheticist features that mark their formative works to increasingly uncompromising experiments with language and form. This is evident in Joyce's turn from the Flaubertian naturalism of *Dubliners* (1914) or the d'Annunzian aestheticisim of *A Portrait of the Artist as a Young Man* (1916) to the epic compendium of styles that is *Ulysses*, and on its completion to the even more wayward "Work in Progress" that eventually became *Finnegans Wake* (1939), a project that dismayed even admirers of *Ulysses* such as Pound, Eliot, Harriet Weaver, and Joyce's brother Stanislaus. This extremism is evident in a different way in the work of Yeats as the courtly pre-Raphaelite tints and Celticism of his early career are left behind from *Responsibilities* (1914) and *The Wild Swans at Coole* (1919) onwards. One of the few Nobel laureates to become more rather than less experimental after winning the prize, Yeats moved from the abrasively anti-modern rhetorics of *The Tower* (1928) or *The Winding Stair* (1933) to the belligerently eugenicist idioms of "On the Boiler" or *Purgatory* (both 1938). This continuous drive to experiment with new forms is also true of O'Casey, who would spend the remainder of his career in London after Yeats refused to stage his *The Silver Tassie* in the Abbey in 1928. Although O'Casey's removal to London places him in the company of fellow southern Irish Protestants such as Elizabeth Bowen, John Eglinton, George Russell (AE), St. John Ervine, and James Stephens, who all took up or maintained residence in England after the formation of the Irish Free State, O'Casey stands out from the rest

by virtue of the fact that his work became ever more militantly avant gard-
ist in the 1930s and 1940s. When Wyndham Lewis remarked in *Time and
Western Man* (1927) that "Joyce and Yeats are the prose and poetry respectively of the Ireland that culminated in the Rebellion," he might have added
that O'Casey was that rebellion's theatrical counterpart.[10] Lewis's point
was not that Joyce or Yeats were mouthpieces of the Sinn Féin insurrection,
but that their works were possessed of the same kind of anti-English, anti-
imperial, and incendiary spirit that had motivated the Irish revolt, and that
these writers had done as much by their works to destabilize the world of
English letters as Irish secession had done to diminish the British state.

The third generation of Irish modernists was born between the last
decade of the nineteenth century and 1916. Leading figures here include
Seán Keating (b. 1889), Thomas MacGreevy (b. 1893), Evie Hone (b. 1894),
Mainie Jellett (b. 1897), Elizabeth Bowen (b. 1899), Norah McGuinness
(b. 1901), Francis Stuart (b. 1902), Brian Coffey (b. 1905), Samuel Beckett
and Máirtín Ó Cadhain (both born 1906), Louis MacNeice (b. 1907), Denis
Devlin (b. 1908), Francis Bacon (b. 1909), Flann O'Brien (b. 1911), Oisín
Kelly (b. 1915), and Louis le Brocquy and Seán Ó Riordáin (both born 1916).
Many of the painters in this group trained in England and France, and most
were deeply influenced there by cubism and abstract art, although Keating's
paintings combine the heroic energies of Soviet proletarian art with Irish
revivalist motifs, and Kelly's sculptures *The Children of Lir* (1964) and *Jim
Larkin* (1977) also marry revivalist or revolutionary themes with modernist
impulses. The writers of Irish Catholic background who worked partly or
fully in the Irish language – Ó Cadhain, O'Brien, and Ó Riordáin – made
their literary careers in Ireland even though they were profoundly estranged
from the post-independence culture they inhabited. All three produced fine
work, but even the best of that work has something of the desperation of
an embattled minority; none of the Irish-language writers, for example,
attained the elevated tone of the Scottish poet Sorley MacLean, also writing
in Gaelic in the 1940s and 1950s, whose work possesses a grander Yeatsian
sense of worldly assurance.[11] The English-language writers of Catholic
background – MacGreevy, Coffey, and Devlin –spent part of their careers in
Europe, but they found employment in the Irish public service or academia;
this, together with their various interests in Catholicism, reflecting a less
absolute rejection of the new state than that expressed by Joyce or Beckett.
The major Irish Protestant writers in this grouping, Bowen, Stuart, Beckett,
and MacNeice, were even more alienated from the new Ireland than were
their Catholic-born counterparts: Bowen spent most of her literary career
in London; Stuart, Australian-born, educated in England, and a convert to
Catholicism in 1920 when he married Iseult Gonne, spent the World War

II period in Germany, where he collaborated with the Nazi régime; Beckett emigrated to Paris in 1927 and remained there, working between Paris and London and the United States for the rest of his life; MacNeice was fascinated by Ireland and Yeats, but it was in the English company of W. H. Auden and Stephen Spender that he perfected his craft. Like Ó Cadhain and Ó Ríordáin, Bowen, Beckett, and Bacon belonged to remaindered communities marooned in the "cold war" climate of post-partition Ireland. Yeats's authoritative sense of commanding the Irish scene seems to have been alien to the tempers or aspirations of all of these writers and painters.

Temperamentally, politically, and stylistically, this third group is a diverse one by any measure. But its members all matured professionally and artistically after the formation of the Irish Free State and after both the Irish Revival and international modernism had already shed much of their earlier radical novelty and iconoclastic panache. The Great Depression, the crisis of European liberalism, the rise of fascism and communist authoritarianisms, and the post-revolutionary conservatism of the Irish Free State and Northern Ireland were probably formative events for this generation; World War II would change its world even more cataclysmically than World War I had done that of its predecessors. Tyrus Miller has suggested that "[i]n their struggle against what they perceived as the apotheosis of form in earlier modernism, late modernists conjured the disruptive, deforming spell of laughter." Repudiating the high modernist's aesthetics of formal mastery, late modernists, Miller observes, deployed satiric and form-breaking strategies to undo the cohesion of earlier modernist styles and "to deflate [their] symbolic resources." Late modernism constitutes, he proposes, a fissile crisis of modernism; it is a modernism that no longer looks to art to restore significance to a broken universe but that strives rather to express "a world in free fall."[12] Conceived in these terms, Irish late modernism's relationship to earlier modernism is as complex and perhaps as antagonistic as the literature of the Irish counter-revival is to revivalism; a spirit of backlash against outsized antecedents and the styles they cultivated informs both.

Individual distinctions acknowledged, third generation family resemblances become apparent in this light. There is something leached about Irish modernism in this latter phase. Black comedy and satiric deflation is crucial to late modernist style, most obviously in the works of O'Brien and Beckett, but also in Patrick Kavanagh's single modernist-style work, *The Great Hunger* (1942), in Ó Cadhain's single masterpiece, *Cré na Cille* (1949), and in Bacon's series *Head I* to *Head VI*, painted in the 1940s. The cool aristocratic poise that characterizes Bowen's writerly persona and literary style sets her work at a distance to that of this late modernist generation, and her hauteur in some ways brings her closer to the dandyism of Wilde or the mandarin aloofness of Yeats or Joyce than to her immediate peers. Nevertheless, Bowen is essentially an ironist, and the frosted sparkle of her prose never conceals that her obsessive theme is breakdown; the desire of a Shaw or Wilde or Egerton to scandalize bourgeois opinion, Yeats's or Synge's heroic styles, Joyce's totalizing ambitions – these are all as alien to Bowen as to her generation more broadly. *The Last September* (1929), *The House in Paris* (1935), and *The Death of the Heart* (1938) are studies in orphaned drift, and drift functions as a kind of de-structuring structure for Bowen. There are many grand houses in her novels, but there is something funereal about all of them and their dissolution signifies not only the unravelling of the Ascendancy class, but also that of the totalizing aspirations of classical realist and high modernist forms. After the 1930s, the absolutism of the earlier high modernist conception of art survives strongest in the works of those committed to extreme politics – Ó Cadhain to militant republicanism, O'Casey to communism, Stuart to fascism. But in these cases, a sense of systematic breakdown and maverick isolation is also pervasive. Even when desolation was their theme, Yeats or Joyce reached towards grander achievement and greater stylistic mastery as they aged; their successors mostly lack their antecedents' redemptive faith in art and make dissolution their absolute. Like admirals who can prevent the capture of their argosies only by sinking them, the late modernists seem obliged to sabotage or even scuttle their arts to save them.

The paradox of the Yeats-Joyce modernist generation is that all the major figures were deeply ambivalent about Ireland and mostly scornful for one reason or another of what the national revolution had accomplished, but their works, as Lewis noted, had nevertheless been infused by the brash rebelliousness of the moment when the Irish political and modernist artistic revolutions first made their mark. The paradox of the figures that belong to the third generation is that they made their careers in an era when modernism was already winning elite acceptance in Western Europe and the United States but when such canonization was increasingly difficult to dissociate from a sense of failure as the world plunged into a second catastrophe. Put another way, from the 1930s onwards Ireland certainly produced a greater quantity and variety of modernist works and did so across a wider spectrum of the arts than it had done earlier, but if this means that Irish modernism's career may be considered increasingly a "success story," then one of the things that divides the third generation is how various artists responded to that "success."

One response was to accept the cultural capital already accrued and to consolidate the achievement. The establishment of the Irish Academy of Letters by Yeats and Shaw in 1932 is an early example of such consolidation;

the founding of the *Irish Exhibition of Living Art* in 1943 by Mainie Jellett, Norah McGuinness, Louis le Brocquy, and others is another instance; as was the representation of Irish modernist artists at Venice Biennales and World Fairs from this period onwards. Modernism in such instances becomes increasingly affiliated with the new Irish state and is exhibited at home and abroad as part of its claim to international legitimacy, cultural modernity, and entrepreneurial innovation. But an opposite, and arguably aesthetically more successful, response was to cultivate an assiduous ethic of failure. This was the route pursued by Beckett, the most celebrated figure in this later cohort, and the strategy that allowed him eventually to shake off Joyce's influence to achieve a late modernist oeuvre of world distinction. Famously contrasting Joyce's tendency to work towards "omniscience and omnipotence as an artist" with his own exploitation of "impotence" and "ignorance,"[13] Beckett's stress on privation and his tendency to move restlessly from one medium to another might seem merely an idiosyncratic response to the dilemmas of the time were it not for the fact that several other Irish late modernist works of the same era also share something of this quality. In other words, Kavanagh's anti-Yeatsian and Eliotesque *The Great Hunger*, O'Brien's *At Swim-Two-Birds* (1939), *The Third Policeman* (1940, posthumously published 1967), or *An Béal Bocht* (1941), Ó Cadhain's *Cré na Cille*, or even Bacon's *Head VI* (1948) or *Study after Velázquez's Pope Innocent X* (1953), all share with Beckett an aesthetic that stresses grotesque morbidity, defaced or debased form, or an austere gallows humour of failure and abjection. To corral these works in this manner may appear forced, but what they have in common is the degree to which they repudiate any redemptive sense of Ireland or Christianity or humanism or the body, and the frustrated antagonism they display towards their respective artistic media. In the major works of Kavanagh, Beckett, Bacon, O'Brien, and Ó Cadhain, the reader will find little or none of Wilde's purpled jubilance, Synge's assonantal extravagances, Yeats's *sprezzatura*, Joyce's intellectual omniverousness, or even Fitzgerald's vermillion passages. When institutional consecration had become the paradoxical response to modernist rebellion, failure and abjection became modernism's last cards to play, and even that hand would soon be played out. "Fail again, fail better" might be this latter generation's motto – a slogan not likely greatly to appeal to Wilde or Shaw, Yeats, or Joyce.[14]

IV

After the early modernist panache of the parvenu and the high modernist mandarin boom, the late modernist bust? Something of this perhaps, but not only this of course. For a time at least, Dublin, after its long post-1800 decline, to on the mask of a literary capital, London and Paris appearing from 1890 to 1950 less like remote or unreachable capitals of world culture than offshore training-schools or inevitable sites of consecration for a succession of Irish talents. For a time, the broken-voiced Patsy Calibans of the nineteenth century became the mellifluous "lords of language" ushering in the twentieth century. In 1900, Ireland was known to the wider literary world primarily as the place where Richard Brinsley Sheridan, Oliver Goldsmith, Edmund Burke, or Thomas Moore had been born before taking their inevitable paths to London, or where Jonathan Swift had wasted to madness. By the 1950s, Irish writers had given to Europe and the world several great modernist oeuvres that it was still struggling to assimilate, while across the Atlantic Irish Americans such as Sullivan, Chopin, O'Neill, and Fitzgerald had made their own contributions to the modern architecture and literature of the United States. "We speak a language that was English," Pound had declared in 1929; by the 1950s that claim had been largely made good. By then, the Irish and the Americans had detonated the old London-centred world of English letters to make way for a language and literature much less restrictively "English" than anything that had existed earlier. But while these developments were underway, the old European world literary system had also come asunder, and in the new world order that was emerging from the wreckage, New York and Moscow were the ascendant neo-imperial world cities, and in their shadows the writers and artists of the "Third World" were cultivating their own revivals or beginning to make their own voyages in. Modernism may have been invented in Europe and its peripheries, but from the 1920s onwards, and especially after the mid-century, the United States claimed modernism as its own, acquiring its archives, housing its sacred artefacts, crafting its grand narratives. In this changed world, Irish artists would have to find new paths to follow, new ways to disport themselves. But where exactly literary and artistic Ireland located itself on the map of that new world order in the aftermath of modernism remained unclear; perhaps it remains so today.

NOTES

1 Ezra Pound, "How To Read," *New York Herald Tribune*, 1929, collected in T. S. Eliot, ed., *Literary Essays of Ezra Pound* (New York: New Directions, 1968), 33–4.
2 For useful overviews see Giovanni Arrighi, *The Long Twentieth Century* (London: Verso, 1994) and John Darwin, *The Empire Project: The Rise and Fall of the British World-System 1830–1970* (Cambridge: Cambridge University Press, 2009).

3 Pascale Casanova, *The World Republic of Letters*, M. B. DeBevoise, trans. (Cambridge, MA: Harvard University Press, 2004), chapters 1–3.

4 Perry Anderson, "Modernity and Revolution," *New Left Review* 144 (March–April 1984), 96–113 and Franco Moretti, "World-Systems Analysis, Evolutionary Theory, *Weltliteratur*," in David Palumbo-Liu, Bruce Robbins and Nirvana Tanoukhi, eds., *Immanuel Wallerstein and the Problem of the World: System, Scale, Culture* (Durham, NC: Duke University Press, 2011), 67–77.

5 W. B. Yeats, "Hopes and Fears for Irish Literature" in John P. Frayne, ed., *Uncollected Prose by W. B. Yeats* (London: Macmillan, 1970), 248–50, 248, 250.

6 On the Famine and modernism, see the "Introduction" to this volume, and also Luke Gibbons, "Montage, Modernism and the City," in *Transformations in Irish Culture* (Cork: Field Day/Cork University Press, 1996), 165–9.

7 On the Irish in London, see Jonathan Schneer, *London 1900: The Imperial Metropolis* (New Haven, CT: Yale University Press, 1999), 162–83. On nineteenth-century American conceptions of Irish culture, see Christopher Dowd, *The Construction of Irish Identity in American Literature* (New York: Routledge, 2011).

8 For a wider survey, see Alex Zwerdling, *Improvised Europeans: American Literary Expatriates and the Siege of London* (New York: Basic Books, 1998).

9 Letter to Harriet Shaw Weaver, *Letters of James Joyce*, vol. I, Stuart Gilbert, ed. (London: Faber and Faber, 1957), 276.

10 Wyndham Lewis, *Time and Western Man* (London: Chatto and Windus, 1927), 93.

11 See Patrick Crotty, "Sorley MacLean/Somhairle Mac Gill-Eain," *Times Literary Supplement*, 12 July 2012, 3–5.

12 Tyrus Miller, *Late Modernism: Politics, Fiction and the Arts Between the World Wars* (Berkeley: University of California Press, 1999), 19.

13 Israel Shenker, "A Portrait of Samuel Beckett, Author of the Puzzling *Waiting for Godot*," *The New York Times*, 6 May 1956, 1, 3.

14 Samuel Beckett, *Worstward Ho* (London: John Calder, 1999), 7.

3

RÓNÁN MCDONALD

The Irish Revival and Modernism

I

The "Irish Revival" and "modernism" are an unlikely pairing. For the major critics of modernism in the mid-century, like Richard Ellmann or Hugh Kenner, the Irish modernists were modern insofar as they transcended their national background. Whereas the towering Irish modernists, James Joyce and Samuel Beckett, took their lead from international, cosmopolitan, and generally metropolitan artistic currents, the revivalists were, in this view, nationalist, valorizing a rural and premodern Ireland swathed in cultural purity and twilit nostalgia. The opposition, often calcifying into reductive duality between Joyce the pioneering modernist and W. B. Yeats the belated Romantic, was buttressed variously by antipathy to the Revival by major modernist figures including Joyce himself, Beckett and Ezra Pound, and by the humanist universalizing approach of American criticism in the aftermath of World War II. What could be less "modernist" than that völkisch and insular movement against which many subsequent Irish writers, realist and experimental, set their teeth and often aimed their scorn? What is less "revivalist" than the deracinated Parisian bohemians, cocking a snoop at the provincial, confessional, conservative backwater that they had been so eager to escape?[1]

In the current critical climate, however, the two concepts have switched their polar charge from repulsion to attraction. The "Revival," far from the opposite of "modernism," is now typically regarded as an incubatory moment of it, its anti-modern ideology of a piece with the modernist disdain for bourgeois values and prefabricated realist forms. "What 'British' modernism there was in the late nineteenth and early twentieth centuries" asserts Terry Eagleton, "was largely of Irish origin."[2] What shifts in critical perspective allowed such a turnaround? How and why does the cleavage between Irish Revival and modernism now emphasize the joints rather than the divisions?

The Revival, or certain aspects of it, was caricatured and simplified by its detractors. Analysis of the historical context reveals that the cultural environment in Ireland from the 1890s to the 1920s, the decades usually signaled by the "Revival," saw multifarious, hydra-headed enterprises, sometimes conflicting, sometimes synergetic. The cultural energies and anxieties that underpinned some of these enterprises resemble the wider European crisis of modernity, albeit shot through with the specificities of cultural nationalism and Ireland's political struggles of the time. Both modernism and revivalism, though often seeking out the new and innovative, are wedded in their very warp and weft to ideas of the old. A central ideological plank of both movements is recoil, even horror, from aspects of the modern world, its homogeneity, its mindless mercantilism, and its materialist disenchantments. Both the Irish Revival and European modernism have aesthetic roots in French Symbolism and in the work of Darwin and Nietzsche; both reject empiricism, realism, and linear temporality; both seek alternatives to modern epistemologies; both are attracted to primitivism, and mythology and the occult, often as alternatives to conventional religion. And straddling both movements, fitting all these descriptors, stands Yeats, a dominating figure in both the Irish Revival and European modernism, though also, ironically, responsible for some of the later fixed ideas about the Revival that would allow for its tenacious caricature. In what follows, I hope first to explain why the Irish Revival and Irish modernism were construed as antithetical movements, and then to elucidate some of the contemporary tendencies in literary studies that have authorized a more dialectical sense of the connections between the two.

II

The Revival originates in the poems and ballads of Young Ireland, the antiquarianism of John O'Donovan (1806–61) and Eugene O'Curry (1794–1862), and the heroic histories of Standish James O'Grady (1846–1928). Despite this initial backward look, Ernest Boyd's early history of the movement, *Ireland's Literary Renaissance* (1916), emphasizes the "modernity" of the Revival compared to the Young Irelanders of the 1840s. However, it focuses on the national precedents for the national movement, obscuring the European context of which the Revival also, vitally, partook. From the influence of Henrik Ibsen on the Abbey Theatre to the Austro-Hungarian precedents for Arthur Griffith's idea of a dual monarchy, we now recognize that the ideas inspiring early-twentieth-century Irish cultural and political separatism were often international.

Moreover, "nation building" can never simply be about a backward look, but must also be orientated toward the present and future. The sense of cultural possibility, of the inadequacy of inherited or imported forms and themes, was common to the Irish Revival and modernism. Both these variegated "movements" were shaped by societies and associations, small magazines and publishing ventures. It is tempting to follow Yeats's lead and see the Revival resulting from unmoored political energies after Charles Stewart Parnell's death in 1891; but this is contested terrain.[3] At that time, several currents developed that sought to identify and celebrate a distinctly Irish mode of expression and thought: in literature, in theatre, in sport, in the Irish language, in economic organization. Yeats recalls being struck with "the sudden certainty that Ireland was to be like soft wax for years to come."[4] The malleability metaphor cleaves to the modern, suggestive of possibility and indeterminacy, rather than the fixed identity of essentialist nationalism. In 1892, Yeats set about molding the wax, founding the London-based Irish Literary Society with T. W. Rolleston and the veteran Young Irelander Charles Gavan Duffy, and the National Literary Society in Dublin, with Douglas Hyde as its first president. Hyde's inaugural lecture, "The Necessity of De-Anglicising Ireland" (1892), one of the early Revival manifestos, asserted the need to recover Irish language and Irish customs and to resist the widespread mimicry of English taste. A key revivalist note had been struck – home rule, suspended in politics, would be achieved in culture.

Yeats's wax attracted more than literary or dramatic hands. John Millington Synge captured the synergy between cultural, social, and economic movements when he claimed of the Gaelic League, the Irish Agricultural Organisation Society, and the literary movement: "it is hard to find someone who is involved in only one of them, without also being interested in the others at the same time."[5] While these organizations had common members, there were also divisions, resentments and cultural distinctions. The Gaelic League, the movement to revive and promote the Irish language, was founded by Hyde and Eoin MacNeill in 1893, and would eventually thwart Hyde's vision of nonalignment by becoming closely associated with nationalist politics, prompting his resignation in 1915. The League became the cultural home of middle-class Catholic nationalism, which took a suspicious stance toward the mandarin "Anglo-Irish" Revival led by Yeats and Lady Gregory, and stood against Yeats's credo that a truly indigenous literature could be created in the English language. But the Gaelic Irish Revival was not, by that token, culturally protectionist or insular. Progressive Irish language revivalists like Patrick Pearse opposed Anglicization while embracing cosmopolitan values, seeking an Irish literature that would resist English imitation but for that very reason form part of European modernism.[6]

Therefore to imagine the Anglo-Irish and Gaelic-Irish Revivals as homogeneous forces lining up against one another is to underestimate how much common purpose they shared and also how much internal conflict there was on each side. A glance at the signal artistic institution of the Anglo-Irish Revival, the Abbey Theatre, reveals contesting positions and aesthetic agendas from the start. Yeats sought to incarnate an ideal, mythic theatre of the elite, written in verse with subjects from Irish mythology, but other early Abbey playwrights, such as Edward Martyn or Padraic Colum, were drawn to naturalist plays of rural life. The division between real and ideal, a drama of verisimilitude versus one of mythic verity, was a feature of the Abbey's early development. That these controversies would resolve into a predominantly realist, rural ethos, with a high quotient of "PQ" (peasant quality), meant that the Abbey's repertoire would later slide into self-caricature.

Later realist writers like Sean Ó Faoláin and Patrick Kavanagh and experimental modernists like Joyce and Beckett could invoke the caricature of a mistily romantic Revival not least to make space for their own creative projects. In that respect the Revival was constructed around an Oedipal opposition: those who came after sought to demythologize it, to contrast its investment in legend and folklore to the mess and murk of lived experience. So Seán O'Casey's Dublin plays contrast revivalist-nationalist rhetoric of heroism with the squalid horrors of actual political violence; later, Kavanagh's images of emotionally impoverished rural life repudiate the bucolic Arcadian ideal of the twilighters.

There are those who reject the Revival in the name of a harder social realism and those who reject it for avant-garde modernism. Firmly in the latter camp is Beckett, whose essay "Recent Irish Poetry" (1934) establishes an opposition between the benighted and sentimental "antiquarians" of the Revival and the modern poets he prized, those who were aware of "the rupture of the lines of communication," who were emboldened enough to recognize the ineffability and truculence of the modern world.[7] Beckett's essay sets up an opposition between revivalism and modernism akin to that between local and metropolitan, delusory and profound. It was a mode of thinking that echoed a commonplace modernist hostility for the provincial, articulated for instance by Pound's heralding of Joyce as one of the European moderns, rather than an "institution for the promotion of Irish peasant industries."[8]

But the adoption of this binary by the young Beckett belies the influence on him of figures like Yeats, Synge, and O'Casey. His youthful visits to the Abbey Theatre were formative and it is not hard to hear echoes of Synge, the playwright who influenced him above all, in Beckett's tramps and vagrants.[9] Equally, Joyce's early modernist disdain for the provincial revivalist ethos in "The Day of the Rabblement" (1901) and "The Holy Office" (1904) is complicated by the tautly responsive depictions of revivalist debates and personalities in *Ulysses* (1922). Episode Nine, "Scylla and Charybdis," contains ripe parodies of Lady Gregory's Kiltartanesque Hiberno-English, but it also puts Stephen Dedalus in dialogue with John Eglinton (William Magee) and Æ (George Russell), tacitly acknowledging that there is more to the literary movement than flowery-tongued peasant exoticism. Russell and Magee were both friends of Yeats and key figures of the Revival, and they took opposing views on its direction, with Magee urging it to repudiate its Celticist, cultural nationalist orientation for a more universal and scientific ethos.[10] As Emer Nolan has pointed out, for all his studied internationalism and rejection of Irish insularity, Joyce's relationship to the Revival and to Irish cultural nationalism defies easy binaries.[11] Stephen Dedalus's famous imperative at the end of *A Portrait of the Artist as a Young Man* (1916), "to forge in the smithy of my soul the uncreated conscience of my race" can, like Yeats's wax, be read both in revivalist and modernist terms.[12]

If there are revivalist influences even in the most deracinated of the Irish modernists, then equally the great revivalists are attuned to the forces and concerns of international modernism. Synge wrote of Irish peasantry and was a founder of the Abbey with Yeats and Lady Gregory, but his work confounds the realist-idealist aesthetic divisions of that theatre. Unlike many of his fellow Protestant playwrights, he resisted "a purely, fantastical, unmodern, ideal, spring-dayish, Cuchulanoid National Theatre" and avoided direct treatment of Irish legend until his last, uncompleted play, *Deirdre of the Sorrows* (1910).[13] Like Joyce or T. S. Eliot, his work infuses mythic elements into contemporary settings and idioms. *The Playboy of the Western World* (1907) evokes Christian and Oedipal archetypes without ever congealing into allegory. The metatheatrical, symbolical, strategically irresolute aspects of *Playboy* underwrite its status as a postcolonial modernist play.[14] With its unsettling tragic and comic hybridities and its mixing of squalid social conditions and inflated poetic language, the play brings opposing tropes into explosive contact with each other, highlighting the precarity of all identities and the contingency of dramatic representation.

The cases of Synge and Hyde, both Protestant masters of the Irish language, indicate that the Anglo-Irish and Gaelic Irish Revivals do not line up neatly with Protestant versus Catholic divisions. But as bourgeois Catholic nationalism in Ireland gained political and cultural traction, sectarian divisions in the cultural and language movements emerged. At critical moments, such as during the *Playboy* riots, mutual mistrust broke into direct confrontation. Such moments allowed self-identifying "Irish-Irelanders" like D. P. Moran to deride the Revival as a project for an alien Ascendancy, more interested in self-serving romanticism and a foreign readership than in the lived experience of the real Ireland. If modernist critics saw the revivalists as mystifiers obsessed with provincial fantasy and romance, the Irish-Irelanders saw them as too detached, insufficiently immersed in the life of the real, if often hidden, Ireland. In Daniel Corkery's view, colonized Ireland is more plastic, more uneven, more traumatized than the sentimental versions promulgated by the twilighters: "Everywhere in the mentality of Irish people are flux and uncertainty. Our national consciousness may be described, in a native phrase, as a quaking sod. It gives no footing."[15] The "quaking sod" (the metaphor evokes soft Irish bogland), unlike Yeats's soft wax, indicates a precarious subjectivity rendered invisible and inarticulate by foreign dominance. The Revival project, he holds, is insufficient for the complexity of the condition in which Ireland emerged into modernity. Corkery sees the revivalists (though he makes a special case for Synge) as Ascendancy eavesdroppers inadequate to the opacity of a nation finding its identity in the aftermath of colonization.

Irish-Irelanders, deracinated Protestant *avant-gardistes*, counter-revival realists, American humanist literary critics, modernist poets and Marxist-republican critics: diverse sources over the twentieth century equated the Revival with cultural nostalgia and reactionary obfuscation, and ipso facto with the anti-modern and the anti-modernist. How then has it come about in the last twenty years or so that the Irish Revival is regarded as a signal aspect, even one of the incubators, of modernism?

III

Part of the answer lies in the rise of two approaches to literary studies in recent decades that have exploded simplistic conceptualizations of the Revival: cultural theory on the one hand and a renewed historicism on the other. Throughout the academic study of literature and the arts, critical priorities have shifted from the discrete, hermetic artwork onto the social condition and intellectual contexts from which texts emerge. In Irish studies, this has rendered visible the intertwined subterranean roots of seemingly opposed movements. So, for instance, the Revival's indebtedness to such discourses as primitivism, spiritualism, evolutionism, and feminism reveals it as part of a broader European, modernist interchange of ideas. Conversely, but consistently, the image of historically uncontaminated modernist writers, who have transcended local or national concerns, has also been radically challenged. In the Irish case, the rise of a theoretically supple historical approach has demonstrated, first of Joyce and then of Beckett, their inseparability from Irish cultural, social, and postcolonial contexts.[16] In short, over the last twenty years, critical attention has shifted from the apparent collision between the Irish Revival and international modernism to their previously obscured collusions.

This wider shift in cultural scholarship has meant that Revival studies and modernist studies look not just at the "highest" artistic achievements in formalist terms but also at institutions, material culture, pamphlets, and popular receptions. This has resulted in taxonomic shifts and definitional recalibration. The "Revival" has come to refer to the Irish Agricultural Organisation Society and the Gaelic Athletic Association as well as to the early poems of Lady Gregory or the translations of Hyde. This scholarly attention has overhauled understanding of what should be included in the Revival, when it begins and ends, and what constitutes its underpinning ideologies. Declan Kiberd's seminal *Inventing Ireland* (1995) emphasizes the Revival's imaginative orchestrations, locating it within the struggle for Irish independence that partook of the wider international emergence of post-colonial modernity. Subsequently, scholars have sought to recover demotic cultures and neglected figures, allowing us to rediscover, for instance, forgotten women writers and artists, or to learn how the northern Revival differed from its Dublin counterpart.[17]

One key effect of the changed emphasis is to expose common intellectual heritages. For instance, we recognize that the interest in folk cultures, the esoteric and the primitive that marked the Anglo-Irish literary movement was also a strong influence on iconic modernist works such as Igor Stravinsky's *Le Sacre du Printemps* (1913) and the paintings of Paul Gauguin. A work like Sinéad Garrigan Mattar's *Primitivism, Science and the Irish Revival* (2004) demonstrates revivalist indebtedness to these discourses, despite the efforts of Yeats and others to disparage materialism and empiricism. Gregory Castle's *Modernism and the Celtic Revival* (2001) also looks at scientific influences in the Revival, in this case anthropology and ethnography. Castle's analysis is animated by the postcolonial paradigms that gained traction in Irish studies in the 1990s, and he argues that anthropology afforded the revivalists with scientifically grounded means to confront and combat ideologies of British imperialism.[18]

The rise of postcolonial theory as a frame within which to understand Irish society, together with corresponding scholarly work that associates modernism with the emergence of the nation state, has, as noted earlier, drawn Ireland's fin-de-siècle cultures into modernist debates. Reading revivalist works as expressive of a postcolonial condition brings them closer to the sites of colonial modernity, redressing, again, the notion that modernism was, solely, a metropolitan, European enterprise.[19] In this way, *pace* Corkery, the cultural Revival can be regarded not as the expression of a dying Ascendancy colonialism but as an early postcolonial struggle toward self-articulation in a hybridized, colonial language, a perspective that was implicit early on in Boyd's *Ireland's Literary Renaissance*, written closer to the period under consideration and hence alert both to its complexity and its novelty.

The Irish Revival depended on a sense of cultural possibility emerging from modernization, reconfiguration of class structure and a heightened urban-rural divide. These conditions accord with an influential Marxist explanation for the development of modernism: combined but uneven social development in which contradictory social conditions are generated by the asymmetrically accelerated entry into modernity of different sections of society. In such circumstances, art gravitates toward ruptured representation, seeking out the avant garde and experimental, the better to express contradictory social conditions. Eagleton summarizes the applicability of this model in the Irish case:

> In an illuminating essay, Perry Anderson has sketched what he sees as the three preconditions conditions for a flourishing modernism: the existence of an artistic *ancien régime*, often in societies still under the sway of an aristocracy; the impact upon this traditional culture of breathtakingly new technologies; and the imaginative closeness of social revolution. Modernism springs from the estranging impact of modernizing forces on a still deeply traditionalist order, in a politically unstable context which opens up social hope as well as spiritual anxiety. Traditional culture provides modernism with an adversary, but also lends it some of the terms in which to inflect itself.[20]

Ireland in the Revival period, Eagleton contends, met the conditions described here by Anderson, and it was the intensity of the clash between the modern and the non-modern elements in Irish society that stimulated both revivalist and modernist projects alike. This argument chimes with that of a number of other critics of the 1990s who saw the irregular and fragmented social conditions of post-Famine Ireland as inhospitable to realist forms.[21] In brief, the broad application of cultural theory, social analysis, and historical analysis exposed the intertwined roots of the Irish Revival and international modernism.

These connections have also been reinforced in both fields – revivalist and modernist studies – by the ethos of expansion, border-crossing, and interdisciplinarity that pertains in the humanities as a whole.[22] Literary studies, suffused as it has been by values of inclusivity rather than selection, has grown more capacious, turning its attention not just to obscured voices and forgotten figures but also to previously neglected forms – letters, diaries, notebooks – and to the material, institutional, and intellectual histories that shape literary production. High modernism was traditionally conceived as an elite grouping of mandarin bohemians; the "Irish Revival" as a select cabal of Anglo-Irish artists. Both these conceptions have been roundly exploded by scholarly research and cultural theory eager to historicize and broaden its purview.

But as the Irish Revival and international modernist studies have both been extended in new directions, how has this affected questions of artistic value and evaluation? The "Irish *Literary* Revival" often loses the middle term in historically orientated scholarship.[23] The generation of critics who elaborated the old definitions of "modernism" (leading figures include Eliot, Edmund Wilson, Clement Greenberg, and Theodor Adorno) were typically preoccupied with the "exclusive," with the finest art of the age if not of all ages and, above all, with the capacity of art to resist the coarsening of culture by consumerism. This vertical axis, with its insistence on formal and stylistic accomplishment, was a key aspect of high modernism, a synchronic bulwark against diachronic leveling.

Contemporary humanities research is, however, uncomfortable with such elitist discriminations, prioritizing instead inclusivity, representativeness, and social and historical relevance. "Expansion" in literary studies has flattened earlier "vertical" distinctions. Clearly this has particular implications for modernism and the Irish Revival, which so often styled themselves, or were styled by others, as hieratic, elite literary movements, at the high cultural side of a "great divide."[24] Both Pound the modernist and Yeats the revivalist deplore the vulgarities of popular taste and the mass market. Both seek the thickened textures and allusiveness of modernist verse a redoubt against the vulgar middle class. In other words, the new modernist and new revivalist studies, with their breaking down of high-low cultural distinctions, brush against the normative grain of many of the traditionally canonical modernist writers.

Historicism has allowed us to see how the literary works of the Revival and modernism have common tributaries. Yet the slackening of interest in literary value, or at least the turn in the academy from explicitly addressing artistic success or failure, may have militated against the specificity or singular stature of the great works of the Revival and modernism. Yeats, Joyce, and Beckett certainly have huge academic and cultural status, but much of it is self-sustaining, deriving from inherited cultural capital rather than renewed canonical interrogation. Most of the attention given to these three writers in recent years has deployed historicist methods, rather than formal or evaluative criticism. However, there are signs in some quarters of a development beyond historicism or an attempt to render history more intimate with artistic form and literary singularity.[25] This development opens fresh possibilities for understanding the modernism-Revival nexus.

For all the expansive ethos of the "new modernist studies," the concept of modernism is shot through with connotations of literary weight, international currency, and formal achievement. Notable recent studies have made this connotation explicit, affirming at the same time that modernist achievement lies in confronting the recalcitrance of representation. For commentators such as Gabriel Josipovici and T. J. Clarke, modernist art asserts the ineffability and alterity of the world, the vagaries of alienated capitalism or desacralized modernity, and the limited possibilities of expression.[26] It is this pained acknowledgment that throws modernist literature into audacious experimentation, an effort to grasp a reality that proves ever elusive.

This version of modernism echoes Beckett's claim that there has been a "rupture in the lines of communication," which only the serious and aware artists recognize (an awareness from which he excludes the "antiquarians" of the Revival).[27] However if, as Max Weber held, modern rationality has brought about "the disenchantment of the world," then many major works of the Irish Revival can, *pace* Beckett, be understood as part of a wider modernist reaction to this disenchantment.[28] The Irish Revival's overlap with modernism surely lies in part in the pessimism, the tragic note, running through many of the major revivalist writers.[29] In many cases, this aspect has a gothic overture, the doomed big house narrative of the declining Ascendancy. But it also feeds some of the most accomplished revivalist art. Beckett praises the painter Jack B. Yeats, brother of the poet, because he "brings light, as only the great dare to bring light, to the issueless predicament of existence."[30] Disagreeing with his friend Thomas MacGreevy's assessment, Beckett insists that Yeats's art has nothing to do with his Irishness. But Beckett also finds modernist opacity elsewhere in the revival's most celebrated works, such as the "dramatic dehiscence" he discerns in O'Casey's *Juno and the Paycock* (1924).[31]

Seamus Heaney has written of the "unconsoled modernity of Yeats's achievement."[32] Yeats declares at the start of his career that, against the "grey truth" of a world dominated by materialist science, "words alone are certain good."[33] But his poetry, at its best, continually questions the assertions of artistic power, notwithstanding the oratorical hauteur of his persona. His investment in the imagination and the power of poetic utterance is inseparable from a contrary guilty recognition of ineffability and contingency. He registers the modern schism between fact and value, between the way things are and the way human ethical or poetic sensibility would wish them to be. "We pieced our thoughts into philosophy," he writes in "Nineteen Hundred and Nineteen" (1921), "And tried to bring the world under a rule / Who are but weasels fighting in a hole."[34]

For all its idealism and mission, for all the sense that it heralded a beginning, revivalist art is at its most "modern" when alert to the contradictions and conflict that spiraled into barbarity and bloodshed, in both Europe and Ireland. In that sense, the revival is most modernist when it is most attuned to its own precariousness, its own failures. The modernist incubus in the Irish revival, then, is that which is aware of the mismatch between word and thing, between imagination and reality or, as Synge suggests in that most totemic revivalist text, *The Playboy of the Western World*, between the gallous stories of art and the dirty deeds of history.

NOTES

1 Richard Ellmann, *James Joyce* (New York: Oxford University Press, 1959); Hugh Kenner, *The Pound Era* (London: Faber and Faber, 1971); Ezra Pound, *Literary Essays*, T. S. Eliot, ed. (London: Faber and Faber, 1954); James Joyce, *Occasional, Critical and Political Writing*, Kevin Barry, ed. (Oxford: Oxford University Press, 2008); Samuel Beckett, *Disjecta: Miscellaneous Writings and a Dramatic Fragment*, Ruby Cohn, ed. (London: John Calder, 1983).

2 Terry Eagleton, *Heathcliff and the Great Hunger* (London: Verso, 1995), 297.

3 Roy Foster contends that the intense cultural activity before the death of Parnell confounds the Yeatsian narrative. *Words Alone: Yeats and his Inheritances* (Oxford: Oxford University Press, 2011).

4 W. B. Yeats, "Ireland After Parnell," Book II of *The Trembling of the Veil* (1922), *Autobiographies* (London: Macmillan, 1955), 199.

5 J. M. Synge, *Collected Works* vol. II: *Prose*, Alan Price, ed. (Gerrards Cross: Colin Smythe, 1982), 382. The fullest treatment of the connections in P. J. Mathews, *Revival: The Abbey Theatre, Sinn Féin, the Gaelic League and the Cooperative Movement* (Cork: Cork University Press/Field Day, 2003).

6 Philip O'Leary, *The Prose Literature of the Gaelic Revival, 1881–1921: Ideology and Innovation* (University Park: Pennsylvania State University Press, 1994).

7 Beckett, *Disjecta*, 70.

8 Ezra Pound, "*Dubliners* and Mr. James Joyce," *The Egoist* I, 14 (July 15, 1914), 267.

9 James Knowlson, *Damned to Fame: The Life of Samuel Beckett* (New York: Simon and Schuster, 1996), 71.

10 The debate between Eglinton, Æ, and Yeats on the Revival is recorded in John Eglinton et al., *Literary Ideals in Ireland* (London: T. Fisher Unwin, 1899).

11 See Emer Nolan, *James Joyce and Nationalism* (London: Routledge, 1995).

12 James Joyce, *A Portrait of the Artist as a Young Man* (London: Penguin, 1992), 276.

13 J. M. Synge, *Collected Letters*, 2 vols., Ann Saddlemyer, ed. (Oxford: Clarendon Press, 1983–4), I: 74.

14 On Synge as a postcolonial writer producing modernist stagecraft, see Declan Kiberd, *Inventing Ireland* (London: Jonathan Cape, 1995), 166–88.

15 Daniel Corkery, *Synge and Anglo-Irish Literature* [1931] (New York: Russell and Russell, 1965), 14.

16 Indicative scholarly works include Nolan, *James Joyce and Nationalism*; Andrew Gibson, *Joyce's Revenge: History, Politics, and Aesthetics in Ulysses* (Oxford: Oxford University Press, 2002); Seán Kennedy, ed. *Beckett and Ireland* (Cambridge: Cambridge University Press, 2010); and Emilie Morin, *Samuel Beckett and the Problem of Irishness* (Basingstoke: Palgrave Macmillan, 2009).

17 Karen Steele, *Women, Press and Politics During the Irish Revival* (Syracuse: Syracuse University Press, 2007); Eugene McNulty, *The Ulster Literary Theatre and the Northern Revival* (Cork: Cork University Press, 2008).

18 Sinéad Garrigan Mattar, *Primitivism, Science and the Irish Revival* (Oxford: Oxford University Press, 2004); Gregory Castle, *Modernism and the Celtic Revival* (Cambridge: Cambridge University Press, 2001).

19 Laura Doyle and Laura Winkiel, eds. *Geomodernisms: Race, Modernism, Modernity* (Bloomington: Indiana University Press, 2005).

20 Eagleton, *Heathcliff*, 297. Perry Anderson, "Modernity and Revolution," *New Left Review* 144 (March-April 1984).

21 For example, David Lloyd, *Anomalous States: Irish Writing and the Post-Colonial Moment* (Durham, NC: Duke University Press, 1993); Seamus Deane, *Strange Country: Modernity and Nationhood in Irish Writing since 1790* (Oxford: Clarendon Press, 1997).

22 For example, an ethos of "expansion" is explicitly welcomed by Margaret Kelleher in "Introduction: New Perspectives on the Literary Revival" *Irish University Review* 33, 1 (Spring/Summer 2003), vii–xii; and by Douglas Mao and Rebecca L. Walkowitz, "The New Modernist Studies" *PMLA*, 123, 3 (May 2008), 737.

23 Edna Longley, "Not Guilty," *The Dublin Review* 16 (Autumn 2004), 17–31.

24 Andreas Huyssen, *After the Great Divide: Modernism, Mass Culture, Postmodernism* (Bloomington: Indiana University Press, 1986).

25 Pascale Casanova, *Samuel Beckett: Anatomy of a Literary Revolution*, Gregory Elliott, trans. (London: Verso, 2007); Derek Attridge, *The Singularity of Literature* (London: Routledge, 2004).

26 For instance, T. J. Clarke, *Farewell to an Idea: Episodes from a History of Modernism* (New Haven, CT: Yale University Press, 1999); Gabriel Josipovici *What Ever Happened to Modernism?* (New Haven, CT: Yale University Press, 2011).

27 Beckett, *Disjecta*, 70–1.

28 Max Weber, "Science as Vocation," *From Max Weber: Essays in Sociology*, H. H. Gerth and C. Wright Mills, eds. (New York: Oxford University Press, 1946), 155.

29 Rónán McDonald, *Tragedy and Irish Literature: Synge, O'Casey, Beckett* (London: Palgrave Macmillan, 2002).

30 Beckett, *Disjecta*, 97.

31 Beckett, *Disjecta*, 82.

32 Seamus Heaney, "W. B. Yeats," *Field Day Anthology of Irish Writing*, Volume II, Seamus Deane, ed. (Derry: Field Day, 1991), 789.

33 W. B. Yeats, *The Variorum Edition of the Poems*, Peter Allt and Russell K. Alspach, eds. (New York: Macmillan, 1957), 45–57.

34 Yeats, *Variorum Poems*, 429.

4

BARRY MCCREA

Style and Idiom

I

In the opening decades of the twentieth century, Irish literature enjoyed a success that was unprecedented and turned out to be unrepeated. In some respects, the causes of this success are mysterious. It is not enough to suggest, as W. B. Yeats and others did, that the political vacuum left by the demise of Charles Stewart Parnell in 1891 simply enabled cultural activity to take center stage. But one way or another, a collision between local nationalist political concerns and international literary currents produced an unusual focus in Irish writing on questions of style and idiom. The European avant-garde sense of language as exhausted and enervated, and the concomitant longing for spiritual renewal through new languages of art, coincided with the Irish nationalist search for an autonomous mode of cultural expression, and in particular with the vexed question of a national language.

The Irish language movement, whether one welcomed or rejected its specific proposals, was a natural conductor for the feelings, both anxious and utopian, which the question of language provoked for European modernists in the early twentieth century. For many, though by no means all, Irish writers, their relationship to the Irish language gradually became an unavoidable question on which they had to take a position. The major contribution that the Irish language made to modernist Irish literature in English had little to do with any innate characteristics of the language itself and more to do with the paradoxical linguistic ideology that accompanied Gaelic revivalism and was popularized by the language movement: the idea that English, even though it was the native (and usually only) language spoken by most Irish people, the language they dreamed in, lived in, had been raised in, was yet "foreign"; and that a more authentically "native" language, in the form of Irish, could be deliberately (re)acquired to replace it. Although nationalist in its origins, this idea has much in common with the contemporaneous ideas of psychoanalysis whereby the language of our conscious minds is radically foreign to that of our unconscious.

As the national question became increasingly framed by the language question, there arose an ideological dissonance between the language people actually spoke – overwhelmingly English – and the language they felt they ought to be speaking. As the Irish language rapidly disappeared as a commonly spoken vernacular and the idea that it should be preserved or revived became increasingly mainstream, Irish writers were confronted with basic linguistic questions that their Anglophone counterparts from England and the United States did not face – which language to write: the language they knew best, English; or the language to which they felt (or felt they should feel) a spiritual loyalty, Irish? If Irish, then what kind of Irish, a language hard to learn, rarely heard in daily life, and which, in its surviving vernacular form, had fragmented into a patchwork of remote dialects? If English, what form of English, one that would be fit for literary purposes but also feel indigenous to the nation? In other words, just as symbolists and avant gardists on the continent were seeking to create new languages of art, the Irish were concerned, on several adjacent fronts, with forging new literary languages for the nation and for its literature.

Attempts to find a face-saving solution to the challenge of the national language were inherently unsatisfactory. Hiberno-English was not a historic dialect, like Scots or Sicilian, which could be turned immediately to literary purposes, but a form of creole that had developed out of a traumatic linguistic history. Ever since English had first been widely adopted by Irish people, some two or three centuries previously, they had spoken it in their own way, as all learners of foreign languages do, imposing the sounds and structures of their mother tongue on the target language. The result, according to the most *ultra* thinking in the Gaelic League, was a population deprived of a mother tongue at all, stuck in a no-man's-land that was neither Irish nor English.[1]

Yeats, a poor linguist who never mastered Irish, wrote in a letter to *The Leader* in 1900 that "[T]he mass of people in this country cease to understand any poetry when they cease to understand [Irish]."[2] While Hiberno-English was the de facto language of the people, it did not feel as though it embodied the people or their history, but was rather, through the heavy imprint of the lost language on its syntax, vocabulary, and phonology, a very potent sign of how this history had been obliterated. Yeats was haunted by the language question throughout his career, and his ideas about both Irish and Hiberno-English were vexed and changeful. At times he thought that the latter might be cultivated as an indigenous literary language, like Scots, but he also longed for the former. He could not speak Irish and never quite adopted the "dialect" as his own medium. The longing for a purer literary idiom can be felt in many of his most famous poems, including "The Lake Isle of Innisfree" (1893) and "Sailing to Byzantium" (1928). Yeats, nonetheless, was the only major Irish modernist to be the author – as so many American, British, German, and French modernists were – of a signature style. His high Irish style of English, identical to standard English in grammar and phonology, yet with a recognizably Irish diction, became a distinct model of Irish writing. But, unlike in other places, the production of an idiosyncratic style turned out not to be the major achievement of other strains of Irish modernism, and Yeats is an exception in this regard. What was distinctive about Irish modernism was rather the development of a relationship to style and idiom as things to be manipulated and deployed at will, in the manner we now associate with postmodernism.

II

It was precisely the unsatisfactory nature of Yeats's solution to the question of a national language that opened the way for the radical new relationship to literary language that was the hallmark of the great achievements of Irish modernism that followed him. In fact, what began as a way out of the unsolvable problem of a national language became an imagined solution to the problems of language and signification that were so central to modernist thought.

The idea that even one's mother tongue was somehow not native to oneself meant that style and idiom were up for grabs in a radical, liberating way. This is perceptible even in a writer as early and as apparently disconnected from Ireland as Oscar Wilde. Through his father, who wrote studies of ancient Irish archeology and, especially, his mother, a collector of Irish folklore, a militant nationalist and a writer of patriotic verse, Wilde had been exposed to the ideology of cultural revival. Although he was proud to style himself an "Oxonian" and thoroughly embedded himself in the English social and cultural world, he was also marked by his own sense of the English language being somehow foreign to him. He wrote to Edmond de Goncourt: "I am Irish by race, but the English have condemned me to speak the language of Shakespeare."[3] The Picture of Dorian Gray (1890), published only a couple of years before the foundation of the Gaelic League, is set wholly in England, without the slightest trace of Ireland or its speech. Yet, however flippantly he might have meant his comment to Goncourt, in terms of the question of style, the novel's strange world owes much to the Irish linguistic predicament. Unlike Yeats, Wilde never cultivated a grand style of his own, but rather developed a method of staging style itself. Wilde's idiom becomes flat and awkward as soon as he tries to find a neutral or objective omni-scient narrative perspective. In *Dorian Gray* or *A Woman of No Importance* (1893), the paradoxes and epigrams – self-conscious style – are attributed to individual witty characters, such as Lord Henry Wotton, Lord Illingworth, or Mrs. Allonby, with other characters playing the "straight" men and women who represent normality. But in both works, Wilde shows difficulty in handling a neutral or normative idiom to narrate or stage these charac-ters. The first half of *A Woman of No Importance* consists largely of these witty, amoral characters delivering crackling lines to the audience, while the second is concerned with the working out of a paternity and marriage plot with an apparently serious moral message. It is clear which has the upper hand; Lytton Strachey commented that its "epigrams engulf [the plot] like the sea."[4] More strikingly, in *Dorian Gray*, while the scandalous paradoxes of the dialogue sparkle and seduce, and while the outrageously allegori-cal plot certainly engages the reader, the narrative voice that recounts the story is curiously blank and colorless, sounding at times almost embarrassed at the banality of its job. Wilde's understanding of the literary possibilities of style takes a leap forward in *The Importance of Being Earnest* (1895), which resolves this tension between the style of the characters and the idiom of the narrative in which they are embedded. Rather than characters pre-senting us with their own individual styles of speaking (and dressing, and living), in *Earnest* the characters and the plot seem not only subordinate to the style but to be produced by it. The "real world" and the real characters behind the masks have become, like the portrait in the attic, locked away to preserve the artifice of the rest. The play is a staging of language and style as things supreme in themselves.

Something similar may be said about an apparently very different play-wright, John Millington Synge, whose own literary career began as a project of language-learning and became a project of language-creating. From the very start, Synge had an unusually linguistic conception of his literary career. His Irish, painstakingly acquired, was at the center of his literary forma-tion; in his first creative years, including much of the time he spent in Paris, everything was secondary to his efforts to improve his command of Irish. In some ways, his learning of Irish was his literary apprenticeship. Yet he never sought to write in the language; he learned Irish so that he could write English. In theory, Synge's compromise was to write in the Hiberno-English "dialect." This Irish English had been employed in literature for colorful or comic effect as early as the seventeenth century, and the popular view of Synge is that he harnessed this unloved speech for high literary purposes. This is only partly true. The language of his plays is an English that follows the syntax of the Irish language and is shaped by the sounds of Irish, and even imports many words directly from it, just as the spoken English of Ireland does. Hiberno-English, in one sense, was now being used as though it were the language of Racine. At the same time, Synge was from an Anglo-Irish family that would never have spoken anything like this dialect themselves. In writing Hiberno-English, he was writing his dialogue in what was, if not quite a foreign language, an idiom far removed from his own intimate world. It is no surprise that he attracted accusations of inauthenticity, notably from St. John Ervine, for whom Synge's idiom was "contrived literary stuff, entirely unrepresentative of peasant speech."[5]

Moreover, as Declan Kiberd shows, the language of Synge's characters resembles the kind of English spoken by the Irish peasantry, but it is far from identical with it.[6] Synge uses words translated from Irish that had in reality never entered the lexicon of Hiberno-English; he even invents words. Most of all, his idiom cleaves more closely to Gaelic syntax than the English actually spoken in Ireland ever did. It is not always clear whether the characters are really speaking the local form of English or whether they are "really" supposed to be speaking an Irish that is being translated for us.

Synge's project is ultimately modernist and not Romantic. Not only is his dialect something he himself never spoke naturally, it was a language no one ever spoke in real life either: his is an English haunted by a knowledge of and longing for Irish rather than an attempt to represent faithfully an Irish version of spoken English. It is this elaborate inauthenticity that makes Synge's work so modernist in inclination, and makes it so different from the superficially comparable projects of Romantics such as Robbie Burns, who elevated his native Scots dialect of English to a literary medium again, or Italians such as Giuseppe Gioachino Belli and Carlo Porta who did the same for local Italian dialects. It was not Synge's realistic experience of Hiberno-English dialect that drove him to write. It was, instead, the experience of learning Irish, his "native" yet foreign language, that provided the key impulse for his innovation in English. Unable to write in Irish and finding it unacceptable to write in standard English, Synge did not create a signature style, like Yeats, as the language of his characters does not pretend to be his own, but he created a personal, constructed literary idiom.

Like Synge, the project of Sean O'Casey, who wrote a generation later and looked to the Hiberno-English of the Dublin slums, seems at first sight to be an elevation of the "low" vernacular of the Irish poor to high literary ends. But all of O'Casey's plays are characterized by an extreme tension between high tragedy and comical farce. His male characters are often vainglorious buffoons who have much in common with the stage Irishman with which Hiberno-English had long been associated. At the same time, O'Casey's work-shy men, who seem to function as symbols of paralysis and destructive self-delusion, are also highly articulate, at times even magnificently poetic.

O'Casey produced a number of overtly experimental, sometimes expressionist works. But even in his best-known popular plays, idiom is implicitly their subject as well as the medium of the dialogue. What we see from Lady Gregory to Synge to O'Casey is not the gradual refinement of a dialect for literary purposes, as Yeats would have wanted, but the evolution of a relationship to language and style as a mode of native literary expression in itself. In other words, what starts as an apparently nationalist attempt to find and refine a native Irish idiom in English is transmuted into a peculiarly modernist understanding of language. In O'Casey, this is in evidence in the way other stylistic registers and vocabularies are incorporated and parodied in sometimes lengthy set pieces. In *The Plough and the Stars* (1926), for example, we are given the violent nationalist rhetoric of Pearse, Marxist jargon in the mouth of the Covey, and the upper-class, Anglo-Irish diction of the "Woman from Rathmines." This dialogical technique suggests that the perspective of the play, which seems to be so rooted in a single idiom – that of the Dublin proletariat – is in fact outside all styles and registers, but chooses to reproduce and deploy them for different purposes.

By the same token, even though O'Casey's great achievement is the manipulation of the Dublin "dialect" for poetic drama of real literary quality, all of his plays, *Juno and the Paycock* (1924) perhaps most of all, simultaneously deal with the inherent mockery in such a project. The recurring figure of the articulate buffoon, exemplified in *Juno* by "the Paycock" (i.e. peacock) Captain Boyle, a spinner of colorful language and supposedly epic stories, teaches the audience to be wary of linguistic virtuosity and thus of the epic pretensions of the whole play. O'Casey's plays mount the spectacle of various high-minded rhetorics only to show them cruelly deflated and bankrupt; the uneasy, unarticulated suspicion thus runs through his drama that his cultivation of the vernacular of the urban poor for high literary purposes might also be susceptible to similar critique.

III

This model of writing, in which all styles and registers are available to be deployed according to the will of the writer, whose own voice never appears, may have contributed to the enduring myth of the figure of the writer in Ireland as a mysterious and powerful entity. It certainly was a myth beloved of many, none more so than of James Joyce. Joyce disliked what he regarded as the patronizing posturing of "dialect" writing, and he looked outside Ireland, and outside the English literary tradition, to French naturalism and

Scandinavian realism, for his stylistic models. But the language revival movement was a powerful force in the cultural milieu where Joyce was formed, and he was never able to ignore it. Like Yeats, Joyce had inconsistent positions with regard to the language. He and his brother Stanislaus entered themselves as Irish-speakers on the 1901 census, when James was nineteen; neither of them could speak the language, so this must be taken as a statement of an ideological conviction of some sort. Joyce attended classes in the Gaelic League, and although he firmly rejected the project of reviving Irish as a backward and naive ideal, his work was thoroughly affected, right to the end, by the ideology of the language movement.

Like other modernists, whatever their final position on the revival, Joyce was prey to uncertainty about what position to take about Irish, and – by extension – about English. One of the most quoted passages in Irish literature is the moment in *A Portrait of the Artist as a Young Man* (1916) when Stephen Dedalus, discussing the word "tundish" with the Dean of Studies, an English priest, reflects with some bitterness that "the language in which we are speaking is his before it is mine."[7] This fundamental doubt, especially when compounded with the complex linguistic life Joyce went on to lead for the greater part of his life, had the effect of making style, idiom, and language itself into subjects to be investigated and staged as though from outside. *Ulysses* (1922) is the work of Irish modernism that most obviously takes style as its subject, and self-consciously showcases a gallery of styles, registers, idioms, and rhetorical cloaks to generate its meaning, such as the language of sentimental women's magazines in "Nausicaa," of provincial journalism in "Eumaeus" or of nationalist hyperbole in "Cyclops." In Joyce, these styles function as complex signifiers in themselves. Even the first three chapters of *Ulysses*, the "Telemachiad," which appear to offer the stylistic stability (and thus narrative security) missing from the rest of the novel, do nothing of the sort. The apparently sober, unshowy tone of the novel's opening seems to be narrated in the style that Joyce boasted he liked to employ to write about Dublin, one of "scrupulous meanness."[8] However, the style of the opening is far odder than it appears. The use of the word "untonsured" to describe Buck Mulligan, for example, looks like a scrupulously realist word, but is quite the contrary, conjuring in the reader's mind an image of its opposite.[9] Karen Lawrence points out that phrases such as "he said sternly" or "he cried briskly," and many others like them that litter the "Telemachiad," are "the unsophisticated prose of fourth-rate fiction; a novel that begins this way parodies its own ability to tell a story."[10]

In *Dubliners* (1914), Joyce had pioneered a radical use of the free indirect style he admired in Flaubert. In the stories, the language used by an apparently external, objective, neutral narrative voice is subtly infused with the kind of idioms and vocabulary the character currently being narrated would use. What attracted Joyce to free indirect style in the first place when he adapted it for *Dubliners* was the way it made language and material reality inseparable. In *Ulysses* he takes this so far that the novel seems to have a consciousness of its own. In "Telemachus," free indirect style is pushed to a new level again, whereby the supposedly neutral third-person narrative is inflected not merely by the diction and worldview of the characters it is talking about but also by the intentions of the prose itself. Here the intention of the prose is to begin a story, and thus its base idiom is a "young" naive style.

Even in their most straightforward narrative moments, both *Ulysses* and *A Portrait* wholly abandon the possibility of a novel having a single "native" idiom that a writer might adapt and stretch for all of his purposes, as Yeats did in his poetry, or as Marcel Proust, Joyce's great rival in literary Paris, did in his *A la recherche du temps perdu* (1913–27). There is no natural or native idiom in *Ulysses* from which the later pastiche chapters depart. As in *Portrait*, the style is the content. The author does not have one style that his genius will manipulate, but is rather an "arranger," to use David Hayman's term, who has no native idiom but is thereby freed to choose from the whole global range of existing idioms and styles as he wishes.[11]

In "The Dead," Gabriel Conroy is confronted by his friend Molly Ivors, a Gaelic Leaguer who tells him that he is a "West Briton" and that Irish is his "own language." Gabriel replies testily but uncomfortably: "if it comes to that, you know, Irish is not my language."[12] He will not learn Irish or become a Gaelic revivalist, but he has still been confronted by the notion that his native English might be foreign to his soul. By the same token, Joyce never properly learned Irish and never espoused its revival, but he remained touched and thoroughly influenced, not by the Irish language, but by the dream that the language represented. The language of *Finnegans Wake* (1939) both is and is not English. To the extent that it *is* English, it is clearly an Irish form of it, although it is sometimes difficult to pinpoint exactly why. The rhythm and sounds of Hiberno-English thump like a drumbeat through the flowing babble of the text. The setting, characters, and underlying language of the *Wake* are produced by Ireland, yet the novel simultaneously avoids having to choose among English, Irish, or other languages. Like Synge, Joyce began as a learner of languages and ended as a creator of his own. Unreadable and widely unread as it may be, *Finnegans Wake* offered the most radical and dazzling solution to the challenges posed by the ideology of the Irish language movement.

The *Wake* is also the work that most overtly shows the unusually polyglot character of Irish modernism, a literary tradition produced in a place without a securely defined official language or natural vernacular. This multilingualism also characterized Joyce's intimate life. The increasing experimentalism of his writing not only comes out of his desire to be always at the avant garde, but also reflects what his mind had become. Edwardian Dublin and early-twentieth-century Hiberno-English constituted the original, formative ground of that mind, its deepest structuring system, but that ground was buried now in thick layers of languages and experiences alien to that world but intimate to the writer. The *Wake* is in part an autobiographical working through of the author's own dizzyingly polyglot life, but the utopian aspirations of Gaelic revivalism are also woven through it.

IV

If the loss of Irish, and the elusive nature of this lost language was formative of Irish modernism in English (and French), one might reasonably imagine that those who did write in the ancestral tongue, the object of such intense linguistic and nationalist projections, were free (or deprived) of these linguistic doubts. This has often been the view from outside the language. But twentieth-century literary Irish was not a normal language either, and choosing to write in Irish was not a straightforward choice. Unlike in Protestant Wales or Scotland, which had robust liturgical traditions in Welsh and Gaelic, no written standard had existed for Irish for several centuries, and very few native speakers were literate in their own language. As a living tongue, Irish had survived only as a disparate collection of local spoken dialects and micro-dialects spoken in disconnected pockets of the country.

The first task facing the movement to promote Irish as a national language was to establish a written standard.[13] In the first part of the twentieth century, anyone writing Irish was dealing with a literary language that needed to be (re)constructed; the question of where authentic Irish was to be found – in eighteenth-century literary conventions, in a living spoken dialect (but if so, which one?), in synthetic modern versions – plagued potential writers of Irish. The Connemara novelist Máirtín Ó Cadhain, widely considered the most successful modernist prose writer in Irish, responded by showcasing the variety of forms that the language could take. A native speaker from the heart of the biggest Irish-speaking community in Ireland, the highly educated Ó Cadhain was in the rare position of being able to call linguistically on the resources of a whole imagined Gaelic world. His work is rooted in the Connemara Gaeltacht where he grew up and in its dialect, but, whereas finding any sort of natural idiom in Irish was an impossible challenge for the great majority of writers, in his masterpiece, *Cré na Cille* (1949), Ó Cadhain includes a wide range of registers and styles of the language, including Scots

Gaelic and historical forms. But this linguistic vitality also came out of his clear sense that the rich and varied Gaelic-speaking reality he was able to summon was a linguistic universe that, other than in his own imagination, had passed.[14]

Ó Cadhain, however, along with Máirtín Ó Direáin and Séamus Ó Grianna, was unusual in that he was a modernist Irish-language writer brought up in a native Irish-speaking community. By the 1940s, when modernist literature was first written in Irish, the number of native speakers was dwarfed by the masses who had learned Irish as a second language. The great majority of the literary activity that took place in Irish over the course of the twentieth century was produced by (and effectively also for) people who had learned it as a second language. Indeed, some poets who wrote in Irish may have been attracted to it precisely because it offered the chance to forge, in a sense, their own private poetic languages, divorced from the language of daily life, even if patriotic considerations made it taboo to state (or even think) this explicitly.

Similarly, hesitation about establishing a literary standard produced endless and seemingly parochial arguments about correct or incorrect usage and so on, but the linguistic self-doubt such dispute aggravated was also productive in a way that parallels Irish modernist writing in English. The particular instability that bedeviled attempts to found a modern literature in Irish chimes with the philosophical crisis of faith in language in general, which was central to European modernism. To choose to write in Irish can even be considered to have been a modernist as well as a patriotic choice.

The first and greatest modernist poet in Irish was a nonnative speaker, Seán Ó Ríordáin, who was tormented all his life by a sense that his Irish was faulty or even "diseased" and by what seemed to him an almost sinful longing – never succumbed to – to write in his native English. But even though the native Irish of west Kerry was an object of desire and envy for Ó Ríordáin, he wrote in an idiosyncratic form of the language, an invented idiolect that no one had ever spoken. He was the object of savage criticism and equally passionate defense for his peculiar idiom. The poet Máire Mhac an tSaoi declared that Ó Ríordáin's poems were not written in Irish at all, but in a kind of "Esperanto."[15] The problem that exercised, and indeed seems to have tacitly confused readers on both sides of the disagreement about Ó Ríordáin, was that of how to differentiate between what were simply lexical or syntactical errors made by someone who had not been fully brought up in the language – a "foreigner's" mistakes, as it were – and what could be viewed as deliberate experimentation within an existing language framework. This would be an easy distinction to draw in languages such as English or French (Nabokov and Beckett being cases in point). But for a language that had disappeared as living speech from everywhere but a few scattered communities with little formal culture, the very existence of a normative framework, at least on a national level, was not given. Another way of saying this is to wonder, as some critics did, who exactly the implied reader of Ó Ríordáin's work was.

But, from a modernist point of view, such doubts might be both tormenting and productive. Ó Ríordáin was haunted by the sense that the language in which he wrote was fallen and faulty; his response to this doubt – using Irish to create a private poetic language that had no speakers or implied reader in the real world – has something in common with Joyce's project in *Finnegans Wake*, and with other modernist experimentations with poetic language, such as surrealism or hermeticism, driven by the impossible desire to find or forge an autonomous language of art.

NOTES

1 See Philip O'Leary, *The Prose Literature of the Gaelic Revival, 1881–1921: Ideology and Innovation* (University Park: Penn State University Press, 1994)

2 *An Duine is Dual: Aistí ar Sheán Ó Ríordáin*, Eoghan Ó hAnluain, ed. (Dublin: Clóchomhar, 1980), 98.

3 *Switching Languages: Translingual Writers Reflect on Their Craft*, Steven G. Kellman, ed. (Lincoln: University of Nebraska Press, 2003), xiii.

4 Richard Ellmann, *Oscar Wilde* (New York: Knopf, 1988), 378.

5 See Declan Kiberd, *Synge and the Irish Language* (London: Macmillan, 1993), 204.

6 Kiberd, *Synge and the Irish Language*.

7 James Joyce, *A Portrait of the Artist as a Young Man* (London: Penguin, 2003), 204–5.

8 James Joyce, *Selected Letters*, Richard Ellmann, ed. (London: Faber and Faber, 1992), 83.

9 James Joyce, *Ulysses*, Hans Walter Gabler, ed. (New York: Random House, 1986), 3.

10 Karen Lawrence, *The Odyssey of Style in Ulysses* (Princeton, NJ: Princeton University Press, 1981), 9.

11 David Hayman, *Ulysses: The Mechanics of Meaning* (Madison: University of Wisconsin Press, 1982).

12 James Joyce, *Dubliners* (London: Penguin, 1992), 189.

13 On the lack of a standard and its effects on Irish language prose, see Máirtín Ó Cadhain, "Irish Prose in the Twentieth Century," in *Literature in Celtic Countries*, J. E. Caerwyn Williams, ed. (Cardiff: University of Wales Press, 1971), 141–2.

14 Ó Cadhain, "Irish Prose in the Twentieth Century," 144.

15 Máire Mhac an tSaoi, "Scríbhneoireacht sa Ghaeilge Inniu," *Studies: An Irish Quarterly Review*, 44, 173 (Spring 1955), 88.

PART II

Genres and Forms

5

LAURA O'CONNOR

W. B. Yeats and Modernist Poetry

I

Widely acclaimed as a major modernist and a foundational Irish-national poet, W. B. Yeats is essential to any discussion of Irish-modernist poetry. However, among the major Irish modernists – Yeats, James Joyce, and Samuel Beckett – only Joyce's modernism is uncontroversial, not least for generational reasons. Yeats was born twenty years before and Beckett twenty years after most of the acclaimed high modernists, who, like Joyce, were born in the 1880s. A Victorian and self-professed "last Romantic" as well as a modernist, Yeats upsets the supposition that modernism constitutes a radical departure from what precedes it. Yeats's publishing career corresponds exactly with the c.1890–1939 periodization of modernism: Oscar Wilde favorably reviewed Yeats's *The Wanderings of Oisin* in 1889, and – at Yeats's request – "Under Ben Bulben" was published in Irish newspapers after his death in 1939. Although Beckett is less known for his poetry than for his prose and plays, his poems in English and French extend from the prize-winning "Whoroscope" (1930) to "Comment Dire" (1989), so that their joint poetic production spans a century. Sanctioned by the expansionist trend of new modernist studies, many critics treat "modernism" as covering the long twentieth century, or as radical aesthetic responses to modernity from roughly Charles Baudelaire to the present. This essay adopts that longer perspective, but concentrates on the 1930s–1950s period, between the heyday of 1920s high modernism and the second efflorescence of Irish poetry in the late 1960s.

The 1930s–1950s post-independence period is at the heart of an ongoing canonical debate about the application of the "Irish modernist" rubric to an experimental strand of Irish poetry. "Modernist" has been deployed to distinguish a group of Paris-based expatriates from other Irish poets of the 1930s and to authorize a genealogy of "true" modernists by retroactively linking a Paris coterie – primarily Denis Devlin and Brian Coffey, along with

Thomas MacGreevy and Blanaid Salkeld and, above all, the by-then lion-
ized Beckett – to the experimental poetics envisioned by the poet-editors of
the New Writers Press, Michael Smith and Trevor Joyce. In an oblique yet
cunning stratagem to endow the nascent avant-garde group with Beckett's
imprimatur, Smith and Coffey reprinted a little known essay by Beckett,
"Recent Irish Poetry" (1934) in the New Writers' journal, *The Lace Curtain*
(No. 4, 1971), to endorse their agenda for innovation.[1] Beckett's essay praises
Devlin and Coffey as "without question the most interesting of the younger
generation of Irish poets" because they comprehend "the rupture of the lines
of communication" and "the breakdown of the object" in salutary contrast
to the "flight from self-awareness" evinced by "our leading twilighters"
whose (insular) Irish residency and themes consign them to "antiquarian"
status.[2] The revisionist version of Irish modernist poetry was recognized,
with reservations, by Alex Davis and Patricia Coughlan's 1995 essay collection, *Modernism and Ireland: The Poetry of the 1930s*, and, because it
dovetails with a longstanding alignment of modernism with cosmopolitanism and Ireland with traditionalism, it became a critical orthodoxy.[3]

All literary genealogies and canons highlight some and occlude other
aspects of the field in question, but this problem is exacerbated by the valorizing valence of "modernist," which functions here and elsewhere as a desir-
able and resilient "brand" of literary distinction. "Irish" and "modernist"
are opposed where the latter is assumed to mean "international," although
the symbiosis between them has boosted the mutual stature of both since the
postwar expansion of Anglo-American liberal arts education. The tension
between "Irish" and "modernist" can be seen in how critics often downplay
the nationality of eminent "international" modernists. Thus Joyce's unmis-
takably Irish avant gardism is commonly attributed to his émigré status,
whereas the epithet "Beckettian" is a byword for a condition of alienated
postnational modernity. Furthermore, Joyce, Beckett, and their advocates
tend to emphasize their ultramodernism to widen the gulf separating them
from Yeats and their revivalist precursors. "Recent Irish Poetry" draws on the
polarizing rhetoric of modernist manifestoes to rally an enlightened déraciné
Irish vanguard against its derogated antithesis, a retrograde neo-Yeatsian
cultural nationalism and revivalism. The polemic denounces neo-Yeatsian
bards without quite distinguishing their host from the "antiquarian" stigma
assigned to his pullulating fleas, while the "leading Twilighters" tag elides
the vibrant mixed registers of the Yeatsian oeuvre, including the formidable
late poetry.

The "national"/"international" dichotomy disregards the finest Irish
modernist poet of the decade after Yeats, Louis MacNeice. Coughlan and
Davis omit MacNeice "because, despite his poetry's complex negotiations

with his Irish background" his career unfolded largely "within English cultural problematics," leaving it open to conjecture whether his exclusion from both the Paris-centered modernists and the Free State-oriented nationalist camps is attributable to his affiliation to Northern Ireland or to the English Macspaunday poets.[4] Although Beckett finds "much in Mrs. Blanaid Salkeld's *Hello Eternity* (1933) that is personal and moving," Coughlan and Davis concede that she and others "are inevitably squeezed out of the binary accounts (whether Revivalist/modernist or Northern/Free-State-based)" of Irish literary history.[5] Moreover, the partisan binary elides the differences within both factions and effaces their commonalties.

The polemical binary needs to be replaced with a more temperate and nuanced critical analysis, one that entails reappraising Yeats's relationship to a set of values that appear to spurn him. I first explore the enduring yet controversial symbolic influence of the bardic Yeats-persona on Yeats's reception, and on the enhanced international profile of Irish poetry and literature. The next section examines how a range of mid-century poets turn to Joyce and T. S. Eliot to negotiate the moral, cultural, and political prescriptivism of the Catholic Church and Orange Order in a partitioned Ireland. Finally, I explore how women's marginalization from Irish public and literary spheres and the masculinist bias of literary canonization obscured the work of mid-century Irish women poets and spurred the efflorescence of feminist poetry and critique in the early 1970s.

II

Yeats harnessed the combined symbolic capital of the modernist institution of "major author" and the Irish institution of "national poet" to secure international and national recognition for his role as a nation-builder and to buffer his creative autonomy against partisan pressures. A sacral aura surrounds the "great" modernist opus or writer, and the major high modernists – Eliot, Joyce, Virginia Woolf, Yeats, Gertrude Stein, Ezra Pound – form a loose clerisy of canon-makers whose *ex cathezra* judgments (Beckett's pun) make them gatekeepers to literary acclaim. The "first principle" of Yeats's poetics was to render the poet-persona "part of his own phantasmagoria" and to transform the phantasmagoric Yeats-in-the-oeuvre (persona and style) into "something intended, complete" over the course of his career.[6] Yeats and Joyce alike conceived the task facing them as writers and the task confronting the colony and as-yet-unconstituted Irish nation as symbiotic inaugural acts of "forg[ing] in the smithy of my soul the uncreated conscience of my race."[7] Although their self-canonizing modes of remaking their bicultural colonial heritage are strikingly different, they both embed an

79

autobiographical writer-persona in localized Irish settings peopled with historical and fictional personages, and envisage their recursive refashionings of the national bard and Dubliner personae as a decolonizing literary praxis. Their combined endeavor made Irish topography, legend, history, and vernacular Irish-English part of the Anglophone literary imagination, and Irish poets benefit from, but are also potentially constrained by, the market niche created by the "Irish" brand.

In *A Survey of Modernist Poetry* (1927), which first applied the "modernist" rubric to the period, Laura Riding and Robert Graves place Yeats among those with "neither the courage nor the capacity to go the whole way with modernism."[8] Yet because modernism lies in its "independence," "intelligent ease," and the enlargement of "the limits of reference, diction, and construction in poetry," and "the best poets ... can be called modernist if only because they are good, and because what is good always seems advanced," the 1923 Nobel Laureate nevertheless makes the grade.[9] Neither this nor Beckett's criticism would have ruffled Yeats. He habitually invokes modernity to lament its depredations, theatricalizes his poet-persona as a revenant from a bygone age, and would rather serve as modernist "antitype" than prototype. A curmudgeon who fulminates against "modern heterogeneity" as he stands observing "discordant architecture, all those electric signs" on O'Connell Bridge, he once astounded Woolf by declaring that it would take thirty generations of associative accretions before the steamroller could replace the spade as a fit symbol for poetry.[10] An archaic modernist, innovative traditionalist, and populist elitist, Yeats's relish for adversarial stances is a rare unequivocal modernist trait. A contrarian in both the colloquial and Blakean senses of the word, Yeats maintains that "[w]e make out of the quarrel with others, rhetoric, but of the quarrel with ourselves, poetry" by struggling "to the death" with a series of masks and daimonic muses to create a "contrapuntal" verse that combines past and present into "a vivid speech that has no laws except that it must not exorcise the ghostly voice."[11]

Yeats first "found [his Irish] theme" when introduced by John O'Leary to the Young Ireland poets' mode of "speak[ing] out of a people to a people ... behind [whom] stretched the generations."[12] The Yeats-persona discourses with an apostrophized Irish people in the communal mode of the Young Ireland poets and of Walt Whitman's performative constitution of a national poem in *Leaves of Grass* (1855–92), and at the same time conveys the oracular aura of a druidic Gaelic *file* (poet-seer). He made the Sligo locale of his childhood legendary by transposing local orature[13] into literature in *The Celtic Twilight* (1893). Yeats contends that the disjunctive transposition of peasant idiom into print renders the inflections of passionate utterance audible on the page because the confrontation between "the old world that sang and listened" and the "world that reads and writes" is an ever-present "antagonism" in Irish imagination and intellect.[14] Translating between spoken and literary idioms was Yeats's primary means of developing a "contrapuntal" Irish-English literary vernacular, which blends "the ghostly voice(s)" of vestigial Gaelic syntax, song-meters, and vehement Irish speech into the measured cadences of canonical English verse.[15]

Adept at cultivating multiple overlapping audiences, each aware of its coexistence among others, Yeats understood the need to harness established forums and traditions to underwrite and amplify his hieratic authority. He realized early that "if Ireland would not read literature it might listen to it, for politics and the Church had created listeners[;] [he] wanted a Theatre – [he] had wanted it for years," and fine-tuning acoustic intimacy between poet and audience was crucial to his literary praxis.[16] The ideal of a theater for mediating the vatic authority of resonant symbolism became increasingly pressing when Yeats realized the necessity to translate and retell Irish myth and legend in an English "with an indefinable Irish quality of rhythm and style" to establish a parallel "de-Anglicizing" platform to the Gaelic revival.[17] The deliberate fashioning of a hybrid English on the Abbey stage was crucial to the formation of Synthetic Scots, Northumbrian English, and African-American vernacular Englishes, as was attested, respectively, by modernists Hugh MacDiarmid, Basil Bunting, James Weldon Johnson, and Sterling Brown.

The *topos* of the Yeats-persona in colloquy with his Irish-national audience simultaneously creates a forum for perpetuating his symbolic afterlife in the Irish imaginary and relays the scene of bardic rapport to an international readership. The hyperbolic performance of the bardic Yeats-persona in "The Tower" (1928) and "Under Ben Bulben" (1939) dictating his "will" and orchestrating his posterity to a summonsed Irish assembly, comprised of ancestral, unborn, local, and diasporic auditors, provides such a platform. The Yeats-in-the-tower persona displays the aristocratic hauteur of a hereditary bardic caste and the Anglo-Irish Ascendancy as he formally bequeaths the bardic mantle to the "young upstanding men" who succeed him. No Oedipal upstart shall usurp such assured supremacy.

W. H. Auden's "In Memory of W. B. Yeats" honors and dethrones the apostrophized dead poet by restating the exhortational trimeters of "Under Ben Bulben['s]" in his own words: "With your unconstraining voice / Still persuade us to rejoice."[18] The elegy's double-voiced praise-abuse conveys mixed messages about Yeats's influence and the influence of poetry as such, including the reassuring assertion that "[t]he words of a dead man / Are modified in the guts of the living" and the blunt refutation of the oeuvre's implicit counter-assertion: "For poetry makes nothing happen." MacNeice, whose modernist verse embraces the discordancy of urban modernity and the "incorrigibly plural" heterogeneity "of things being various" relates to Auden's skeptical estrangement.[19] In his monograph, *The Poetry of W. B. Yeats*, MacNeice recalls that when he first read *The Tower* (1928) as an Eliot-obsessed young poet, it seemed "frigid, unsympathetic" and "mannered," whereas he now finds similar "mannerism" in Eliot.[20] Yeats eludes easy cat-egorization, MacNeice astutely observes, because he is "peculiar – almost, indeed, self-contradictory – in that he fuse[s] Symbolist doctrine with nation-alist doctrine."[21]

"To Ireland in the Coming Times" (1892) restates in verse Yeats's defense against O'Leary that his study of "magic" is essential to "what [he] believe[s] to be a greater renaissance – the revolt of the soul against the intellect – now beginning in the world."[22] The "red-rose-bordered hem / Of her" blends Rosicrucian symbolism and the Dark Rosaleen, a sovereignty muse of the Jacobite *aisling*, to represent archaic poetic wisdom. Yeats mounts a meta-metrical argument that the poet's ability to plumb "the deep" of "unmea-sured mind" (the *Anima Mundi* / Great Memory evoked by symbols) shall distinguish his "rhymes" over those of his Irish precursors:

> *Nor may I less be counted one*
> *With Davis, Mangan, Ferguson,*
> *Because, to him who ponders well,*
> *My rhymes more than their rhyming tell*
> *Of things discovered in the deep,*
> *Where only body's laid asleep.*[23]

Anima Mundi is often imagined as a store of visual images and symbols, but the sonorous dimension of Great Memory also matters. Evocative intona-tional cadences and resonant timbres or idioms arouse a responsive com-munal chord among those who experience a similar attunement. Even at its most vestigial, a reflex spark of familiarity enkindles a sense of belonging among those who harken to the bard's register. "The Symbolism of Poetry" (1900) and "Per Amica Silentia Lunae" (1917) theorize how the "indefin-able yet precise emotions," "moods," or "daimons" evoked by harmonious relations of sounds, colors, and forms prolong "that moment of creation" through rhythm "hushing us with an alluring monotony, while it holds us waking by variety" so that "the mind liberated from the pressure of the will is unfolded in symbols."[24] Rhythm, rhyme, and symbol – the heightened formal elements of verse – stimulate the reverie-like state in which individ-ual and collective memory coalesce and reconfigure the subliminal recep-tivity that orients aisthesis. It is at this subliminal "gut" level of aesthetic receptivity that the living modify the poet's words, and the makers of symbolic art (*poietes*) "are continually making and unmaking mankind."[25] Such vatic utterance posits a mode of address apt to a place of public assembly.

The conception of the poet as a public bard making common cause with "the people" (construed by their poet as a nation in the oeuvre) and a vatic Symbolist en*chant*ing readers/listeners into receptivity, categorically rejects the dominant Anglo-American supposition that the efficacy of poetry has diminished. The positioning of the bardic Yeats-persona in the twilight mists of the Celtic fringe at the farthest remove from the metropolitan hubs of modernism exaggerates the poet's archaized peripherality, but the poet's belief that "the supernatural can at any moment create new myths" inures him to modernist pessimism about poetry's futurity.[26] Yeats exerts strong influence on cultures where orature commingles with literature, and thus his oracular modes of address, apocalyptic imagery, and use of traditional lyric are emulated, even as early as the 1930s, by such poets as Gladys Casely Hayford (Sierra Leone) and Herbert Dhlomo (South Africa). Yeats's influence on twentieth-century postcolonial poetics, despite his neocolonialist and antidemocratic proclivities, derives from a resonating symbolism and a "tradition"-sanctioned belief that poetry can foster collaborative political action. The tone of aggrieved entitlement that laces Yeats's declarations on behalf of "we Irish" blends aristocratic *noblesse oblige* and the pride of a bardic elite with the indignant riposte of a downtrodden people. The precedent of Yeatsian bardic authority exemplifies how writers can combine international literary eminence with the oppositional iconoclasm and novelty of hitherto lesser-known traditions to secure "major" status for minority literatures.

III

The role of community and creed in an era of secularization is a recurrent topic of modernist debate. Poetry was frequently posited as a secular surrogate for abandoned or shattered religious faiths. Whereas some poets turned to theosophy, Eastern religions, and alternative spirituality, others viewed orthodox Christianity as a repository of common allusion, resonant symbolism, and ritual. Yeats's pursuit of "magic" and theosophy to counteract his father's agnosticism held little pertinence for Irish writers immersed in Christianity. Joyce's anatomy of the combined effects of Catholicism, nationalism, and colonialism on the moral and aesthetic development of the (male) artist in *A Portrait of the Artist as Young Man* (1916) was embraced, by contrast, as a personal *Bildung* of their own religious, moral, and civic conflicts by many Irish Catholics. Eliot's conversion to Catholicism conferred modernist legitimacy on traditional religious practices, and the exploration of ritual in his verse-plays and liturgical cadences such as those in "Ash Wednesday" drew on a resonant prosodic memory for churchgoers.

Questions of community and creed were greatly complicated for Irish modernists by Ireland's long history as a theater of conflict between Reformation Europe, the British Empire, and native resistance. The conflict intensified in Victorian Ireland as a result of the "devotional revolution," the post-Famine shift from vernacular to the Rome-regulated Catholicism that brought about a massive increase in religious vocations, church-building, and attendance at the newly instituted Tridentine Latin mass. The Catholic hierarchy strove to reinforce the coupling of "Irishness" and "Catholicism" in the public mind, and assumed control over education, social welfare, and the regulation of marriage, sexuality, and family.[27] The concerted effort to consolidate Catholic hegemony provoked a Unionist backlash against Home Rule as Rome Rule. The clashing valences of "1916" in Unionist and Nationalist cultural memory – the enormous sacrifice of loyalist Ulstermen's lives at the Somme on the one hand, and the Easter Rising with its iconography of a Cuchulain-Christ redeemer and a mariolatrous Mother Ireland on the other – sowed opposing myths of foundational blood-sacrifice that contributed to transforming Orange-Unionist and Catholic-nationalist politics into warring "creeds" and ethno-religious factionalism that were institutionalized by the sectarian partitioning of Ireland in 1922.

For MacNeice, "the rector's son, born to the Anglican order, / Banned for ever from the candles of the Irish poor," the sectarian border compounds the alienation of growing up in a segregated community ("Carrickfergus" (1937). In "The Glens" (1942), John Hewitt wishes without optimism that the "tally" of Irish Catholics' "savage history of wrong" could be redressed.[28] He checks the conciliatory impulse with a reminder of his irremediable difference from them, "Not these my people, of a vainer faith / and a more violent lineage," and his fear of coerced conformism: "I fear their creed as we have always feared / the lifted hand against unfettered thought." In this account, northern Protestants imagine that Catholics – despite their alienation from property and thralldom to their creed – enjoy, unlike them, an inalienable sense of "rootedness" and belonging to community.

Patrick Kavanagh, a Catholic small farmer on the southern side of partitioned Ulster, conforms to the image of indigenous poet. Kavanagh practices a bardic tradition of praises and dispraises, but he strongly dissents from nationalist ideology and detests Yeatsian and revivalist idealizations of the self-sufficient peasant. His caustic persona as a satirist is counterbalanced by a religious sense of the miraculous and the numinous, "Wherever life pours ordinary plenty" ("Advent"), in celebratory epiphanies such as the Canal

Bank sonnets.[29] The satiric title of "The Great Hunger" (1942) excoriates the repressive legacy of the devotional revolution. Its opening line, "Clay is the word and clay is the flesh," evokes the tactile earthiness of protagonist Patrick Maguire's "sensuous groping fingers" gathering potatoes and planting seeds while also recalling liturgical refrains of death and incarnation.[30] Like many rural bachelors of the era, Maguire "made a field his bride."[31] A vignette of Maguire in his mid-thirties augurs a bleak future that exposes the wanton denial underwriting romantic portrayals of a carefree peasantry:

> Sitting on a wooden gate,
> Sitting on a wooden gate,
> Sitting on a wooden gate
> He rode in day-dream cars.
> He locked his body with his knees
> When the gate swung too much in the breeze.
> But while he caught high ecstasies
> Life slipped between the bars.[32]

Maguire disavows his hunger for emotional and sexual intimacy until it is too late. Destitute of affection, the aged bachelor garners some compensatory comfort from his respectability as a church usher.

The psychological toll of Catholic guilt and shame is a recurrent theme for Austin Clarke. "Ancient Lights" recounts a childhood confession when he was manipulated by the priest's insinuations into confessing "immodest" touch before he had any concept of what that might mean.[33] The confessor's prurience produces the boy's guilty sense of innate bodily sinfulness. The striking dissonance in Clarke's poetry between clear-sighted satire and lacerating self-recrimination is symptomatic of a pervasive internalized guilt and shame, whose psychocultural toll has really only come into focus since the 1990s, when public trust in the institutional apparatus of the Catholic Church imploded as a result of sex-abuse scandals and the 1998 Belfast Agreement created a political framework for easing North/South sectarian tensions.

Independence brought an upsurge of translation activity, both for international diplomacy and for promoting Gaelic literature. Translation offered Clarke a vehicle for gaining critical distance, and he ironizes the contemporary Church's erotophobia by juxtaposing it with life-affirming romances from medieval monastic Ireland. Clarke's prosodic experiment as a poet-translator – he subordinates semantic equivalence to preserving the assonantal patterning of Gaelic verse-forms – was censured by Irish modernists, and Beckett's unaccountable personal antipathy toward Clarke has made him a primary target of the "antiquarian" stigma.[34] The categorical cosmopolitan/nationalist divide has precluded the pairing of Devlin and

Clarke for critical consideration, although they share a deep affinity for intricate verbal patterning and both invoke medieval Irish monasticism to bracket Jansenist Irish Catholicism as aberrant. Paris offered Devlin and Coffey access to an intellectual Catholic tradition that was conspicuously absent from top-down Tridentine Catholicism, which helped to relativize devotional Irish Catholicism. Working between languages and writing English in a Francophone milieu gave them an enabling sense of linguistic estrangement that accentuated the kinship between composing and translating poetry. Coffey translated Stephane Mallarmé and Paul Éluard, Devlin translated Saint John Perse, and they collaborated on an unfinished project of translating the French Symbolists into Irish.

Kavanagh and Devlin turn to the pilgrimage at St. Patrick's Purgatory, Lough Derg, to set penitential Irish Catholicism in a comparative European context. Lough Derg's rich literary and religious intertextuality extends back to the middle ages, when Dante's *Commedia* was influenced by legends about knights' extreme ordeals in an island cave there, which was believed to be an entrance to purgatory.[35] The Lough Derg pilgrimage ritualizes self-mortification: circuiting barefoot around stone-bed "stations" over a three-day fast, itself beginning with a thirty-six hour vigil, pilgrims recite "a hundred decades / Of rosaries until they hardly kn[o]w what words mean," and intone "I renounce the World, the Flesh, and the Devil" at regular intervals.[36] Devlin's "Lough Derg" (1946) approaches the penitential site from "mullioned Europe shattered," acutely aware that the neutrality of the Free State he serves as a diplomat isolates it from its own European past.[37] The final stanza of Kavanagh's "Lough Derg" (1942) likewise signs off on "June nineteen-forty-two / When the Germans were fighting outside Rostov," so that the island pilgrimage serves ambiguously both as atonement for Ireland's self-sequestration and as a means of ironizing the pettiness of the pilgrims' private intercessionary pleas against the enormity of Europe's travails.[38] A dense palimpsest of intertexts, Devlin's "Lough Derg" reads as if successive versions were repeatedly reworked so as to open up additional semantic resonance. Readers pause on his epithet for contemporary Irish missionaries, "doughed in dogma," for example, as aural and graphemic tacks of association slide the "dog" in "dogma" back to "dough" to connote doctrinal kneading into lumpish pliancy.[39]

The centrality of shared allusive domains and of coteries to avant-garde and minority literary formations can be seen at play in two later adaptations of the "Lough Derg" intertext. Seamus Heaney's "Station Island" (1984) plumbs the religious and literary dimensions of the "confession" genre to compose a self-canonizing poetic autobiography in the Irish-modernist mode. Heaney develops Kavanagh's poet-pilgrim persona, Yeats's colloquys with shades, and the architectonics of Eliot's *Four Quartets* into the poet-speaker's purgatorial circuitings, which conclude by Joyce's shade enjoining him to quit "doing the decent thing."[40] The liminal lake-isle sanctuary on the southern side of partitioned Ulster emblematizes the sundering of Northern Catholics from the "local" pilgrimage site and the minority-poet-spokesperson's ambivalence about his "[e]scape from the massacre" by migrating to the South.[41]

Beckett adapts Devlin's Biblical allusion in "Lough Derg" that depicts God as a sadistic trifler – "Europe that humanized the sacred bane / Of God's chance who yet laughed in his mind / And balanced thief and saint: were they this kind?" – into a structural "key" for *Waiting for Godot*. The motifs of salvation, damnation, death, and vigilant waiting retain a religious residue in *Godot*, despite Beckett's nihilistic deployment of the hermeneutic crux. It is intriguing to imagine the theological discussion and banter that arose out of Joyce and Beckett's abandoned, though psychoculturally resonant, Catholicism and Protestantism on the one hand, and Devlin, Coffey, and MacGreevy's observant Catholicism on the other.

Beckett's poetry is composed in an anti-lyrical, minimalist, and meta-linguistic idiom in the zone of recursive play between poem and poetics, English and French. The speaker of "Comment Dire" / "What is the Word" (1989) stutters like a struggling language-learner or an aphasic subsiding into wordless oblivion. The French solecisms wryly imply that the poet-translator has not quite mastered his adopted vernacular, while the emphasis on the French-derived "folly" in the original calls attention to English's dependence on loanwords. The contrast between the clever allusions and gleeful Joycean word-play in "Whoroscope" (1930) and the spare French lyrics in *Poèmes 1937–1939* suggests that Beckett's switch to French "sans style" was perhaps made to escape the loquacious and connotative excess (for him) of Irish varieties of English. Theater was as crucial for Beckett as it had been for Yeats. The plays dramatize human dependence on auditors to corroborate existence. The later prose is increasingly punctuated by pauses for auditory feedback and hesitant silence. Beckett's prose paradoxically conveys the acoustic sonority and lyricism spurned by his poems to create the bardic ambiance of the overheard voice in *Company* "[m]urmuring now and then, Yes I remember."[42]

Overt textuality also characterizes Coffey's poetry, a philosopher whose foregrounding of the word may derive from the dissertation on Thomas Aquinas he wrote under Jacques Maritain. Coffey's term for his Pablo Neruda translations – "rendering" – takes translation to be a dedicated act of "reading" that requires one to *rend*, to tear apart, the original to *render* a version that conveys some sense of the whole. His astringent syntax and avoidance of punctuation uses the white space of the page to set each word apart. An infinitesimal pause after each word inflects the meter, a rending to indicate the imperceptible interval "between now no longer and not yet now."[43] The representation of Devlin's untimely death in Coffey's "Advent" (1975) as an "act of vanishment" smoothes the harshness of "vanquish" and "banish" without effacing it to prepare for the recognition of "vehement" finality:

> to where eye cannot enter when no sound returns not
> a silence   nothingness
> more vehement than our whole knowing how it was here[44]

The verse invites readers to undertake the rending/rendering task of the translator by actively recreating the poem as a torn body of sound.

Coffey's poetry blossomed in the 1970s, when he became a bridge between the Beckett circle of the 1930s and the New Writers poets who set themselves against the Yeats-Heaney poetry establishment, not least by reprinting Beckett's "Recent Irish Poetry." Coffey's participation in both coteries gave him an invigorating circle of first readers and association with both groups' profiles, two advantageous footholds in the institutions of modernist and Irish letters that eluded mid-century women poets.

IV

The patriarchal ideology of the Catholic-Nationalist South and Protestant-Unionist North subordinated women to the role of family nurturer and marginalized their cultural and political agency from the public sphere. The bardic genealogy invoked by Yeats in "To Ireland" likewise precludes women's right to become "True brother of a company / That sang, to sweeten Ireland's wrong." Masculinist bias also permeates modernism. Insecurity about the ascendancy of women writers and popular imputations of poetry's effeminacy lent a resurgent machismo to becoming a "major" modernist or producing a modern epic, as indicated by Joyce's jubilant remark that *The Waste Land* "ends the idea of poetry for ladies."[45] Furthermore, women poets published during the 1930s and 1940s – including Salkeld, Mary Devenport O'Neill, Rhoda Coghill, Máire Mhac an tSaoi, Sheila Wingfield, and Freda Laughton – enjoyed neither their precursors' optimism that the coeval suffragist and cultural-nationalist movements would bring about social change, nor their successors' access to second-wave feminist critique and transnational civil rights movements. Their poetry disappeared from public consciousness until recuperative feminist research republished a selection in the 2002 *Field Day Anthology of Women's Writing and Traditions,* and their out-of-print verse was known only to a handful of scholars before the 2012 publication of Lucy Collins's critical anthology, *Poetry by Women in Ireland 1870–1970*.[46] Archival research into this "missing" generation reveals a consistent pattern: the poets were more often marginalized from journals and contemporary anthologies, disproportionately omitted from subsequently updated anthologies, and subjected to more sexist reviews than were their pre-independence female precursors.[47]

Several poets turned to mythic personae and the dramatic monologue as a vehicle for sidestepping the gender bias that associates the first-person lyric "I" with a "he" bolstered by "not-she" status and for a deflected exploration of transformational lyric subjectivity. Yeats's tactic of harnessing the vituperative energy and transgressive sexual morality of the Crazy-Jane persona against Church-State sanctimony offers contrastive ground for interpreting their strategies of indirection. Katherine Arnold Price spent three decades revising "Curithir and Liadain" (1925, 1957), a retelling of Kuno Meyer's translation of a ninth-century romance between monastic poet-lovers. Price develops the dialogical device of direct self-disclosure in the original to explore Liadain's interpretation of her chequered relationship with Curithir. The restless self-analysis of the nun-lover-poet persona approaches the sexuality of single women from different vantages than the privations of Kavanagh's Maguire. Price's generation included college-educated women who chose professional over domestic lives; women who shunned the role of deferential wife and self-sacrificing mother; nuns; women widowed by the European wars, and women whose access to contraception bestowed sexual freedoms long enjoyed by men. In a philosophic idiom redolent of Marianne Moore's "Marriage" (1923), Price's speaker chafes against convention and the regulation of sexual relationships:

> Must the private spirit live by something public,
> Something shared, made valid by common acceptance?
> None could come nearer than Curithir; but he went away.
>
> I wanted to move always further into pure being.[48]

Price's Liadain owns her grief and emotional vulnerability, and prevails to "put a scansion even on disaster."

Máire Mhac an tSaoi's choice of Irish as a literary vernacular paradoxically preserved her public visibility in Ireland where she features on school curricula. She adopts "Máire Ní Ógáin" – like "Crazy Jane," a moniker for a foolish or loose woman – to stage an elaborate confessional performance in "Ceathrúintí Mháire Ní Ógáin" ("Mary Hogan's Quatrains," 1956).[49] Writing for a small readership of Irish readers, a community whose members tend to know one another's affairs, she conveys what is probably an open secret in a forthright yet coy "don't ask, don't tell" performance. The "Máire Ní Ógáin" persona simultaneously exploits and satirizes the kind of public complicity that refrains from acknowledging what it wishes to suppress.

Salkeld's "Arachne" (1955) launches a metapoetic spin on the feminized crafts of weaving and provisioning. The Arachnean dance of dispersal and realignment sketches and dodges entrapment by rupturing the sonnet form with off-course tacking and line-casting:

> Let them fly. So long as she keeps her stand.
> Mere radii – (centrifugal, her force) –
> Puffed by her fiery breath off – they course

The closing couplet shows the speaker poised within a "still centre," though in a repose that acknowledges an unsatiated appetite for a predatory kill:

> She could wish centripetal force, though ... to suck
> One late fugitive ... into her still centre.[50]

Much of the middle-generation women's verse in Collins's anthology bears the hallmarks of modernism, including ruptured syntax, conceptual diction, erudite allusion, and ironic juxtaposition. Their subversive irony and indirection often fell on deaf ears, however. Thus an otherwise laudatory review of Salkeld's *Hello Eternity!* (1933) regrets the misleading impression created by the "bold impudence" of the title.[51]

Women's limited access to the bardic or priestly authorities so commonly associated with the Irish male poetic persona lay behind the sixteen-year-old Medbh McGuckian's decision, made at a reading by Heaney in 1966, that becoming a poet would be "the second best thing to becoming a priest."[52] In the early 1970s she joined Ciaran Carson and Paul Muldoon in a writer's group with Heaney and they remain a vital primary audience for her. Around the same time, Nuala Ní Dhomhnaill joined a group of Cork university poets who challenged conservative revivalists by creolizing Gaelic poetry with 1960s counter-cultural argot. They activated an untapped audience of passive bilinguists by widely distributing their journal, *Innti*, and holding agitprop readings in city pubs. The transformation of newspapers' "women's pages" into organs of feminist consciousness-raising and the founding of the Irish Women's Movement in 1970 inspired poets to play their part *qua* poets by attempting to undo the patriarchal conditioning of language and literary conventions.

The masculinist bias of the Irish bardic poem has received sustained feminist critique since the 1980s, most notably by Eavan Boland in her 1987 manifesto-poem "Mise Eire" ("I am Ireland") and critical prose.[53] "Mise

Eire" contests Patrick Pearse and Yeats's appropriation of Eire's archaic matriarchal prerogative to authorize leaders and poets. Boland invokes her representative experience as a suburban mother to sanction her bardic prerogative to speak on behalf of the nation's silenced women. Ní Dhomhnaill also seizes bardic authority, but because her poetic tradition is steeped in the patriarchal *aisling* genre – then the object of radical feminist critique – she does so through a Jungian exploration of the dark vertiginous energy of the cailleach/sovereignty goddess in *Feis* (1991), arguably the most ambitious major opus in twentieth-century Irish-language poetry. McGuckian emerged "in some degree a priest" from a harrowing experience of parturition and post-partum psychosis, filled with hallucinations of the Virgin Mary, which culminated with the revelation "that birth, death, and orgasm were all exactly the same sensation," a bodily knowledge she makes the invincible ground of her poetic authority.[54] These feminist revisions of the bardic poem strive to unleash the "muse energy" (McGuckian and Ní Dhomhnaill's term) enshrined behind an obfuscating veneration of motherhood, and claim that maternity and poetic authority are mutually empowering, not incompatible or conflicting. They locate the priestly vatic function within the fecundity of the female body, and demand and secure access to the kinds of public hearing afforded by the pulpit, the hustings, and the literary canon.

V

Defining features of Irish modernist verse include commitments to radical linguistic and generic experiment and engagement with public issues. Yeats's youthful dream of a theater to congregate an audience of listeners was realized not only through the Abbey, but also by developing a form of bardic authority that combined an abrasively political poetry with the Symbolist "magic" of visual and aural evocation. His engagement in public debate through poetry and political advocacy secured acceptance for the neo-bardic role of poet as public intellectual, and was an influential counterexample to strands of modernism that divorced poetry from political engagement or ceded the general public to popular genres. Yeats's Symbolist theory of aesthetic receptivity sets a high premium on the acoustic and dialogical dimension of literature, an emphasis retained and developed in new directions by Joyce and Beckett, whose prose is widely acclaimed as "lyrical." By attending to the acoustic dimension of their work, I hope to have shown how the distinctly Irish-modernist achievement of "the bardic," broadly conceived, imparts and fosters a habit of attentive listening across the range of genres.

The generation that came after Yeats hewed closer to the examples of Joyce and Eliot, though they also drew heavily on the bardic mode of satire to critique and castigate post-revolutionary stagnation, censorship, and repression. They explored the resilient hold of religious tradition on inspiring and inhibiting the psyche while dealing with how the sectarian partitioning of Ireland had revived post-Reformation struggles for institutional hegemony in ways that isolated Ireland from secular European modernity. The institution of "the bard" in the Irish-language and neo-modernist tradition is a bastion of male exclusivity, making it a valuable trope for shoring up "traditional" male privilege when gender roles were being transformed by feminist activism and modernizing forces. Despite the setbacks to mid-century women's creative agency, their poetry displays buoyant pleasure in the refuge afforded by poetry for exploring subjective interiority, even as they exploit formal means to question their confinement. They were not prolific, and their near-erasure from the literary canon created an absence for their successors that stimulated a concerted creative and critical effort to redress the material and psychological barriers that discourage women from seeking, and realizing, their full poetic authority.

NOTES

1 See Trevor Joyce, "New Writers' Press: The History of a Project," *Modernism and Ireland: the Poetry of the 1930s*, Patricia Coughlan and Alex Davis, eds. (Cork: Cork University Press, 1995), 276–306; 296. The poets have since regrouped around Cork's annual SoundEye poetry festival.
2 Samuel Beckett, "Recent Irish Poetry," Ruby Cohn, ed. *Disjecta: Miscellaneous Writings and a Dramatic Fragment* (New York: Grove Press, 1984), 70–1.
3 Coughlan and Davis, *Modernism and Ireland*, 11.
4 Coughlan and Davis, *Modernism and Ireland*, 11.
5 Beckett, *Disjecta*, 74; Coughlan and Davis, *Modernism and Ireland*, 10.
6 W. B. Yeats, *Essays and Introductions* (New York: Macmillan, 1961), 509.
7 James Joyce, *A Portrait of the Artist as a Young Man*, Seamus Deane, ed. (New York: Penguin, 1992), 276.
8 Laura Riding and Robert Graves, *A Survey of Modernist Poetry* (London: William Heineman, 1927), 176.
9 Riding and Graves, *A Survey*, 178–80.
10 Yeats, *Essays*, 526; Virginia Woolf, *The Diary of Virginia Woolf*, vol. 3 (1925–1930), Anne Olivier Bell, ed. (New York: Harcourt Brace Jovanovich, 1980), 330.
11 W. B. Yeats, *Mythologies* (New York: Macmillan, 1959), 331; Yeats, *Essays*, 524.
12 Yeats, *Essays*, 510.
13 "Orature," used to avoid the literocentric bias of "oral literature," refers to orally transmitted legend, lore, and traditions.
14 W. B. Yeats, *Explorations* (New York: Macmillan, 1962), 205–6.
15 Yeats, *Essays*, 524.
16 W. B. Yeats, *Autobiographies* (New York: Macmillan, 1955), 396.

17 See Yeats's letter to *United Ireland* (1892), *Uncollected Prose* vol. I, John P. Frayne, ed. (New York: Columbia University Press, 1970), 255–6.

18 W. H. Auden, *Selected Poems*, Edward Mendelson, ed. (New York: Columbia University Press, 1979), 83.

19 Louis MacNeice, "Snow," in *Selected Poems*, Michael Longley, ed. (London: Faber and Faber, 1988), 23.

20 Louis MacNeice, *The Poetry of W.B. Yeats* (New York: Oxford University Press, 1941), 135.

21 MacNeice, *Poetry of W. B. Yeats*, 32.

22 *The Letters of W. B. Yeats*, Allan Wade, ed. (London: Rupert Hart-Davis, 1954), 211 (July 23, 1892).

23 W. B. Yeats, *The Poems*, Daniel Albright, ed. (London: Everyman, 1990), 45.

24 Yeats, *Essays*, "Symbolism," 159.

25 Yeats, "Symbolism," 157.

26 Yeats, *Essays*, 185.

27 See Kevin Whelan, "The Cultural Effects of the Famine," *The Cambridge Companion to Modern Irish Culture*, Joe Cleary and Claire Connolly. eds. (Cambridge: Cambridge University Press, 2005), 137–54.

28 *The Selected John Hewitt*, Alan Warner, ed. (Belfast: Blackstaff Press, 1981), 54.

29 Patrick Kavanagh, *The Complete Poems*, Peter Kavanagh, ed. (Newbridge, Co. Kildare: Goldsmith Press, 1972), 125.

30 Kavanagh, *Poems*, 79, 85.

31 Kavanagh, *Poems*, 81.

32 Kavanagh, *Poems*, 91.

33 Austin Clarke, *Selected Poems*, Hugh Maxton, ed. (Dublin: Lilliput, 1991), 84.

34 See W. J. Mc Cormack, "Austin Clarke: The Poet as Scapegoat of Modernism," Coughlan and Davis, *Modernism and Ireland*, 75–102.

35 See Peggy O'Brien, *Writing Lough Derg: From William Carleton to Seamus Heaney* (New York: Syracuse University Press, 2006), 73.

36 Kavanagh, *Poems*, 110, 107.

37 Denis Devlin, *Collected Poems of Denis Devlin*, J. C. C. Mays, ed. (Dublin: Dedalus, 1989), 123.

38 Kavanagh, *Poems*, 123.

39 Devlin, *Poems*, 134.

40 Seamus Heaney, *Station Island* (London: Faber and Faber, 1984), 93.

41 See "Exposure," *North* (London: Faber and Faber, 1975), 73.

42 Samuel Beckett, *Company* (New York: Grove Press, 1980), 16.

43 Brian Coffey, *Poems and Versions 1929–1990* (Dublin: Dedalus, 1991), 140.

44 Coffey, *Poems*, 144.

45 Quoted in Michael North, *Reading 1922: A Return to the Scene of the Modern* (Oxford: Oxford University Press, 1999), 174.

46 *The Field Day Anthology of Irish Writing: Irish Women's Writing and Traditions*, vol. V, Angela Bourke, et al., eds. (Cork: Cork University Press, 2002); Lucy Collins, ed. *Poetry by Women in Ireland: A Critical Anthology 1870–1970* (Liverpool: Liverpool University Press, 2012).

47 Anne Mulhall, "'The well-known, old, but still unbeaten track': Women Poets and Irish Periodical Culture in the Mid-Twentieth Century," *Irish University*

Review 42, 1 (2012), 32–52; 42. See Mulhall's citations for related scholarship by Kathy D'Arcy, Anne Fogarty, Susan Schreibman, and Moynagh Sullivan.

48 Bourke, *Field Day Anthology*, 1027.

49 Máire Mhac an tSaoi, *An Paróiste Míorúilteach: Rogha Dánta / The Miraculous Parish: Selected Poems*, Louis de Paor, ed. (Dublin: O'Brien Press, 2011), 88–96.

50 Blanaid Salkeld, *Experiment in Error* (Aldington, Kent: The Hand and Flower Press, 1955), 4.

51 Mulhall, "Women Poets," 42.

52 "*Comhrá*: A conversation between Medbh McGuckian and Nuala Ní Dhomhnaill, edited, with a foreword and afterword, by Laura O'Connor," *The Southern Review: Special Issue on Irish Poetry* 13, 3 (1995), 581–614; 592.

53 Eavan Boland, *New Collected Poems* (New York: W. W. Norton, 2008), 128–9.

54 McGuckian, *Comhrá*, 596.

6

EMER NOLAN

James Joyce and the Mutations of the Modernist Novel

I

James Joyce always looms large in critical discussions of English-language modernism, alongside other radical literary innovators of the early-twentieth-century novel, such as Marcel Proust, Virginia Woolf, Gertrude Stein, Alfred Döblin, D. H. Lawrence, John Dos Passos, and William Faulkner. However, it is a more troublesome and certainly less tried exercise to place Joyce in the context of a specifically Irish literary modernism. For example, the Irish modernist triad of W. B. Yeats, Joyce, and Samuel Beckett does not harmonize quite as well as the usual transnational groupings and not only because of the chronologies involved. These three did not just pursue parallel if distinct projects: Joyce defined himself in part against Yeats; Beckett certainly defined himself against Joyce. The various genres of Irish modernist writing, therefore, did not evolve along independent paths but instead were regarded from the outset as being at odds or even in contest with each other. The poetry and drama of Yeats were influenced by European aesthetic trends such as symbolism but were also strongly associated with the movement for national cultural revival in Ireland. Poetry in particular was seen as a key medium (along with music) in which the traditional spirit of the Irish people could be preserved and renewed. The Irish modernist novel, in its emergent, pre-Joycean form and in Joyce's own early work, was much indebted to French experimental naturalism. However, in contrast to the revivalists, Irish novelists were evidently mainly committed to a skeptical investigation of modern Irish society and to a dissident individualism rather than to any collectivist cultural project. Recently, critics have emphasized that Joyce's major works are in fact intricately bound up with the story of Ireland's political revolution in the early twentieth century.[1] But he is still neither generally understood as emerging from any national tradition nor as inspiring a school of literary descendants, but rather as having invented the iconic modernist novel of twentieth-century Irish fiction.

As my title suggests, the history of modernist Irish fiction can be understood as a sequence of mutations. All of Joyce's major works – *Dubliners* (1914), *A Portrait of the Artist as a Young Man* (1916), *Ulysses* (1922), *Finnegans Wake* (1939) – are magnificent, but before and after that we have a number of key novels by other Irish writers, none of which achieves equal resonance or scale; nor do any others, it seems, occupy comparably important historical moments. Works that could rival his epic range or ambition flourished mainly outside Ireland and even outside Europe; examples include Dos Passos's *The U.S.A. Trilogy* (1930–6), Miguel Ángel Asturias's *Men of Maize* (1949), or Gabriel García Márquez's *One Hundred Years of Solitude* (1967). But there are, of course, worlds elsewhere, in Irish as in modern fiction generally, in which Joyce is not the only presiding deity. For example, the Irish novelists George Moore and Elizabeth Bowen combined elements of nineteenth-century Anglo-Irish Big House fiction with narratives of individual and particularly of women's development. Moore's *A Drama in Muslin* (1886) and Bowen's *The Last September* (1929) are set against the backdrop of the Land War and the Anglo-Irish War, respectively. Both novels accept the near-inevitability of a Catholic-dominated independent Irish state. But Moore and Bowen concentrate on exploring the issues of female education and the possibilities of upper-class marital happiness in prose that is finely attuned to the nuanced inner lives of the chief women protagonists. It is made clear that such heroines need to flee both Ireland's existing neo-feudal regime and its coming popular democracy. Joyce, on the other hand, gave the representation of the new popular culture of an emerging modern Ireland a central thematic and formal significance. But novelists in a post-Joycean line who shared his preoccupations with satirizing revivalist idealizations of Irishness or with the comedy of Irish linguistic performance struggled to match the hazardous odysseys of his mature fiction. Even remarkable works such as Flann O'Brien's *At Swim-Two-Birds* (1939), Máirtín Ó Cadhain's *Cré na Cille* (1949), or Beckett's *Trilogy* (1951–3) offer only partial or negative responses to Joyce's explorations. This chapter examines the French-influenced realism best developed by Moore and Bowen, the more radically avant-garde modernism cultivated by Joyce, and the various modes of satiric late modernism essayed by Joyce's Irish successors.

II

The success of the realist novel from the early eighteenth century onward was bound up with its aspiration to depict individual characters inhabiting material and social circumstances that were highly recognizable to new middle-class readers. However, as Jesse Matz observes, modernist novelists announce an absolute break with the realism or "Victorianism" that preceded them; with its emphasis on subjectivity, flux, and on its own status as art, the modernist novel promises an escape from the complacency or moralism of traditional fiction.[2] However, Matz further suggests that all of these supposedly modernist tendencies were in fact inherent in the very form of the novel.[3] Indeed, it is has been noted that some eighteenth-century authors with Irish associations, such as Jonathan Swift or Laurence Sterne, were foremost among those who exploited or satirized the anarchic or destabilizing possibilities of the form at an early stage.[4] There are also important connections between realist and modernist form and ideologies of national identity in the nineteenth and twentieth centuries. Realism acknowledges that there is a limit to the capacity of the individual for unfettered self-development.[5] She or he must explore the conflict between the desiring self and the demands of society against the particular context of the "community in anonymity" of the modern nation.[6] For example, in the *Bildungsroman*, the individual's freedom is sometimes destroyed but more often realized in chastened form within the national constraints of his or her natal society. There is a paradox here. On the one hand, in its commitment to everyday language and ordinary social worlds, the novel is remote from the fetishization of folk culture or the notions of continuous national character that seem so important to the ideology of nationalism. On the other hand, more than any other literary form, it is equipped to capture the richly detailed lifeworlds of modern people, the intricacies of local relationships and a specific geography that typically embraces both town or village and the metropolitan world beyond. Thus, the realist novel provides narrative bearings in a reasonably comprehensible historical world, where time and place intersect. The modernist novel, by contrast, seems to be self-consciously postnational – preoccupied with philosophical issues concerning consciousness and representation, set in the derealized worlds of the modern city and often imbued with a new sense of imperial or global space (as in the works of Joseph Conrad or Lawrence). Thus the position of the modernist novel in any national canon was bound to be different to that of the realist novel. But any conjugation between fictional form and national identity is always intricate.

Take the case of the Protestant, Anglo-Irish population of Ireland, originally descended mainly from English planters and colonists. From Maria Edgeworth's *Castle Rackrent* (1800) to Bram Stoker's *Dracula* (1897), this group produced almost all of the most accomplished Irish novels written between the Act of Union and the Land War. Anglo-Irish fiction weakened the ideology of an "English people in Ireland" by showing how far the former settler class had in time diverged from its metropolitan counterpart.

These novels exposed as an illusion the survival in Irish conditions of a confident landed class of the kind we find in the English novel from Jane Austen's *Pride and Prejudice* (1813) to George Eliot's *Middlemarch* (1874). However, such fictions also provided an unsurpassed expression of an anxious, hybrid Anglo-Irish identity; no other form matched their account of this caste's ambivalence toward both England and the indigenous people who worked on their land and in their houses. Anglo-Irish writers would eventually make a distinctive contribution to a wider, transnational modernist sensibility – including the Gothic of vampires and haunted mansions of Stoker or Sheridan Le Fanu and the sense, in Bowen and others, of the evaporation of agency in the face of an inescapable history. And feminist critics are now beginning to trace the connections between Bowen's Anglo-Irish cultural identity and issues of sexual politics relevant to both her Irish novels and those set in England or elsewhere.[7]

In the case of the fiction authored by Irish Catholics, beginning in the second decade of the nineteenth century, the relationship between the novel and varieties of Irish nationalism is similarly complex. The efforts of early Catholic novelists such as John and Michael Banim to emulate Walter Scott in producing coherent national allegories in realist forms remained frustrated; their deference to Scott and other British models was burdensome. The great national Irish novel of the pre-Revivalist period was *Knocknagow* (1873) by the Fenian leader Charles Kickham, the best-selling work of Irish fiction in Ireland and Irish-America until the middle of the twentieth century. This sentimental novel about a village community in Tipperary generally endorsed the new Catholic bourgeois settlement that had painfully evolved from the upheavals of failed rebellion, the Great Famine and near-continuous agrarian unrest in the nineteenth century. But the narrative also itemizes the cost of such an endorsement. The novel's repression of the Gaelic past and of recent historical trauma is at times shockingly self-conscious in its advocacy of active forgetting; Kickham also sponsors the use of music to preserve the essential "spirit" of the past while not paying too much attention to what actually happened. The chief components of the social and political aesthetic of *Knocknagow* – and of its reception – were the subordination of individuality to the requirements of communal consensus and survival and the functional importance of storytelling in confirming a shared set of values between the audience and the artist who created the story.[8]

Nothing could be further from the world of Moore, the novelist who made the achievement of self-consciously "modern" fiction one of the goals of the Irish Literary Revival. (In the National Library episode in *Ulysses*, Stephen Dedalus resents the high opinions of Moore held by the local literati: "Our national epic has yet to be written, Dr Sigerson says. Moore is the man for it."[9]) The most important reorientation of the notion of a radical cultural difference that distinguished Ireland from Britain or even other European countries was achieved in the period of the revival – between the death of Parnell and the publication of *Ulysses*. The major revivalist artists were for the most part Protestants who had become nationalists at least in a cultural sense. Their fascination with Gaelic or premodern culture, and their apotheosis of the west of Ireland as one of its sole surviving spaces in modernity, was expressed most memorably in the poetry of Yeats or the plays of J. M. Synge rather than in any form of narrative fiction. But Moore wrote a memoir of revivalist Dublin, *Hail and Farewell* (1911–14), in which he provocatively allocated to himself the central role in the movement that was generally granted to Yeats.

Moore came from a family of Catholic landlords in County Mayo; during the Land War, he was outraged that his bohemian life studying art in Paris was rudely interrupted when the tenants on his estate began withholding their rents. Moore therefore became, in his own view, a direct "victim" of the political movements that would eventually deprive the landlords of their estates. But in his fiction, as Terry Eagleton argues, Moore often demonstrates a striking "negative identification" with people who had been marginalized for quite different reasons, and especially with women such as the eponymous English servant in *Esther Waters* (1894) or Rose Leicester in *The Lake* (1905).[10] In *A Drama in Muslin*, which opens in an English convent school, Moore provides an early example of the female Catholic *Bildungsroman* that would be developed later by prominent Irish novelists, including Kate O'Brien and Edna O'Brien. He also revamps the Anglo-Irish novel by his use of naturalistic techniques and by drawing on topics dear to late-nineteenth-century feminism. Moore's work presents the Ascendancy class as doomed. This fate is understood as a historical necessity; the question of the justice of the cause of the dispossessed majority does not arise. Moore instead devotes most of his energy to exposing the real conditions of upper-class girls in the fashionable society centered on Dublin Castle. Here we first encounter motifs that are recurrent to the point of obsession with Moore: for example, the horror of enforced celibacy for the girls destined not to find husbands and the misery of unwanted pregnancy. It is precisely such themes of sexual denial or repression that were in time to become central to many twentieth-century Irish novels in which the lack of healthy marriages and the emotional abuse of the young were taken to be definitive and revelatory of the condition not just of the privileged but of the mass of Irish people.

In *A Drama in Muslin*, Moore describes how the peasants in their cabins or the poor on the streets of Dublin gaze in an apparently threatening fashion at the "silken exquisites who, a little frightened, strove to hide themselves within the scented shadow of their broughams."[11] However, the significance of this Irish underclass hostility is uncertain. Are they the unwitting or the vengeful agents of the imminent destruction of upper-class privilege, or is there here a promise that at least one blessing of this long-anticipated upheaval will be the release of women of the gentry from ennui or sexual exploitation? The same question also lurks in Bowen's *The Last September*, which records the attraction for Lois, the young Anglo-Irish woman, of the "violent realness"[12] of the subterranean Ireland that she encounters in the form of the ultramasculine figures of the republican rebels who flit through the gardens and across the countryside surrounding the family estate. Bowen sought not only to expose the oppression of women in its subtle or crude forms, but also to suggest that any society guilty of such oppression was itself radically insecure or doomed. In her work, buildings and indeed the whole physical infrastructure of class and power become fractured and vulnerable to ruin as readily as the human psyche or body. Lois has the fine antennae capable of registering this process, which is happening in and beyond her; but she is also aware of the limitations of the Ascendancy and imperial male world that confines her to such luxuriant sensitivity and indeed of her own inability to articulate her plight. *The Last September* does not tell us about Lois's ultimate fate. However, other Anglo-Irish women writers gave more direct answers to related questions about the coming sexual regime of modern Ireland. For example, in Emily Lawless's *Grania* (1891), the tragic story of a young Aran Islander, it is clear that the author believes that the new Ireland will be worse rather than better for women; she suggests that domination by Catholic, middle-class men (here represented by the heroine's sadly inadequate lover Murdough) will be more disabling than rule by the landlords from their Big Houses.

Alice Barton, the central woman character in *A Drama in Muslin*, seeing the lives of her sister and many of her friends destroyed by sexual ignorance and hypocrisy, marries an English doctor and goes to live in suburban London. She wants to be a writer as well as to find romantic fulfillment; similarly, Rose in *The Lake* seeks not just emotional but intellectual satisfaction when she runs away to Europe with her lover. Like Dorothea Brooke in *Middlemarch*, Alice seeks individual fulfillment in a vocation that involves sacrificing class privilege in a companionate, bourgeois marriage. (However, in keeping with Moore's disenchanted naturalism, Alice's partner has none of Ladislaw's youthful charm, and he is not even her first choice of husband.) Here Moore demonstrates how he has been influenced by the crucial dramatizations in Victorian domestic realism of the conflicts between romance and women's vocations. Few modern Irish novelists linger over the sufferings of middle-class women who attempt to stray into male-dominated areas of culture or who struggle to live happily or productively in the modern world; nor did social conditions in Ireland often provide much material basis for such efforts at self-liberation. Joyce's notions of what a woman could or should be are generally considered to be much grander and more emancipatory than those of other male writers. But in elaborating these, he showed little interest in what feminists or others may have had to say about what women actually wanted. So despite Joyce's early admiration for Henrik Ibsen and for the naturalistic drama or novel with its depictions of rebellious women protesting against constrictive social conventions, there is no equivalent in his work to the moment in *A Doll's House* (1879) when the heroine abandons her husband and family with a final slam of the door. Thus, for Nuala O'Faolain the major Irish modernists were a "great and elegant series of chauvinists" and their domination of the literary field, she contends, was not enabling for Irish women's fiction.[13] Moore's and Bowen's novels owe debts, respectively, to French naturalism and aestheticism, and to Bloomsbury modernism, but in aesthetic terms both are more radically "modern" than radically "modernist." Whether a promising mode of Irish realism of the type they developed was really cut off by Joyce's achievement to the detriment of the Irish social or women's novel is an interesting question. It must be said, however, that Joyce's work was much more thoroughly immersed in middle- and lower-middle-class Ireland than was that of either Moore or Bowen, and in some respects, therefore, his work delivered not only a terrifically radical jolt to the modern novel generally but to Irish cultural sensibilities more specifically.

III

Joyce paid a rival's hostile attention to some of Moore's fiction. He wrote to his brother from Rome about how tiresome he found *The Lake*, mocking all the talk in the novel about art, literature, and Italy, where "they drink nice wine instead of horrid black porter."[14] But these jokes at the expense of Moore's "cosmopolitanism" reveal something about the uses to which Joyce will eventually put his own Irish subject matter. An earlier Irish critical tradition concentrated on Joyce's supposed celebration of a broader European modernity as an emancipatory alternative to the constrictions of nativist "tradition." However, he is now primarily understood as the Irish artist who most profoundly absorbed and most memorably represented the historical experiences of colonial underdevelopment, economic peripherality, and cultural trauma. Thus, Joyce is now the central figure in recent reconceptualizations of modernity and modernism in Irish criticism, and has enjoyed renewed influence in other areas of contemporary Irish Studies including visual art, cinema, and philosophy.[15] As such, he is usually regarded less as a model for other Irish writers than an essential part of the very context in which they are read.

We have seen that in departing from the traditions of novelistic realism, Joyce breaks the alliance between the realist-naturalistic novel and feminist individualism. Instead, his fiction reorders the established representation of the relation between the sphere of privacy, one of the creations of bourgeois civilization, and that of the public world. We might even argue that ultimately, in *Ulysses* and *Finnegans Wake*, the distinction between these two realms is so effectively dissolved that the public sphere becomes the site of the most profound emotional connections and authentic identities. The idea of the domestic space is subjected to a sustained irony; No. 7 Eccles Street, the kitchen, and the bedroom, are counterpointed against the pub, the newspaper office, the church, and the graveyard so that the intimacies that were once proper to the former sphere are fully realized only in the latter. In these works, an idea of Ireland quite different to that of Moore or Bowen, or indeed Yeats, becomes "home."

From the moment in *A Portrait of the Artist* that Stephen Dedalus – then a young boy from a comfortable suburban house being educated among a privileged Catholic elite at boarding school – first encounters the voluble world of his father and his associates, it is clear that this group will be crucial to the development of Joyce's fiction. These are men that know themselves to be living in post-heroic times. During the boy's first Christmas vacation from school, the bourgeois comfort of the family dining room is upended by the raw, aggressive emotion that Stephen hears in the voices of his father and his friends as they mourn their lost leader, Parnell. The child has never encountered anything like this bitter hostility within his family circle, especially between the men and his aunt; crucially, this is the first time the harsh, demotic language of Irish men enters his consciousness. Mr. Casey tells of spitting in the eye of the woman who called Kitty O'Shea a bad name and he blasphemes with the terrible words "No God for Ireland! ... Away with God!"[16] As Dante correctly prophesies, the boy will "remember all this when he grows up ... the language he heard against God and religion and priests in his own home," for this Irish family cannot be free of politics, not even (as Mrs. Dedalus pleads) "for one day in the year."[17] From the outset, such violent language is associated with the sins but also the suffering fallibility of the father; it is also associated with the story of Ireland and with the traditions of Whiteboyism and Fenianism in the Dedalus as in the Joyce family. Yeats famously traced the movement for cultural revival in Ireland back to this same moment of traumatic loss that followed the death of Parnell.[18]

In *Dubliners*, Joyce insists that to fill this vacuum with what aspiring poet Little Chandler in "A Little Cloud" calls the "Celtic note"[19] could only be a distraction and delusion as no such pliant aesthetic could redeem the broken lives of the inhabitants of this dark, provincial city. Joyce sets out to satirize the degenerate condition of this group as it is made manifest in their political discourse in "Ivy Day in the Committee Room" or in the ignorant and hypocritical talk about religion in "Grace." But, as suggested by the "journey westward"[20] at the conclusion of the final story, "The Dead," complications emerge in relation to Joyce's view of this project of cultural renovation. He never again attempts the kind of direct appropriation of the revivalist or religious motifs evident in the final lines of "The Dead" (although some of these will reappear in a much more mediated form in the evocations of Ireland's early Christian Golden Age in *Finnegans Wake*). Instead, Joyce's anti-heroic mode becomes comic rather than satiric – if *Dubliners* is the hangover, *Ulysses* is the party (showing the verbal inventiveness and imaginative appeal of this shabby, jokey, sometimes fairly savage crew of Dubliners). In *Ulysses* and *Finnegans Wake*, Joyce answers his friends from *A Portrait* – the socialist McCann's accusation that he was "an anti-social being, wrapped up in [him]self" and the declaration by Davin, the naive country boy, that that "[y]ou're a born sneerer.... Our day will come yet, believe me."[21] Joyce's cultural accomplishment is intimately related to the achievements of people like these two men during the period when *Ulysses* is being written (1914–22) – the novel salutes, imitates, and downgrades their successes in a single ambiguous tribute.[22]

Yet, amidst all this transformation, a dualistic conception of gender still remains as a structural underpinning for both these national epics. Joyce borrows from the verbal performances typical of the male-dominated pubs and streets of Dublin to elaborate his accounts of the shared histories and the ongoing conflicts that define this community. He accomplishes this by using a huge range of parodic, ironic, and polyvocal styles that are better accommodated in modernist rather than realist modes of narrative. This constitutes his main contribution to the reformulated "Irishness" of the "Irish" modernist novel. Taken together with his parallel descriptions of Leopold Bloom as the possessor of a supposedly less-locally inflected modern consciousness, Joyce's investigation of the Irish crowd comes to be regarded, along with some other key works, such as T. S. Eliot's *The Waste Land* (1922), as central to a broader modernist encounter with twentieth-century mass culture. But in contrast to the crowded homosocial public worlds depicted by Joyce, sexual comfort and transcendent historical wisdom are associated with the singular female presences of Molly Bloom or Anna Livia Plurabelle. Although these are at least in part avatars of a national community conventionally symbolized by a woman (Mother Ireland), the narratives (especially in the *Wake*) ultimately yield to these Olympian "feminine" perspectives on the inevitability of historical recurrence and on the endless capacity of human civilization to renew itself.

Slavoj Žižek argues that the sense of a shared culture in nationalist discourse is bound up with a collective sense of a national "Thing." He suggests that:[23]

> "If we are asked how we can recognize the presence of this Thing, the only consistent answer is that the Thing is present in that elusive entity called 'our way of life.' All we can do is enumerate disconnected fragments of the way our community organizes its feasts, its rituals of mating, its initiation ceremonies, in short, all the details by which is made visible the unique way in which a community *organizes its enjoyment*."

It seems plausible to contend that the novel is a privileged vehicle for the identification of such a national "Thing" in modern Irish culture. There are significant parallels, for example, between the portrayal of a reconstituted village life in Kickham's *Knocknagow* and Eamon de Valera's much later declarations about Ireland as a place where sturdy youths and comely maidens dance at the crossroads. But given Joyce's hostility to any Gaelicist or pastoral vision of Ireland and his once-secure reputation as a subversive demythologizer of nationalism, it is perhaps all the more surprising to note the significant continuities between Kickham's experimental epic and *Ulysses* in their respective portrayals of the "way of life" of Irish people. Some of these continuities are explained by Joyce's preservation of elements of an older communal or small-town life within his representation of the metropolis. Both novels, for example, draw on an established group repertoire of gossip, anecdote, and song. Verbal or musical performances bind people together and distract from or assuage the prevailing conditions of poverty and anomie. This is how this particular community, in Žižek's phrase, organizes its enjoyment. One difference is that the people in the village of Knocknagow congregate in each other's kitchens, in the fields or at the church they all attend, whereas in Joyce's Dublin the focus is on the much more segregated space of the pub. There the "shared" culture is based far more on the language and rituals of men and focused to an extraordinary degree on the consumption of alcohol (Bloom's relative abstemiousness in relation to drink is balanced by his far keener interest in other consumerist pleasures, such as food, home improvements, and erotic literature). Kickham's main concern in the area of sexuality is to argue for the importance of affectionate, companionate marriages rather than the mercenary unions that were encouraged by the necessity of preserving small family landholdings and by a Church that was anxious to de-emphasize sex as such in the interests of preserving the moral virtue of the community. In Joyce, all this social polemic about Irish sexuality has been displaced onto the figure of Molly. At one level, she represents something far more complex than the bourgeois ideal of companionate marriage, but she also stands for an even more elusive dream of libidinal and emotional fulfillment.

IV

The post-Joycean Irish modernist novel, especially as represented by Flann O'Brien, concentrates in any event on the scenes of masculine community, with all the opportunities they represent to exploit the comedy of Hiberno-English in its demotic forms. O'Brien abandons Joyce's ambitious aesthetic program for the novel and develops only the localism and humor of his predecessor's works. He has no place for the elevated view of femininity in Joyce and instead reduces sex to the status of a dirty joke in *At Swim-Two-Birds*. Both Stephen and Bloom in their different styles ruminate about women as life-givers in *Ulysses*. Stephen's anxiety about the role of woman in reproduction is alleviated by his reflections on the Trinity, a much preferable grouping to him than the Holy Family that was the image by which the "mob of Europe"[24] had debased Christianity. In *At Swim*, O'Brien dismisses the whole sentimental business of childbirth and motherhood – for example, he introduces a character who rails against the "tedious anachronism" of child-rearing and laments that children cannot be born "already matured, teethed, reared, educated, and ready to essay those competitive plums which make the Civil Service and the Banks so attractive to the younger breadwinners of today."[25] *At Swim-Two-Birds*, *The Third Policeman* (1967), or *An Béal Bocht* (*The Poor Mouth*) (1941) are primarily concerned with the deflation of grandiosity – including that of the Irish Gaelicists and nationalists who tried to create a "pure" Ireland and of Joyce who proposed in *Finnegans Wake* to make the little world of Ireland an everywhere. In O'Brien's work the mob is not in the least menacing but neither has it any other role in history; instead, it has become the risible public with no time for anything that is "high-falutin.'"

Mikhail Bakhtin has suggested that the literary genre of the novel arises largely out of a reaction against earlier forms such as the epic or the romance; in displacing these older genres, the realist novel ultimately becomes the key form of narrative for modern societies.[26] But modernist novelists, anxious to assert the literary-aesthetic dimensions of the novel as a form and skeptical of realism's capacity to represent the ruptures and shocks of modernity, embarked on a subversive deconstruction of inherited novelistic traditions.[27] In the Irish situation, Joyce is not so strongly marked by any argument with earlier Irish *novels*. He almost completely ignores the Anglo-Irish novelistic tradition and, while he criticizes Moore and presumably never regarded *Knocknagow* as a model, we can now see that his work nevertheless does combine elements of Moore – naturalism and aestheticism – with elements of Kickham's popular sentimentality. Joyce's later experimental ventures apparently isolated him as an artist, but his embrace of epic forms embedded him as the narrator of the collective story of the Irish people. Still, like the early realist novelists, he does carry on a battle with other *genres* – in this case, those usually associated with the rival modernism of the Irish literary revival. Joyce's more ambitious successors in fiction evidently have to discover for themselves a distinctive way of pursuing this same mission. Chronologically, Beckett's career precedes O'Brien's, but it is perhaps better understood as the last in a series of Irish modernist experiments. Beckett is the only legatee of the revivalist-modernist period in Ireland who successfully pursues an innovative aesthetic project of his own; alone among later Irish writers, he is acknowledged as having contributed to the evolution of European literature in the era of the Cold War.

Perhaps there was no real alternative to Joyce's mock or anti-heroic treatment of Irish culture in the novel form. Certainly, while there were a few novelists committed to revivalist aesthetics, the results were mixed. As Seamus Deane has argued, writers found it impossible to make "the conjunction between the myths of the past and the actualities of the present ... effective within a single work": instead, this effort produced a schismatic divide in the work of several novelists, including James Stephens, Eimar O'Duffy, and Brinsley MacNamara, between "fantasies of peculiarly whimsical purity and realistic novels of a determined grimness."[28] The comic treatment of Gaelic legends or motifs, following especially from the "Cyclops" chapter in *Ulysses*, proved to be a good deal more productive.

O'Brien plays endless variations on such techniques. In *The Poor Mouth*, the inhabitants of the Gaeltacht have so completely internalized accounts of themselves by the revivalists (and later their own writers) as the only "real" Gaels that they die in their droves at their Gaelic *feiseanna* (or festivals) from excess of speaking Irish and endless Irish dancing in the rain.[29] In *At Swim*, while one of the characters, Shanahan, professes his admiration for the unrelenting poetic lamentations of a revived Finn MacCool, he still asks: "But the man in the street, where does he come in?" Shanahan prefers a "pome about a thing that's known to all of us" with its refrain: "A PINT OF PLAIN IS YOUR ONLY MAN."[30] O'Brien mocks both revivalist genres and Joyce's encyclopedic world epic, parading a dingy demotic ordinariness which deflates both.

Ó Cadhain's *Cré na Cille* ("Graveyard Clay") also depends on gossip, story, and anecdote to create its version of a national affective community.

But – in this case – the talkers, more mixed in gender terms, are literally extinct, discoursing from their coffins in a Connemara cemetery. The novel – the outstanding achievement of Irish-language modernist fiction – represents a further play on revivalist and Joycean motifs. *Cré na Cille* is written in an exuberant, vernacular form of Irish; thus, the novel apparently belies doubts about both the capacity of the language to survive and its adaptability to modern literary forms. But while Irish lives on, the people who speak it are dead. As Clair Wills points out, *Cré na Cille* consists largely of monologue rather than dialogue, each character dwelling obsessively on his or her own concerns and memories.[31] The buried villagers may resemble the communal storytellers of Synge, Joyce, or Flann O'Brien but, like Beckett's later tormented narrators, they are abjectly isolated selves afflicted by the most painful kind of immortality.

Beckett started his career in fiction with an experiment in counter-revivalist comedy, *Murphy* (1938). After his escape from Dublin to London, while tied to the rocking chair in his garret, Murphy tries to isolate his Cartesian consciousness that cannot achieve the bodiless purity it desires. This might appear to be an advance précis of Beckett's entire career – exile from the ersatz Celticism and from the ignorant complacency of the Irish cultural scene to a radical and impossible exile from material reality, specifically that of the body. As Hamm declares in *Endgame* (1957): "You're on earth, there's no cure for that!"[32] Murphy asks that his ashes be flushed down the toilet in the Abbey Theatre after his death; his ironic fate, anticipating Beckett's own in some respects, is to be always returned to what he so vehemently repudiates.[33] Like Joyce, Beckett responds to various literary forms that were being created or revamped in the Ireland of his day; unlike Joyce, he experiments not just with the short story or the novel but also with drama. All of these genres only barely survive the vampiric action of the internal monologue (or soliloquy) that is the formal counterpart of the voracious consciousness that Beckett wants both to explore and to obliterate. This consciousness can envision satisfaction only in the silence of extinction. The recurrent figure, out of Synge and Yeats, of the eloquent tramp, becomes a dominant presence.

Beckett showed some affinities with the Anglo-Irish fictional tradition in his own "Big House" novel, *Watt* (1953), but this – like *Murphy* – proved another false start. In the mature *Trilogy*, composed in French and subsequently translated, the titles (*Molloy, Malone Dies, The Unnamable*) indicate the process of unnaming, a final release for the consciousness of any connection with "character" and "history." Arguably, Beckett shows a settler-colonial identification with, but alienation from, the landscape (especially of the Dublin and Wicklow mountains) which is the best correlative of that space called the "Beckett Country."[34] This beloved terrain is particular and specific, but never totalized or historically "placed" as "Joyce's Ireland" is. Joyce has a sense of a maimed tradition, but a tradition nevertheless rather than just an absence. This is not to say that for Beckett's people the trauma of historical dispossession was greater. But the extinction of their ownership of Ireland in the early twentieth century was indeed final, and this created a certain intimacy with extinction that was also, for different reasons, a European experience. Beckett's postwar dramatic masterpieces, from *Waiting for Godot* (1953) and *Endgame* onward, have clearly influenced contemporary Irish plays as the rabidly eloquent monologues of Tom Murphy, Conor McPherson, or Martin McDonagh attest. There is no comparable impact in the Irish novel, although Beckett's presence is tangible in fiction elsewhere.[35]

V

So who was "right," so to speak – Joyce or Beckett? Which version of modernism spoke more fully to twentieth-century modernity and the Irish experience of same? Literary-critical accounts of high modernism today acknowledge that its major ambitions belong now to history, while nonetheless enjoying what Fredric Jameson calls the "libidinal charge" that remains associated with the very "trope of modernity."[36] In relation to Ireland, interpretations of Joyce or Yeats can show how the losses of colonial experience still inspired magnificent works full of confident cultural self-assertion, including *Ulysses* or Yeats's "The Statues" or "Under Ben Bulben" from *Last Poems* (1939). But while historians of modernism can sometimes ignore Beckett, he is inescapably part of the story of modernism in Ireland. This seems to guarantee that the outcome of the Irish modernist adventure appears inevitably to be an anticlimax. Responding not primarily to events in Ireland, but to the changed conditions of Europe, Beckett is – as Jameson argues – a key figure in the emergence of a "late modernism" that no longer strives after "aesthetic totality or the systematic and Utopian metamorphosis of forms."[37] All accounts of Irish modernism concluding with Beckett end on a dying note – the failure of art is tragic, and so of a piece with the failure of everything else. Does the history of twentieth-century Ireland prove that Joyce was wrong to imagine that the Irish would find their own way to process or imagine modernity – or merely their own jokes and codes and solidarities to survive it? Even to ask this question is an acknowledgment of the impact and success of that series of brilliant experiments with the form of the Irish novel that Joyce is understood to have begun and Beckett to have terminated.

NOTES

1 For example, see the essays on Joyce in Seamus Deane, *Celtic Revivals* (London: Faber and Faber, 1985); for a later volume that collects essays by a range of contributors to postcolonial Joyce studies, see also Derek Attridge and Marjorie Howes, eds. *Semicolonial Joyce* (Cambridge: Cambridge University Press, 2000).

2 Jesse Matz, "The Novel," in David Bradshaw and Kevin J. H. Dettmar, eds. *A Companion to Modernist Literature and Culture* (Oxford: Blackwell, 2008), 215–26; 215.

3 Matz, "The Novel," 223.

4 On Irish writers' resistance to realist literary forms, see Terry Eagleton, "Form and Ideology in the Anglo-Irish Novel," in *Heathcliff and the Great Hunger: Studies in Irish Culture* (London: Verso, 1995), 145–225; especially 149.

5 See Franco Moretti's *The Way of the World: The* Bildungsroman *in European Culture* (London: Verso, 1987).

6 Benedict Anderson has outlined the specific contribution of the novel (together with the newspaper) to "the remarkable confidence of community in anonymity which is the hallmark of modern nations," in *Imagined Communities: Reflections on the Origin and Spread of Nationalism* (London: Verso, 1983), 40.

7 Only two of Bowen's ten novels are set in Ireland. Heather Laird addresses the apparent split between "Irish" readings of Bowen's fiction and readings more attentive to such crucial preoccupations as same-sex desire. See "The 'Placing' and Politics of Bowen in Contemporary Irish Literary and Cultural Criticism," in *Elizabeth Bowen*, Eibhear Walshe, ed. (Dublin: Irish Academic Press, 2009), 193–207, especially 202–4.

8 See accounts of the Banims and Kickham in Emer Nolan, *Catholic Emancipations: Irish Fiction from Thomas Moore to James Joyce* (Syracuse, NY: Syracuse University Press, 2007), chapters 2 and 3.

9 James Joyce, *Ulysses* [1922], Hans Walter Gabler, ed. (London: The Bodley Head, 1996), 158.

10 Eagleton, "Form and Ideology," 219.

11 George Moore, *A Drama in Muslin* [1886] (Gerrards Cross: Colin Smythe, 1981), 171.

12 Elizabeth Bowen, *The Last September* [1929] (London: Penguin, 1942), 49.

13 Nuala O'Faolain, "Irish Women and Writing in Modern Ireland," [1985] in Angela Bourke et al., eds. *The Field Day Anthology of Irish Writing: Irish Women's Writings and Traditions*, vol. 5 (Cork: Cork University Press, 2002), 1601–5; 1603.

14 James Joyce, *Selected Letters*, Richard Ellmann. ed. (London: Faber, 1975), 99, 106.

15 For examples, see Luke Gibbons, "Montage, Modernism and the City," *Transformations in Irish Culture* (Cork: Cork University Press, 1996), 165–9; and the studies of Irish artists included in Christa-Maria Lerm Hayes, *Joyce in Art: Visual Art Inspired by James Joyce* (Dublin: Lilliput, 2004).

16 James Joyce, *A Portrait of the Artist as a Young Man*, Seamus Deane, ed. (London: Penguin, 1992), 39.

17 Joyce, *A Portrait*, 33.

18 W. B. Yeats, *Autobiographies* (London: Macmillan, 1955), 559.
19 James Joyce, *Dubliners* [1914], Terence Brown, ed. (London: Penguin, 1992), 69.
20 Joyce, *Dubliners*, 225.
21 Joyce, *A Portrait*, 191, 218, 220.
22 These characters are based on Joyce's friends Francis Sheehy-Skeffington and George Clancy; see Joyce, *Portrait*, 307–8n, 309n.
23 Slavoj Žižek, *Tarrying with the Negative: Kant, Hegel, and the Critique of Ideology* (Durham, NC: Duke University Press, 1993), 201.
24 Joyce, *Ulysses*, 170.
25 Flann O'Brien, *At Swim-Two-Birds* [1939] (London: Penguin, 1967), 41.
26 See M. M. Bakhtin, *The Dialogic Imagination*, Michael Holquist, ed., Caryl Emerson and Michael Holquist, trans. (Austin: University of Texas Press, 1981).
27 See Matz, "The Novel," 216–17.
28 Seamus Deane, *A Short History of Irish Literature* (London: Hutchinson, 1986), 200.
29 Flann O'Brien, *The Poor Mouth* [1941], Patrick C. Power, trans. (London: Paladin, 1988), 58–9.
30 O'Brien, *At Swim*, 76–7.
31 Clair Wills, *That Neutral Island: A Cultural History of Ireland during the Second World War* (London: Faber and Faber, 2007), 340.
32 Samuel Beckett, *Endgame* in *The Complete Dramatic Works* (London: Faber and Faber, 1986), 118.
33 Samuel Beckett, *Murphy* [1938], (New York: Grove Press, 1957), 269.
34 See Eoin O'Brien and David Davison, *The Beckett Country: Samuel Beckett's Ireland* (Dublin: Black Cat Press, 1986); for a selection of recent essays that read Beckett in an Irish or a postcolonial context, see Seán Kennedy, ed., *Beckett and Ireland* (Cambridge: Cambridge University Press, 2010).
35 John Banville is usually regarded as the contemporary Irish novelist most influenced by Beckett.
36 Fredric Jameson, *A Singular Modernity: Essay on the Ontology of the Present* (London: Verso, 2002), 34.
37 Jameson, *A Singular Modernity*, 166.

7

BEN LEVITAS

Modernist Experiments in Irish Theatre

What makes modern theatre modernist? One might say: when theatre makes its presence felt. The reflexive awareness and formal renewals of modernism, its resistance to routine mimesis, become in the theatre a complex calling-of-attention not merely to issues of style, but also of enaction and social function. Theatre, unlike bookish literature, is a social art, a discipline of shared imagination and physical display, with a built civic presence and a place of public gathering. Modernity itself is its fabric. In Ireland that meant highly charged material: Irish theatrical experimentation is inevitably bound up with participation in the politics of representation, emerging as it did in a period of national reappraisal and revolution. Irish theatre's instinct for troubling involvement not only kept politics productively uneasy, but inclined toward a modernist scrutiny of its own processes. From Wilde and Shaw, through the nascent controversies of the Abbey Theatre and the scenic innovation of the Gate, and onward past Beckett's bleak hinterland, what constitutes our category challenges narrow definition. This modernism acts in a broad spectrum of theatricality, ranging from distending adaptations of realism to the avant garde, and from the poetics of symbolism and expressionism, to an awareness of the role of theatre practitioners beyond the theatre, in the public realm. And it is characteristically a metatheatre, one that finds strange perspective in the formal and social parallax.

Irish theatre, because of these relevancies and reflexivities, is a protagonist in the wider story of theatrical modernism that exerted early influence. Wilde's reputation as an Anglophone dramatist rests on the ironic refinements of his comic plays, such as *Lady Windermere's Fan* (1892) and *The Importance of Being Earnest* (1895), with their aphoristic counterpunches and startling shifts from sentimentality to cool heterodoxy. Such plays play with the performance of self, with the presentation of public and private personas, and authentic falsity: "being natural" as Mrs Cheveley declares in *An Ideal Husband* (1895), "is such a very difficult pose to keep up."[1] But it is *Salomé* (published 1893, first performed 1896) that emerged as an ur-text of European modernist theatre, bringing embodiment to an emerging symbolist tradition – the biblical subject already handled by Gustave Flaubert, Stéphane Mallarmé, and Joris-Karl Huysmans.[2] Wilde's theatricalisation brought new potency to the tetrarch Herod's court, with its echoes of imperial decadence, the necrotic appetites of the play's eponymous sexual predator, and the contrast with the divine asceticism of the prophet Jokanaan. Its reputation was irresistible, receiving its first production – Wilde was still imprisoned – at the Théâtre de L'Oeuvre, Paris under the direction of Aurélien Lugné-Poë, before being lifted into iconic status by Max Reinhardt's Berlin productions (first at the Kleines Theater, and then at the Neues Theater in 1902–3 from whence it toured Europe). The symbolic operations of a language only partially able to intuit the world is set against physicality, manifest onstage in an embodied exhibition of released erotic energy. Mallarmé's literary-symbolist assertion that the dancer is "not a woman who dances ... but a metaphor"[3] is challenged and compromised in the phenomenology of felt theatre. It was no accident that the play's influence was magnified by propagation into other performance forms – Richard Strauss's opera of 1905 and the *Ballets Russes* dance version, choreographed by Boris Romanov of 1913.

Salomé is a play in which language already distrusts its power when confronted with an ambiguous body: a staged presence that both symbolizes sensuality and manifests it. Salomé's first approach to Jokanaan is a failed attempt at metaphorical seduction. Jokanaan's body is initially describable – "white like the lilies" and "like the snows" – but then moves beyond description – "roses ... are not so white," "nor the feet of the dawn ... nor the breast of the moon." Finally, following his rejection of her approach, indescribably horrible: "a whited sepulchre, full of loathsome things." Apprehending the body, Salomé is left without words to equate with the object of desire: "There is nothing in the world so white as thy body," "so black as thy hair," "so red as thy mouth."[4] In the final scenes, speech is overtaken by dance, and dialogue is abandoned for vocabularies of movement and of immobility. Salomé's visceral liveness is set against the dismembered death's-head of Jokanaan, and her own final stillness once she is crushed by soldiers' shields. The transgressive display of female sexual power emerges as a short-lived challenge to normative Christian codes of denial and puritan hostility. The tragedy is one of a double lack, the dislocation between physical and metaphysical realms in which each becomes a negation of life: the ascetic's refusal and the hedonist's insistence both culminating in the darkest of ironies, necrophilia.

Reconciliation and failure of reconciliation of text and body are central to Irish theatrical modernism. But *Salomé* is also interventionist: beyond the concern with poetry and corporeality, it engages issues of censorship and acceptability, directly connecting with a penumbra of discourses around the theatre. Written first in French, *Salomé* was identified as transgressive by the British censor, the Lord Chamberlain, and refused licence until 1931 (the Dublin public saw it three years sooner). Subsequently, Wilde's incarceration inevitably placed his work within the context of his fall from grace; its subsequent afterlives in European theatre were inevitably allegorized by the playwright's death, crushed as it were under the shields of late-Victorian morality. His entire life might be considered a paratheatrical operation. As he put it in *De Profundis* (1905): "I was a man who stood in symbolic relations to the art and culture of my age."[5]

In this, Wilde and Shaw were close associates. Wilde's comedies offered a playful twist on modern dramatics; Shaw similarly would devise a studiedly realist *mise en scène*, only to overlay situation and dialogue with intentionally excessive rhetorical panache. He, too, tested the boundaries of acceptability: the insouciant portrayal of brothel Madam as a captain of industry in *Mrs Warren's Profession* (published 1898; first performed in 1902) fell foul of the Lord Chamberlain in 1893. As in *Pygmalion* (1913), agencies of speech had contagious, transformative power. *Man and Superman* (1905) was innovative in its refusal of plot and suspense, a celebration of philosophical fantasy that threatened to expand indefinitely. The prolix elaboration of his "metabiological pentateuch" *Back to Methuselah* (1922) stretched the point as if trying to reach the date when that sequence ends, AD 31920. Such strategies were part of a deeper impulse to blur the difference between narrative play and public intervention. If the sexual politics of Wilde's fall constituted a charged atmosphere through which his works would be absorbed, the social politics of Shaw's rise was energized by the prefaces, the pamphleteering and theatrical intrusion into public debates. He declared in *The Quintessence of Ibsenism* (1891): "the point to seize is that social progress takes effect through the replacement of old institutions by new ones."[6] True to his word, he inaugurated a tradition of political theatre at the Royal Court, London. The point was opinion formation, the enacted act of persuasion, and Shaw commanded attention. Prime Minister Arthur Balfour went to see Shaw's discussion of the "Irish Question," *John Bull's Other Island* (1904) five times – and took with him the Liberal opposition leaders Henry Campbell-Bannerman and Herbert Asquith.

Wilde and Shaw were Irish without being Irish revivalists. Nevertheless, their dazzling displays laid the ground rules for Irish modernist theatricalities: poetics and embodiment; metatheatrical reflexivity; paratheatrics and social involvement. The tensions implicit in these elements were amplified once Irish modernity did evolve a theatre it could call its own. In the context of cultural nationalism, the recognition of theatre's potency as a socially engaged medium made it a politically charged arena. Sure enough, the first production of the Irish Literary Theatre (ILT) in 1899, Yeats's *The Countess Cathleen*, drew controversy for its apparent exploitation of still-resonant Famine contexts for the purpose of showcasing symbolist tropes of artistic and aristocratic detachment. A polar opposite emerged in the 1902 debut performance of the ILT's long-lived successor, the Irish National Theatre Society. Yeats and Lady Gregory's one-act *Cathleen ni Houlihan* electrified radical nationalists with an incendiary combination of peasant realism and a symbolist incursion from an old woman whose mythic personification of Ireland demanded blood sacrifice to win national redemption. The poetic incantation formally asserted the force of literary evocation over realist depiction: speech that is not only capable of provoking action, but immediately involving and being action:

> They that had red cheeks will have pale cheeks for my sake; and for all that, they will think they are well paid.
>
> > [*She goes out; her voice is heard outside singing.*
> > They shall be remembered for ever,
> > They shall be alive for ever,
> > They shall be speaking for ever,
> > The people shall hear them for ever.[7]

The role had been given to Maud Gonne, the well-known republican firebrand, doubling its symbolist and avant-gardist potencies. Gonne produced a metatheatrical performance that was aware, even propagandistically proud, of its formalistic power as mythic national symbolism, yet was at the same time paratheatrical in stepping out of the fictive frame toward public speech, taking a revolutionary message directly to the audience.

Cathleen ni Houlihan's radical form won wide praise but the consensus was short-lived. As performed idealism, it was quickly taken up by nationalist voices keen to repeat its exemplary heroics. Propagandist Celtic theatrics were a performance staple in the hands of activists such as Bulmer Hobson, Alice Milligan, and Patrick Pearse, but their "archaic avant-garde"[8] became constrained by stilted virtue: challenge to social, sexual, or religious norms was not their point. (A more Ibsenite republicanism would be found at Edward Martyn's Hardwicke Theatre, where Thomas MacDonagh's *Pagans* and Eimar O'Duffy's *The Phoenix on the Roof* tested the waters in 1915.[9]) Lady Gregory experimented briefly with curious dramas of unreliable hearsay, *Spreading the News* (1904) and *Hyacinth Halvey* (1906), but in future kept clear of experimental realms. Yeats meanwhile retreated quickly toward Irish mythologies retold in the symbolist spectrum. The most successful – *The*

King's Threshold (1903), and *On Baile's Strand* (1903) – are allegories of political detachment rather than provocation.

The Abbey Theatre's forceful cultural centrality was secured, not by the single-minded republicanism of *Cathleen ni Houlihan*, but by J. M. Synge's dissident avant-gardism. Synge evolved rapidly from the representational security of his first works, *In the Shadow of the Glen* (1903) and *Riders to the Sea* (1904), toward an emphasis on perception as a shifting process rather than a fixed position. Importantly, reception became as much a subject as a consequence of his theatre. His evocation of rural Ireland, by turns unsparingly naturalistic and lyrically romantic, was initially admired but carried an emancipatory conviction and sexual frankness that was less welcome: the comic portrayal of adultery in *In the Shadow of the Glen* made plenty of enemies among conservative nationalists. The criticism that quickly surrounded such work braced Synge's formative convictions into more experimental directions. A traveller by inclination, at home in Wicklow, Dublin, and Paris, Synge's response was to remake his understanding into the unstable terrain of his masterpieces *The Well of the Saints* (1905) and *The Playboy of the Western World* (1907), in which the social position of imaginative power has become unsure. Vision in these plays is altered in use. Martin and Mary Doul of the *Well*, whose blindness is cured but who, in the light of their experiences, prefer to fade back to blackness, testify to the pleasures of imagination freed from social mores and jealousies. A wry critique of censorious watchfulness operates, as well as the shock of new ways of looking: as Martin Doul says, "there's few sees anything but them is blind for a space."[10] But at the end of the play the couple are cast out, in a critique of moral presumption on both sides: the people of the village shed any hope of change with their expulsion, while the Douls' departure is an ill-fated escape to delusional beauty. The twin tragedy suggests that the capacity to alter reality must work with hard facts of privation and death.

The *Playboy of the Western World* took this idea further again. Christy Mahon evolves from a guilty parricide to proud idol to scapegoat. Observing himself in the looking-glass he recognises reality as a pliable distortion: "it was the divil's own mirror we had beyond, would twist a squint across an angel's brow."[11] By the final scenes, of the binding and burning of Christy at the hands of his adoptive community, the Abbey audiences were themselves drawn into outraged intervention, shouting down the play. Violent rejection onstage and off is enjoined. Synge's provocation effected what he declared the following day – "an event in the history of the Irish stage."[12]

That shift from play to event marks out Synge's disruption of the complicities of representational form. No sooner had Molly Allgood/Pegeen declared, as if policing the borders between art and life, "there's a great gap between a gallous story and a dirty deed,"[13] than provocation to active interruption collapses such boundaries. Lady Gregory famously sent a telegram to Yeats, "Audience broke up in disorder at the word shift,"[14] but it would have been more accurate had she left "word" out of the sentence: Synge's shift is between the performed and the performative, as the play is arrested and the event begun. The *Playboy* carries this history, is always spectrally attended by its initial reception, but is much more than an Irish *épater le bourgeois*. Pegeen's closing line, "I've lost him surely,"[15] is echoed by Christy's embrace of empty power over his father and a romping lifetime devoid of intimacy. It bespeaks, rather than the victory of bridling modernist over staid public, a shared loss in mutual dismissal. From this point of view, the civic disturbance of "*Playboy* week" is not an amplification of tragic severance, but a comedic restoration of possibility. Provoking the riot, Synge's incitement interrupts disengagement by reengaging his public in a common manifestation of performed ideas.

Synge's breadth of influence in European modernism is testament to the variety in his work: Bertolt Brecht picked up on his sense of reflexive contingency, Federico García Lorca on his combustible mix of folk idiom and sex, Antonin Artaud on the riotousness. Yeats's reading of the *Playboy* was no less formative; for him, the play was about holding out and winning out to become the "master of all fights." "[I]t became possible to live" he declared, "when I had learnt all I had not learnt in shaping words, in defending Synge against his enemies."[16] In effect, he constructed a new final act starring himself: the *Playboy* debates, held at the end of the week of disturbances, in which he held sway in a theatrical parliament of warring opinion. This paratheatrical Yeats appears to counterpoint some of his symbolist staging strategies. While his drama, like the ship in *The Shadowy Waters* (1906), grew more pale and distant by degrees, his public persona grew, in inverse proportion, ever more combative.

The conjunction in Yeats of artist and public man is worth pondering, as it is inflected through his later theatre. In his early attempts to minimize physical presence in the symbolic reaches of his work, Yeats had National Theatre actors resist realism by restricting their movement as much as possible. The practice of rehearsing in barrels encapsulates the disembodying literary emphasis of his drama. But there are echoes of Alfred Jarry's and Edward Gordon Craig's ideas of the actor as "übermarionette," defamiliarising the body to emphasise the disorientations of modernity[17]; while Vsevolod Meyerhold's principles of bio-mechanics at the Moscow Art Theatre became a more overt expression of a similar distrust of natural movement. Yeats and Meyerhold both worked with Craig, whose use of hinged flats to create lighted screens for Yeats's *The Hour-Glass* in 1911 marks a process of syncretic reformulation following Synge's death. Yeats's poetry began to take on more edge, inflected by his fractious civic role; and his theatre changed again, catalyzed by the discovery of Noh theatre, via Ezra Pound. The raft of tensions between public space, the body, and the written and spoken word could be bound together. Following that other great "disturbing event," the revolutionary insurrection in Dublin during Easter 1916, the negotiation of symbolic and social realms was ever more urgent.

Yeats's association with Craig had suggested a new role for light in *mise en scène*, but the theatre he developed during the revolutionary period (1916–21) began by jettisoning symbolic light altogether. "The most effective lighting is the lighting we are most accustomed to in our rooms. These masked players seem stranger when there is no mechanical means of separating them from us," he deliberated.[18] In pulling drama out of the theatre and into lived space (albeit the chandeliered drawing room of Lady Cunard), Yeats was exploring a new interface between representation and presence.[19] What became *Four Plays for Dancers* (1921) are conceived not as a product or function of a designated theatre space, sequestered within civic, institutional walls, but an intrusion into the real, a stark display of the puzzling durability of the playing out of tales, begun with a spare statement of scenic poetry:

> The three musicians enter slowly. One carries a black cloth. He stands in the middle of the space. The others stand on either side and slowly unfold the cloth till a part of the stage is hidden. As they unfold it they move backward and outward so that the cloth makes an angle.[20]

Yeats's cloth acts as a symbol and manifestation of the fabric of being and imagination, revealing lived space as performance space, but only as the exterior enfolds the subjective, offering the display of unseen possibility. The tension between, on the one hand, the force of the symbolic (poetic speech, mask, archetype, and mythic character) and, on the other, the power of immersive somatic elements (music, decorative design, and, crucially, dance), is both the formal substance and the thematic matter of the enacted tales.

In *At the Hawk's Well* (1916), an archetypal study of an empty quest for immortality that denies fullness of life (the irony is that the well is also a metaphor for lost time), the young hero and Old Man also face an incursion into their reality. The story is disrupted by the bewitching distraction of the Hawk's dance – initially performed by Michio Itō, who possessed what Yeats called a "minute intensity of movement" – producing a mesmeric cessation of narrative. The dance is both symbolic of and embodies sensual life, bridging the phenomenon of the objective body in space and the symbolic abstraction denoting the unavoidable, immortal principle of mortality.

"O God," as the first musician says, "protect me / From a horrible death-less body / Sliding through the veins of a sudden."[21] The tension is further tested in *The Only Jealousy of Emer* (1922), a play of sexual fidelity and the fidelity of memory in which Fand, the Woman of the Sidhe, dances to draw Cuchulain into thoughtless physicality, with all the depthlessness of beauty.

Demonstration rather than evocation brought a new emphasis on wid-ening theatrical vocabularies, moving from dialogue to broader modern-ist aesthetics. The combinations of myth, music, lyric, and dance produced a minimalist *Gesamtkunstwerk* from which language is decentred. *At the Hawk's Well* was a collaborative work, requiring Yeats's text, Edmund Dulac's design, and Itō's dance; *The Only Jealousy* was later developed in response to a production devised by Albert van Dalsum, performed in Amsterdam in 1922, and in particular to five masks by Hildo Krop.[22] The result, *Fighting the Waves* (1929) was to be "more occasion for sculptor and dancer, for the exciting dramatic music of George Antheil"[23]; it too advanced from the association with Itō to a more thorough involvement dance via Ninette de Valois, whose ballet school had been brought within the ambit of the Abbey in 1927.[24]

At the Hawk's Well and *The Only Jealousy of Emer* enact symbolisms interposed with ambivalent embodiments; *The Dreaming of the Bones* (published 1919, first performed 1931) and *Calvary* (published 1921, first performed 1954) extended the interface into sociocultural process, into political and religious realms. In *The Dreaming of the Bones* the resonance is directly with the culmination of the Easter Rising in 1916 and intima-tions of the approaching War of Independence. The spirits of Diarmuid and Dervorgilla dance to be forgiven by a young rebel; cursed never to touch, they almost touch the imagination of the political mind. But the political mind is obdurate: "I had almost yielded and forgiven it all."[25] At first sight this might seem a rebuke to shrill extremists, a plea for a quietening of great hatreds. But it also warns of peril in the partnering of forgiveness with for-getfulness, when "the enemy has toppled roof and gable."[26] Here is a guard-ing of political priority, restraining both symbolic myth and beauty that in unremembering physicality suspends the world. Confronting the conscrip-tion crisis in 1918, Yeats could forcefully state of the play, "recent events have made it actual."[27]

In fact, "recent events" were increasingly interpreted as engaged in perfor-mance as well as being represented by performance. The Easter Rising had been quickly interpreted in theatrical terms, as a gesture of redemptive defi-ance, while the War of Independence and subsequent Civil War were waged not just through military attrition, but with strategic deployment of spectac-ular violence, of propaganda and acts of persuasive display.[28] Conversely, social space was contested and, with it, the running of theatres. *Feiseanna* were proscribed; curfews pared away at social time, turning out-of-hours cultural traffic into trespass. As elsewhere in Europe, the sense of increasing interpenetration between modes of performance and politics was particularly felt in the theatre, which in the 1920s processed these shocks. But, whereas in Europe social upheaval seemed a new normality, the Irish Free State began after the Civil War to consolidate Ireland's socially conservative dispensation. Irish modernity hatched its particular modernisms, which, rather like its revolution, were typified by partial rather than radical transitions.

Sean O'Casey's plays began, with *The Shadow of a Gunman* (1923) and *Juno and the Paycock* (1924), to update Synge's sensibility of contingent realism to revolutionary change. Shifting self-image and class image are combined into social instability and crisis, memorably figured in *Juno* as the "terr...ible state o'... chassis!"[29] *The Plough and the Stars* (1926) was a challenging piece of postrevolutionary reassessment: the misery and comedy of the tenements underpin a critique of war weighed on the scales of social justice. But the play also pushed beyond a straightforward realism toward a form of modernist hiatus, a temporary disjuncture intruding in realist convention that would be more fully found in *The Silver Tassie* (1929). In the second act of the *Plough*, the portrayal of Dublin life at the time of the Easter Rising produced the first Abbey riot since the *Playboy*.[30] Revered symbol and despised body are set side by side, the iconic tricolour brought within the pub, while Rosie Redmond the prostitute plies her seductions in ribald music-hall song. From outside the pub, the voice of Pearse presents a slice of verbatim theatre, importing the force of his instantly recognizable rhetoric, but simultaneously signaling its remoteness from a multivalent Ireland. Act II is, however, overtaken by the realities of conflict, and by Act IV the British occupation of the city replicates the confinement of curfew Dublin. Bessie's death drives home the final nail; until that point, Nora's distraught outbursts are a ghost of expressionist release. But faced with the motionless body on stage, Nora begins to speak for a reluctant audience: "don't leave me here to be lookin' and lookin' at it!"[31] In *The Silver Tassie* violence blasts a much bigger hole in realist tropes: Act II opens out to the battlefield, pictured in pastiche ritual and shattered song. But representational narrative returns and encases it too, as if in metal, just as "Dreams of line, of colour, and of form" are fastened into choral worship of the Howitzer that dominates the stage: "Jail'd in thy steel are hours of merriment / Cadg'd from the pageant-dream of children's play."[32] Afterward, Harry Heegan wakes to the hospital ward and the wheelchair, and the repressions of a new reality. An expressionist world appears, only to be swallowed up in refusal to face the war and its complex of terrors.

Yeats's excoriation of the Dublin audience over the *Plough* was another purposeful paratheatrical display. But he too closed the door on expressionist possibility at the Abbey by refusing not just *The Silver Tassie* but also Denis Johnston's *The Old Lady Says "No!"* (1929). O'Casey's and Johnston's works betrayed discomfort in a climate increasingly monitored by the Free State's censorious eye. Although Lennox Robinson had opened a radical valve in 1918 at the Peacock Theatre, where the Dublin Drama League could perform modernists such as Luigi Pirandello, August Strindberg, Ernst Toller, and Eugene O'Neill, the initiation of state subsidy in 1926 forced the Abbey into dulling negotiation.[33] The appetite for continental expressionism reveals impatience with habits of rural realism that, Yeats and O'Casey apart, came to dominate. As the Drama League's natural successor, the Dublin Gate Theatre became the viable alternative to the Abbey's staid attitudes. Erstwhile stalwarts such as Denis Johnston and Mary Manning transferred their allegiance forthwith.[34]

The shift away from the National Theatre also allowed other aspects of theatricality to emerge from the shadow of the play-text. From the start, the Gate Theatre prospectus very deliberately claimed modernist cachet: "It is proposed to open the Dublin Gate Theatre Studio in October, 1928, for the production of modern and progressive plays, unfettered by theatrical convention."[35] Yet its leading lights Micheál Mac Liammóir and Hilton Edwards were actors, scenographers, and directors, rather than writers. Both revelled in the opportunity to present full-blooded expressionist productions, opening by degrees to a wider vocabulary of theatrical presentation, and specifically intent on exposing naturalism as merely another formal style. What Hilton Edwards in 1934 called "the 'Theatre Theatrical'"[36] radically recalibrated any notional opposition between realism and modernism toward a spectrum on one palette.

The Gate's emphasis chimed with Artaud's maxim "it is the *mise en scène* that is theatre, much more than the written and spoken play."[37] Works were selected to test the boundaries of the possible. Their opening production was Henrik Ibsen's *Peer Gynt* (1876) featuring a cast of forty-eight on a thin strip of the Peacock stage. (Such epic instincts would be reinforced when the Gate moved to the Rotunda buildings, with a twelve-hour cycle of *Back To Methuselah* over three nights in 1930.) The restless exploratory staging of expressionist fare – O'Neill, Elmer Rice, Karel Čapek, Georg Kaiser – brought a new recognition of modernist theatrical vocabularies, particularly evident when the Gate found a native expressionist to include in its repertoire. *The Old Lady Says "No!"* was a metatheatrical indictment of Abbey rhetoric. Johnston's dream play presented nationalist theatricality itself as complicit in structuring Irish delusion, romantically lost in a fantasy past, and fantastically removed from the mundane bitterness of the present. In a Pirandellian blurring of stage reality and dream world, an actor playing Robert Emmet, deliriously concussed, roams a Dublin textured in quoted text and iconic idols. A scathing reincarnation of an "old tattered" Cathleen ni Houlihan appears, roaming the streets, singing snatches of ballads and Yeatsian verse between begging for coppers.[38] Opinion of the play was divided: Joseph Holloway, the veteran theatre diarist, was not alone in his short shrift, describing it as "a mad-house play for muck minded people!"[39] Constance Curran, the critics' critic, rhapsodised at length in the *Irish Statesman*:

> The play turns back on itself and phrases recur in new contexts in iridescent pattern. The characters, trailing the clouds of their old glory, are like those Chinese boxes ... the language gross, poetic, pseudo-poetic and grave ... from Irish folk songs through Callanan, Moore, Mangan, Blake, Swift, Sheridan, Wilde, Joyce, Shaw, Yeats, and O'Casey to Tim Healy.[40]

But what Holloway and Curran did agree on was the brilliance of the staging. Expressionism brought fresh aesthetics, particularly Edwards's technically assured simulation of space and atmosphere through light. The careful control in his almost abstract-expressionist colour composition is evident in his account of the *Peer Gynt* revival in 1932:

> Settings, costumes and lights were unified by being limited to two distinct and contrasting colour schemes ... lighting that varied from the deepest blue of night to the palest steel with no suspicion of any other colour. For the desert scenes, every tone of red and amber with lighting varying from deep orange to straw ... and later the solitary white of Peer, presently submerged in the red and gold of his oriental clothes and finally emerging once more in a single note of white.[41]

Edwards acted in conjunction with the stage design of Mac Liammóir, characterised by his fluent quotation of modernist stylistics. He could evoke Aubrey Beardsley in his designs for *The Importance of Being Earnest*, deploy a fairground pastiche of Henri Matisse and Jean Cocteau for Ferenc Molnár's *Liliom* (1909, Gate production 1934) or turn from the ornate Celtic revivalism of his own *Diarmuid agus Gráinne* (the inaugural production of the Irish-language theatre, Galway 1928) to Bauhaus functionality for Kaiser's futuristic *Gas* (1918, Gate production 1930).[42] Taken together, they produced a flexible stage practice that included expressionism within a wider category of the formally theatrical, making no style off limits for inventive exploration.

Importantly, all of Wilde's oeuvre could thus be returned to the theatrical repertoire: *Salomé* in a landmark statement of intent in 1928 and the comedies in frequent revival. The centrality of Wilde was bound up with a pragmatic performance of sexuality and national identity. Mac Liammóir's Irishness was a pose; although he maintained until his death that his boyhood was spent in Cork, he was born and raised in Kensal Green, London. His only Irish connection was found through a close friendship to an immigrant family in nearby Kilburn, woven into a formatively theatricalised experience as a childhood actor.[43] On the other hand, Mac Liammóir and Edwards's homosexual relationship became a tacitly understood aspect of their dual personas. Resonant fascination with the mask of Yeatsian revivalism and the posture of Wilde were to be expected, allowing as they did a space of uncertain display within which Mac Liammóir and Edwards could practice their sexual, as well as their professional, partnership.

This dimension of the Gate could also provide occasion for women to step beyond of the role of modernist performer (a genealogy here of Maud Gonne, Molly Allgood, de Valois, Billie Whitelaw) into authorial control. Manning's knowing satire on the caged ambitions of young Dublin, *Youth's the Season ... ?* (1931) crisply caught the moment. The effusive, camp excess of Desmond Millington and the brittle wit of Toots Ellerslie suggested a hopeful alliance and challenge to gender norms. Closeted domestic interiors in Acts I and III are (again) suspended in Act II for a freely drawn scene of cocktail-party fluidity before returning for brutal closure. The nascent literary intellectual Terence Killigrew, attended by his silent shadow Horace Egosmith, self-coruscates toward a concluding suicide. Manning's final comment on the position of women was not positive: the play's chill coda is Toots's frantic "I can't unlock the door! Help me Desmond! Somebody! Let me out!"[44]

The Gate's first decade was pursued with ferocious energy: 127 productions by the end of 1938, by which time its invention was flagging. But it put Yeats on his mettle, helping provoke a late burst of innovation. Attending the Abbey in August 1934, Samuel Beckett, aged twenty-eight, saw *Resurrection* (1934) and *The King of the Great Clock Tower* (1934). He had just received a commission to write on the censorship laws for the *Bookman* and noted, half approvingly, the elder statesman's latest attempts to provoke hostility with his late reprise of Salomé's death's-head dance: "the Valois rolling her uterine areas with conviction. And Dolan chanting what Yeats, greatly daring, can compose in the way of blasphemy, making the Christ convert the Plato."[45]

Beckett's debt to Yeats, particularly to the late play *Purgatory* (also attended in debut, 1938), was echoed in his own versions of the reiterative violence of perpetrator and victim: Pozzo and Lucky in *Waiting for Godot* (1953) and Hamm and Clov in *Endgame* (1957). Arguably, however, it is the culmination in Beckett of the suggestive tension between corporeal presence and structures of language that sets him in the tradition of outward-looking Irish modernism. Beckett is Irish-European – like Wilde he chose French as well as English for his linguistic medium – like Synge, Yeats, and Johnston, his work keeps dialogue with the somatics of music and movement so central to the dynamic theatrical modernism of the continental avant garde. Beckett's late transition to theatre came at least in part as a consequence of the limitations of the written word. The need to produce silence and absence as opposed to mere blankness was a crucial point of transition. He wrote to Axel Kaun in 1937:

> Is there any reason why that terrifyingly arbitrary materiality of the word surface should not be dissolved, as for example the sound surface of Beethoven's Seventh Symphony is devoured by huge black pauses ... it can only be a matter of somehow inventing a method of verbally demonstrating this scornful attitude vis-à-vis the word. In this dissonance of instrument and usage perhaps one will already be able to sense a whispering of the end-music or of the silence underlying all.[46]

The "dissonance of instrument and usage" that Beckett would seek to construct came through a recognition that silence could be achieved only through presence: silence, unlike blankness, was contextually constituted in the possibility of sound, requiring the manifest failure of speech. It was the capacity for theatre to demonstrate enduring failure that gave it the ability to confront the limits of art. Theatre alone of the literary modernisms would express that aspect of modernity that had as its symptom the failure of modernism itself. Lucky's first-act monologue in *Waiting for Godot* suggests the misfiring engine of Ireland's modernist eloquence (with Pozzo the expectant English audience),[47] as the language of Joyce and Synge stutters to a halt: "the skull the skull the skull the skull in Connemara."[48] But a characteristic exchange between Estragon and Vladimir acts out alternatives:

> Estragon: Off we go!
> *They embrace. They separate. Silence.*
> Vladimir: How time flies when one has fun!
> *Silence.*[49]

Estragon and Vladimir articulate intent, only to lapse into ineffective stasis, yet they also occupy the space that thickens with quiet purposelessness. The brief choreography of their affectionate gesture emphasises an obstinate persistence of life even as signification founders. If earlier explorations of the tensions between symbolic and somatic life had been generated by strategies of interruption – of narrative halted by dance, or even by riot – here the arrest is permanent.

Beckett's theatre thus fits within an Irish tradition of ambivalently physical theatre. Indeed, its physicality is selected from all possible media for the
specific capacity to show that ambivalence. Just as Beckett moved from the
novel to the theatre to accomplish substantial silence, his restless selection
of alternative media – of radio for *All that Fall* (1957) and *Embers* (1959),
of television for *Eh Joe* (1965) of film for *Film* (1965) – are always meta-
formally attuned, each commenting on the specific demands and limitations
that each medium makes on perception and its processes. It is a process
particularly evident where Beckett comments on mixed-media formalism,
most notably in *Krapp's Last Tape* (1958), with its fascination found in
live listening to the disembodiments of sound recording. But just as with
the dancers of Wilde and Yeats, or the anti-heroes of Synge and O'Casey,
Beckett's figures have embodied presence rendered ambiguous by an always-
also-symbolic aspect. In *Waiting for Godot*, Gogo and Didi, if down at heel,
are free of limb; but Pozzo and Lucky suffer creeping incapacitation. Beside
Hamm's immobility in *Endgame*, Nag and Nell dwell in bins, like two of
Yeats's actors in barrels. From half-buried Winnie in *Happy Days* (1961)
to *Play's* trio of potted heads (1963), Beckett's figures are typically less and
less dancer, more and more mask, as if progressively necrotised by symbolic
form. The occlusion of physical presence both emphasises the incomplete
condition of being – the disembodied mouth of *Not I* (1972) calling attention to a fragmentary understanding of self – and also reasserts its existence
as a broken remainder.

Beckett's longevity made him contemporary with a wide array of Irish
dramatists in the late twentieth century. In such company, it is noticeable
that Beckett's modernism was no less self-consuming in its paratheatrical
aspect – silence and curtailed speech were performatively exported beyond
the theatre walls. Even *Catastrophe* (1982) and *What Where* (1983),
which might be said to overtly repoliticize his form, both attack censorship through self-accusatory condemnations of theatrical interrogation.
Thus Beckett made reticence his loudest declaration of intent.[50] Not so with
the noisy legion of dramatists whose emergence coincided with new political crises in Ireland north and south from the 1960s on: Brian Friel, Tom
Kilroy, Stewart Parker, or Frank McGuinness – or of the avowedly activist interventions of Charabanc and the Field Day Theatre Company. Here
the alternative testing of performance-public dynamics present in earlier
Irish modernisms persisted in rich variety. A search for continuity would
be found less in Beckett than in the radical pairings of Sean O'Casey with
the People's Theatre in Newcastle-upon-Tyne in the 1940s, or of Brendan
Behan with Dublin's Pike Theatre and Joan Littlewood's Theatre Workshop
in the 1950s.

Ireland's late modern theatre has been most modernist when adhering to its rich tradition of theatrical flexibilities, literary and physical. The bed-bound storytellers voiced by Tom Murphy, Sebastian Barry, and Enda Walsh echo Beckettian immobility, but as a point of access to Irish memory that would be otherwise forgotten and misheard. Elsewhere the occult lyricism of Marina Carr's ghost plays owes much to Yeats's gift for creating unnerving presence, while Synge can be detected in Martin McDonagh's ingenious travesty of archetypes. This bastard modernism of Ireland also encompasses the directorial legacy of the Gate, that counterbalance of practitioners to playwrights evident for instance in the stagings of Garry Hynes, whose epic cycles *DruidSynge* (2005) and *DruidMurphy* (2012) recall the scale of Edwards-Mac Liammóir ambition. No less notice should be taken of the lineaments of dance theatre that stretch from the work of Michael Keegan-Dolan and Fabulous Beast back to *Salomé*. The modernist logic of encroaching absence is thus offset from the first by the physical bodies it cannot erase. The 1973 production of Beckett's *Not I* at the Royal Court was heightened by the obliteration of all light in the auditorium (exit sign bulbs removed),[51] but the intensity of focus on Billie Whitelaw's adrift illuminated mouth, remained inextinguishable – like a new Saturn that cannot consume all her children.

NOTES

1 Oscar Wilde, *Complete Works of Oscar Wilde* (London: Collins, 1966), 487.

2 Petra Dierkes-Thrun, *Salomé's Modernity: Oscar Wilde and the Aesthetics of Transgression* (Ann Arbor: Michigan University Press, 2011), 15–55.

3 Stephane Mallarmé, *Mallarmé in Prose*, Mary Ann Caws, ed., (New York: New Directions, 2001), 109.

4 Wilde, *Complete Works*, 559.

5 Wilde, *Complete Works*, 912.

6 George Bernard Shaw, *The Quintessence of Ibsenism* (London: Walter Scott, 1891), 94.

7 William Butler Yeats, *The Variorum Edition of the Plays of W. B. Yeats*, Russell K. Alspach, ed., (London: Macmillan, 1966), 229.

8 Terry Eagleton, *Heathcliff and the Great Hunger* (London: Verso, 1995), 273.

9 W. J. Feeney, *Drama in Hardwicke Street: A History of the Irish Theatre Company* (Rutherford: Fairleigh Dickenson University Press, 1984), 84.

10 J. M. Synge, *Collected Works*, vol. 3, *Plays*: Book 1, Ann Saddlemyer, ed., (London: Oxford University Press, 1968), 154.

11 Synge, *Collected Works*, vol. 4, *Plays*: Book 2, Saddlemyer, ed., (London: Oxford University Press, 1968), 95.

12 J. M. Synge, *The Collected Letters of J. M. Synge*, vol. I, *1871–1907*, Ann Saddlemyer, ed., (Oxford: Oxford University Press, 1983), 285.

13 Synge, *Collected Works*, 4, 169.

14 Lady Gregory, *Our Irish Theatre* (London: Putnam, 1913), 67.

15 Synge, *Collected Works*, 4, 173.
16 William Butler Yeats, *J. M. Synge and the Ireland of his Time* (Dublin: Cuala, 1911), 13.
17 Olga Taxidou, *Modernism and Performance: Jarry to Brecht* (London: Palgrave, 2007), 23–34.
18 Yeats, *Variorum Plays*, 399.
19 Michael McAteer, *Yeats and European Drama* (Cambridge: Cambridge University Press, 2010), 93.
20 Yeats, *Variorum Plays*, 398.
21 Yeats, *Variorum Plays*, 409–10.
22 Roselinde Supheert, *Yeats in Holland, The Reception of the Work of W. B. Yeats in the Netherlands before World War Two* (Amsterdam: Rodopi, 1995), 134–59.
23 Yeats, *Variorum Plays*, 567.
24 Richard Taylor, *The Drama of W. B. Yeats: Irish Myth and the Japanese Nō* (New Haven, CT: Yale University Press, 1976), 162–70; Sylvia C. Ellis, *The Plays of W. B. Yeats: Yeats and the Dancer* (London: Macmillan, 1995), 227–9.
25 Yeats, *Variorum Plays*, 775.
26 Yeats, *Variorum Plays*, 773.
27 R. F. Foster, *W. B. Yeats, A Life: II The Arch Poet* (Oxford: Oxford University Press, 2003), 126.
28 Paige Reynolds, *Modernism, Drama, and the Audience for Irish Spectacle* (Cambridge: Cambridge University Press, 2007), 116–55.
29 Sean O'Casey, *Collected Plays* I (London: Macmillan 1949), 89.
30 Nicholas Allen, *Modernism, Ireland and Civil War* (Cambridge: Cambridge University Press, 2009), 50–2.
31 O'Casey, *Collected Plays* I, 260.
32 Sean O'Casey, *Collected Plays* II (London: Macmillan, 1948), 54.
33 Lauren Arrington, *W. B. Yeats, the Abbey Theatre, Censorship, and the Irish State: Adding the Half-Pence to the Pence* (Oxford: Oxford University Press, 2010).
34 Brenna Katz Clarke and Harold Ferrar, *The Dublin Drama League, 1918–1941* (Dublin: Dolmen, 1979), 20.
35 National Library of Ireland, Ms 33,038.
36 "Production," *The Gate Theatre, Dublin*, Bulmer Hobson, ed. (Dublin: Gate Theatre, 1934), 22.
37 Antonin Artaud, *The Theater and Its Double* (New York: Grove, 1958), 41.
38 Denis Johnston, *The Old Lady Says "No!"*, Christine St. Peter, ed., (Washington, DC: Catholic University of America Press, 1992), 70.
39 The Diaries of Joseph Holloway, 4 July 1929. National Library of Ireland, Ms 1929.
40 *Irish Statesman*, No. 15, 13 July 1929.
41 "Production," *Gate Theatre*, 34.
42 Dublin Gate Theatre Papers, Northwestern University Library, Mss L1.15; H3.L; LF3a.
43 Christopher Fitz-Simon, *The Boys: A Biography of Micheál Mac Liammóir and Hilton Edwards* (London: Nick Hern, 1994), 20–2.

44 Mary Manning, "Youth's the Season...?," in *Plays of Changing Ireland*, Curtis Canfield, ed. (New York: Macmillan, 1936), 404.

45 *The Letters of Samuel Beckett 1929–1940*, Martha Dow Fehsenfeld and Lois More Overbeck, eds. (Cambridge: Cambridge University Press, 2009), 216.

46 Dow Fehsenfeld and More Overbeck, *Letters*, 518–19.

47 Fredric Jameson, *A Singular Modernity: Essay on the Ontology of the Present* (London: Verso, 2002), 201.

48 Samuel Beckett, *Waiting for Godot* (London: Faber and Faber, 1965), 44.

49 Beckett, *Waiting for Godot*, 76.

50 Alan W. Friedman, *Party Pieces: Oral Storytelling and Social Performance in Joyce and Beckett* (Syracuse, NY: Syracuse University Press, 2007), 143–79.

51 James Knowlson, *Damned to Fame: The Life of Samuel Beckett* (London: Bloomsbury, 1996), 595–9.

8

LUKE GIBBONS

Visual Modernisms

In 1942, a limestone panel depicting the Celtic sun god Lugh launching three aircraft was placed over the doorway of the new Government Buildings on Kildare Street, Dublin. The national airline, Aer Lingus, was then in its infancy, but the art deco lintel, carved by the sculptor Gabriel Hayes, provided a utopian glimpse of the future: like aviation, visual modernism promoted internationalism, but also drew on the past to fuse myth and technology, and to bring Irish culture into contact with the new self-images of an age.

The image was often ahead of its time in twentieth-century Ireland, thus forging important links between visual culture and modernism. Although the highpoint of Irish modernism is associated with the literary achievements of James Joyce and Samuel Beckett, the modernist turn was signalled earlier in the literary innovations of George Moore, and in Moore's writings on the visual arts based on his time in Paris in the 1870s, where he counted Édouard Manet and Edgar Degas among his friends. Moore's book *Modern Painting* (1893) introduced French Impressionism to the Anglophone world, and contained discussions of Manet, Degas, Claude Monet, and Camille Pissarro, as well as chapters on "The Camera in Art," "Sex in Art," and "The New Art Criticism."[1] Degas, Manet, Monet, and James McNeill Whistler were among the artists exhibited at the *Modern Paintings* exhibition in Dublin in 1899, but Moore's critical taste was not given full curatorial expression until Hugh Lane's *Exhibition of Pictures presented to the City of Dublin to form the nucleus of a Gallery of Modern Art* in 1904. Lane, a nephew of Lady Gregory, had amassed an impressive collection of modern art and this influential show included masterpieces by Manet, Degas, Monet, Pisarro, Pierre-Auguste Renoir, and Jean-Baptiste-Camille Corot, as well as important Irish painters, including Roderic O'Conor, Nathaniel Hone, Walter Osborne, William Orpen, John Lavery, and John B. Yeats. Lane's exhibition was part of an ambitious plan to build a gallery of modern art in Dublin showcasing his valuable collection, but Dublin Corporation stalled on the project. This famously provoked W. B. Yeats's ireful "September 1913," but also prompted Lane to bequeath thirty-nine key pictures in his collection to the National Gallery in London. Lane added a codicil stipulating that the paintings be returned to Dublin if a suitable gallery was built to house them, but the codicil was not witnessed, and Lane's death in the sinking of the *Lusitania* in 1915 brought a premature end to the possibility of Dublin acting as an outpost for modern art in early-twentieth-century Europe.[2]

Post-impressionism and academic realism were dominant styles in the early twentieth century, but even before World War I, a number of artists, including May Guinness and Mary Swanzy, had gravitated towards international modernism. Guinness was the first practicing artist to introduce a modernist sensibility into Irish art, encountering the work of Henri Matisse, Raoul Dufy, and other Fauvists at the Salon d'Automne following her 1905–7 stay in Paris, and then the more radical Cubism of Pablo Picasso and Georges Braque. Her composition *The Infant* (1905), showing a woman reading to a child, is comprised of intersecting planes balanced through linear rhythms and blocks of colour, and is one of the earliest fully realized Irish modernist paintings: "the first of her race," as James White declared at her *Memorial Exhibition* in 1956, "to paint her way into the heart and spirit of the new movement of the 20th century."[3] This early work prefigures the handling of colour and line in her later distinctive blend of Fauvism and Cubism. Guinness returned to France between 1922 and 1925 to study with the Cubist painter André Lhote. Her younger contemporary Swanzy also studied in Paris at this time, visiting Gertrude Stein's salon and incorporating elements of Paul Cézanne, Paul Gauguin, Matisse, Picasso, Braque, and, in particular, Robert Delaunay (with whom she exhibited at the Salon des Indépendants in 1914) into a technique in which sweeping arcs and angular planes intersected to animate the pictorial field.[4]

Marianne Hartigan has noted "that it was women who were the catalysts for the introduction of modernism into Irish art," and attributes this to their immunity from the public compromises necessary for a career in art: a female artist "did not have to bow to academia to make a living as a painter, but could afford to experiment and explore new methods."[5] These women were mostly from well-off Protestant backgrounds and this allowed for the kind of independent travel that freed more adventurous artists from the conservatism of Irish art schools. In 1920, Evie Hone and Mainie Jellett travelled to Paris to study with André Lhote, both having spent time in London art schools (Jellett studying with Walter Sickert), but France sparked a radical transformation in their work. The classical austerity of Lhote's Cubism lent itself to a purist style that suited the formal rigour of Jellett's and Hone's sensibilities. Within a short period, both had gravitated towards the more abstract but more fluid compositional style of Albert Gleizes, another leading Cubist. Gleizes's "Rustic Cubism" was influenced by Henri Bergson's theory of the "flow" of experience, and was also drawn to both Celticism and Catholic medievalism, all of which proved very fertile ground for the development of a distinctive Irish Cubism.[6] In the hands of Jellett, spatial planes and blocks of colour were imbued with rhythm and harmony, imparting a tonal quality to otherwise severe geometric abstractions. Curvilinear and angular patterns added vitality to her spatial compositions, attenuating the vestiges of figuration. Jellett's spiritual orientation embraced elements of Celticism and Christian devotion, particularly in recurrent treatments of the Madonna and Child, and on her return to Ireland she sought to reconcile modern European influences with Irish visual traditions: "If a Celtic artist of the 8th or 9th century were to meet a present day Cubist or non-representational painter, they would understand one another."[7] Hone's spiritual quest led to her conversion to Catholicism, and to the discovery of a new powerful visual medium in stained glass: in 1933, she joined An Túr Gloine, the pioneering stained glass studio set up by Sarah Purser (also an early visitor to Paris, and friend of Degas and Berthe Morisot). Hone's outstanding skill led to important religious commissions for church buildings and, most famously, for the east window of the chapel at Eton College.

Jellett and Hone exhibited their early Cubist work at the Society of Dublin Painters in October 1923, alongside work by Harry Clarke, Paul Henry, Grace Henry, Letitia Hamilton, Harriet Kirkwood, and others. The exhibition elicited mocking responses, provoking AE (George Russell) to write scornfully of finding "Miss Jellett a late victim to Cubism in some subsection of this artistic malaria."[8] Thomas MacGreevy defended the audacity of the exhibition, however, writing in the short-lived Dublin avant-garde periodical, *The Klaxon*, that it challenged not only the relation of art to the objective world but also to subjective life: "That the freedom from subject [matter], from painted psychology, from symbolism, has heightened the aesthetic value of her work is not, I think, to be doubted by anyone who has seen the pictures she has exhibited during the past four or five years."[9] MacGreevy repudiated the idea that modernism had retreated into subjectivity, proposing instead that "psychology has been subordinated to [the] aesthetic," a hollowing-out of the self later noted by his friend Beckett in Irish poetry of the 1930s.[10]

Borrowing a phrase from Joyce, Dorothy Walker identified "structural rhythm" as a recurrent principle in Irish modernism, pointing to a tendency to offset formal rigour by the fluidity and "lyrical force" of improvisation, and it is in this light that Eileen Gray's innovations in design and architecture in the 1920s are best viewed.[11] Born in Enniscorthy in 1878, Gray first experienced the shock of modernity on a visit to the spectacular Palace of Electricity at the *Exposition Universelle* in Paris in 1900. Like other Irish modernists, she attended art school in London and Paris and settled in France in 1907, training first in the specialist craft of lacquer, before moving into furniture design and interior décor. Gray's stylistic breakthrough came with her Transat chair design (1925), which combined the clean lines of a skeletal frame with the sunken curve of the seat, modelled on ocean liner deck-chairs. Breaking from the austere geometry of the De Stijl movement, the tactile quality of Gray's chair made it (in Philippe Garnier's rewording of Le Corbusier) "a machine for sitting in."[12] Gray's subsequent move into architecture placed her at the centre of the modern movement in the 1920s. In the design for her house overlooking the sea at Roquebrune-Cap-Martin in the south of France, E-1027, she drew once more on a nautical look, the tiered levels of the house simulating the superstructure of an ocean liner. Le Corbusier decorated the walls of the house with murals, and built his own rural retreat in the vicinity. Gray's best-known exercises in minimalism are the combination of vertical angles and curvilinear planes in her side-table designs for E-1027, using glass, chrome and tubular steel. *The Eileen Gray, Pioneer of Design* exhibition, organized by the Royal Institute of the Architects of Ireland at the Bank of Ireland in Dublin's Baggot Street in 1973, marked a belated Irish recognition of her achievements (she died in 1976).[13]

Irish architecture was the public face of visual modernism as demonstrated in the vast Shannon hydroelectric scheme at Ardnacrusha, Co. Clare (1925–9).[14] Notwithstanding its doctrinal conservatism, the Catholic church was also receptive to these trends, Barry Byrne's startling art deco church of Christ the King (1931) in Cork being rivalled by the extravagant use of mass-spectacle, neon-displays, aircraft flyovers, and broadcasting during the Eucharistic Congress in Dublin in 1932. Commissions for Evie Hone's stained glass were bound up with this forward-looking strand, as was the acceptance (on loan) of Georges Rouault's controversial *Christ and the Soldier* (also known as *Christ in His Passion)* (1930) by St. Patrick's College, Maynooth, following its rejection by the Municipal Gallery of Modern Art, Dublin, in 1942. Part of the appeal of modernism to religious authorities was the universalism of its spiritual elements (emphasized by artists such as Wassily Kandinsky and Rouault) but the paradox in Ireland was that a Celtic inflection, influenced by the revival, was considered by the Catholic church to bring an unwelcome national orientation, reconnecting the image with the material culture of politics and history.[15]

The architect Michael Scott became one of the most articulate exponents of modernist principles in the interwar period, inviting Walter Gropius to

Dublin in 1936 to lecture on the "International Style."[16] In 1939, Scott designed the concrete, glass, and steel Irish pavilion for that year's New York World Fair, whose curvilinear shamrock outline could be recognized only from the air. Scott invited Seán Keating and Maurice McGonigal to paint murals for the pavilion, which was also a showcase for work by Hone and Jellett. Hone executed her monumental *Four Green Fields* stained glass tableau, now in Government Buildings, Merrion Street, Dublin, whereas the murals of Irish cultural, rural, and industrial life devised by Jellett for the fair enjoyed another outing at the 1938 *Empire Exhibition* in Glasgow. Scott's landmark building, the Dublin central bus station, Busáras, was built between 1945 and 1953, the austerity of an L-shaped glass and concrete main building being counterpointed by the curved, scallop effect on the canopy over the boarding area.[17]

Although visual modernism is frequently equated with Cubism, abstraction, and spatial form, expressionism also exerted an influence on Irish culture in the early decades of the state, particularly in theatre through the pioneering efforts of the Dublin Drama League. Productions at the Peacock Theatre such as Georg Kaiser's *From Morn to Midnight* (1927) and Ernst Toller's *Hoppla, We're Alive!* (1929) called for striking sets that attracted European-inspired artists like Harry Kernoff and Norah McGuinness to stage design.[18] McGuinness, born in Derry, studied initially in Dublin with Harry Clarke and was also a protégée of Lhote's school in Paris. In much of her work, she fuses Cubist compositional techniques with a vivid colour sense akin to that of expressionism. She exhibited at the Wertheim Gallery in London and the Paul Reinhardt Gallery in New York but, in addition to stage design, also worked in shop window display for Altman's and Helen Rubenstein in New York, as well as Brown Thomas in Dublin – another indication of the manner in which the unavailability of a public career in the academy forced modernist artists to work in commercial life, or in other cultural forms.[19]

The crossing of expressionism and Cubism in Irish modernism was not confined to theatre and the visual arts but also informed one of the few indigenous film productions of the interwar years, Denis Johnston's *Guests of the Nation* (1935), a silent adaptation of Frank O'Connor's 1931 short story of the same name. Shot on 16mm, with a scenario by Mary Manning, the film lacked professional production qualities but more than compensated with compelling performances (especially from Barry Fitzgerald). The low-budget production also showed considerable visual sophistication, as in the expressionist use of shadow and silhouettes, cutaways to highlight emotionally charged objects (clocks, footprints), and montage sequences of extreme close-ups cut in an almost Cubist compositional style. Johnston went on to act in Brian Desmond Hurst's 1935 film version of John M. Synge's *Riders to the Sea* (1904) but devoted his creative energies to becoming one of Ireland's leading dramatists, never realizing the cinematic potential shown in his improvised silent film.[20]

Although expressionism is usually seen as a mainland European "import" to Ireland, the painting career of Jack B. Yeats shows that while international currents exerted an influence, stylistic breakthroughs also arose from indigenous cultural impulses. Yeats's late style shows affinities with the Austrian expressionist Oskar Kokoschka who visited Ireland as early as 1928, but there is no record of the painters having met on this occasion, or of Yeats's early familiarity with Kokoschka's work (though they became friends later in life). Critical accounts of Yeats tend to identify early representational or illustrative work with his formative phase during the Irish revival, but attribute the growing consciousness of form and preoccupation with paint as a medium in mid-career to a subjective turn.[21] However, the pictorial abandon and density of paint in Yeats's late work suggests another possibility: that the recourse to form is not a retreat into subjectivity but a more complex, painful engagement with the Ireland of his time. Thomas MacGreevy's determination to claim Yeats as "Ireland's national painter" was famously opposed by Beckett's counter-claim that Yeats's formal experimentation marked him out as a leading European modernist, but it may be that it is the obliquity singled out by Beckett that carries the deepest engagement with Irish culture.[22] The challenge to representation derived not just from the international style but from a crisis of representation in Irish culture itself, produced by the fissures of the Civil War and the contested legitimacy of the new repressive Free State. Beckett noted, like many others, that abstraction marked the end of representation; but, rather than seeing this as cause for celebration, it was as if art was in mourning for the "lost object."[23] The object for Beckett migrated to form: commenting on Joyce's *Work in Progress*, he wrote: "Here form *is* content, content *is* form. You complain that this stuff is not written in English. It is not written at all.... His writing is not *about* something, *it is that something itself*."[24] The recourse to form, in other words, was not a retreat from external reality but a means of expressing truths that lay beyond the surface appeal of realism.

It is usual to note a transition from line to colour midway through Yeats's career, but the end of the line was already apparent in the seeming indeterminate shapes that begin to appear in his sketchbooks in response to political upheavals in Ireland. MacGreevy remarked of the events of the Irish Revolution that they were "too obscure to have become completely articulate in art," but it was this obscurity that Yeats articulated in his formal strategies.[25] Beckett wrote of the "space that intervenes between him [the artist] and the world of objects" as a "no-man's land, Hellespont or vacuum, according as he happens to be feeling resentful, nostalgic or merely depressed. A picture by Mr Jack Yeats, Mr Eliot's 'Waste Land' [1922], are notable statements of this kind."[26] If the desolation of World War I lies behind "The Waste Land," the violence of the Irish Revolution and the Civil War haunted the no-man's land of Yeats's later work. As he moved away from representation, there is an increased reliance on memory rather than observation, but these reminiscences are increasingly lodged in the physical gestures of paint on canvas resembling the body's own relation to expression. The obscuring of content does not mean it has been spirited away, but that is has been pressed – one might even say repressed – into form. Instead of a subjective vision, "de-materialization" of content is accompanied by an increased materialization of surface, paint, and application. Energy, rhythm, and movement are manifested in colour and composition, but with the blocking off – or blocking in – of subjectivity, politics is rerouted into the material texture of the medium. As John Berger wrote following his meeting with Yeats in 1956, the painter's work is marked not by inwardness but by an "outward-facing expressionism [that] is the natural style of art for previously exploited nations fighting for independence."[27]

It is in this charged recourse to form that MacGreevy also discerns the red hues of World War II in Yeats's powerful *Tinker's Encampment: the Blood of Abel* (1940). In this work, the coagulated paint and riot of colour bear witness to the ferocity of "faction" fighting on a global scale, but the flashlight held by a child in the bottom corner raises the possibility, however remote it seemed at the time, of a space beyond representation – a world beyond the carnage. As the turbulence in Irish life passed out of content into form in Yeats's work, politics had less to do with overt subject matter (though such topics continued to present themselves) than with the fall-out from the revolution that informed even the most desultory, everyday scenes.

If, as Jim Shanahan notes, "applying 'Irish' or any other national designation to any form of modernism appears on first consideration to be an oxymoron,"[28] then the impact of the White Stag movement on Irish art during World War II might have something in common with another animal species of oxymoron, the Irish bull. That an initially foreign group represented a high point in Irish modernism is one paradox: that the group flourished during the "Emergency" of World War II, when Ireland was supposedly cut off from the outside world, is another.[29] Originally comprising of two émigrés who arrived in Ireland in 1940, Basil Rákóczi and Kenneth Hall, the movement is credited with opening Irish art to the latest currents in European modernism, particularly those influenced by psychoanalysis and expressionism. The unusual title and personal names suggested exotic origins but the group was entirely British, Rákóczi changing his name from Beaumont to that of his Hungarian father in the 1930s (but also maintaining an attachment to Ireland through his Cork-born mother). The strong interest of the movement in psychology led to a cultivation of child-like qualities in art, and to attempts to capture early or unconscious formative experiences: "a strange world," wrote Rákóczi, "in which the familiar blends with the weird, fragmentary, infantile memories."[30] Stylistically, this took the form of an expressionist use of line, influenced by Kandinsky or Paul Klee, as well as colour, which lent itself to primary shapes such as the circle, triangle, and, closer to child-psychology, aspects of the human face, including the all-seeing eye.

The adoption of the term "subjective art" was in keeping with this psychological approach, suggesting that the turn to inner life rather than public culture was the only course open to a modernist aesthetic in a peripheral country such as Ireland. The irony here is readily apparent, as it was in Irish public culture that the group attained its highest profile. In due course, Irish artists identified with the White Stag movement, most notably Patrick Scott, then in his early twenties, Thurloe Connolly, Ralph Cusack, the composer and painter Brian Boydell, and others. Building on early shows in 1940, the efforts of the group culminated in the *Exhibition of Subjective Art*, held in Dublin in January 1944. The influential English critic Herbert Read wrote the introduction to the catalogue, which was later expanded as "On Subjective Art," in *The Bell* magazine in Ireland, and in Cyril Connolly's periodical *Horizon* in England.[31]

Institutionally, modernism attracted little support in academic art circles and one of the few outlets was provided by the Society of Dublin Painters, founded in 1920 by Paul Henry, Jack B. Yeats, Mary Swanzy and others. The rejection of two paintings by Louis le Brocquy, *The Spanish Shawl* and *Image of Chaos*, by the Royal Hibernian Academy in 1942, and further rejections of le Brocquy and Nano Reid in 1943, showed that Irish modernism was still in the margins. To redress this deficit, the first *Irish Exhibition of Living Art* was held in September 1943, featuring le Brocquy, Jellett, Hone, Reid, McGuinness, Jack Hanlon, and Patrick Scott among the seventy-four Irish artists on display – "the most vital and distinguished exhibition of work by Irish artists that has ever been held," in the words of the *Irish Times* – and the organizers constituted themselves as a committee, with Jellett as chair.[32] The exhibition showcased the range of modernist strands in Irish art: Cubism and Fauvism (Guinness, Jellett, Swanzy, McGuinness, Reid), expressionism (Jack B. Yeats), surrealism (Colin Middleton, Nick Nicholls),

White Stag-affiliated artists (Patrick Scott, Connolly, Cusack), and social realism (Sean Keating's *Tip Wagons at Poulaphouca*).

The anomalies of Irish visual modernism, and the politics of national canon formation, are perhaps most apparent in the career of le Brocquy (1916–2012). During the post-World War II period in which he established a reputation as a British painter, le Brocquy merited inclusion in the modernist canon, as in the *40 Years of Modern Art* show at the Institute of Contemporary Arts, London in 1948. His subsequent return to the Irish art world in the 1960s led to a pre-eminence at home that was achieved, however, at the cost of his international reputation, as if, re-enacting earlier critical responses to Jack B. Yeats and the White Stag group, modernism and Irish culture were mutually exclusive.[33] Herbert Read's popular Pelican book, *Contemporary British Art* (1951), includes le Brocquy, Francis Bacon, and the Northern Irish sculptor F. E. McWilliam in a list of artists displaying surrealist qualities, but proposed that they did not constitute a vigorous surrealist movement "due to anti-organizational traits in the *English* character rather than to any absence of appropriate talent."[34] F. E. McWilliam was the only Irish visual artist directly associated with the surrealist movement on these islands, arising out of his involvement with the *International Surrealist Exhibition* (1936) organized by Read and others in London. Influenced by Constantin Brancusi and Alberto Giacometti, McWilliam was a friend and contemporary of Henry Moore, and while maintaining a high international profile throughout his career, is perhaps best known in Ireland for his sculpture of the Irish legendary figure, Princess Macha, at Altnagelvin Hospital, Derry, in 1957. McWilliam's friend, William Scott, born in Scotland but raised in Fermanagh, also figured prominently in Read's modernist British canon, and established a distinctive style in elemental still lifes, embodying sensual colours and shapes in a figural abstract style seen to telling effect in his massive mural commissioned also for Altnagelvin hospital (1958–9). Other Irish artists worked in surrealist idioms but took their bearings from the European mainland, Nevill Johnson from a surrealist exhibition in Paris, and Colin Middleton from a trip to Belgium. Middleton's work is indebted to René Magritte, and Johnson's apocalyptic *Europe 1945* (1945) to dystopian Salvador Dalí-esque landscapes.[35] It is easy on this account to see how modernist developments are attributed to external connections, whereas Irish culture is considered – at most – to be responsible for content, or the forces that drove artists to search abroad for inspiration in the first place.

For this reason, it is not surprising that Louis le Brocquy's Irishness, when it was acknowledged, was linked to the Romantic Ireland of W. B. Yeats and James Stephens, author of *The Crock of Gold* (1912). That this militated against the very idea of modernism was underlined by Read, recounting his early encounters with the artist:

> The painter from Joyce's Dublin did seem when I first met him in 1944 to have some qualities of Celtic origin. His images might have been found in a crock of gold, and both Yeats the poet and his brother the painter might have been amongst his ancestors. But since then le Brocquy's art has become emancipated from provincial myth and is now both independent and universal.[36]

In this formulation, le Brocquy's modernist universality is only achieved at the expense of his Irishness (that is, "provincial myth") – a shedding of nationality not required in the case of British artists. That the universality of the image might consist in a cross-cultural capacity to address different visual communities, rather than aspiring to a generalized humanism or formalism, is not considered. Cultural diversity is more in keeping with vernacular modernism rather than high modernism, and is latent in le Brocquy's *Tinker* series, the same theme that allowed Jack Yeats, in *Tinker's Encampment* (1941), to bridge the local and the universal. Le Brocquy's encounter with a tinker encampment in Tullamore in 1945 inspired a series of more than twenty paintings dealing with the "freedom" of the Traveller lifestyle – an ambiguous freedom, as Ernie O'Malley wrote at the time, not unlike that enjoyed by the artist as outsider.[37] Yet in its theme of outcasts, the *Tinker* series also visualized the fate of the dispossessed of Europe in the aftermath of World War II, a far cry from any form of aesthetic nomadism.

A similar range of national and international references cross-cut le Brocquy's most famous painting, *A Family* (1951), which won the Prealpina prize at the Venice Biennale in 1956. Initially painted for the Festival of Britain exhibition, *Sixty Paintings for 1951*, it was exhibited at le Brocquy's first major Irish show in the Victor Waddington Gallery, Dublin, in 1951. The stark grey finish and elemental figures, exposed under stark electric light, were conceived, as le Brocquy himself noted, in the face of atomic threat and the social upheavals of World War II: "it was painted while contemplating a human condition stripped back to Paleolithic circumstances under the electric light bulbs."[38] As Medb Ruane has suggested, the forlorn family in a bedroom resembling a hospital setting also acquires a local resonance in that it was painted at the height of the controversy surrounding the Mother and Child Scheme in Ireland in 1951, when the Catholic church sought to prevent the family from coming under the provision of the welfare state – a fact that may explain Dublin Corporation's refusal to accept an anonymous donation of the work for the Municipal Gallery of Modern Art in 1952.[39] It is not that local and universal interpretations contradict each other; instead, they point to a wide cross-cultural range of reference, complemented by the compositional debt to Manet's *Olympia* (1863), and Picasso's *Guernica* (1937). In this, le Brocquy's work challenges the prejudice that marginal locations militate against international status: the unspoken assumption here is that *some* locations matter more than others, particularly those of the metropolitan centre.

Although Francis Bacon's reputation was made entirely in England, he was born in Dublin and lived in Kildare and Laois during the War of Independence and the Civil War period. His renderings of the body as a theatre of pain suggest a world not unlike that of Beckett, in which subjectivity offers no repose. "What directly interests [Bacon]," wrote Gilles Deleuze, "is a violence that is involved only with colour and line: the violence of a sensation (and not of a representation), a static or potential violence, a violence of reaction and expression."[40] Inner experience is not the domain of psychology but of physiology, as if the raw experience of pain does not make it to the mind but is dispersed throughout the body in lesions of shape and colour. Jellett's and Hone's recoil from a crumbling Anglo-Irish world encouraged a flight into spirituality and even a measure of accommodation with the Catholic church, but in Bacon's work, the "Popery" of his studies of Velázquez's Pope Innocent X summons up a chamber of horrors reminiscent of the Protestant Gothic imagination of nineteenth-century Ireland.[41] For all the immediacy of sensation, Bacon's evisceration of images has as much to do with the stylistic codes of genre and the artistic canon (Diego Velázquez, Nicolas Poussin, Sergei Eisenstein) as with reflexes of the nervous system. Loss of self is closer to the bone than self-expression, as befits an artist who looked to the crucifixion for a self-portrait: even in his particular studies of individuals, wrote Ernst van Alphen, Bacon displays the "power of the portrait to threaten subjectivity."[42]

The *Irish Exhibition of Living Art* was the driving force in extending the boundaries of modernism in Irish art from its founding in 1943, under the stewardship of Norah McGuinness who succeeded as chair following Mainie Jellett's untimely death in 1944. The commercial patronage required to bring this art to the buying public was significantly expanded with the opening of the Waddington Gallery (the main outlet for Jack B. Yeats), and the Dawson Gallery in 1944, whose position in the forefront of contemporary Irish art was shared with the David Hendriks Gallery (opened in 1956). It is striking that as Abstract Expressionism, the last phase of high modernism, was becoming hegemonic on the international scene during the Cold War, Celticism also came in from the cold in the *Rosc* exhibitions, designed to open an insular Irish art scene to the most dynamic currents in the international art world. "Rosc" means the "poetry of vision" in the Irish language, but that was the extent of the concession to Irish modernism in the first two *Rosc* exhibitions in 1967 and 1971. The ambitious scheme to showcase international art on a grand scale was the brainchild of Michael Scott and the distinguished Irish-American critic and curator, James Johnson Sweeney (former director of the Museum of Modern Art in New York, and former curator of the Guggenheim Museum).[43] The initial *Rosc* exhibition opened at the Royal Dublin Society (RDS) in late 1967, and featured some of the biggest names in modern art: Pablo Picasso, Joan Miró, Karel Appel, and Bacon (seen as international rather than Irish), as well as icons of the American avant garde such as Willem de Kooning, Barnett Newman, Kenneth Noland, Robert Rauschenberg, Roy Lichtenstein, and Jim Dine.

The longstanding perception that contemporary Ireland was inimical to the spirit of modernism informed the decision to exclude Irish artists from the first two *Rosc* shows (although the motif and installation schemes for the first two exhibitions were designed by Patrick Scott, who had also trained as an architect). To compensate for this, the selection jury took the controversial decision to exhibit the glories of ancient "Celtic" art alongside contemporary international works – the transience of the modern borrowing the aura of artefacts that stood the test of time, whereas Irish "vision," in turn, basked in the reflection of international style, as if making up for the lost ground of centuries. This conjunction of the archaic and the avant garde was consistent with the modernist fascination with primitivism, but was also in keeping with formalist criticism that looked to art solely for its internal qualities, abstracted from historical or cultural contexts. Prehistoric gold artefacts, stone carvings, and early Christian decorative and religious objects were lifted out of their material or cultural settings to be placed alongside the modernist bravura of the work on show at the RDS. In some cases, this involved physical lifting, leading residents in Carndonagh, Co. Donegal, to organize a sit-in around a high cross to prevent its removal to Dublin. In other cases, the borrowing was institutional, but the response was also less than enthusiastic: the director of the National Museum refused to let objects steeped in heritage leave the museum, even though they were organized in a special exhibition to complement the RDS show. Some ancient artefacts were eventually installed in the exhibition alongside contemporary works "to demonstrate," as Dorothy Walker wrote, "that the art of past can share both spirit and appearance with the art of the present."[44] Although appearing to validate the Irish visual imagination, the exhibition did the opposite, divesting the image in Ireland of all claims to be modern in the name of antiquity.

The controversy surrounding *Rosc* was a minor affair but a symptom nonetheless of a crisis within the dehistoricizing tendencies of modernism. The rise of pop-art, minimalism, and conceptual art challenged the self-contained nature of the high modernist aesthetic, raising questions relating to spectatorship, the canon, and gallery space theorized in Brian O'Doherty's publication, *Inside the White Cube* (1976), and Rosalind Krauss's "expanded field" of sculptural space.[45] Under postmodernism and postcolonialism, this opening up was extended to wide-ranging reappraisals of regional and vernacular modernisms, culminating in the critical storm that followed the Museum of Modern Art exhibition, *"Primitivism" in 20th Century Art: Affinity of the Tribal and the Modern*, in New York in 1984. These critical turns signalled, in different ways, the end of high modernism, showing a new sensitivity to place and region, as in Kenneth Frampton's concept of "critical regionalism," or, in postcolonialism, to the effects of globalization on the excluded "others" of Western modernity.

As a riposte to the exclusion of Irish artists in the second *Rosc* of 1971, Brian O'Doherty, one of the Irish artists who enjoyed an international reputation, curated *The Irish Imagination* exhibition at the Municipal Gallery in the same year, showcasing the best in contemporary Irish art. In the exhibition catalogue, O'Doherty noted the absence in Irish art of many of the vogues and "isms" that featured on the international scene, but added that this was not necessarily a failure to "catch up"; it may have been a refusal to settle for "doppelganger provincialism."[46] In the 1960s, for example, Patrick Scott's experiments with soaking paint in umprimed canvas paralleled the acclaimed staining techniques of Helen Frankenthaler and Morris Louis, but did not derive from them.[47] By the same token, the Paris-based artist Michael Farrell drew on Celtic curvilinear designs in his abstract *Pressé* works but, like Robert Ballagh, gradually moved towards more figurative, highly stylized large canvases gesturing towards Pop Art, in response to the political conflict in Northern Ireland. In seeking to account for distinctive strands in Irish modernism, the recourse to Celticism became a standard trope, but, from a postcolonial position, this might be reconcepualized as an assertion of peripheral modernism, attesting to the power of marginal cultures to negotiate, with different degrees of success, the terms of their own diverse engagements with dominant international styles and, indeed, new realignments of cultural capital under globalization.

In 1977, the third *Rosc* exhibition opted for the inclusion of Irish artists for the first time, selecting O'Doherty (now "Patrick Ireland") and James Coleman in an exhibition devoted primarily to contemporary European art. O'Doherty featured the *Rope* drawings that became a stylistic signature of his work, and Coleman exhibited his black and white film installation, *Box (ahhareturnabout)* (1977), a landmark in contemporary Irish art. *Rosc* 1980 featured a wide range of Irish artists including Coleman, le Brocquy, Michael Craig-Martin, Patrick Scott, William Scott, Cecil King,

Nigel Rolfe, Robert Ballagh, Alastair MacLennan, and "the most 'Irish' of all, Sean Scully, who true to Irish paradox, has become an American citizen," and whose striped patterns of line and colour broke new ground in Irish abstraction.[48] In 1984, Dorothy Walker could proclaim that the monolith of modernism was broken up to introduce a welcome diversity, illustrated by German New Expressionism, Italian Trans-avant-garde, French New Figuration, and other geographical modernisms.[49] That cultural crossings may have their own irony is clear from the relocation of the emigré Francis Bacon's studio to the Dublin City Gallery The Hugh Lane in 2001, the exhibition space that arose from Lane's shattered hopes for Irish art. Out of such debris and displacements, Irish modernism itself was made.

NOTES

1 George Moore, *Modern Painting* (London: Walter Scott, 1893).

2 Robert O'Byrne et al., *Hugh Lane: Founder of a Gallery of Modern Art for Ireland* (London: Scala, 2008).

3 James White, "Introduction," *May Guinness Memorial Exhibition Catalogue* (Dublin: Dawson Gallery, 1956).

4 Mary Swanzy, *Retrospective Exhibitions of Paintings* (Dublin: Municipal Gallery of Modern Art, 1968); Julian Campbell, *An Exhibition of Paintings by Mary Swanzy, H.R.H.A (1882–1978)* (London; Pyms Gallery, 1986); Alan and Mary Hobart, *An Exhibition of Paintings by Mary Swanzy, H.R.H.A (1882–1978)* (London; Pyms Gallery, 1998).

5 Marianne Hartigan, "Irish Women Painters and the Introduction of Modernism," in James Christen Steward, ed., *When Time Began to Rant and Rage: Figurative Painting from Twentieth-Century Ireland* (London: Merrell Holberton, 1998), 64.

6 Bruce Adams, *Rustic Cubism: Anne Dangar and the Art Colony at Moly-Sabata* (Chicago: University of Chicago Press, 2004).

7 Bruce Arnold, *Mainie Jellett and the Modern Movement in Ireland* (New Haven, CT: Yale University Press, 1992), 181.

8 *Irish Statesman*, 27 October 1923, cited in Arnold, *Mainie Jellett*, 80.

9 Thomas MacGreevy, "Picasso, Maimie [sic] Jellett and Dublin Criticism," *The Klaxon*, 1 (1923–4), reprinted in Fintan Cullen, ed., *Sources in Irish Art* (Cork: Cork University Press, 2000), 254.

10 MacGreevy, "Picasso," 255. See also Samuel Beckett, "Recent Irish Poetry" (1934), in *Disjecta: Miscellaneous Writings and a Dramatic Fragment*, Ruby Cohn ed. (London: John Calder, 1983), 70

11 Dorothy Walker, "The New Tribalism," *Rosc: The Poetry of Vision* (Dublin: Rosc, 1984), 20. The phrase is Stephen Dedalus's from the "Circe" chapter in James Joyce, *Ulysses* (1922).

12 Philippe Garnier, *Eileen Gray: Design and Architecture 1878–1976* (Cologne: Taschen, 1993), 7–8.

13 Dorothy Walker, "L'Art de Vivre: The Designs of Eileen Gray (1878–1976)," *Irish Arts Review* 15 (1999), 118–25.

14   Sorcha O'Brien, "Technology and Modernity: The Shannon Scheme and Visions of National Progress," in Linda King and Elaine Sisson, eds., *Ireland, Design and Visual Culture: Negotiating Modernity*, 1922–1992 (Cork: Cork University Press, 2011), 59–74.

15   For the conflict between revivalist and "universalist" elements in religious design, see Mary Ann Bolger, "The Ephemera of Eternity: The Irish Catholic Memorial Card as Material Culture," in King and Sisson, eds., *Ireland, Design and Visual Culture*, 235–50.

16   Ellen Rowley, "The Conditions of Twentieth-Century Irish Architecture," in Enrique Juncosa and Christina Kennedy, eds., *The Moderns: The Arts in Ireland from the 1900s to the 1970s* (Dublin: Irish Museum of Modern Art, 2011), 418–28; Paul Larmour, *Free State Architecture: Modern Movement Architecture in Ireland, 1922–1949* (Oysterhaven: Gandon Editions, 2009).

17   It is striking that this juxtaposition of curve and cube also features in Kevin Roche's design of the Convention Centre, Dublin, one of the few architectural showcases of the Celtic Tiger era. Roche, born and educated in Ireland, achieved international eminence as an architect working in the United States: see Ellen Rowley, "From Mitchelstown to Michigan: Kevin Roche's Formative Years," in *Irish Journal of American Studies* (Summer 2009).

18   Elaine Sisson, "Experimentalism on the Irish Stage: Theatre and German Expressionism in the 1920s," in King and Sisson, eds., *Ireland, Design and Visual Culture*, 39–58.

19   Anne Crookshank, *Norah McGuinness: Retrospective Exhibition* (Dublin: Trinity College, 1968); Marianne Hartigan, "The Commercial Design Career of Norah McGuinness," *Irish Arts Review* 3 (1986).

20   Kevin Rockett, "Guests of the Nation," *The Irish Filmography* (Dublin: Red Mountain Media, 1996); Kevin Rockett, Luke Gibbons, and John Hill, *Cinema and Ireland* (London: Routledge, 1988), 60–2.

21   Thomas MacGreevy, *Jack B. Yeats: An Appreciation and an Interpretation* (Dublin: Victor Waddington Publications, 1945), 26–7.

22   MacGreevy, *Jack B. Yeats*, 10; Samuel Beckett, "MacGreevy on Yeats" (1945) and "Hommage à Jack B. Yeats" (1954), in Roger McHugh, ed., *Jack B. Yeats: A Centenary Gathering* (Dublin: Dolmen Press, 1971).

23   Samuel Beckett, "Les peintres de l'empêchement," *Disjecta*, 136, translated in David Lloyd, "Republics of Difference: Yeats, MacGreevy, Beckett," *Field Day Review* 1, 64.

24   Samuel Beckett, "Dante ... Bruno. Vico ... Joyce," *Disjecta* 27.

25   MacGreevy, *Jack B. Yeats*, 26.

26   Samuel Beckett, "Recent Irish Poetry" (1934), *Disjecta* 70

27   John Berger, "Jack Yeats" (1962), in *Selected Essays and Articles: The Look of Things* (Harmondsworth: Penguin, 1972), 59.

28   Jim Shanahan, "'Vivid Irish History': Frank Mathew's *The Wood of the Brambles* and the Prehistory of Irish Modernist Fiction," in Edwina Keown and Carol Taaffe, eds., *Irish Modernism: Origins, Contexts, Publics* (Oxford: Peter Lang, 2010), 33.

29   Clair Wills, *That Neutral Island: A Cultural History of Ireland During the Second World War* (London: Faber, 2007), 283–7.

30   Basil Rákóczi, "Painting the Unconscious," *Commentary* (January 1942), cited in Róisín Kennedy, "Experimentalism or Mere Chaos? The White Stag Group

and the Reception of Subjective Art in Ireland," in Keown and Taaffe, *Irish Modernism*, 184.

31 Herbert Read, "On Subjective Art," *The Bell* 7, 5 (February 1944), 424–9; 'Art in Crisis,' *Horizon* (May, 1944), 336–50.

32 S. B. Kennedy, *Irish Art and Modernism 1880–1950* (Dublin/Belfast: Hugh Lane Municipal Gallery/Institute of Irish Studies, Queen's University, 1991), 121.

33 Lucy Cotter, "Ambivalent Homecomings: Louis le Brocquy, Francis Bacon and the Mechanics of Canonization," *Field Day Review* 7 (2011), 171–202.

34 Herbert Read, *Contemporary British Art* (Harmondsworth: Penguin, 1951), 34 (My emphasis).

35 Riann Coulter, *The Surreal in Irish Art* (Banbridge: F. E. McWilliam Gallery and Studio, 2011).

36 Herbert Read, *A Letter to A Young Painter* [1962], cited in Cotter, "Ambivalent Homecomings," 178.

37 Earnán O'Malley, "Louis le Brocquy," *Horizon* xiv: 79 (July 1946), in Cormac K. H. O'Malley and Nicholas Allen, eds., *Broken Landscapes: Selected Letters of Ernie O'Malley 1924–1957* (Dublin: Lilliput, 2011), 396.

38 Cited in Róisín Kennedy, "Made In England: The Critical Reception of Louis le Brocquy's *A Family*," *Third Text* 19, 5 (September 2005), 475.

39 Medb Ruane, "Le Brocquy *A Family*," *Irish Arts Review* 19, 1 (Summer 2002), 23, cited in Róisín Kennedy, "Made in England," 475.

40 Gilles Deleuze, *Francis Bacon: The Logic of Sensation*, Daniel W. Smith, trans. (London: Continuum, 205), xii.

41 Fionna Barber, "Disturbed Ground: Francis Bacon, Traumatic Memory and the Gothic," *The Irish Review* 39 (2008), 125–38. Affinities between Bacon's work and anti-Catholic rituals of the Orange Order are discussed in Lynn Brunet, *"A Course of Severe and Arduous Trials": Bacon, Beckett and Spurious Freemasonry in Early Twentieth-Century Ireland* (Bern: Peter Lang, 2009).

42 Ernst van Alphen, "The Portrait's Dispersal: Concepts of Representation and Subjectivity in Contemporary Portraiture," in Joanna Woodall, ed., *Portraiture: Facing the Subject* (Manchester and New York: Manchester University Press, 1997), 246.

43 Dorothy Walker, "Rosc," in *Modern Art in Ireland* (Dublin: Lilliput, 1997).

44 Dorothy Walker, "Rosc," 113.

45 Brian O'Doherty, *Inside The White Cube: The Ideology of Gallery Space* (Santa Monica: The Lapis Press, 1986), based on three influential articles originally published in *Artforum* in 1976; Rosalind Krauss, "Sculpture in the Expanded Field," *October* 8 (1979), 30–44.

46 Brian O'Doherty, "The Native Heritage," *The Irish Imagination 1959–1971* (Dublin: Municipal Gallery of Modern Art, 1971), 20.

47 Christina Kennedy, "Modernism and Beyond: the 1960s and '70s," in Juncosa and Kennedy, eds., *The Moderns*, 209.

48 Dorothy Walker, "The New Tribalism," 22.

49 Dorothy Walker, "The New Tribalism," 20.

PART III
Constituencies

9

ANNE FOGARTY

Women and Modernism

I

There is no gainsaying the pre-eminence of W. B. Yeats, James Joyce, or Samuel Beckett in the history of Irish modernism, yet the privileging of this male-centred literary canon and its aesthetic precepts blocks from view a women's modernism frequently rooted in popular literary modes. However, the reconceptualization of several crucial aspects of modernism in recent decades, together with the archival work of literary critics and historians who have reclaimed forgotten corpuses of writing, permit us now to consider Irish modernism in a more inclusive fashion and to take better account of the achievement of women artists. The new modernist studies dispute the idea that there is a homogeneous modernism, positing instead the existence of overlapping movements driven by congruent agendas and objectives. The work of Irish women modernist writers forms one such intersecting narrative: a contour of development may be tracked from the decadent writing of George Egerton in the 1890s, to the novels of Elizabeth Bowen published from the late 1920s to the 1960s, to the experimental journalism and short stories by Maeve Brennan produced from the 1940s to the 1970s. Because these artists have often been considered piecemeal or their achievement scanted, any overview offered in this chapter must perforce be speculative and tentative.[1]

In *The Gender of Modernity* (1995), Rita Felski usefully reminds us that the history of women's experience of modernity is not of a piece with their involvement in modernism.[2] These processes may intersect but are nevertheless distinct formations. Felski's disentangling of the high modernist moment from the manifold ways in which the impact of modernity was represented by women authors is vital because it allows us to inspect cultural pathways and politically grounded textualities that broaden the facets of Irish cultural history. The depiction of the shock of the new in late-nineteenth- and early-twentieth-century works and the radical feminism enunciated in different forms by New Woman and revivalist writers produce the conditions that make this modernism possible. In addition, the questioning of the notion of the self-sufficient author by feminist criticism led to the recognition that coteries, collectives, political and social movements, and campaigns for social justice all nurtured modernist creativity. One of the striking features of singular female artists such as Alice Milligan, Lady Gregory, Eva Gore-Booth, and Dorothy Macardle, who all produced work during the Irish literary revival, was that they contributed as much to collective political endeavours as to the creation of an oeuvre of their own. Their political activism served as a spur for their experimental writing that has palpable modernist hallmarks.

J. C. C. Mays has postulated that modernism in Ireland is a broken formation, at once proleptic and belated.[3] Modernism, he suggests, appears to arrive prematurely because of the social and political upheavals of post-Famine Ireland. But it also makes its presence felt *post hoc* and continues to inform literary production from the 1930s to the 1970s. These ruptured trajectories are all the more borne out by the successive waves of activity that can be picked out in the collective contribution made by Irish women artists to modernism. Although continuities between the writers in different eras may be established, careers often peter out and significant corpuses of work vanish from view. Nevertheless, two significant phases within the history of women and Irish modernism may be discerned: a first era of production spans the period from the late nineteenth century to the 1930s and includes the writings of Egerton, Katherine Cecil Thurston, Eva Gore-Booth, Gregory, and Macardle; the second phase from the late 1930s to the early 1970s may be seen as a recrudescence of modernism that encompasses the work of Bowen, Kate O'Brien, and Brennan. Notably, the women of the earlier period marry political activism, feminist advocacy, and engagement in the public sphere with artistic experimentation. Although generally less politically active than its predecessors, the group of writers that emerges in the mid-twentieth century self-consciously carries forward the earlier modernist quarrel with literary form while continuing to undermine artificial divisions between high art and popular culture and to unpick the ideological stances that insist on the fixity of gender roles and of national and sexual identities. Moreover, several of these second-generation writers connect with the aspirations of their predecessors through their questioning of nationalist values and simplified notions of home, identity, and belonging. In particular, the evincing of an array of feminist concerns interlinks women writers in the founding and belated phases of modernism and forms a distinctive substratum in their work. This feminocentrism challenges and supplements the views of sexuality and femininity put forward by male artists. An additional overarching aspect of the diverse women who contribute to Irish modernism at different junctures from the 1890s onwards, and which connects them with male counterparts such as Oscar Wilde, Yeats, and Beckett, is their interest in intermediality. The creative talents of these writers often span several fields – such as acting, painting, directing, and musicianship – and their writings frequently integrate the visual and performing arts and draw on their techniques and idioms to extend the possibilities of linguistic representation.

II

New Woman's fiction and the Irish literary revival are generally treated as movements separate from modernism and running athwart it, thus often obscuring the experimentalism of female artists who played with artistic form. However, texts written by women impelled by the ideas of both of these cultural moments are shaped by avant-garde presumptions that may be identified as modernist, and they are also frequently imbued with anti-imperialist, socialist, and counter-hegemonic political ideals that give added traction to their radicalism. The unstable social background and migrant existence of one of the key exponents of New Woman writing, Mary Chavelita Dunne Bright (1859–1945), who wrote under the pseudonym George Egerton, inform her short stories, which highlight subaltern perspectives and the untameable aspects of female desire and fluidly interweave numerous transnational locations, including Ireland and Norway. Born in Australia to an Irish father and Welsh mother, she possibly spent time as a child in Chile before receiving a Catholic education in Dublin. As an adult, she lived and worked variously in Germany, New York, London, and Norway. Her sojourn in Norway and a liaison with Knut Hamsun brought her into contact with the innovations of Scandinavian literature. But while her fictions are demonstrably influenced by the naturalism and expressionism of Knut Hamsun, Henrik Ibsen, Bjørnstjerne Bjørnson, and August Strindberg, they are above all imbued with Nietzschean thinking. The restless heroines of her stories chafe against domestic confinement, seek an outlet for their desires, and are generally in quest of emancipation from social and sexual constraints. In "The Regeneration of Two," the final tale in *Discords* (1894), Fruen adapts a Nietzschean slogan and proclaims the overturning of all values as the basis for revolutionizing the position of women.[4] The New Woman envisaged by Egerton is defined by her femininity, her unruly desires, and her hybrid racial identity. The women in her stories are frequently depicted as exotic and dark-skinned or conceived of as gypsies and witches. "A Cross Line," the opening tale of *Keynotes*

(1893), which is set in Millstreet, County Cork, scandalized Victorian readers because the heroine explicitly pursues an extramarital affair, is repelled by maternity, and flagrantly indulges in erotic fantasies.[5] The Irish bogland backdrop typifies the non-metropolitan environments favoured by Egerton. In keeping with these off-centre locations, she foregrounds the carnality of her unconventional female protagonists who resolutely seek to escape the control of husbands and lovers. The radical feminist ethos of Egerton's work is conjoined by its formal innovativeness. Her tales anticipate facets of the modernist short story in their eschewal of structured plots, their fascination with psychologism, and their deployment of elusive leitmotifs and frequent gaps and ellipses.

In her novels, Katherine Cecil Thurston (1875–1911), who stemmed from a Catholic nationalist background, her father twice holding the lord mayorship of Cork, merges genres in startling ways to subvert views of sexual identity. She eschewed the cultural politics of the revival and, moving between domiciles in London and Waterford, produced novels that straddle the popular and the literary. Her ability to blend and fuse genres to create accomplished hybrid modes is evident in her two final novels, *The Fly on the Wheel* (1908) and *Max* (1910).[6] *The Fly on the Wheel* combines naturalism with sensationalism and aspects of a New Woman narrative to explore the existential dilemmas of an impoverished heroine who falls in love with a married man. Jane Miller has argued that a modernism of content may be detected in the British Edwardian novel, which precedes the modernism of form ushered in by Virginia Woolf, amongst others.[7] The radical upturning of realist form associated with Joyce and Woolf, Miller contends, does not happen all at once but is effected as a gradual transition by the recurrent undermining of conventions by many of the predecessors of the modernists. The crises evinced in Thurston's final novels and her stretching of familiar forms to breaking point corroborate Miller's proposition that the ruptures of high modernism are prepared for by other modernist moments in which traditional modes are parried and negotiated. In a manner that anticipates Joyce's dissection of Dublin in *Dubliners* (1914), *The Fly on the Wheel* produces a scabrous account of the provincialism of Waterford society and clinically dissects the way in which a conservative Catholic middle class has gained a stranglehold on the commercial interests of the city. Stephen Carey is forced to assume control of his siblings and of the family fortunes following the death of his father and the simultaneous collapse of his building business. His self-abnegation and undeviating sense of duty have enabled him to become a successful figure and to promote the fortunes of his brothers. Patriarchy, as embodied by Carey, is sanctioned as a supreme social good and is the motor force of emergent middle-class Irish values. Alongside its needling satire, Thurston's novel also uncovers the contradictions that trouble the brittle realities of a society whose value system depends on the rigid maintenance and policing of sexual roles. Stephen has married Daisy, whom he sees as his chattel; her attractiveness and subservience merely reinforce his authority and virility. However, he is catapulted into crisis when he falls in love with Isabel Costello, a penurious, orphaned local woman who has returned to Waterford from Paris and who had previously been attached to his brother, Frank, a liaison of which Stephen had disapproved and sought to end.

By contrast with Stephen, Isabel is bohemian and rebellious. Her sexual power is depicted as emanating from her close association with nature, the body, and untrammelled instinct. However, Eros and chaotic libidinal forces are given only momentary sway as they are associated with facets of modernity from which this emergent community shields itself. An abruptly aborted elopement by the lovers in Stephen's car dramatizes the simultaneous lure and fear of the modern. The ideological claims of reason, religion, and family reassert themselves at the close and Stephen abjures Isabel as a consequence, thus rescuing himself from the world of instinct and passion. The end of the novel complicates naturalism's characteristic drive towards tragic climaxes. The culminating scene, in which Isabel commits suicide by drinking a glass of wine she has laced with poison, is endowed with a symbolic resonance that is teasing and cryptic as the heroine sees in the glass "the warmth, the redness, the glory of the sun."[8] Isabel's death thus becomes a form of apotheosis or of *jouissance* even while it is also suggested that she is a sacrificial victim who has been punished for exposing the weak underside of patriarchy and the deadly compromises that underpin the proprieties of middle-class sexuality.

If realism, as Elizabeth Deeds Ermarth holds, is founded on a consensus about the conditions of perception, then Thurston's fiction unravels such consensus because of her fusion and overlaying of genres and her recognition of the way in which desire and female difference undermine bourgeois facades and conventions.[9] *Max* takes bohemian Paris as its locale and focuses on the ambiguous sexuality and indeterminate identity of the main protagonist who is training to be an artist. In his guise as a "boy," Max strikes up a close friendship, which has pronounced homoerotic undertones, with Edward Blake, an Irishman. But Max turns out to be a woman in disguise who has fled an unhappy marriage; in a pivotal disclosure scene, his neighbour Jacqueline helps restore his covert female identity. This femininity, however, is not treated as an essence nor does it herald a return to a stable self. Instead, it becomes the subject of Max's art when he sets out to paint his counter-self, Maxine. Sexual roles, it is inferred, are imagined and performative in nature, not biological givens. In a plot that evidently shadows Wilde's *The Picture of Dorian Gray* (1890), Blake falls in love with the painting of Maxine, whose subject he holds to be Max's sister and insists on meeting her. These double roles are merged as Blake finds that Max and Maxine are the self-same person, but even though this resolution has been read as the restoration of heterosexual norms, the final ecstatic union between the lovers is still entangled with the ambivalent sexual fantasies and masquerades that have been toyed with up to this point. Thurston's unconventional novel daringly broaches homosexual desire and queer love while simultaneously deconstructing the meaning of femininity. Moreover, by having the portrait of Max as Maxine come to life and find fulfilment, Thurston reverses the tragic trajectory of *Dorian Gray* and establishes a transgressive imaginary space in the Irish novel where queer sexual identities and homosexual desire are encompassed in a covert and carefully coded fashion.

Unlike Thurston, who had little truck with cultural nationalism, the female playwrights who participated materially in the building up of an indigenous Irish theatre movement were motivated by the struggle for political independence and the desire to harness communal energies to contest the injustices of British colonial rule. Although the quest for national freedom has primacy in their writing, it is entwined with the conjoint, even if at times conflicting, endeavour of achieving parity and freedom for women. In fact, the faultlines between nationalism and feminism in part account for the modernist impulses in the work in question. Hailing originally from a Northern Methodist family, Alice Milligan (1866–1953) became an ardent convert to the nationalist cause and was multiply engaged as political agitator, historian, journalist, poet, musician, pamphleteer, artist, director, and writer of fiction. Her unorthodox novel, *A Royal Democrat* (1890), fuses fantasy and speculative history with a "story of Ireland" fiction and evinces Milligan's readiness to play with fictional form. The text is set in the imagined future of the 1940s and tracks the story of Arthur, the republican heir to the British throne, whose recalcitrant thinking seems a consequence of his part-Irish descent. Shipwrecked off the Donegal coast, he travels around the west of Ireland under the assumed name of Cormac King and consorts with nationalist rebels, eventually getting drawn into an armed insurrection near Derry during the still ongoing Land War. He is imprisoned with the other rebels but his life is saved by Nola Shane, the Irish woman with whom he has fallen in love, who reveals his true identity. Divergent political aims are harmonized in the fanciful ending: a Home Rule Bill is passed enabling the foundation of an Irish Parliament in 1948, while the heir to the English throne is permitted to abdicate in favour of his cousin Friederike, who has been ruling on his behalf. The latter befriends Nola following Cormac's death and adopts her as confidante. Monarchism, republicanism, the Irish Home Rule cause, and feminist liberation are thus reconciled in this playfully futuristic fiction.

But Milligan's most experimental work, as Catherine Morris has contended, takes place in the realm of community theatre.[10] Milligan directed memorable and ground-breaking productions of her own pageants and short plays based on Celtic myths that were styled in the manner of the tableau vivant and borrowed from techniques deployed in the magic lantern shows she frequently organized for the Gaelic League. These stagings made use of multimedia effects and drew on aspects of modernist drama in their commingling of the visual and performing arts and their reliance on fragmentation. "Erin Fettered, Erin Free" was one of the most well-received of Milligan's silent but potent tableaux and was performed for the feminist company *Inghinidhe na hÉireann* in Dublin in August 1901. The redolent image of an imprisoned Ireland transformed into a vision of freedom carried the overt burden of nationalist aspirations but more covertly of suffragette hopes. A further feature of Milligan's productions that transfixed her contemporaries was her deployment of the vernacular and demotic. Yeats records in his *Autobiographies* that a performance of Milligan's *The Deliverance of Red Hugh O'Donnell* in 1901 left him with "his head on fire" and provided him with the impetus to establish the Irish National Theatre.[11]

Yeats's striking image of Eva Gore-Booth (1870–1926) as "withered old and skeleton-gaunt" has lastingly memorialized her, but elided her achievements as an artist.[12] Gore-Booth's remarkable career as a social reformer, suffragette, pacifist, nationalist, and mystic informs her poetry and drama, which are imbued with a dissenting vision and a queer sexuality and shaped by a formal experimentalism. Born into a Protestant, Anglo-Irish landowning family in Lissadell, County Sligo, she rejected this privileged existence on political grounds.[13] In conjunction with her partner Esther Roper, with whom she lived in Manchester, she agitated for female suffrage and workers' rights, and organized community-based educational groups and amateur theatrical societies especially for women. She co-founded the radical feminist journal *Urania*, whose manifesto took inspiration from Katherine Cecil Thurston's *Max* by identifying as one of its chief aims the abolition of the differences between men and women. A play, *Fiametta*, probably composed in the 1900s and published posthumously, depicts the damaging effects of marriage on the heroine Gertrude Fane, an actress whose name echoes that of the hapless Sybil Vane in *Dorian Gray*, but whose fate pointedly reworks the death by suicide of Wilde's protagonist.[14] This feminist metadrama, which also incorporates Wilde's *An Ideal Husband* (1895) as an intertext and combines suffragette agitprop with aspects of Ibsenite naturalism, interweaves Gertrude's struggle to cast off the role of wife with a narrative tracking her efforts to embody on stage the otherworldly figure of Fiametta. The indeterminate ending gestures at the possibility of utopian renewal as Gertrude escapes society to fuse, in the manner of Peer Gynt, with an elemental and empowering natural sphere and to make common cause with her sister, who has protectively defended her rights to freedom as a woman and an artist. Gore-Booth's other plays that retell stories from Celtic mythology are distinctive, as Cathy Leeney has contended, because of their innovative use of scenography and their experimentation with the symbolic dynamics of dramatic space.[15] Gore-Booth exhibits in this manner the influence of European Symbolist writers on her compositions and of avant-garde developments in modern theatre with which she would initially have come into contact when attending productions of Richard Wagner in Bayreuth in 1895. In her *Unseen Kings* (1904) and *The Buried Life of Deirdre* (c. 1911, never performed) stage space is freed from the constraints of naturalism and set in a dialectic with an off-stage imagined zone endowed with a potent and feminine Otherness.[16] Furthermore, Gore-Booth radically recasts the Celtic myths that she dramatizes in these two works because of the prominence given not only to the central female figures of Niamh and Deirdre but also to their interrelationships with other women.

Like Gore-Booth, Lady Gregory (1852–1932) was from a Protestant land-owning background – she managed an estate at Coole Park, County Galway, after the death of her husband, Sir William Gregory – and worked to promote cultural nationalist ideals, but she demurred from any overt espousal of feminist aspirations. Gregory's stylistic innovations have often been overlooked because of her links with the Ascendancy, her seemingly traditional views of gender roles, and her apparent acceptance of an ancillary role in the development of the Abbey Theatre that she co-founded. However, her self-deprecatory comments about her literary aspirations in her memoirs belie the radical strains in her plays and the degree to which she engages with what Marshall Berman has dubbed "the melting vision" of modernity.[17] In *Our Irish Theatre* (1913), she notes that she had to abandon her decidedly radical intention to write "a play for a man and a scarecrow only," but nonetheless affirms her continuing belief in the necessity for experimentation.[18] Her plays, in fact, put pressure on differing theatrical forms while also interrogating the ways in which women are used to shore up myths of masculinity and to indemnify notions of national identity. Moreover, many of her works specifically focus on outlawed or disempowered women, including Gormleith, Dervorgilla, and Grania. Gregory's ascetic tragedy, *The Gaol Gate* (1906), centres on two illiterate women, Mary Cushin and her daughter-in-law, Mary Cahel, who have been summoned to a gaol in which son and husband, Denis Cahel, is incarcerated.[19] On arrival, they learn that Denis has been hanged, but their tragic mood is mitigated when they realize that he has not turned informer on his neighbours. The mother's assumption of the traditional role of the keener who will celebrate the dead man at the end of the play starkly indicates that women can play a part within a patriarchal world only by accepting their secondariness. Female eloquence is thus revealed to be founded on silence and suppression and questions are simultaneously raised about the nature of heroism and the cathartic function of tragedy. *Grania* (published 1912), a chamber play that was never staged during Gregory's lifetime, depicts the eponymous heroine as a wayward New Woman torn between sexual desire and a need for autonomy.[20] When the dying Diarmuid fixates on Finn, thus completely discounting Grania, the heroine recognizes in a painful epiphany the degree to which male rivalries determine the oppressive structures of a heroic culture in which women are scapegoated or sidelined. At the end of the play, Grania self-consciously robes herself in her golden dress, an erstwhile sign of power, forces Finn to accept her as his consort, and faces the laughing mockery of his troops. Her moral compromise, allied with the metatheatrical devices of the donning of a costume and of disembodied laughter, underscores the sense of feminine alienation that dominates the ending of this modernist chamber play that resonates with the work of Ibsen and Strindberg.

In *Earth-Bound: Nine Stories of Ireland* (1924), the historian and fiction writer Dorothy Macardle (1889–1958) uses notions of collective production, colloquy, and mystic communion to underpin the interlinked tales.[21] Written during her imprisonment in Kilmainham and Mountjoy jails from 1922 to 1923 for her anti-Treaty sympathies, Macardle's stories are dedicated to fellow republicans while the text itself is a chain of narratives told by various male and female narrators to an audience of fellow-Irish emigrants in the Philadelphia abode of Una and Frank O'Carroll. Realism breaks down and shades into Gothic in these texts, which deal with the recent and ongoing traumas of the War of Independence and Civil War, and in which ghosts from the Irish past frequently intervene in the present. Despite the republicanism that imbues the collection, the penultimate story, "The Portrait of Roisin Dhu," strikingly critiques the reliance of an Irish nationalist aesthetic on idealized images of femininity.[22] Nuala, the Blasket Island woman who has posed for Hugo Blake's portrait of Roisin Dhu, dies of unrequited love for the artist while he in turn is haunted by her memory and commits suicide. Even though Blake's painting mesmerizes the audience that views it in America, the story pointedly represents the myth of Mother Ireland as pernicious for artist and subject alike and uncovers the human costs of a political philosophy that discounts emotions and sublimates sexuality. In the diasporic setting conjured up by *Earth-Bound*, the rationalized modernity of contemporary Philadelphia is troubled by the haunted landscapes, historical spectres and the unfinished revolutionary business of Ireland.

III

Tim Armstrong has contended that artists who followed in the wake of the founding generation of modernism whose work reaches a pinnacle in 1922 are beset by their belatedness.[23] However, belatedness is not just a lack; it also becomes an animating force for the women whose texts were published from the late 1920s onwards. Joyce, moreover, seems to replace Wilde and Yeats as the lodestone for the writing produced in this period. Bowen, Kate O'Brien, and Brennan all carry forward and renew the legacy of modernism in these decades, as do several other key figures such as Mary Manning, Teresa Deevy, Blanaid Salkeld, and Sheila Wingfield, whom space does not permit me to discuss here.

The problem of belatedness was at once a besetting aesthetic problem and a peculiar facet of the personal history of Bowen (1899–1973) who, as the final descendant of an Anglo-Irish family, inherited the estate of Bowen's Court in north County Cork. The troubling dimensions of a colonial family history and the prospect of the imminent loss of her ancestral home are registered in the Gothic disturbances in her novels, in their non-linear plots, and in the manner in which space and time are frequently disrupted. In *The Last September* (1929), the events of which take place on the crumbling estate of Danielstown during the War of Independence, Lois Farquar finds herself paralyzed in a world of self-cancelling interrelationships. Variously connected with a web of figures including her fiancé, the British soldier, Gerald Lesworth, Daventry, a shell-shocked private who has survived World War I, and an Irish gunman on the run, she is also caught up in the erotic force-field of the bisexual Marda Norton and the unfinished romances of her dead mother, Laura. Portia Quayne, the orphaned heroine of *The Death of the Heart* (1938), whose naive, unvarnished diary sends shockwaves through her brother's household, is similarly trapped in mirror worlds from which there seems to be no egress as she pieces together an existence that replicates the life of Anna, her hostile stepmother. Stella Rodney in *The Heat of the Day* (1949), a novel set in 1942, is torn between the blandishments of the sinister secret agent Harrison and her lover, Robert Kelway, who turns out to be a Nazi spy. Bowen's work disturbs the decorum of realist fiction by making her characters permeable and porous and by endowing houses and objects with an uncanny agency that supersedes that of her protagonists. In *A World of Love* (1955), the unaddressed and abandoned love letters of

Guy Danby, who has died in World War I, discovered in Montfort, a decaying Irish mansion, galvanize the emotions of all of the females in the novel, including those of Maud, the fey young girl who finds them. The uncanny Guy is emblematic of the reverberating aftermath of twentieth-century historical trauma but, the final scene, which takes place in a newly opened Shannon Airport, also foregrounds the dislocations of the modern with its discomfiting ability to reduce both present and past to enigmatic traces. Bowen's final novel, *Eva Trout* (1968), with its inarticulate giantess heroine and her misplaced bisexual passions, continues the author's experimentation with novelistic form and her persistent dismantling of the traditional contours of character and of bourgeois proprieties. The discontinuous plot of Bowen's final fiction particularly relies on abruptly changing visual scenes and on cinematic jump-cuts to depict the absurd world inhabited by her childlike central protagonist.

Like several other women modernist writers, Kate O'Brien (1897–1974) overlays different genres in her fiction thereby creating suggestive dissonances. Several of her works trouble the parameters of the *Bildungsroman* and jarringly interfuse romance with naturalism. In addition, O'Brien pointedly problematizes heterosexual identity and uses queer moments to unsettle conventional views of femininity and to raise ethical questions about the marginalization of the subaltern. The free movement in her fiction between Irish and European locales challenges the insularity of Free State Ireland and essentialist views of nationality. In *Mary Lavelle* (1936), the world of the Irish Catholic heroine is turned upside down when she becomes a governess in Bilbao and embarks on an affair with Juanito, the married son of her employer.[24] The otherness of Basque culture and the queer potential of erotic love dislodge the fixities of her middle-class Irish milieu. In a crucial scene, pleasure and the aesthetic are troublingly mixed in the violent rituals of the bullfight, while the open ending suggests that the planned progression of the heroine towards marriage at home has become an impossibility. In *The Land of Spices* (1941), O'Brien reworks Joyce's *A Portrait of the Artist as a Young Man* (1916), restaging it in a girls' boarding school in Mellick, her fictionalized rendering of Limerick.[25] The novel intertwines the fate of Mère Marie-Hélène, the English reverend mother of this Irish institution run by Belgian nuns, with that of Anna Murphy, a local girl. Queer love and the vocational pursuit of art and the intellectual life are endowed with disruptive but transformative potential in this text. In this manner, O'Brien carries forward and revises aspects of Joyce. Like him, she troubles the developmental story underlying the European *Bildungsroman* and also upturns the expectations of the nationalist novel, which posits a congruence between individual and nation. Her heroines achieve freedom through affective growth, through their implication in queer sexual alliances, and through breaking with nationalist imperatives and the embracing of make-shift transnational identities.

The oeuvre of Maeve Brennan (1917–93) gives heightened expression to the endeavours of a belated modernism to renegotiate but also to continue the initial formal and thematic concerns of this movement. Brennan, who stemmed from a Republican family, was born in Ranelagh, Dublin, but spent her formative years and adult life in the United States, working as an editor at *The New Yorker* for a significant phase of her career. The throwaway and absurdist journalistic fragment, the short story and the novella are the particular literary modes that Brennan cultivates. In reinventing them, she wins from them peculiar dimensions while carrying forward the determination of the modernist writer to renovate inherited genres so that they more adequately convey the dislocations and impermanence of modern life. Crucially, her work is transatlantic and marries renderings of destitution in downtown New York with haunting excavations of suburban Dublin and the debilitating structures of Irish family life. Brennan's succinct columns in *The New Yorker* written between 1953 and 1968, which hinge on fragile apercus, evince a fascination with the phantasmagoria of city life and the evanescence but centrality of the everyday.[26] Like her short fiction, they capture the existential underpinnings of urban living. Where transient and vanished spaces crystallize facets of life in New York in the 1950s and 1960s, images of domestic entrapment, diminution, and silence render the peculiarities of existence in Ranelagh in her short stories. Several linked stories, which originally appeared in *The New Yorker* and were republished posthumously in *The Springs of Affection* (1997), circle anxiously and obsessively around the increasing misery and attenuated existences of two families, the Derdons and the Bagots. "Family Walls" (1973) deploys images of silence and immurement to foreground the passivity and anomie of Rose Derdon, whereas in "The Springs of Affection" (1972) the sinister regrouping of the furniture of the dead Delia and Martin Bagot by Min, the latter's malevolent and emotionally rapacious sister, in her apartment in Wexford vividly concretizes the depleted milieu of yet another symbolically resonant female figure.[27] Brennan's work, whether centring on unhappy wives in Ranelagh, the floating perceptions of a jobbing journalist walking the streets of New York, or fractious maids in wealthy American households, remains true to the radical legacy of modernism in its concern to give expression to the everyday and the marginal, to rework literary modes in fresh and arresting ways, to produce work that is international and diasporic, and to track the enlivening but also debilitating effects of the modern, especially on the lives of women.

NOTES

1   For a different genealogy of the history of women and Irish modernism, see Paige Reynolds, "'Colleen Modernism': Afterlife in Irish Women's Writing," *Éire-Ireland* 44 (2009), 94–117.

2   Rita Felski, *The Gender of Modernity* (Cambridge, MA: Harvard University Press, 1995), 1–29.

3   See J. C. C. Mays, "Introduction," to James Joyce, *Poems and Exiles* (Harmondsworth: Penguin, 1992), xvii–xlvii.

4   George Egerton, "The Regeneration of Two," *Keynotes and Discords* (London: Virago, 1983), 241.

5   George Egerton, "A Cross Line," *Keynotes and Discords*, 1–36.

6   Katherine Cecil Thurston, *The Fly on the Wheel* (New York: Dodd, Mead and Company, 1908); *Max* (New York: Harper and Brothers, 1909).

7   Jane Eldridge Miller, *Rebel Women: Feminism, Modernism and the Edwardian Novel* (Chicago: Chicago University Press, 1994), 1–9.

8   Thurston, *The Fly on the Wheel*, 336.

9   Elizabeth Deeds Ermarth, *Realism and Consensus in the English Novel: Time, Space and Narrative* (Edinburgh: Edinburgh University Press, 1998), 3–37.

10 See Catherine Morris, *Alice Milligan and the Irish Cultural Revival* (Dublin: Four Courts Press, 2012), 221–77.

11 W. B. Yeats, *Autobiographies: Memories and Reflections* (London: Macmillan, 1955), 449. For the play that had such an impact on Yeats, see Alice Milligan, "The Deliverance of Red Hugh O'Donnell," *Irish Weekly Freeman*, 15 March 1902.

12 W. B. Yeats, "In Memory of Eva Gore-Booth and Con Markiewicz," Daniel Albright, ed., *The Poems* (London: Everyman, 1990), 283–4.

13 See Sonja Tiernan, *Eva Gore-Booth: An Image of Such Politics* (Manchester: Manchester University Press, 2012).

14 Sonja Tiernan, ed., *Fiametta: A Previously Unpublished Play by Eva Gore-Booth* (Lewiston, NY: Edwin Mellen Press, 2012).

15 Cathy Leeney, *Irish Women Playwrights 1900–1939: Gender and Violence on Stage* (New York: Peter Lang, 2012), 59–96.

16 Eva Gore-Booth, *Unseen Kings* and *The Buried Life of Deirdre*, in *The Plays of Eva Gore-Booth*, Frederick S. Lapisardi, ed. (Lewiston, NY: Edwin Mellen Press, 1991), 1–21 and 149–216.

17 Marshall Berman, *All That is Solid Melts into Air: The Experience of Modernity* (London: Verso, 1982), 90–8.

18 Lady Gregory, *Our Irish Theatre* (New York and London: G. P. Putnam's Sons, 1913), 57.

19 Lady Gregory, *The Gaol Gate* in *The Collected Plays II: Tragedies and Tragic-Comedies*, Ann Saddlemyer, ed., (Gerrards Cross: Colin Smythe, 1979), 3–10.

20 Lady Gregory, *Grania* in *The Collected Plays II: Tragedies and Tragic-Comedies*, 11–46.

21 Dorothy Macardle, *Earth-Bound: Nine Stories of Ireland* (Worcester, MA: The Harrigan Press, 1924).

22 Macardle, *Earth-Bound*, 90–101.

23 Tim Armstrong, *Modernism* (London: Polity Press, 2005), 35–41.

24 Kate O'Brien, *Mary Lavelle* (London: Virago, 1984).
25 Kate O'Brien, *The Land of Spices* (London: Virago, 1988).
26 Maeve Brennan, *The Long-Winded Lady: Notes from The New Yorker* (Boston: Houghton Mifflin, 1998).
27 Maeve Brennan, "Family Walls" and "The Springs of Affection," *The Springs of Affection: Stories of Dublin*, 159–80 and 296–343.

10

LOUIS DE PAOR

Irish Language Modernisms

The spectre of a "lost" Gaelic language and civilization haunting the imagination of English-speaking Ireland is a persistent feature of Anglophone Irish writing, providing a highly productive sense of linguistic and cultural disinheritance and a simultaneous sense of liberation from received language and tradition. One of the most remarkable features of Irish language writing in the modern period is a sense of the enduring authority and continuing availability of Irish as a vehicle for literary expression. It might be argued that this confidence conceals a repressed anxiety about the diminishing resources of the language, but for all the heated debates about tradition and modernity that persist right through the period under review, the legitimacy of the language itself is rarely contested. Despite Máirtín Ó Cadhain's assertion that it is difficult to do your best in a language that might predecease you,[1] most writers in Irish in the first half of the twentieth century seem less anxious about the incapacity of an endangered language than they are about their own ability to deploy and replenish its considerable resources.

For all the recent work by Philip O'Leary and others, there is still a tendency to see disputes among early language revivalists as a struggle between nativists committed to protecting the Irish language and its traditions from outside influence, and progressives determined to liberate the language and its literature from a preoccupation with rural pieties. Risteard de hIndeberg's review of Pádraig Mac Piarais's/Patrick Pearse's collection of short stories, *Íosagán agus Scéalta Eile* (1907), is often cited as typical of the reactionary response to innovation of any kind: "If Irish literature is the talk of big broad-chested men, this is the frivolous petulancy of latter-day English *genre* scribblers, and their utterance is as the mincing of the under-assistant floor-walker in a millinery shop."[2] De hIndeberg went beyond those who opposed English cultural influence to express a more fundamental opposition to modern European ideas and poetics: "The resuscitation of the Irish language is not merely a protest against English and Englishmen. It is of far deeper significance for it opposes itself squarely to the modern European spirit, whether it finds expression in current thought (as it is called), in philosophy, in ethics, or in aesthetics."[3] De hIndeberg's radical traditionalism failed to derail the revolt initiated by Mac Piarais in his poems and stories, and in editorials published during his stewardship of the Gaelic League's *An Claidheamh Soluis* (1903–09). Mac Piarais rejected the folktale as "an echo of old mythologies," unsuitable as a model for contemporary fiction, and traditional style as "the *debris* of an antique native culture ... a peasant convention, which in its essentials, is accepted by the folk everywhere." And he went on to decouple the terms "Irish" and "traditional": "'Traditionalism' is not essentially Irish.... The traditional style is not the *Irish* way of singing or declaiming, but the *peasant* way; it is not, and never has been, the possession of the nation at large, but only of a class in the nation."[4]

Frank O'Brien has argued that Mac Piarais pioneered the short story in Irish before it had established itself as a major literary form in English, and that his views on the relationship between the living speech of the Gaeltacht and the language of literature were more nuanced than the fetishization of Kiltartanese by many of his Celtic Twilight contemporaries writing in English: "the Irish prose of tomorrow ... will be found in the speech of the people, but it will not be the speech of the people; for the ordinary speech of the people is never literature, though it is the stuff of which literature is made."[5] It is a useful refinement of the argument of An tAthair Peadar Ó Laoghaire (1839–1920) that a new literature in Irish must draw on the living speech of the Gaeltacht rather than the literary language of the eighteenth century, bypassing the nineteenth-century decline in the language and its literature, to create new work that was adequate to its own time and place. Ó Laoghaire's novel *Séadna* (1904) is the story of Goethe's Faust heavily inflected by the treatment of the same theme in Irish folklore, further proof of the dynamic possibilities of a new relationship between the Gaelic vernacular and European traditions.

Mac Piarais is the most influential critic of the Revival period. Central to his poetics is the idea that modernization of literary form and style in Irish requires a deeper engagement with precedents in the native tradition and a realignment of the relationship with contemporary Europe that had been disrupted by English colonialism:

> Two influences go into the making of every artist, apart from his own personality, if indeed personality is not in the main only the sum of these influences: the influence of his ancestors and that of his contemporaries. Irish literature if it [is] to live and grow, must get into contact on the one hand with its own past and on the other with the mind of contemporary Europe.... This is the twentieth century; and no literature can take root in the twentieth century which is not of the twentieth century. We want no Gothic revival.[6]

In 1903, he rebuked those who confused "Anglicisation" and "cosmopolitanism":

> We fear that in Ireland, "cosmopolitanism" … is only another word for Anglicisation, and that the "world" of which "we" are citizens is that portion of the British Empire which – we speak metaphorically – lies between Westminster and Fleet Street.… Do you seriously contend that we should be wise to cut ourselves adrift from the great world of European thought? … Were we then completely aloof from European thought when we were Irish, and are we more in touch with it now that we are more than half English?[7]

Although Mac Piarais was among the first to import the European short story into Irish, his stories remain stubbornly conventional in their validation of traditional community values, and morally conservative despite their technical innovation. The best of his poems, however, are exemplary instances of the integration of older Gaelic and contemporary European models. The language of "Mise Éire" is the everyday spoken language of the Gaeltacht, heightened by references to Cúchulainn and the Hag of Beare, and by the adaptation of the sovereignty myth of early and medieval Gaelic poetry to articulate a sense of personal and national crisis that is urgently contemporary. "Fornocht do Chonac Thú" draws on the conventions of the medieval courtly love tradition to interrogate the tension between the beauty of the world and personal sacrifice leading ultimately to death. The language of the poem successfully integrates the archaic and the contemporary while following the regular metre of the aristocratic love poems of early modern Ireland. The formal control adds considerably to the sense of self-repression, which is the poem's subject.

For Mac Piarais and his peers among the elite of progressive Irish nationalists, products of the British colonial education system, access to English and continental literatures was part of their cultural inheritance as subjects of empire, while traditional literature in Irish, whether oral or written, had to be rediscovered and rehabilitated through individual and collective effort. In that context, those arguing for a resuscitation of native models might even be presented as more radical than their cosmopolitan counterparts. In any event, as Philip O'Leary reminds us, progressive and nativist refer more to fluctuating positions than to stable ideologies, as individual writers and critics move from one position to the other in different debates.[8] The "aggressively cosmopolitan" Pádraic Ó Conaire (1882–1928), for example, announced that he would "build a wall around Ireland! A wall thirty cubits high, the same as Tibet … a wall of brass around it. I wouldn't let in an idea. Not an idea mind you, from the outside world."[9] In a 1908 essay, the same writer pointed to the example of nineteenth-century Russian literature and its preoccupation with darker aspects of human psychology and behaviour as a model for prose writers in Irish:

> Nuair a thángadar aníos as an bpoll 'n-a rabhadar ag cuartughadh bhí rud salach smeartha a raibh dealbh duine air aca agus ghlaoidheadar amach i n-árd a ngotha: Seo é an duine! Seo é an fear! Seo í an fhírinne! Ach ní mórán áird a bhí ortha ar dtús. Do ceapadh go raibh an rud salach smeartha ró-ghránda le bheith 'n-a fhear ... Ach ní raibh na hughdair úd, Gogol agus an dream a tháinig roimhe, go faitcheach scáthmhar. Do mhionnuigh agus mhóidigh siad go raibh an fhírinne faighte acu, agus tháinig Tourgéníbh agus móran eile 'n-a ndiaidh le cruthughadh go raibh an ceart aca – go raibh an mhaith agus an uaisleacht taobh istigh de shalachar agus de ghrándacht an deilbh úd a bhí fáighte aca.

> [When they came up out of the hole in which they were searching, they had a filthy, smeared thing with the shape of a human being, and they cried out at the top of their lungs: Here is the human! Here is the man! Here is the truth! But they weren't paid much attention at first. It was thought that the filthy, smeared thing was too ugly to be a man. But those authors, Gogol and those who preceded him, were not fearful or timid. They vowed and they swore that they had found the truth, and Turgenev and many others came after them to prove that they were right – that the good and the noble existed within the filth and ugliness of that form that they had found.][10]

Ó Conaire's novel *Deoraíocht* (1910) is formally untidy but psychologically compelling in its exploration of the degradation of a Connemara man rendered paraplegic by a motor accident in London. The physical disintegration of the central character is accompanied by an existential crisis of identity as he descends into the grotesque underworld of a travelling freak show. Despite the clumsiness of its structure, the novel's interrogation of dislocation and despair, of marginalization and isolation, is in keeping with the central preoccupations of European modernism. Ó Conaire is the outstanding Irish language prose writer of the Revival period. That the setting for his stories is often rural rather than urban makes them no less modern in their representation of existential crisis and the oppressive burden of social convention, of human beings shadowed relentlessly by their own imminent self-destruction.[11]

If the achievements of Revival writers in Irish do not finally match those of their counterparts writing in English, it is the absence of a sufficient body of significant work in poetry and prose that would vindicate either of the competing ideologies that reduces the battle between progressive and conservative positions to caricature, rather than the ideologies themselves. As Yeats and Synge demonstrated, a naive preoccupation with rural peasant life was not an impediment to producing literature of a high order. Irish language writers of the earlier period were nonetheless involved in a radical experiment to accelerate the transition from traditional oral modes to modern literary forms of composition and transmission. For at least one of the more accomplished and combative conservatives, Séamus Ó Grianna, the move was too precipitous. If Irish literature had been asleep for 300 years, he argued, "shílfinn go bhfuil sé contabhairteach a cur ar chosaibh anáirde agus an codladh in a súilibh. B'fhéidir gur síos in súmaire a thuitfeadh sí leis an deifre" [it would seem to me dangerous to set it galloping with sleep still in its eyes. Perhaps it would fall into a bog-hole in its haste].[12] Protagonists on all sides of these debates were conscious of the international contexts of their disputes. Brian Ó Conchubhair has drawn attention, for instance, to the influence of German philologist Max Müller's idea that dialect represents the dynamic principle of a living language on the revivalist preoccupation with cultural authenticity and the cult of the native speaker.[13]

In that regard, the Blasket autobiographies of Tomás Ó Criomhthain (1856–1937), Peig Sayers (1873–1958), and Muiris Ó Súilleabháin (1904–50), published between 1929 and 1936, might be seen as the apotheosis of the native Irish speaker. These cross-cultural collaborative texts are the product of contact between the islanders and a succession of European, English, and Irish visitors infatuated by traditional community life as an antidote to modernity.[14] If modernism has always included a strong anti-modern element, the image of life on the Great Blasket contained in these works is carefully constructed to satisfy the expectations not only of Irish cultural nationalists but of an international audience weary of modernity. Although they are hardly modernist in the usual sense, they represent a radical moment of transition in Gaeltacht literature from oral to written forms of self-representation. The celebration of social solidarity in these books is at odds with Seosamh Mac Grianna's (1900–90) autobiographical account of a native speaker from Donegal determined to assert his own absolute freedom from convention in *Mo Bhealach Féin* (1940), a disturbing portrait of an alienated anti-hero in the most unlikely surroundings, whether attempting to lead a black resistance movement in Cardiff, or rowing across the Irish Sea in a stolen boat.

Although critics generally identify the modernist period in Irish language writing as extending from the outbreak of World War II to the beginning of the Troubles in the north of Ireland, the chronology is useful but imprecise. Mac Piarais and Ó Conaire emerged during the Revival period (1893–1939), but there are modernist elements in both their critical and their creative writing, and there are protomodernist and antimodernist features in the work of Liam Gógan (1891–1979). Gógan favoured a return to earlier Irish models of language and metre and argued vehemently against adopting modernist techniques and attitudes that were symptomatic of a general moral collapse following two world wars. As Ireland, he insisted, had been spared the horror of these wars, there was no justification for Irish poets to follow the bad example of their European counterparts in abandoning established conventions. An accomplished lexicologist, he invented the term "poblacht" (republic) and proposed "bithiúnachas" or "blackguardism" as an Irish term for "existentialism."[15]

It is nonetheless true that the generation of writers in Irish who established themselves during and after the war years were better placed than their predecessors to integrate contemporary European thought and influence with detailed knowledge of traditional writing in Irish. There are, however, significant differences between their work and that of their European counterparts, an inflection that reflects the specificity of local circumstances as well as their own individual life experience and patterns of imagination. Máirtín Ó Direáin (1910–88) may have been well-read in existential philosophy, but his exploration of dislocation and alienation in a city where everyone is isolated in the prison cell of an attenuated self derives from the personal trauma of moving from Inis Mór, the largest of the Aran Islands, to the mainland cities of Galway and Dublin. His sense of displacement speaks to the experience of several generations of Irish people, but the economic crises that make migration a persistent feature of the Irish historical experience are very different from the political upheavals and the ideological and philosophical changes that took place elsewhere in Europe in the first half of the twentieth century. Seán Ó Ríordáin's (1916–77) search for a stable authentic self as the cornerstone of personal and literary integrity chimes with a key element of the modernist predicament, but the crisis of identity is precipitated by personal illness, coupled with linguistic and cultural uncertainty. Máire Mhac an tSaoi (1922-) explores the intimate and transgressive experience of women in a way that is consistent with the modernist rejection of traditional morality, but her experience of the aftermath of war in Paris seems to have confirmed her commitment to the established conventions of the Irish language, and the imagined stabilities of traditional Gaeltacht community life. There is little sense among modern poets in Irish of the crisis of confidence in language itself, which is such a pronounced feature of European modernism, although Mhac an tSaoi has acknowledged a growing doubt in her previously unshakeable conviction in the authority of the Gaeltacht world she encountered as a child:

Mhaireas os cionn leathchéad bliain ins an chluthaireacht san, á iompar timpeall liom im intinn go dtí gur dhúisíos ó chianaibhín agus go bhfuaireas mo chruinne ché leata ar an aer agus ceiliúrtha. Tá sé ródhéanach agam malairt timpeallachta a chuardach. Deirtí go mba phioróid é an cainteoir dúchais deireannach a mhair de chuid Bhreatain Chorn, agus gur chónaigh sé i Ringsend. Mise an phioróid sin.

[I lived in that warmth for more than fifty years, carrying it around with me in my head until I woke a short while ago and found my world scattered to the wind, dispersed. It is too late for me to look for another habitat. It used to be said that the last native speaker of Cornish was a parrot and that he lived in Ringsend. I am that parrot.][16]

Ó Ríordáin is exceptional in this regard, as linguistic instability is central to his achievement. His early work, in particular, is idiosyncratic and iconoclastic in its attempt to articulate a poetic imagination that does not, and cannot, fully inhabit a language "that is half-mine."[17] His struggle with religious authority is part of an existential and ultimately unresolved conflict between the desire for personal freedom and the overweening authority of church, community, language and tradition. In a series of long poems in his debut collection, *Eireaball Spideoige* (1952), he veers between the security and stability of religious and moral convention and the persistent need for individual liberty. Seán Ó Tuama has suggested that "Oíche Nollaig na mBan" is "possibly the first poem in the Irish language where the existence of eternity and of a supernatural creator is openly refuted."[18] Whatever the outcome in any individual poem, the resolution is always temporary as Ó Ríordáin's imagination is defined by the conflict between irreconcilable contradictions.

Religious doubt is, for the most part, more a matter of momentary despair than of ideological conviction among modernist poets in Irish. Even Ó Ríordáin's interrogation of religious belief is different from that of his European counterparts for whom the existential crisis of meaning is predicated on the non-existence of a divine creator. There is little interrogation of religious belief in Ó Direáin's poems where God is a presiding presence against which to measure human frailty in a world that has slipped the moorings of traditional morality. Mhac an tSaoi celebrates the rituals of religion in some of her poems while flouting conventional morality in others. In later poems, such as "Bás mo Mháthar" and "Moment of Truth," she questions the existence of God but never fully commits herself to agnosticism.

While poetry is the most productive genre from the 1940s through to the 1960s, the single greatest achievement in Irish in the modernist period is the fiction of Máirtín Ó Cadhain (1906–70). Although his work is less formally experimental than is often suggested, Ó Cadhain drew on his encyclopaedic knowledge of the Irish language and its oral and written literatures, and a broad range of European writing in several languages to explore the conflict between personal desire and social conventions in traditional rural and modern urban communities. Although many critics have argued that his creative work and his political activities were entirely separate – "It is as if Hans Christian Andersen had another life as an agitator and a terrorist"[19] – Ó Cadhain is a writer *engagé* whose work is informed by political anger against social injustice[20]. In that and in his exploration of the Kafkaesque world of state bureaucracies and the alienation of those trapped within them, he is at one with many of his European contemporaries. His work is characterised by a restlessness of form as though his narrative imagination could not be adequately contained within the established limits of either the short story or the novel. While *Cré na Cille* (1949) has been compared to *Ulysses* (1922) for its linguistic exuberance, the narrative structure, which relies almost entirely on dialogue among the dead, owes as much to the verbal jousting that is a characteristic feature of Gaeltacht culture as it does to avant-garde experimentalism.

Instability of form is also characteristic of the work of Brian Ó Nualláin/ Flann O'Brien (1911–66) who drew on a scholarly understanding of early Irish literature in *At Swim-Two-Birds* (1939) and on a comprehensive knowledge of autobiographical writing in Irish in *An Béal Bocht* (1941), "a prolonged sneer" at the excesses of language revivalists, and a parody of Ó Criomhthain's *An tOileánach* (1929), "the superbest of all books I have ever read."[21] The contradictory relationship with the Irish language and its literature is characteristic of Ó Nualláin, who remained alert to the enduring capacity of the language for creative expression and the hypocrisy of half-hearted attempts to revive it. *At Swim-Two-Birds* draws much of its structural coherence from the tales of medieval and early modern Irish that Ó Nualláin had studied as a student to provide its own idiosyncratic critique of modernist and postmodern approaches to narrative. *An Béal Bocht* is a masterclass in pastiche in which textual authority overruns the human capacity to generate meaning from direct encounters with reality, and characters become trapped in a prison-house of literature where stereotype reigns supreme.

If the war years mark the emergence of modernism as the prevailing aesthetic and metaphysical climate of poetry and prose in Irish, it reaches a cusp in the 1960s, a high point that also marks the beginning of its decline. Ó Direáin's *Ár Ré Dhearóil* (1962) and Ó Ríordáin's *Brosna* (1964) represent a significant departure from the earlier work of each of the two poets, a breakthrough that turned out to be more final than it must have seemed at the time, while Máire Mhac an tSaoi would not publish a sequel to *Margadh na Saoire* (1955) until *Codladh an Ghaiscígh agus Véarsaí Eile* (1973). The title poem of Ó Direáin's collection provides his fullest exploration of the predicament of the uprooted countryman, adrift and unmanned in the godless city. There are strong traces of misogyny in the exploration of compromised masculinity in a world where men are reduced to the menial routines of sterile clerical work, while women have recourse to the consolations of higher education and travel, "I gcúiteamh na gine / Nár fhás faoina mbroinn, / Nár iompair trí ráithe / Faoina gcom" / To compensate for the child / That did not grow in their womb, / That they didn't carry nine months / In the hollow of their bodies].[22] Ó Ríordáin abandoned the prefabricated metres, which were so heavily criticised in his early work in favour of more flexible rhythms determined by the material of each individual poem, effecting a temporary reconciliation between convention and iconoclasm, between the promiscuous resources of English and the more resistant capacity of Irish, before capitulating to the allure of an idealized Gaeltacht where the language of community remains intact, continuous with its own history and place. The rejection of Shelley, Keats and Shakespeare, and the embrace of community, tradition, language and convention advocated by the poet in "Fill Arís," are at odds with the conflict between irreconcilable opposites, which provides the creative dynamic in the best of his poetry and prose. Ó Cadhain's late flourishing produced two outstanding collections of stories in *An tSraith ar Lár* (1967), which includes a sequence of interconnected stories that articulate the experience of a rural community in transition, and *An tSraith dhá Tógáil* (1970), which extends the exploration begun in his earlier work of male characters trapped by personal incapacity in the wheels of a dehumanizing bureaucracy. There is a significant change in Ó Cadhain's technique in the later stories towards a non-realistic style appropriate to the surreal experience of characters alienated from self and community, and increasingly detached from reality. His ability to adapt Irish to the modern urban bureaucratic world confirms an enduring confidence in the capacity of language to articulate even the most dehumanizing and apparently meaningless aspects of the modern experience.

The 1960s also saw a continuation of the modernist experiment with form among younger writers, including Breandán Ó Doibhlinn (1931–), Diarmuid Ó Súilleabháin (1932–85), Eoghan Ó Tuairisc (1919–82) and Seán Ó Tuama (1926–2006). Ó Tuama's engagement with French theatre during his time in Paris in the mid-1950s led to a succession of plays that explored contentious social issues, from the predicament of unmarried mothers in *Is é Seo m'Oileán* (1961) to that of a homosexual priest in *Déan Trócaire ar Shagairt Óga* (1970). The stage directions to *Corp Eoghain Uí Shúilleabháin* (1963) indicate that the mock tragedy should progress from *allegro* to *scherzo* to *andante* against a set in the manner of Salvador Dalí. *Moloney* (1956) and *Gunna Cam agus Slabhra Óir* (1956) provide an interrogation of Irish history and the heroic, while *Iúdás Iscariot agus a Bhean*

(1967) continues the preoccupation with religious and existential themes, as the mental breakdown of the actor parallels that of the character Judas.[23] Ó Tuama's first collection of poems *Faoileán na Beatha* (1962) is formally dexterous, but contains little of the religious scepticism or, indeed, the agnosticism that characterize his later work.

Ó Tuairisc's output during this period is prodigious and includes two novels, three plays, and a collection of poems, in addition to his work in English. The verse play *Na Mairnéalaigh* (1960) contrasts political idealism and economic reality as an elderly couple who have escaped a sinking coffin-ship cross paths with the boat carrying Daniel O'Connell's remains to Ireland. *Cúirt an Mheán Oíche* (1962) juxtaposes contemporary attitudes to sexuality with Irish mythology to highlight the opposition between poetic idealism and pragmatic realism.[24] *Lá Fhéile Mhichíl* (1963) draws on Eliot's reading of Milton's involvement in the English Civil War to investigate Ó Tuairisc's idea that "[e]very man, not dead to generous feeling, must sympathise with Satan against the Omnipotent."[25] The novels *L'Attaque* (1962) and *Dé Luain* (1966) focus on the interior lives of the central characters to dramatise the historical experience of 1798 and 1916 respectively, providing a more human perspective on suffering and sacrifice beyond the rhetoric of idealism. The interrogation of heroic values is a central preoccupation of the ex-soldier Ó Tuairisc, and the long poem "Aifreann na Marbh" on the bombing of Hiroshima in his debut collection *Lux Aeterna* (1964) the pinnacle of his achievement in that regard.[26] It provides a counterpoint to a more sympathetic critique of the heroic in an Irish nationalist context in the novels, as the glories of European and Irish history and culture are undermined by an act of barbarism that derives from, and ultimately, negates, the achievements of western civilization. That the poem follows the structure of a requiem mass is partly ironic, but there is a sense throughout that religious faith and ritual may provide the only consolation for human suffering. Both Ó Tuairisc and Ó Tuama continued their formal and linguistic experiments into the 1970s and 1980s and it is in their work, and that of Máire Mhac an tSaoi, that we find the most accomplished late modernist writing in Irish. The humanist confrontation with mortality following the collapse of religious belief is central to Ó Tuama's poetic project in *Saol fó Thoinn* (1978) and *An Bás i dTír na nÓg* (1988), while Ó Tuairisc's last novel, *An Lomnochtán* (1977), articulates the growing consciousness of a child in a fragmented language that is both psychologically and linguistically plausible.

From the alienation of Ó Conaire's outcasts and Ó Direáin's countryman adrift in an urban wasteland, to the religious doubt and resistance to traditional morality in Mac Grianna, Ó Ríordáin, Ó Tuama, and Mhac an tSaoi; from the exploration of compromised masculinity and dehumanizing bureaucracies in Ó Direáin and Ó Cadhain, to the experiment with language and form in Mac Piarais, Ó Conaire, Ó Cadhain, Gógan, Ó Nualláin, Ó Ríordáin, Ó Tuairisc, Ó Tuama, and, indeed, the Blasket autobiographies; writers in Irish provide their own imaginative responses to European modernism. Given the very different historical circumstances of Ireland in the first half of the twentieth century, the situation of the language itself, and the preoccupations of each individual writer, it is hardly surprising that Irish language modernisms should be comparable to, and yet, distinct from, European, and indeed, Anglophone Irish modernisms. The relative stability of religious belief, for instance, confirms the continuing centrality of religion in Irish public and private life, while the relentless experimentation with form and technique arises less, perhaps, from a rejection of tradition and convention than from a determination to prove the adaptability of the Irish language to the pressures of the contemporary moment and of the individual writer's imagination. Given the continuing decline in the number of competent Irish speakers under both British and Irish governments, the confidence of writers in Irish in the capacity of the language and its literature is, perhaps, the most distinctive, and the most surprising characteristic of all. It is forcefully expressed, with her customary authority, by Mhac an tSaoi, one of the most transgressive voices in modernist poetry in Irish:

> Is dóigh le daoine nach leor mórtas cine chun an teanga a thabhairt slán. Táim sásta dul i mbannaí gur leor, agus gurb iad na siocaracha idéalacha, rom1ánsúla, seachas aon argóint phraiticiúil faoi ndear í a bheith insa mhaith ina bhfuil sí. Fágann an cúrsa uile ualach trom freagrachta orthu súd a thugann faoi scríobh na Gaeilge. Is é ár ndualgas é a chruthú go bhfuil sí beo, agus tá – an fhaid atáimidne ag plé léi.[27]

> [People think that ancestral pride is not enough to save the language. I'm prepared to swear that it is, and that it is idealistic, romantic, ideas rather than any practical argument that has preserved as much of it as now survives. This places a heavy burden of responsibility on those who would write in Irish. It is our duty to prove that she is alive, and so she is – as long as we continue to care for her.]

It is an attitude that derives as much from the idealism and commitment of early cultural nationalism as it does from the anxieties of the modernist imagination.

NOTES

1 Máirtín Ó Cadhain, *Páipéir Bhána agus Páipéir Bhreaca* (Dublin: An Clóchomhar, 1969), 40.

2 Philip O'Leary, *The Prose Literature of the Gaelic Revival, 1881–1921: Ideology and Innovation* (University Park, PA: Pennsylvania State University Press, 1994), 120.

3   O'Leary, 35.
4   Frank O'Brien, *Filíocht Ghaeilge na Linne Seo* (Dublin: An Clóchomhar, 1968), 31, 32.
5   O'Brien, 36, 30, 31.
6   O'Brien, 31.
7   O'Leary, 56.
8   O'Leary, 14–15.
9   O'Leary, 19.
10 O'Leary, 39.
11 Pádraigín Riggs, *Pádraic Ó Conaire: Deoraí* (Dublin: An Clóchomhar, 1994). Ó Tuama reminds us that Ó Conaire's early stories of personal disintegration and social dysfunction predate Joyce's representation of urban paralysis in *Dubliners*. *Aguisíní*, (Galway & Dublin: Centre for Irish Studies & Coiscéim, 2008), 59.
12 O'Leary, 466.
13 Brian Ó Conchubhair, *Fin de Siècle na Gaeilge: Darwin, an Athbheochan agus Smaointeoireacht na hEorpa* (Indreabhán: An Clóchomhar, 2009), 193–236. Ó Conchubhair argues that revivalists were aware of fin-de-siècle anxiety about cultural and linguistic hybridity, and of European debates about miscegenation and degeneration driven by social Darwinism.
14 John Eastlake, "*The* (Original) *Islandman*?: Examining the Origin in Blasket Autobiography," in Nessa Cronin, Seán Crosson, and John Eastlake, eds., *Anáil an Bhéil Bheo: Orality and Modern Irish Culture* (Newcastle: Cambridge Scholars Publishing, 2009), 241–56.
15 Tomás Mac Síomóin, "Stoirm Scéine agus Dún Uí Dhireáin," in Caoimhín Mac Giolla Léith, ed., *Cime mar Chách: Aistí ar Mháirtín Ó Direáin* (Dublin: Coiscéim, 1993), 29.
16 Máire Mhac an tSaoi, *An Paróiste Míorúilteach/The Miraculous Parish* (Dublin & Indreabhán: O'Brien Press & Cló IarChonnacht, 2011), 23.
17 Ó Ríordáin's linguistic anxiety is explored in several poems, including "A Theanga seo Leath-liom," from *Brosna* (Dublin: Sáirséal & Dill, 1964), 25
18 Seán Ó Tuama, *Repossessions: Selected Essays on the Irish Literary Heritage* (Cork: Cork University Press, 1995), 16.
19 Cian Ó hÉigeartaigh, "Máirtín Ó Cadhain: Politics and Literature," *Canadian Journal of Irish Studies*, 34, 1, Spring 2008, 29.
20 Seán Ó Tuama, "A Writer's Testament," in *Repossessions: Selected Essays on the Irish Literary Heritage*, 212–18; and Louis de Paor, "Maxim Gorky, Máirtín Ó Cadhain agus Riastradh na Scéalaíochta," *Comhar*, Nollaig 1990, 51–4.
21 Flann O'Brien, *The Hair of the Dogma* (London: Hart-Davis, MacGibbon, 1977), 180, 81.
22 Máirtín Ó Direáin, *Selected Poems/Tacar Dánta*, Douglas Sealy and Tomás Mac Síomóin, eds. (Newbridge: Goldsmith Press, 1982), 73.
23 *Gunna Cam agus Slabhra Óir* had its premiere at the Abbey Theatre in 1956, with Ray McAnally among the cast, and a score by Seán Ó Riada. For further details of Ó Tuama's work, see "Working with Seán Ó Tuama" in Vera Ryan, *Dan Donovan: An Everyman's Life* (Cork: The Collins Press & Everyman Palace, 2008); and Pádraig Ó Siadhail, *Stair dhrámaíocht na Gaeilge 1900–1970* (Indreabhán: Cló IarChonnacht, 1993).

24 Máirín Nic Eoin, *Eoghan Ó Tuairisc: Beatha agus Saothar* (Dublin: An Clóchomhar, 2006), 303.
25 Nic Eoin, 178, 179. See also Máirín Nic Eoin, "Contemporary Prose and Drama in Irish: 1940–2000," in Margaret Kelleher and Philip O'Leary, eds., *The Cambridge History of Irish Literature*, 270–316.
26 See Colbert Kearney, "Between birth and birth, *Lux Aeterna*," *Poetry Ireland Review* 13, Special Eugene Watters Issue, 'The Week-end of Dermot and Grace', 1985, 90–105; and Mícheál Mac Craith, "Aifreann Na Marbh: Oidhe Chlainne Hiroshima," *An Nuafhilíocht, Léachtaí Cholm Cille*, XVII, Pádraig Ó Fiannachta, ed. (Maigh Nuad: An Sagart, 1986), 61–94.
27 Máire Mhac an tSaoi, "Dhá Arm Aigne," *Innti* 11, 1990, 14–15.

11

JOE CLEARY

Irish American Modernisms

I

In 1932, when W. B. Yeats and George Bernard Shaw were founding the Irish Academy of Letters, Shaw nominated Eugene O'Neill and T. E. Lawrence to become associate members. A delighted O'Neill wrote to his son observing that "I regard this as an honor, whereas other Academies don't mean much to me. Anything with Yeats, Shaw, A. E., O'Casey, Flaherty, Robinson in it is good enough for me."[1] When O'Neill later won the Nobel Prize for Literature in 1936, several Irish dramatists, including Shaw, Yeats, and Lennox Robinson, recorded their approval, and O'Neill remarked that he had also been congratulated by the Irish Free State ambassador in Washington (Robert Brennan, former Sinn Féin activist and father of the writer Maeve Brennan) for "adding, along with Shaw and Yeats, to the credit of old Ireland." "What," O'Neill concluded, "could be more perfect?"[2]

In the period between 1890 and the Cold War, when modern Irish literature in English attained an unprecedented stature, several Irish American figures also contributed to the concurrent development of an American modernist culture that was itself remarkably distinguished. Those involved include Kate Chopin (1850–1904), Louis Henry Sullivan (1856–1924), John Quinn (1870–1924), Gerald Clery Murphy (1888–1964), Eugene O'Neill (1888–1953), F. Scott Fitzgerald (1896–1940), Henry Cowell (1897–1965), John O'Hara (1905–70), and Flannery O'Connor (1925–64). Sullivan was a pioneer of American high-rise architecture and an early mentor to Frank Lloyd Wright, who published an appreciative account of their relationship in his *Genius and the Mobocracy* (1949).[3] The son of Irish immigrants, James Quinn, from County Limerick, and Mary Quinlaw Quinn, who had arrived in the United States as a fourteen-year old orphan, John Quinn grew up in Ohio, later becoming a lawyer and art collector in New York, where he did much to promote both Irish and European avant-garde literature and painting.[4] Gerald Murphy was a wealthy Boston-born painter and aesthete who, with his wife Sara Wiborg Murphy, settled in the French Riviera during the 1920s where their home, Villa America, became a meeting-point for the "lost generation" of American expatriates. A painter in the cubist style, Murphy's work is said by some to anticipate American pop art; Sara appeared in several Picasso paintings; the Murphys were the prototypes for Dick and Nicole Diver in Fitzgerald's *Tender is the Night* (1934).[5] Henry Cowell, the son of Carlow-born Harry Cowell, an Irish immigrant printer and writer, was a pioneer of American ultra-modernist music as well as a leading figure in the development of "world music."[6]

The respective contributions of Sullivan, Quinn, Murphy, and Cowell to American modernist architecture, painting, and music are notable. But, like their modernist contemporaries in Ireland, it was in the literary field that Irish Americans made their most sustained mark. Chopin, Fitzgerald, O'Hara, and Flannery O'Connor contributed to the development of the American modernist novel and short story; O'Neill's remaking of American drama would remain unmatched in scope by any later-twentieth-century American playwright. Nevertheless, despite these cumulative achievements, an Irish American literary modernism cannot be conceived in the same way as the roughly contemporaneous African American or Irish modernisms. The Irish Americans did not share an equivalent sense of regional or racial identity, and there was no equivalent either to an Irish or Harlem Renaissance that served as a common crucible of cultural renewal; in fact, Irish American literary historians have lamented that the modernists did not write about Irish American subject matter.[7] So how much beyond their Irish (or in some cases part-Irish) ancestry do the figures listed here actually share? To address this question it will be necessary in the first section of this chapter to consider the general historical conjuncture within which American and Irish American modernism more specifically flourished, and in the later sections to examine how a few key Irish American modernist literary works respond to that broad historical context.[8]

II

"The chief clue to the understanding of most contemporary Anglo-Saxon literature is to be found in the decay of Protestantism" wrote T. S. Eliot in *After Strange Gods* in 1933.[9] Eliot's remark on the connection between the decline of a Protestant religious world view and the emergence of modern liberal humanist sensibility that sought to replace religion with an idea of culture remains suggestive where British, Anglo-Irish, and mainstream Anglo-American modernisms are concerned. The decline of a religious sense of the world was certainly of real importance to Irish

American Catholic writers also, but their situation cannot be comprehended exactly in Eliot's terms as they had never been part of incumbent if historically declining establishment elites in the same way that Eliot and Ezra Pound or Yeats and Samuel Beckett were within their respective cultures. On the contrary, the Irish American Catholic community that took shape in the wake of the Great Famine was associated by the American WASP elites with plebeian squalor and an alien religious despotism. Moreover, as a continuous stream of new Irish migrants arrived in the United States throughout the latter half of the nineteenth century, the American-born Irish Americans always had to contend with recent arrivals from "the old country." The former, as historian Kerby Miller observes, regarded themselves as an exilic and forcibly transplanted race rather than of indigenous American stock.[10] The upshot was a remarkably conflicted identity that had to reconcile an emigrant Irishness associated with all of the vices and virtues attributed to non-modern Hibernian backwardness with an emergent Americanness associated with all of the problems and virtues of advanced modernity. However, it was arguably this bifurcated and radically contradictory inheritance that catalyzed Irish American modernism.

Although many obstacles to Irish assimilation had been overcome by the early twentieth century, it was not until Irish immigration tapered off in the 1920s that native-born Irish Americans finally overwhelmed their immigrant compatriots and forged a more separate identity. Even then, despite the enormous advances made by a small elite penetrating the upper reaches of WASP society, the vast majority of Irish Americans remained working class and the outbreak of World War I, the Easter Rising, and the Irish War of Independence renewed old hostilities on the part of the American Anglophile elites and brought fresh accusations of anti-American and anti-British sympathies. However, the Bolshevik Revolution and the emergence thereafter of the United States as the guardian of "Western Civilization" gradually allowed Irish Americans to deploy their Catholicism to strategically affiliate themselves with American nationalism on the basis of a common anti-Communism. Domestically, the emergence of African Americans after the Great Migration northward as the most radically alienated but politically assertive ethnic minority further facilitated the assimilation of the Irish Americans, allowing them to reposition themselves within the American fold as a model minority both by virtue of their anti-Communism and their commitment to a racially white America.[11]

In the cultural sphere more specifically, matters were further complicated by the advance of secular modernity, the crisis of liberalism represented by World Wars I and II, and by America's "coming-of-age" as a world power in the aftermath of the extended European catastrophe that ran from 1914 to 1945. On the one hand, America's ascendancy in this interval fed an extraordinary sense of national pride, often accompanied by a dismissive sense of European moral rottenness and cultural decline. Nevertheless, the opening up of a new era of American world domination was itself generative of doubts both political and cultural in character: political, because the United States, following Roman precedent, was perceived by critics to be surrendering its foundational republican heritage to become a successor empire to Great Britain and France; cultural, because the American intellectual elites remained troubled by anxiety, most memorably expressed by Alexis de Tocqueville, that while democratic cultures might be vigorously energetic they could never sustain the intellectual sophistication of the aristocratic cultures they would inevitably displace.[12] Thus, the United States might be replacing Great Britain and France as the engine of twentieth-century modernity, but what kind of modernity did it represent and at what cost to its foundational republicanism? And would American democracy ever be capable of fashioning a high culture equal to that of Europe or only some crass simulacrum of same?

These were generalized early-twentieth-century American excitements and anxieties, but Irish Americans experienced them through a particular subcultural filter. For those born to immigrant parents, the immigrant Irish narrative of exilic dispossession and loss and an American narrative of "rags to riches" success earned through hard work offered mutually thwarting legacies because the one narrative insisted on all that was spiritually lost or culturally squandered in pursuit of the American success that the other narrative valorized. Matters were aggravated further by the fact that, as the United States became the guardian-state of liberal capitalist modernity, the Catholic Church, worried about the advance of liberal secularism and consumer materialism, was striking a strongly anti-modern and anti-liberal disposition, as evidenced by Pius X's condemnations of "Modernism" in 1907. Ought the increasingly Irish-dominated American Catholic Church help its denigrated members to assimilate into the American mainstream to reap the benefits of capitalist modernity or work to promote some alternative value-world to that materialism? Finally, the Celticist discourses popularized by Matthew Arnold and Ernest Renan and turned to such prestigious national literary account in early-twentieth-century Ireland by the Irish revivalists represented yet another cultural legacy that pitted the Irish against modernity. Celticism elevated the hostility between Anglo-Saxon and Celt into a grand civilizational clash between a worldly bourgeois materialism and an otherworldly aristocratic spiritualism; this also ramified into an *agon* between Saxon realism and prose and Celtic imagination and poetry, or between a complacent accommodation to modernity and a seeking after something finer. In Ireland, Celticism fashioned a cultural nationalism that espoused the idea of an ancient nation heroically resistant to what Yeats called the "filthy modern tide" of twentieth-century industrial civilization.[13] But in the case of Irish America, the conflict between Saxon materialism and Celtic imagination could not be so easily displaced into a conflict with some foreign entity such as England because the United States was itself a byword for the crass modern materialism that Celticism supposedly spurned; in America, therefore, Celticism involved a quarrel with the idea of America itself.

An ethnic identity so strongly incentivized, on the one hand, to strive to find a place within American liberal capitalist modernity but disposed, on the other, by an assortment of Catholic, Celticist, and Irish exilic discourses to associate America with a debilitated materialism could hardly be a comfortable one. In the case of the Irish American writer or artist with high cultural ambitions in this period, there were good reasons not to embrace an Irish American ethnic identity. To do so was to adopt a history that smacked of a benighted peasant or working-class past, or of the sanctimony of middle-class Catholic respectability, none of these high cultural heritages. But because the United States itself also tended to be associated with mass culture rather than high culture throughout the early twentieth century, there could be no easy trade-off of one half of Irish American identity for another either. Small wonder, then, that some Irish American figures chose not to embrace an Irish American ethnic identity but to try to radically remake and elevate Irishness and Americanness alike. Modernism, as an aesthetic that in most of its manifestations repudiated the immediate past and cultivated a sense of cosmopolitan aspiration, had its attractions here, and this impulse is exemplified in various ways by Sullivan's heroically soaring architecture, Quinn's avid championing of European and Irish avant-garde art, Murphy's hedonism, or O'Neill's titanic effort to elevate the popular commercial Irish and American theatre associated with his father. Another option was to bring the discourses of Irishness (whether in its Celticist, Catholic, or exilic versions) and the discourse of Americanness into mutually interrogative contention, a strategy implicit, as we will see, in Fitzgerald and explicit in O'Neill in his later period. Most Irish American modernists personally broke with Catholicism (for instance, Chopin, Quinn, O'Neill, and Fitzgerald) or were repudiated by it (Fitzgerald was denied a Catholic burial while O'Neill was censured by the Catholic press for his nihilism), but Flannery O'Connor made Catholicism a foundation-stone of her artistic vision. To speak of an Irish American modernism, therefore, is not to denote an art that explicitly identifies with Irish America or that mimetically depicts that ethnic community's lifeworld. Instead, it is to name a constellation of work that channels the seriously contradictory value-systems that Irish Americans had to negotiate into an experimental art that dwells obsessively on the tensions between a ubiquitous capitalist materialism that subsumes and commodifies everything and a sense of yearning for something that materialism can never satisfy.

III

Praised on its publication by T. S. Eliot as "the first step that American fiction has taken since Henry James," *The Great Gatsby* (1925) remains one of the exemplary works of American modernism in the 1920s.[14] In contrast to *This Side of Paradise* (1920), his much more commercially successful first novel that draws overtly on his familial and Catholic backgrounds, there is little direct evidence in *The Great Gatsby* of the concatenation of Irish, Catholic, Celticist, and American forces that shaped Fitzgerald's imagination. However, like *This Side of Paradise*, *The Great Gatsby* is essentially an intensely self-conscious passing narrative in which an ethnic parvenu finds his way into the gorgeous upper echelons of American WASP society, there to discover the great vacuity concealed at the heart of the American Dream. In this sense at least, *The Great Gatsby* can be regarded as merely more successful in covering over its ethnic traces than *This Side of Paradise*, just as its eponymous protagonist has traded the name "Gatz" for the more assimilated "Gatsby."

Even so, Irishness has by no means been entirely elided and there are plenty of knowing winks to the reader. Gatsby has first been set on the road to his success by the uncouth and drunken millionaire Dan Cody – "the pioneer debauchee, who during one phase of American life brought back to the Eastern seaboard the savage violence of the frontier brothel and saloon."[15] Cody carries the name of Irish American entrepreneurial circus-performer of vaudeville Americanness, Buffalo Bill Cody, and thereby hints at the performative nature of identity as such, and simultaneously links Gatsby via this adoptive father with a history of American western frontier violence and eastern showbusiness. Gatsby's shady wealth is also connected to the "small, flat-nosed Jew," Meyer Wolfsheim, a stand-in for Arnold Rothstein, the racketeer who had fixed the World Series in 1919. Wolfsheim associates Gatsby with another recent immigrant ethnicity despised by WASP America for its reputed corruption, pushiness, and mass culture associations. Similarly, when Gatsby stages his opulent parties in East Egg, the mock-epic lists of guests promiscuously mingle some parodically WASP-sounding names with an outlandish mix of non-WASP ethnic interlopers, a significant number of whom appear to be Irish or Jewish:

> A man named Klipspringer was there so often and so long that he became known as "the boarder" – I doubt if he had any other home. Of theatrical people there was Gus Waize and Horace O'Donavan and Lester Meyer and George Duckweed and Francis Bull. Also from New York were the Chromes and the Backhyssons and the Dennickers and Russel Betty and the Corrigans and the Kellehers and the Dewars and the Scullys and S. W. Belcher and the Smirkes and the young Quinns, divorced now, and Henry L. Palmetto, who killed himself by jumping in front of a subway train in Times Square.[16]

To the narrator Nick Carraway, this travesty of a high-society event makes Gatsby's place seem "like the World Fair,"[17] and one party indeed is entertained by a "celebrated tenor [who] had sung in Italian" as well as by the song "Mr Vladimir Tostoff's *Jazz History of the World.*"[18] Jumbling European high culture and African American popular cultures with high- and low-society party-crashers of multifarious kinds, Gatsby's extravaganzas are a microcosm of an America whose magnificence is that it is so lavishly open to all comers but which by the same measure is so mixed in its ethnic composition as to be scarcely a bona fide nation at all, let alone one culturally coherent or sophisticated enough to rule the world. The story of a young midwestern roughneck who has been helped on his way to a fortune by a violent and drunken Irish American millionaire and a crooked Jew, who lives in a house that is "a factual imitation of some Hôtel de Ville in Normandy"[19] and who affects himself "an Oggsford man"[20] after only a brief spell in Oxford, *The Great Gatsby* is not simply a domestic national allegory about the snares of the American Dream but also a caustic commentary on modern American pretensions to emulate European high culture and European world-rule. With his sunshiny cars, faux-French chateau, imported English suits, and faux-English locutions, Gatsby represents more than just new money hoping to marry into old American stock; he is also a figure that represents an arriviste American "New World" whose attempts to mimic old European high culture of a French, English, or Italianate kind always suggest a certain brazen fakery. A Tocquevillian-style embarrassment about the crude vulgarity of American democratic culture and a sense of excitement at its rude energy and openness are consistently counterpointed in this text.

Fitzgerald's capacity to register this epochal situation was almost certainly sharpened by his own family circumstances, which contained *in nuce* something of the wider national drama. His father, Edward Fitzgerald, could trace his American lineage to the seventeenth century and was descended from the Scott Key family of Maryland that counted in its ranks the composer

Francis Scott Key who wrote the lyrics of the republic's anthem, "The Star-Spangled Banner." But Mollie McQuillan, Fitzgerald's mother, was the first-generation daughter of an Irish immigrant to St. Paul, Minnesota, and it was the newly wealthy McQuillans who financially supported the Fitzgeralds when Edward's always-precarious career collapsed in 1908. Writing to John O'Hara in 1933, F. Scott Fitzgerald presented these domestic inheritances as an *agon* between an arriviste "black Irish" vulgarity and an exhausted "old American" gentility that has had its day:

> I am half black Irish and half old American stock with the usual exaggerated ancestral pretensions. The black Irish half of the family had the money and looked down upon the Maryland side of the family who had, and really had, that certain series of reticences and obligations that go under the poor old shattered word "breeding." [21]

Here, as in *The Great Gatsby*, allegiances are slippery. The southern and aristocratic-sounding paternal Fitzgeralds have the pathos of "reticences and obligations that go under the poor old shattered word 'breeding,'" but their ancestral pretensions are (like those of Nick Carraway, who self-consciously cites his own family's dubious claims to Scottish aristocratic ancestry) in any case "exaggerated" in the typical American manner where bloodlines are concerned. The maternal "black Irish" look down with northern and new-moneyed arrogance on the shattered "Maryland side of the family," but it was McQuillan capital nonetheless that allowed Fitzgerald to be educated in the elite New Jersey Newman Catholic preparatory school and that enabled him in 1913 to enter a very Protestant Princeton, the university that he tarried in scarcely longer than did Gatsby in Oxford, but which gave him his first real access to America's WASP elite. Fitzgerald's whole story is that of an arriviste with slender pretensions to aristocratic pedigree or "breeding," but he is an arriviste in an America that was itself a quintessentially arriviste world power after 1918, and which was, like Fitzgerald, all the more headily infatuated with the idea of aristocracy for precisely that reason.

In *The Great Gatsby*, these tensions between a modern and mixed-race America of arrivistes and a would-be aristocratic WASP America seem clearly resolved, at the level of plot at least. When push comes to shove, Daisy Buchanan abandons Gatsby and remains with her muscularly upper-crust and Yale-educated husband Tom Buchanan, a polo-playing plutocrat with aristocratic pretensions who has, retro-style, converted his modern garage into old-world stables. In fact, both Buchanan-besotted working-class lovers, Gatsby and Myrtle Wilson, end up dead, their insinuations into the world of inherited wealth decisively terminated. However, while the narrative firmly strikes down these lower-class attempts at outlandish mobility, Fitzgerald deploys any number of affective strategies to suggest that the death of Gatsby (though not that of Myrtle, who is the greedily consumerist "feminine" verso of Gatsby's grandly "masculine" consumerist expansiveness) is devastatingly tragic.[22] Moreover, while the carelessly cruel Buchanans preserve their enclosed world from Gatsby's predations, that world is depicted as morally repulsive. With his world-affrighted midwestern caution, Nick seems an unlikely elegist for the gaudy Gatsby. But it is precisely this mediating narrator's combination of moral prissiness, social snobbery, homoerotic fascination, and elegiac *tristesse* that makes *The Great Gatsby* such a mesmerically self-conflicted, radically unstable text: it can never celebrate Gatsby without mocking his absurdity, nor condemn him without ruefully granting him epic grandeur.

In an early appreciation written shortly after the success of *This Side of Paradise* and before *The Great Gatsby*, Edmund Wilson, who befriended Fitzgerald at Princeton (and treated him throughout his career with a version of the patrician condescension and admiration with which Nick treats Gatsby), wrote that there were two things essential to any understanding of this author. The first was that he was from a newly wealthy but uncultured Minnesotan background and thus viewed America's eastern elite with the midwesterner's "sensitivity and eagerness for life without a sound base of culture and taste"; the second was that:

> Fitzgerald is partly Irish and that he brings both to life and to fiction certain qualities that are not Anglo-Saxon. For, like the Irish, Fitzgerald is romantic, but also cynical about romance; he is bitter as well as ecstatic; astringent as well as lyrical. He casts himself in the role of playboy, yet at the playboy he incessantly mocks. He is vain, a little malicious, of quick intelligence and wit, and has an Irish gift for turning language into something iridescent and surprising.[23]

Wilson's "sensitivity and eagerness for life" quite precisely describes the qualities that Nick admires in Gatsby – as though Fitzgerald had somehow magnified Wilson's approbation of him into Gatsby's astounding "romantic readiness"[24] and simultaneously converted Wilson's censure of his lack of "a sound base of culture and taste" into the smugness of Tom Buchanan, who despises Gatsby's lack of culture, though Tom is equally deficient. That Wilson should attribute to Fitzgerald "an Irish gift for turning language into something iridescent and surprising" might seem mere Celticism, the same affectation that led Fitzgerald to sign his letters to Wilson "Celtically" and "Gaelically yours."[25] But Wilson's assessment was written in an era in which Wilde, Shaw, Synge, Yeats, and Joyce were all major presences in the literary world and the idea of the Irishman as both sentimentally romantic playboy and astringent cynic comes straight from

Shaw's *John Bull's Other Island* (1904). That Fitzgerald might have learned how to turn a dirty deed into a gallous story from Wilde's *Salomé* (1896) or Synge's *Playboy of the Western World* (1907) or to combine Yeatsian aristocratic yearning after old worlds with Joyce's mock-epic satire of the modern metropolis is therefore hardly fanciful.

Indeed, the ability to turn "language into something iridescent and surprising" is Fitzgerald's major gift as a writer, the Midas touch that transmutes the unlovely story of Gatsby's criminal rise and fatal fixation on Daisy Buchanan into a mordantly gorgeous modernist prose-poem. Moreover, *The Great Gatsby* famously concludes with a tour de force of fine writing that gathers into itself all of those contraries of ecstatic enthusiasm and bitter cynicism that Wilson had noted as it compresses the American story from the wide-eyed Dutch sailors first landing on the green breast of the New World up to Gatsby gazing on Daisy's green light into a mini-epic of the wonder-transfixed arriviste. In this melancholically lyrical ending, Fitzgerald's novel morally repudiates the American Dream; it depends on a ceaseless striving for some chimerical future that merely threatens to make an ash-heap wasteland of a once edenic continent and that sustains a class system as violently hierarchical and rigid as any European aristocracy, but which has no culture or grace worth speaking of. If Gatsby's English suits and French villa are sustained by lower-class Irish and Jewish criminal racketeering, polo-playing Tom's WASP anxieties about the collapse of the white race betray an upper-class crudity that is no more refined; there is a thuggish element to both men. But *Gatsby* stylistically affirms what it morally abhors, granting Gatsby especially, like the arriviste America whose spirit he incarnates, a matchless intensity of aspiration that is deemed somehow to be redemptive, no matter how dubious its ultimate object. The vacillations of an Irish America on the threshold of acceptance into a white America that was itself on the threshold of becoming an imperial world power do much to explain this mixture of enthusiasm and abhorrence that makes Fitzgerald's classic novel the terrifically schizoid text that it is. Intellectually, *The Great Gatsby* cannot reconcile the contradictions between the epic nature of American ambition and the trashiness of its ultimate object; stylistically, it converts these antinomies into a ruefully ecstatic high modernism that remains skeptical of the American idea even as it flamboyantly attests to America's cultural arrival on the world stage.

IV

"Irish-American through and through, with an heroic resentment of the New England Yankee tradition, O'Neill from the start seemed to know that his spiritual quest was to undermine Emerson's American religion of self-reliance."²⁶ This is Harold Bloom's verdict, though Bloom also remarks that: "Perhaps no major dramatist has ever been so lacking in rhetorical exuberance, in what Yeats once praised Blake for having: 'beautiful, laughing speech.'"²⁷ Combined, these assessments suggest that O'Neill was more fiercely skeptical than Fitzgerald about American materialism and individualism, but lacked the "Irish gift for turning language into something iridescent and surprising" that Wilson had praised in the Minnesotan Irishman. There may indeed be a labored earnestness in O'Neill's vision and something unlovely in his language that separates him not only from Fitzgerald but from the more lyrically adventurous versions of Irish modernism more generally. But this is a partial truth. Irish modernism and maybe American modernism too trace a broad curve from linguistic extravagance to linguistic austerity, each graduating from the early hothouse aestheticism of the Decadents and Symbolists to the linguistic minimalism of late modernism, as variously practised by Ernest Hemingway, Beckett, or Flannery O'Connor. It is as though in the fin de siècle contest between the disenchanted dictions of the naturalists and the opulent ones of the aestheticists, the latter had won a temporary ascendancy that prevailed until a brilliant high modernist interval, only then for the evicted naturalists to return after the 1920s and conquer everything. O'Neill's work, due to its earliest debts to Scandinavian and Shavian naturalism, was foundationally affiliated to this linguistically penurious naturalistic world, but it is never at home there. An Irishman bearing the aristocratic surname of Gaelic high kings growing up in Yankee New England, a lapsed Catholic coming of age in an era of Wilsonian Protestantism and Prohibition, a playwright who achieved his best work in the late modernist period but who always retained a high modernist ambition to epic totality, O'Neill, like Fitzgerald, is perpetually at odds with himself and his milieu.

Unlike Fitzgerald, O'Neill was immigrant Irish on both sides. However, the social gap between the severely impoverished family background of his father, James O'Neill, who in 1847 fled the Great Famine from Kilkenny and grew up in the slums of Buffalo, New York, before going on to become a famous actor, and the more prosperous family circumstances of his mother, Mary Ellen Quinlan, meant that he too psychically internalized the divide between lower- and middle-class Irish America. His father's associations with the popular commercial theatre meant that in O'Neill's case the modernist antipathy to popular culture was also a personal affair. It was as though in creating a highbrow American drama he could at once supersede the degraded commercial paternal legacy and a more general Irish association with vaudeville and minstrelsy and simultaneously redeem the father's lost promise to be a great Shakespearean actor, which, according to family legend at least, had been squandered when he committed to play the title role in a long-running Broadway dramatization of Alexandre Dumas's *The Count of Monte Cristo* (1844–5). Like the Abbey Theatre dramatists he admired, Eugene O'Neill was a writer without an available national theatrical high cultural tradition; he had no option but to fashion his art from an eclectic variety of sources ranging from modern naturalism to Greek or Shakespearean tragedy.[28]

Long Day's Journey Into Night (written 1941–2, published and first performed 1956), the work usually considered his masterpiece, converts not only O'Neill's own family and national inheritance but also this complex literary and cultural inheritance into a tale of tragic doom. Before the audience meets the ill-fated Tyrones, it is first introduced to their family library where, as an elaborate opening stage direction stipulates, a portrait of Shakespeare presides over a bookcase comprised of novels by "Balzac, Zola, Stendhal," intellectual treatises by "Schopenhauer, Nietzsche, Marx, Engels, Kropotkin [and] Max Stirner," and plays by "Ibsen, Shaw [and] Strindberg" alongside the poetry of "Swinburne, Rossetti, Wilde, Ernest Dowson [and] Kipling, etc." That library, we are told, also contains "three sets of Shakespeare" and histories by Gibbon, Hume and Thiers as well as the works of Charles Lever and "several histories of Ireland." "The astonishing thing about these sets," the stage directions comment sardonically, "is that all the volumes have the look of having been read and reread."[29] We are not, then, in Gatsby's culturally innocent world in which expensive library books are uncut objects of display, but in a meta-critical world attentive to its own intellectual resources.

Long Day's Journey stresses a generational divide between James and Mary Tyrone and their unmarried sons Jamie and Edmund (the ghost of the dead third son, Eugene, also hovering somewhere near), and the play similarly divides the literary universe represented by the family library into two ages. Presiding God-like above the later works of European letters, Shakespeare belongs to an old world that, for James Tyrone at least, represents an age of healthy literature, and Tyrone *père*, despite Edmund's scorn, even insists, however absurdly, that "Shakespeare was an Irish Catholic" and that "The proof is in his plays."[30] In contrast, James insists, the modern literary world of Voltaire, Schopenhauer, and Nietzsche or Dowson, Rossetti, and Wilde, the writers his sons' love, is a diseased world consumed by a death wish. With his sturdy Irish peasant health and fierce drive for success, James, like his beloved Shakespeare, also seems to possess an old-world vigor, whereas his sons in contrast, as evidenced by Jamie's chronic nihilism and alcoholism and Edmund's consumption, like the modern post-Enlightenment literature they love to recite, are diseased and death-doomed.

Long Day's Journey knows that the fiction that the world can be divided into a pre-Enlightenment age of rude health, high culture, and faith and a post-Enlightenment age of disease, literary decadence, and spiritual disillusion is a convenience only. The legend that James could have been America's greatest Shakespearean actor is another, as is Mary's belief that were it not for her fall into the sordid theatrical world of her husband she might have retained her Catholic faith and the eternal consolation of the Blessed Virgin. These are all threadbare self-deceiving family myths, but they still exert an enormous spell. And while *Long Day's Journey* never invites its audience to credit these myths, neither does it encourage it to view the disenchanted post-Enlightenment world as a welcome escape from such self-delusion. Thus, even though James O'Neill is a land-grasping skinflint who likes to present himself as a grand Old World Irish aristocrat, he nonetheless really does have an earthy peasant energy that his sneering Mephistophelian Irish American son, Jamie, the New World non-believer, lacks. The stage directions tell us that thirty-three-year-old Jamie "lacks his father's vitality" and that the "signs of premature disintegration are on him."[31] As in O'Neill's *The Iceman Cometh* (written 1939, performed 1946), in which Hickey shatters the desperate delusions of the denizens of Harry Hope's bar only to discover than no-one, not even he, can live without pipe dreams, delusion and the disenchantment of delusion seem equally destructive here. Thus, the older generation in *Long Day's Journey* may pine disastrously for faded faiths that the younger generation has outgrown and scorns, but the notion that people can live without belief or even misbelief is itself a delusion, different from others only in being more suicidal.

Where does this dialectic of deluded belief and destructive unbelief leave things? By the final act, set around midnight, all the Tyrone family fictions have long since been shredded: Mary has retreated into drug addiction, the menfolk into alcoholic stupor, and the mutual recrimination that lacerated their daytime conversation now spent too. So sodden and beaten a world ought to run – as perhaps in Beckett – toward total silence or at least that linguistic flatness that Bloom ascribes to O'Neill. But instead O'Neill makes the last act of *Long Day's Journey* the most soaringly poetic in the play; he does so, however, not by means of his own verbal resources but by plundering the late-nineteenth-century Decadents for successive set pieces when Edmund and Jamie, paragons of New World disbelief, recite at length the poetry of Baudelaire, Swinburne, Dowson, and Wilde. The point of this is that once it has dissolved all Old World faiths and melted everything that had once seemed solid into air, the post-Enlightenment New World has nothing left for spiritual or literary resource but to make poetry of its own disenchantment and spiritual penury. To this extent at least *Long Day's*

Journey endorses James O'Neill's Irish conviction that the New World is sicker than the Old, its only surviving creed the debased religion of money, its last great wish a death wish. The play closes with Mary's disconsolate plea for an innocence that belonged to a time before she was pushed out of her girlhood convent and lost her Catholic faith. Lyrical arias of fin de siècle decadence and despair and a real craving for the recovery of a spiritually enchanted universe contend to the bitter end. But what brings down the curtain is not just the pathos of the lapsed Catholic or lapsed believer in the American Dream, but that of a late modernist who knows even the Decadent poetry of despair has also had its day and can no longer shelter anyone from even darker night.

V

For both Fitzgerald's *The Great Gatsby* and O'Neill's *Long Day's Journey Into Night*, a hankering after something irretrievably lost as the price of entry into American liberal capitalist modernity issues in a condition of bewilderment salved only by the saving grace of art or style. The death of mystery and the difficulties of belief in modern America are Flannery O'Connor's fundamental preoccupations, too, although her fictional world is of a low-mimetic kind located in a grotesque backwoods American South that has none of decadent splendor of Fitzgerald's New York nor the high tragic aspiration of O'Neill's tormented Tyrones. "Christian dogma is about the only thing left in the world that surely guards and respects mystery."[32] From this credo O'Connor fashioned a work that is a bizarre legatee to O'Neill's and Fitzgerald's, one that turns back to religion to redeem a world shown to be in desperate need of salvation, though scarcely capable of even grasping what salvation might mean.

O'Connor was born in 1925 in Savannah, Georgia, to Regina Cline and Edward F. O'Connor. Her father died in 1941 of lupus, the fatal disease that she contracted a decade later. As an orthodox Catholic, O'Connor might easily have made her cultural alienation from the religious fundamentalism of the Protestant South her major theme. However, it was not from Protestantism but from liberal humanist and secular America, which all her works savagely rebuke, that O'Connor was really alienated. And she was in any case skeptical of alienation as a cultural standpoint or literary disposition, writing scornfully in an incisive essay that "Alienation was once a diagnosis, but in much of the fiction of our time it has become an ideal."[33] Choosing, therefore, identification with the world of her Southern origins rather than espousing what she regarded as a facilely conventional sense of alienation, O'Connor contended that the Bible Belt was actually a singularly valuable resource for an American Catholic literature, because there the writer could still find the religious enthusiasm, widespread Biblical literacy, and prophetic vision that any Christianity worth its salt always needed. "It becomes more and more difficult in America to make belief believable, but in this the Southern writer has the greatest possible advantage. He lives in the Bible Belt."[34] Yet despite this insistence on its value, it is nearly impossible to tell from O'Connor's fiction whether she really sees the Protestant South as a society still promisingly vibrant with religious feeling or rather as a place that exemplifies the horrible disfigurations of religion in modern times. Her fiction, that is, represents a world so spiritually blasted and morally twisted as to seem to revoke the tribute she pays to the Protestant South in her critical writing. Yet it is always that Protestant South, and not the Catholic world in which she grew up and to which she declared allegiance, that transfixes her literary imagination.

The grandson of an itinerant evangelical preacher, Hazel Motes, the crazed protagonist of O'Connor's *Wise Blood* (1949), returns from World War II an aggressively militant atheist determined to scandalize the Bible Belt of his youth by evangelizing his own faithless faith as preached in his "Church Without Christ," which proclaims that "the blind don't see and the lame don't walk and what's dead stays that way."[35] However, in the seedy city of Taulkinham where he preaches his anti-gospel, Motes makes no impression because the local populace has become so coarsened and incapable of conviction that it regards the heretic and the devout with equal indifference, or is interested in either only as entertainment. As a result, Hazel attracts the attention of a local conman, Hoover Shoats, alias Onnie Jay Holy, who wishes to rename Motes's church "The Holy Church of Christ Without Christ."[36] With a grander name and better marketing, Shoats seems to think, Hazel's preaching zeal can at least be converted into lucrative showmanship. Enraged that religion and heresy alike should be destined to become merely more fodder for the society of the spectacle, Hazel is confounded, his crusade without purpose in an already post-religious universe. Having exposed Asa Hawks, a fake fellow-evangelist who had pretended to blind himself in a Biblical act of Christian faith, Motes withdraws from the world in despair. Eventually, taking on himself the grand gesture of faith that Hawks had only simulated, Motes, in a desperate act of late conversion, limes his eyes till they are sightless. Starting out with a belated mission to scandalize religious sensibility, O'Connor's protagonist does an about turn when he discovers that the much more demanding crusade would actually be to restore that sensibility.

There is a sense, then, in which O'Connor represents the completion of a cycle whereby a modernism that had once found its origins in an attempt to make art do duty for religion now abandons this ambition as hubristic and returns to subserve religion. A low mimetic, hillbilly version of O'Neill's cynical, world-weary Jamie Tyrone, Hazel Motes begins *Wise Blood* as an evangelist of anti-Christian nihilism, but abandons this blasphemous crusade when he discovers its redundancy so as to become a kind of grotesquely self-mortifying Old Testament saint who testifies to faith. Thus, whereas O'Neill's characters in *Long Day's Journey* follow a trajectory that takes them from a condition of already tattered belief into a kind of hellish midnight where every belief is shredded, O'Connor's impulse is to pursue an inverse trajectory that starts with unbelief as a given but then undertakes a difficult journey back to belief. The Protestant South furnishes O'Connor with a landscape she declares hospitable to this quest. But her actual depiction of that South as a place in which religion is either totally dead or survives only in horribly mutilated and shrivelled forms means that any prospect of recovering what has been lost seems ultimately, whatever her declared intentions, as imaginatively remote for O'Connor as for O'Neill. O'Connor, in other words, struggles fiercely to wrest a blessing from her malignant world and to make her readers feel a need for divine grace, even if she can do so only by relentlessly rubbing their noses in the sheer awfulness of their latterday substitute religions. But whether a modern world conceived in such relentlessly grotesque terms can ever really yield a scintilla of grace is questionable.

In a statement cited earlier in this chapter, T. S. Eliot asserted that "The chief clue to the understanding of most contemporary literature is to be found in the decay of Protestantism." For some high modernists, art or culture became a substitute religion, standing in by sheer effort of stylistic will and totalizing ambition for the collapsing faiths of the modern era and giving the twentieth century is own secular equivalent of "sacred texts." For others, the later-period T. S. Eliot himself being the exemplary instance, this was to ask too much of art and the only recourse was to return to a Catholicism or Anglo-Catholicism that had not capitulated, as Protestantism had apparently done, to modern humanism and liberalism. O'Connor is a late modernist after Eliot in the sense that, for her, art can no longer pretend to compensate for religion or to be merely content with expressing a sense of alienation. In *The Great Gatsby*, the gigantically unseeing eyes of Dr. Eckleburg look out like those of a vacuous God over the spreading American wasteland; but in Fitzgerald's novel, this God-abandoned universe is at least relieved by the grandeur, however deluded, of Gatsby's capacity for wonder, and by the sinuous lyrical virtuosity of Fitzgerald's prose. And in *Long Day's Journey*, even a long day's voyage into the dark night of spiritual torment has the mitigating grace of its decadent fin de siècle poetry.

However, neither Gatsby-like attempts to steer between frank cynicism and desperate romance nor borrowing bitter-sweet Baudelaire-style Decadent despair will satisfy O'Connor. These are versions of modernism that rely too much on poetic elan to compensate for what has been spiritually lost to modernity. Thus, O'Connor's signature style is deliberately harsh and non-poetic; her's is brutally anti-lyrical world of freakshows and the grotesque. But something holy, she insists, has somehow to be prised from this degraded material.

In this one respect at least, O'Connor is a Southern Irish American Catholic counterpart to the Southern Irish Protestant Beckett: stylistically, they share an utterly abjected world, a horror of all bogus consolations, the same chilled cerebral comedy, the same renunciation of high modernist pretensions to aesthetic grandeur or totalizing ambition. Beckett, of course, has no wish to proselytize his reader and he looks for no reconciliation with God or miracles of grace, though readers may feel that only this could save his worlds. In her critical writings, O'Connor declares her desire to proselytize and affirms the search for miracle her vocation, and this ought to make her very different to Beckett, yet her work serves its avowed functions only, if at all, by way of the most tortuous negative dialectics. In their different ways, she and Beckett represent a last-gasp modernism resourcefully managing its rapidly diminishing means.

NOTES

1 O'Neill to Eugene O'Neill, Jr., November 11, 1932, in Travis Bogard and Jackson R. Bryer, eds. *Selected Letters of Eugene O'Neill* (New Haven, CT: Yale University Press, 1988), 407. The figures referred to in O'Neill's letter are George Russell (AE), Sean O'Casey, Liam O'Flaherty, and Lennox Robinson.

2 O'Neill to Russell Crouse, November 25, 1936, in Bogard and Bryer, *Selected Letters*, 455.

3 On Sullivan, see Willard Connely, *Louis Sullivan As He Lived: The Shaping of American Architecture* (New York: Horizon Press, 1960); and Frank Lloyd Wright, *Genius and the Mobocracy* (New York: Duell, Sloan and Pearce, 1949).

4 On Quinn, see B. L. Reid, *The Man from New York: John Quinn and His Friends* (New York: Oxford University Press, 1968).

5 On Gerald and Sara Murphy, see Calvin Tomkins, *Living Well Is the Best Revenge* (New York: Viking Press, 1971).

6 On Cowell, see Michael Hicks, *Henry Cowell, Bohemian* (Chicago: University of Illinois Press, 2002); and Joel Sachs, *Henry Cowell: A Man Made of Music* (Oxford: Oxford University Press, 2012).

7 For example, Charles Fanning's *The Irish Voice in America: 250 Years of Irish-American Fiction* (Lexington: University Press of Kentucky, 2000) excludes most of the Irish-American modernist writers discussed here because they do not engage in ethnic representation of a social realist kind.

8 For purposes of abbreviation, the term "Irish American" refers hereafter to Irish American writers of Catholic background. As the case of Cowell reminds us, there are many Irish Americans of Protestant origin, commonly self-designated as "Scots Irish" or "Scotch-Irish." But the writers considered here emerged from an Irish American Catholic background and will be assessed in that context.

9 T. S. Eliot, *After Strange Gods: A Primer of Modern Heresy*, (London: Faber and Faber, 1933), 38.

10 On the Irish exilic narrative, see Kerby A. Miller, *Emigrants and Exiles: Ireland and the Irish Exodus to North America* (New York: Oxford University Press, 1985).

11 See variously Kevin Kenny, *The American Irish: A History* (Harlow: Pearson Educational, 2000); J. J. Lee and Marion R. Casey, *Making the Irish American: History and Heritage of the Irish in the United States* (New York: New York University Press, 2000); and Christopher Dowd, *The Construction of Irish Identity in American Literature* (New York: Routledge, 2011).

12 See Alexis de Tocqueville, *Democracy in America*, Gerald Bevan, trans. (London and New York: Penguin Books, 2003); on American culture, see especially volume 2, part I.

13 See Yeats, "The Statues," in M. L. Rosenthal, ed., *William Butler Yeats: Selected Poems and Four Plays* (New York: Scribner, 1996), 205–6.

14 Cited in F. Scott Fitzgerald, *The Crack-Up*, Edmund Wilson, ed. (New York: New Directions, 1993), 310.

15 F. Scott Fitzgerald, *The Great Gatsby* (Hertfordshire: Wordsworth's Classics, 2001), 64.

16 Fitzgerald, *Great Gatsby*, 40.

17 Fitzgerald, *Great Gatsby*, 52.

18 Fitzgerald, *Great Gatsby*, 31, 33.

19 Fitzgerald, *Great Gatsby*, 5.

20 Fitzgerald, *Great Gatsby*, 46.

21 Matthew F. Bruccoli, ed., *F. Scott Fitzgerald: A Life in Letters* (New York: Scribners, 1994), 233. Cited in Kirk Curnutt, *A Historical Guide to F. Scott Fitzgerald* (Oxford: Oxford University Press, 2004), 23–4.

22 On modernist rhetorics that feminize consumerism, see Rita Felski, *The Gender of Modernity* (Cambridge, MA: Harvard University Press, 1995), 61–90.

23 Edmund Wilson, "F. Scott Fitzgerald," in *The Shores of Light: A Literary Chronicle of the Twenties and Thirties* (New York: Vintage Books, 1961). Cited in Fanning, *The Irish Voice in America*, 247.

24 Wilson, "F. Scott Fitzgerald," 4.

25 See Robert Sklar, *F. Scott Fitzgerald: The Last Laocoön* (New York: Oxford University Press, 1967), 14.

26 Harold Bloom, "Foreword," Eugene O'Neill, *Long Day's Journey Into Night* (New Haven, CT: Yale University Press, 2002), vi.

27 Bloom, "Foreword," viii.

28 On O'Neill, see Louis Sheaffer, *O'Neill: Son and Playwright* (Boston: Little Brown, 1968) and *O'Neill: Son and Artist* (Boston: Little Brown, 1973).

29 O'Neill, *Long Day's Journey*, 11.

30 O'Neill, *Long Day's Journey*, 129.

31 O'Neill, *Long Day's Journey*, 19.

32 Flannery O'Connor, "Catholic Novelists and Their Readers," in *Mystery and Manners: Occasional Prose*, Sally and Robert Fitzgerald, eds. (New York: Farrar, Strauss & Giroux, 1957), 169–90, 178.

33 Flannery O'Connor, "The Catholic Novelist in the Protestant South," in *Mystery and Manners*, 191–207, 199.

34 Flannery O'Connor, *Mystery and Manners*, 201.

35 Flannery O'Connor, *Wise Blood*, (London: Faber and Faber, 1949), 99.

36 Flannery O'Connor, *Wise Blood*, 145.

PART IV

Domestic Receptions, World Imaginations

12

ENDA DUFFY

Critical Receptions of Literary Modernism

Irish modernism and Irish postcoloniality were parallel projects, and the closeness of the cultural and the political realms fostered a tense intimacy between Irish modernism and its Irish readers. In the years before Irish independence, Anglo-Irish critics were inevitably suspicious: Trinity College Provost John Pentland Mahaffy, for example, remarked that "James Joyce is a living argument in favour of my contention that it was a mistake to establish a separate university for the aborigines of this island – for the corner boys who spit in the Liffey."[1] After 1921, readers and critics in the new Irish state had their own suspicions about the evolving work of Irish modernism. No member of the Irish consular staff attended Joyce's funeral when he died in Zurich in 1941. (Lord Derwent, British ambassador to Bern, was there and spoke).[2] In these charged and changing political and cultural contexts, the response of early critics in Ireland to Irish modernism was often suspicious, timid, and ambivalent.

This chapter surveys the turns this timidity took; first, let us consider some further reasons for it. In the small Irish artistic-intellectual world, many of the critics knew the writers well, and personal feelings color their criticism. Thus, for example, the first Irish commentators on Joyce's books had often figured as characters in them, from Oliver St. John Gogarty to John Eglinton. Second, serious critical commentary on Irish modernism was hampered by the sectarian divide in the Irish university system, by the precarious status of the new universities that catered to Catholics, and by the lack of interest on the part of the professoriate in the contemporary Irish cultural scene. Early critiques of Irish modernism appeared in the kinds of venues that championed modernist experiment elsewhere – that is, in little magazines and ephemeral publications. This explains why a sustained critical response to the Revival only emerged belatedly, once the universities, after their 1970s expansions, began to produce an intellectual class ready to offer analyses of Irishness in comparative or global terms. (The notable exception to this academic deficit is Daniel Corkery.) This essay concludes where the academic response begins; it chronicles instead the succession of amateurs, dilettantes, and fellow-writers who improvised the narrative on which the academic critics would subsequently build.

An additional factor in the critics' ambivalence was that they were never sure whether they were writing for an audience at home in Ireland, in which case they might debate a work's impact on the national scene, or for a broader audience, whether British (which demanded its own special tact – or hypocrisy) or American. Note, for example, how many commentators on the Irish Revival – Ernest Boyd, Padraig and Mary Colum, Gogarty – ended by making New York their home. These critics sold a new version of Irishness to Americans; they also partook in a new stage in the movement of transnational cultural capital in the West, in which not only the work of authors from marginal locales, but their critics too, could be deemed of interest, under certain conditions, in the metropolis. In the United States, in the case of Irish culture, this involved the slow acceptance of the Irish immigrant population as part of the American *civitas*. Whether or not they knew it, these critics were part of a cultural turn in the United States whereby, as it's been said eloquently, the Irish became white.[3] Irish literary modernism was not just a local phenomenon but the result of diverse and experimental negotiations between the local situation and the global context; the Irish critical response to it was also formed in such negotiations, and for the criticism, the international quotient was if anything more crucial.

This issue of how the critics' international, and particularly American, audience affected their criticism returns us to this criticism's crux: the particular nature of Irish modernism itself. Irish modernism stands bifurcated by the historical dividing line of the Easter Rebellion and the War of Independence. Its first half, from James Clarence Mangan to Yeats, readily readable as the full-throated textuality of a national cultural revival, is in many ways not conventionally modernist at all. It often explicitly rejects the urban, alienated, lonely, crowded, and bourgeois world of T. S. Eliot, Marcel Proust, Robert Musil, and Virginia Woolf. The second wave of Irish modernism, on the other hand, from Joyce to Beckett and beyond, enters into the forms and attitudes of cosmopolitan modernism with a vengeance, while still maintaining Ireland as its setting. With these successive anticolonial and postcolonial modernisms, the Irish modernist progression has a unique cast. Irish modernist texts had to come to terms with the same social, cultural, and technological transformations that were being charted in cosmopolitan modernist texts – to which one other, epistemic-changing transformation was added: the rebellion and the achievement of independence. Irish literature changed on April 21, 1916. This gave Irish modernism an intense intimacy with political revolution as its central energizing impulse.

Irish criticism of modernism, as much as the literary works themselves, also had the shock of dramatic political change always reverberating through its very structures, and thus had to face a series of specific issues to articulate its ideas. First, was protonationalist "Celtic Revival" literature really modernist at all? Second, was the subsequent wave of more avant-garde Euro-modernism in any sense Irish? Third, should the critic open up the issues at stake in this contradiction for a local audience, or simply flog some well-packaged account of a literary movement's achievement for an international one? Facing this series of unlikelihoods and potentials, Irish critics, like the modernist texts themselves, pivoting around the caesura of independence and *before* and *after* chronotopes of late-colonial struggle and postcolonial disillusion, often retreated instead to the surer ground of an analogous but more superficial debate. That is, they argued about whether Irish writing should be more national, and (in various formulae) local, or whether it should be more cosmopolitan. For one faction, Irish writers were not Irish enough; for another, they were frighteningly insular and provincial: Daniel Corkery versus Seán Ó Faoláin. Whatever the perspective, arguments couched only in these terms often smacked of the insecurity of the marginal. They defer the question of the significance of Irish independence, and thus fudge the crucial issue for a national criticism of how the interaction of literature and politics could generate a specifically local modernism.

The Irish critical response to modernism may be said to have been inaugurated where the previous phase ended, with the activist certainty of the Gaelic League founder Douglas Hyde's *A Literary History of Ireland From the Earliest Time to the Present Day* (1899). Hyde's study is a version *avant la lettre* of Corkery's *The Hidden Ireland* of 1924, without the controversy stirred by the latter. Here, Irish literature ends with the eighteenth-century bardic schools. Reinforcing its work of scholarly reclamation is a nationalist certitude that the long tradition of Gaelic literature gives the Irish a native literary record of which they can be proud. Hyde casts his scholarship, in other words, in the form familiar to celebrations of Irish cultural achievement since the days of Thomas Davis in *The Nation*. The work was meant to appeal to the pride of newly prosperous emigrants abroad as well as to the native Irish, so that it is appropriate that today Hyde's work sits next to the embossed, green-boarded anthologies of Irish writing produced for the immigrant market still to be found in university libraries.

The first wave of modernist Celtic Revival writing aimed to continue the Gaelic tradition, to "Be counted one / With Davis, Mangan, Ferguson" in Yeats's phrase. Yet Yeats's need to claim this inheritance betrays his uncertainty about any seamless continuity, an uncertainty even more evident in the early critical writing of the Celtic Revival era. Ireland's early modernist literature, like that in London, Lisbon, or Chicago, was produced around coteries and printed often in little magazines, where critiques mingled with the literary texts, and where the usual self-regard and infighting of such venues was exacerbated by the small scale of Ireland's literary scene. It was in conditions of such intimacy that "John Eglinton" wrote his most important criticism. Eglinton was the pen name of W. K. Magee, and the Magee/Eglinton difference (the refusal to be "Magee") bespeaks the West-Brit binarism that shadows his writing.

Eglinton is best known for a single critical judgment: as editor of the magazine *Dana*, he rejected the autobiographical sketch by Joyce that subsequently became *A Portrait of the Artist as a Young Man* (1916). Eglinton justified his rejection with a stock anti-modernist jibe: "I cannot print what I cannot understand." Joyce had his revenge by pillorying Eglinton in *Ulysses* as the one who "ask[s] with elder's gall ... holyeyed."[4] He has Eglinton begin his sentences with the very un-Irish "One." Eglinton moved to Bournemouth in 1924, unwilling, he claimed, to live in an independent Ireland. In the 1920s he wrote "Dublin Letters" in *The Dial*, and essays in another, tormented genre that forms part of the Irish response to modernism – memoirs of the famous writer the critic is now proud to have once known. The best, and most embarrassing, of these essays are on Joyce. Critically, Eglinton's free-thinking reasonableness had earlier led him to oppose Yeats's Celtic Twilight effusions. Rather than reinvent a wholly Irish tradition, Eglinton advocated not simply a cosmopolitan outlook, but a Thoreau-inspired universalism; these arguments with Yeats are outlined in his *Literary Ideas in Ireland* of 1898. In that work, Eglinton may have launched the school of Irish modernist critique that bemoans the obsession with Irishness and with Irish nationalism, but his laconic style undercuts his argument. This style turns tormented when he writes on Joyce in *Irish Literary Portraits* (1935). Earlier, in *The Dial*[5] he had berated *Ulysses* on the usual grounds of its modernist novelty, noting that "[t]here is an effort and strain in the composition of this book which makes one at times feel a concern for its author."[6] (Of course, he was not alone in this attitude; George Moore, among other notable Irish writer-critics, also found *Ulysses* "boring ... dirty" and called its author "a nobody from the Dublin docks: no family, no breeding."[7]) Writing in 1929, Eglinton professes to think of Joyce as primarily Catholic: "In him, for the first time, the mind of Catholic Ireland triumphs over the Anglicanism of the English language,"[8] so that he offers Joyce the backhanded compliment that his "Catholic" language marks the triumph of the newly independent Ireland. This might seem like the first statement placing Joyce as a postcolonial writer, but it is born of sectarian snobbery and resentment of his success. Bitterness causes him to claim that Joyce's modernism, far from being progressive, was reactionary. This was the end-point, moreover, of Eglinton's original argument with what he perceived as Yeats's overly local interest in Ireland; he now professes a "distaste" for the Celtic Revival in general. That its most distinguished early literary critic should have been a professed apostate meant that Irish modernism did not have the comfort of support from Irish critics. However, this critique only flourished on the Dublin-London axis; elsewhere, especially for the American audience, Irish Revival writers were lavished with praise.

If Eglinton stands for "enlightened intransigence" in the face of successive waves of modernism, Boyd, in his seminal *Ireland's Literary Renaissance* of 1916, is positively eager to avoid dissent. An *Irish Times* reporter who joined the British consular service, he was sent to Baltimore, and, on resigning in 1920, settled in New York, working as a translator and *littérateur*. Boyd's study tells with extraordinary evenness a tale of Irish cultural success. It characterizes diverse writings as a movement confident in its claim to international attention and refuses any sense of inferiority about Ireland's marginality. But Boyd's book is also almost wholly *un*comparative; it neither presents the new Irish literature as a branch of Britain's, nor does it think of it as part of any international developments, except in the most general of terms. This abjuring of the comparative stance meant that the "modernism" of Irish renaissance writing never had to be faced directly. Boyd's achievement is both highly innovative and monumental: he inaugurated the narrative of the Revival, which – despite new nuances and changes of inflection – is still largely in place a century later. The detrimental influence of *Ireland's Literary Renaissance* lies in its refusal to compare Ireland's with other national literatures. By telling a highly coherent tale of measured development that was more or less wholly local, leading from "Precursors" (Mangan) to "Fathers" (O'Grady) to "Sources" (Hyde) to "Transition Writers" (Allingham) to the Revival in full flower (Yeats and many others) to "The Younger Generation" (the Maunsel poets), he invented a tale persuasive both to Irish nationalists at home and abroad and to literary critics. (He gives short shrift to prose, and dismisses *Dubliners* as "curious studies of lower-class city life."[9]) He leaves in abeyance the question of the particular significance of Ireland's cultural entrée into modernity. Consummate public-relations man of the Revival, Boyd tells a compelling story of enterprising, gradual, and thoroughly successful innovation.

Boyd's is a story of international-level achievement on an island about which few success stories were told. Celebrating successful Irish cultural entrepreneurship has perhaps been the predominant note of Irish literary and cultural criticism since, to such a degree that it appears naturalized. The post-1980s postcolonial turn has, if anything, burnished this narrative, despite asking some serious questions about the political efficacy of each author's work. We need to note, at this remove, whose interests Boyd's work has served and whose it has sidelined. For a start, its stress on how authors achieve success by building on the work of their predecessors introduced a conservative emphasis on literary tradition into Irish modernist letters. Direct discussions of rupture were avoided. This in turn discouraged discussion of other kinds of possible relations between the literary and social, political, or class-based forces. It also played down the impact of events "abroad," that might also account for some of the richness of the new literature.

If Boyd's tour de force seems tailored to audiences abroad, his successors, writing after Irish independence, wrote primarily for a Free State audience concerned with the cultural prospects of the new nation. The representative figures here were Daniel Corkery and his one-time student, Ó Faoláin. Although from successive generations (Corkery, born in 1878, was four years older than Joyce; Ó Faoláin was born in 1900), the two have much in common, even if their critical stances now appear at odds. Both were from Cork, and each brought a blunt provincial perspective to bear on the Dublin scene. Both came from working-class backgrounds and both possessed a surfeit of idealism for the cultural possibilities implied by the founding of the Irish postcolonial state.

Given this idealism, there is much poignance in Corkery's well-argued nativism. Much hard-headed materialist observation of the actual conditions of production of Irish modernist literature underlies his arguments. Corkery is commonly cited today as the starred example of the fundamentalist, insular strain in Irish literary criticism. This reputation was cemented when a 1969 article by L. M. Cullen questioning the historical accuracy of the picture painted in *The Hidden Ireland*[10] became a much-cited opening salvo in the "revisionist" Irish history wars.[11] It is Corkery's *Synge and Irish Literature* of 1931, however, that directly took aim at the critical response to Irish modernism. Declaring at the outset that "A normal literature is written within the confines of a country which names it," he excoriates the Anglo-Irish writers of the literary Revival, who wrote in English, and, as scions of the British-descended aristocratic landlord class that oppressed the native Irish, knew nothing of the peasants or the middle-class Catholics they purported to represent. They were writing neither for those peasants, nor did they have any real sympathy for them. J. M. Synge, alone among the Revival writers, attempted contact with the peasantry, and therefore, Corkery implies, deserves the benefit of the doubt, which this study narrowly gives him. Although moved by *Riders to the Sea* (1904), he speaks of *The Playboy of the Western World* (1907) as "an alien ascendancy's callous caperings,"[12] concluding that "[h]is elimination of the spiritual left a narrowness in ... [his characters]. It is in this way that they are freakish, not in the poetry talk they indulge in nor in their want of practicality in human affairs."[13] This judgment follows from Corkery's opening declaration that "[t]he three great forces ... in the Irish national being ... are (1) the religious consciousness of the people, (2) Irish nationalism, and (3) the land."[14] Corkery's traditionalist nationalism is hardly surprising in the new postcolonial polis. His animus against the ascendancy is reinforced by his class origins, yet he relentlessly transmutes his class consciousness into accounts of "national being."

Despite his insularity, Corkery sounds almost like the young W. H. Auden of the same years, as mandarin modernism gave way to a degree of social awareness after the economic crash. And it is tempting to fantasize that, under better circumstances and with a somewhat altered outlook, Corkery might have grown into the Irish Georg Lukács, or even the Irish Antonio Gramsci. Answering his call for a writer to represent the consciousness of the Irish lumpenproletariat, he might have found Joyce, whose rejection of Christianity he would no doubt have held as alien. That, in this study published ten years after *Ulysses* (1922) appeared, he is still obsessed with Synge, marks his inward-looking critical timidity. Corkery's work, despite his idealism, is largely in the spirit of the 1929 Censorship Act, evidence of a remarkably puritanical fear of modernism whether high or low, as foreign, British, and evil.

Ó Faoláin is generally lauded as the voice of liberal enlightenment standing against this censorship, especially in the pages of the journal *The Bell*. If Corkery is cast as the reactionary nativist, Ó Faoláin seems the sophisticated cosmopolitan battling reactionary philistines. His 1926–9 Harvard period left him with an indelible sense that cultural *nous* must be cosmopolitan and comparative. Importing this sense through his critical interventions in Ireland, he is the figure who had most to do with recasting the debate about Irish modernism as one between native traditionalists and modernist and modernizing cosmopolitans. At the same time, his own fiction, while playfully aware of modernist form-bending, nevertheless marks a retreat to realism from the formidable modernist experimentalism of Joyce, the later Yeats and Beckett. Ó Faoláin gamely acknowledged this, yet – in self-serving mode – he was wont to claim that the fault for not continuing on the modernist path lay not with himself and his generation, but with the post-independence Irish state, with its rigid Catholicism and censorious culture. In a characteristic essay of 1952, for example, he excuses his 1935 novel *Bird Alone*, explaining that because the seduced victim at its heart had hardly been a credible character in the context of the new Ireland, "[o]ne cannot, it is equally obvious, get very far or achieve much variety of action with so strict a morality."[15] In this logic, Joyce's good fortune was that he wrote of pre-independence Ireland. Such special pleading, inaugurated by Ó Faoláin under the aegis of an idea that brilliant modernist writing is simply not possible about or under repressive conditions, has become another master-trope of Irish criticism, granting minor works praise under the self-denigrating assumption that the political conditions they portray allow for nothing better. At its most extreme, in Ó Faoláin's case, this extended to the denigration of Irish culture as a whole for being simply too lacking in finesse for the cosmopolitan artist. Corkery, speaking for the peasant, could denigrate Synge on the grounds that he was not realist enough; Ó Faoláin could denigrate his own work on the grounds that peasant primitiveness, turned into postcolonial puritanism, was good only for old-fashioned realism. Ó Faoláin's cosmopolitanism, like Corkery's insularity, operates as a defense mechanism; its denigration of Irish life as an impossible ground for culture reads "culture" within the Arnoldian framework, and abjures altogether the modernist project of exposing the grounds for modern alienation.

Ó Faoláin was also at the center of a willful refusal on the part of Irish criticism in the mid-century decades to face up to the tremendous advances represented by *Ulysses*, *Finnegans Wake* (1939), and the second wave of Irish modernism. This elision makes Ó Faoláin's literary criticism read quite strangely today. His *The Vanishing Hero: Studies in Novelists in the Twenties* (1956), for example, opens with an invocation of G. E. Moore's *Principia Ethica* (1903) as a defense of individualism, circles around Waugh and others, before staging a showdown between Joyce and Woolf. Woolf is castigated for a lack of mature "faith," while Joyce, with his epiphanies in *A Portrait*, is shown to have bested her by grappling with what Moore had in mind. Despite the brittle theorizing of subjecthood, *The Vanishing Hero* most comes alive when dealing with the more material matter of Woolf's social contacts. She was, after all, to Ó Faoláin's wonderment, actually part of Moore's circle. What clearly strikes Ó Faoláin is that the Irish scholarship boy Joyce, whose poverty is lingered on lovingly, could better Woolf to the point where in *A Portrait* he describes the achievement of a kind of secular priesthood. "Dedalus is the *persona* or mask of a man who has ... more than human pity for the sufferings of humanity," Ó Faoláin declares grandiloquently.[16] But no amount of existentialism can hide the fact that the book that launched the twenties, *Ulysses*, and its hero, Bloom, are entirely missing here. This is a failure of critical nerve by a critic as intelligent as Ó Faoláin. His limited opposition to the new state's philistinism impeded any real breakthrough regarding the potential revolutionary power of Irish modernism in understanding Irish anomie.

By refusing to engage seriously with *Ulysses* and *Finnegans Wake*, the whole range of revolutionary truths about Irish culture Joyce brought to the surface could be ignored by the writer-revolutionaries of the new postcolonial state. Yet this great Joyce rejection was not total. One signal exception was Samuel Beckett, who capped an apprenticeship to Joyce with his essay "Dante ... Bruno ... Vico ... Joyce" written in 1929 for a volume on the project, which would become *Finnegans Wake, Our Exagmination Round His Factification for Incamination of Work in Progress*.[17] "Dante ... Bruno," a star-turn in Irish modernist criticism, is blunt, witty, and workmanlike. Just as, for Beckett, Vico is a "practical roundheaded Neapolitan" (16), Joyce, practical Dubliner in Paris, is portrayed as a modernist who imbeds history, from recent controversy to Viconian cycle, in every fighting word. Beckett ties the language's sensuous obscurity to its role as a vehicle of history. This 1929 text announces the first full-dress gesture of any Irish critic to really face up to the challenge of Joyce's modernism, for Ireland and the world. It asserts that Joyce, as a Viconian, brings out, through the obscurities of his language, the lived history embedded within it.

Two later exemplary studies of Irish modernists appeared in 1941: Louis MacNeice's *The Poetry of W. B. Yeats*, and an essay by Elizabeth Bowen, "James Joyce,"[18] published in *The Bell* after Joyce's death. MacNeice's study[19] has a sub-Auden air (as in Auden's "In Memory of W. B. Yeats" of 1939), but one thickened by MacNeice's allegiance to Yeats as a fellow Irish poet. MacNeice distrusts both Yeats's aestheticism and his Irish nationalism; yet the younger writer's own unclear status, as an Anglo-Irish poet now of "Northern Ireland," granted him a flexible sense of selfhood against which to judge Yeats's various stages of modernist experiment especially in relation to its Irish background. By the end, he is comparing Yeats and Joyce, refusing the usual tendency to contrast them.

This mid-century criticism in which Anglo-Irish writers, displaced, look askance at Irish modernism is even better represented by Bowen's memorial essay on Joyce. This essay is the opening call in modern Irish criticism to welcome wholeheartedly Joyce's *Irish* modernism. Joyce's absence from Ireland, yet his obsessive love for the place, is the central contradiction on which the essay dwells. The argument is that the Irish should have a special affinity for and understanding of Joyce at his most obscure. Bowen is by no means fulsome in her praise; when she claims that "gradually, Joyce withdrew from pity, as he withdrew from Ireland" (240), she is arguing the relation of modernist stylistic obscurity and social clear-sightedness, and she means it as a deep compliment. She relates this to the anticerebral quality of Joyce's style. She is one of the first to celebrate the centrality of humor in Joyce's texts:

> And Joyce had another gigantic faculty – laughter. His laughter ... breaks out in the course of *Ulysses* into a sustained roar. He pounded language to jelly ... to make it tell us what he was laughing at. One may say that he ended by laughing so much that he could not speak. (242–3)

This is a new note in the Irish response to Irish modernism. Bowen steers her argument back to the Irish as readers of Joyce: "The shy thin man with the thick spectacles belonged to us, and was of us, wherever he went" (247). With this essay Bowen unequivocally declares that Joyce is the birthright of the Irish.

Does the story of the rise of an Irish criticism of Irish modernism, then, have a happy ending? For postwar academic literary criticism, Irish modernist culture became a Cold War prize, and the American Yeats and Joyce industries were born. Irish academic critics reacted with skepticism, yet some used the international perspective to launch new attempts at a synthesis of the standard divisions. The finest of these is Vivian Mercier's *The Irish Comic Tradition* of 1962,[20] in which he essays a grand knitting together of the ancient Gaelic tradition beloved by Corkery and the Anglo-Irish Celtic Revival celebrated by Boyd. Time and again, he shows how the chief pleasures of Irish writing in English arise from attitudes developed over centuries in Gaelic literature. Swift knew no Irish, but the Gulliver story may be a version of "the Irish *immram* (voyage) tradition … and the leprechaun material in *Aidheadh Fhearghusa* … some Gaelic student of Swift's acquaintance might have supplied him with a literal translation."[21] The learning is worn so lightly that the connections convince; nevertheless, staging a shotgun marriage of the Gaelic tradition and the new literature, the book tends to generalize about "the Irish mind." Why, for a thousand years, have Irish writers been so comic, is the question Mercier sets himself: "One answer … might be that the Irish mind is innately destructive."[22] By writing an influence study without relating the literature to politics or history, Mercier surrenders the vehemence of Corkery (to whose work his book can be seen as a polite riposte) without gaining the insight that Irish humor is always relearned from previous generations.

Mercier's apolitical politeness, therefore, is his weakness. The Northern Irish Troubles would soon push the next wave of criticism into a forthright engagement with literature's political significance. A radical new school of postcolonial Irish literary criticism, born of the Troubles, was on the horizon, pioneered in the work of Field Day in Derry and the journal *The Crane Bag* in Dublin. It embraced such formerly taboo topics as the relation of political violence and literary culture, and compared Ireland's postcolonial status to that of other nations. It took the interweaving of the personal and the political to be the founding principle of Irish literary culture, brought Joyce's work into the center of these discussions, and read Irish modernist literature as a vital staging ground on which the various cultures on the island of Ireland could hash out new versions of their postcolonial identities. Irish criticism in the years 1900–75, despite its tentativeness, its resentments and its refusal to engage with the most avant garde of Irish post-independence writing, had nevertheless set the stage for this late-twentieth-century movement to theorize the political dimensions of modernist Irish culture in a postimperial frame.

NOTES

1 Richard Ellmann, *James Joyce* (Londan: Oxford University Press, 1959), 59, fn. 1.
2 Ellmann, *James* Joyce, 755.
3 Noel Ignatiev, *How the Irish Became White* (New York: Routledge, 1995).
4 James Joyce, *Ulysses* (New York: Modern Library, 1961), 184.
5 See *The Dial*, lxxii, 6, June 1922, 619–22.
6 *The Dial*, 622.
7 Quoted in Len Platt, *Joyce and the Anglo-Irish: A Study of Joyce and the Irish Literary Revival* (Amsterdam: Rodopi, 1998), 16.
8 Quoted in Joseph Brooker, *Joyce's Critics: Transitions in Reading and Culture* (Madison: University of Wisconsin Press, 2004), 191.
9 Ernest A. Boyd, *Ireland's Literary Renaissance* (New York: John Lane, 1916), 386.
10 Daniel Corkery, *The Hidden Ireland: A Study of Gaelic Munster in the Eighteenth Century* (1924; Dublin: Gill and Macmillan, 1967).
11 L. M. Cullen, "The Hidden Ireland: Re-assessment of a Concept," *Studia Hibernica* xi, 1969, 7–47.
12 Daniel Corkery, *Synge and Anglo-Irish Literature: A Study* (New York: Russell and Russell, 1965), 151.
13 Corkery, *Synge and Anglo-Irish Literature*, 239.
14 Corkery, *Synge and Anglo-Irish Literature*, 19.
15 Seán Ó Faoláin, "Ireland After Yeats (1952)" reprint, *World Literature Today* 63, 2, 1989, 241–5; 244.
16 Seán Ó Faoláin, *The Vanishing Hero: Studies in Novelists of the Twenties* (London: Eyre and Spottiswoode, 1956), 219.
17 Samuel Beckett et al., *Our Exagmination Round His Factification for Incamination of Work in Progress* (London: Faber and Faber, 1929), 5–13.
18 Elizabeth Bowen, "James Joyce," in *People, Places, Things: Essays by Elizabeth Bowen*, Allan Hepburn, ed. (Edinburgh: Edinburgh University Press, 2008), 239–47.
19 Louis MacNiece, *The Poetry of W. B. Yeats* (London: Oxford University Press. 1941).
20 Vivian Mercier, *The Irish Comic Tradition* (Oxford: Oxford University Press, 1962).
21 Mercier, *Comic Tradition*, 188 and 228.
22 Mercier, *Comic Tradition*, 233.

13

MICHAEL VALDEZ MOSES

Irish Modernist Imaginaries

I

Depending on whether its local or cosmopolitan features are emphasized, Irish modernism may appear as an instance of an anti-imperial and postcolonial national literary renaissance or as a harbinger of contemporary world literature. In what follows, I explore how Irish modernism emerged out of a network of global cultural relations, some many centuries old, others that developed shortly before or even contemporaneously with the Irish literary Revival. The long evolution of these networks of exchange was a haphazard, uncoordinated affair involving different and sometimes antagonistic political, religious, cultural, and economic institutions and forces. I suggest that the contemporary emergence of a "world literature," in which Irish modernism has played an important role, has a long history that predates the rise of late capitalism in the twentieth and twenty-first centuries (although capitalism and global networks of commercial exchange played important roles as well). By highlighting the non-teleological and aleatory process by which a complex network of global relations slowly evolved and that provided the matrix out of which Irish modernism emerged, I aim to complicate our understanding of the latter. Irish modernism is no single simple thing, but, rather, a loose set of diverse literary phenomena with tangled, unstable, and sometimes conflicting relations with world literature and global culture.[1] Each Irish modernist negotiated the relationship between a national and a transnational imaginary in a different manner and combined the local and cosmopolitan in novel ways. Each idiosyncratic synthesis offered its author a distinctive array of cultural dividends and liabilities. The sheer profusion of modernist experimentation challenges our customary tendency to categorize Irish modernists as either centripetally nationalist (Yeats and the Revivalists) or centrifugally European and cosmopolitan (Joyce and Beckett).

One problem with our prevailing theoretical models of literary studies is the tendency to posit a homology between the teleological relation of the nation-state and an emergent global ("new world") order on the one hand and that between the old national literatures and a contemporaneous global culture on the other. Just as independent nation-states "inevitably" gave way to a new world order, so too did national literary traditions merge into an organized global literary system – or so the story goes. Even at a time when critics acknowledge the invented character of national identities and seize on their constructed character as a means to legitimize (or subvert) the emergent world culture, this widely circulated narrative tacitly assumes the primacy and political resilience of the nation-state, which remains the historical starting point for and one of the few sources of resistance to globalization. Given that the establishment of national languages, educational systems, and literary and cultural traditions provided the disciplinary and institutional basis for the rise of modern professional literary studies, it is by no means accidental that the nation-state, even in its allegedly weakened condition, continues to provide the cultural horizon against which we view the "rise" of world literature. But what the sovereign claims of the nation-state has tended to obscure is the manifest ways and various means by which political societies, artistic movements, commercial enterprises, religious communities, languages, cultures, and literatures were linked (if not fully globalized) well before the nation-state assumed its privileged position in the late nineteenth and twentieth centuries.[2]

II

The efforts of a heterogeneous group of Irish nationalists including Arthur Griffith, D. P. Moran, Michael Cusack, Douglas Hyde, James Connolly, Hanna Sheehy-Skeffington, Lady Gregory, Patrick Pearse, Maud Gonne, and W. B. Yeats, despite their differing ideas of what the new Ireland should become, attest to a shared desire to revive an ancient Irish nation after centuries of British imperial rule. Paradoxically, even the most avidly "nativist" conceptions of the new nation were often inspired by forms of community that preceded and supplemented (or exceeded) the political-theoretical conception of the bounded territorial sovereign nation. For example, Moran's *The Philosophy of Irish Ireland* (1905), a work that dismissed Yeats's English-language "Irish" literary Revival as a "glaring fraud" and discounted Griffith's celebration of the 1782 Grattan Parliament as a provincial enthusiasm of the Anglo-Irish Protestant elite, would seem to exemplify – both by its title and its strident arguments on behalf of a Gaelicized Irish-speaking Ireland – a particularly restrictive and anti-cosmopolitan conception of the nation.[3] And yet, Moran argues on behalf of a "bi-lingual" Irish people whose resuscitation of their Gaelic heritage will better prepare them for economic modernization on the world stage; indeed, the damage inflicted by the anglicizing of Ireland includes its having prevented Irish-speaking Gaels from fulfilling their destiny as a "potent imperial race" capable of turning "great tracts of the United States" into "Irish speaking and Irish thinking" lands.⁴ Despite his hostility toward the anglicization of Ireland (but not the gaelicization of America), Moran's double-pronged critique of Yeats and Griffith, leaders of the Irish Revival and Sinn Féin, tacitly embraces modes of communal belonging and cultural exchange made possible by the global expanse of the British Empire: the transatlantic settlement of America, the emergence of English as an international language of world trade, the trans-national flow of ideas, goods, technology, and labor.

Moran's call for a "return" to the language, culture, and traditions of "the Gael" envisions an "imagined community" simultaneously more limited and more expansive than the modern territorially bounded nation-state. His Irish version of late-nineteenth-century romantic nationalism makes crucial concessions to the universal aspirations of an earlier eighteenth-century classical Enlightenment ideal: while determined to preserve the "distinctive character, traditions, and civilizations of one's own country," Moran opposes anti-English Irish politicians who foment "hysterical and artificial stimulation of racial hatred," "a bad passion ... absolutely unjustifiable on moral grounds."⁵ In a passage consonant with the writings of his nemesis, Yeats, Moran argues that a distinctively Irish "national character" requires the development of "individuality;" "the highest point ... to which a people can go is the sum of its individualities."⁶ Notwithstanding his enthusiasm for "the racy of the soil," Moran positions himself as an enlightened and liberal defender of individual rights and freedoms. His cultural nationalism embraces "the full breath of the principle of liberty."⁷

Moran's nationalist Gael would settle America, speak English to his financial advantage, and pursue commerce with the great world; but he would also oppose cultural homogeneity and autocratically-imposed social norms (including those promoted by Douglas Hyde's Gaelic League): "uniformity is soul-destroying."⁸ His Irish Ireland will embody a democratic experiment-in-living in which many idiosyncratic versions of Irishness compete in the marketplace of ideas. Citing as precedent the Brehon Laws that "had no executive force behind them," Moran endorses a stochastic and spontaneous bottom-up process that allows Irishness to emerge and be continuously redefined by the uncoordinated efforts of individual Irish citizens.⁹ He justifies this non-teleological and decentralized version of Irish romantic nationalism as the best way to resist a homogenized and moribund world culture that negates national differences and crushes individuality.¹⁰ Moran's Gael, because of his deep-rootedness in the Irish past, turns out to be a secret adherent of the cultural logic of J. S. Mill's *On Liberty* (1859), although Moran might not confess any fondness for its English author.

It may seem perverse to focus on Moran, who was neither a literary modernist, nor a friend of Yeats and his fellow Revivalists at the Irish National Theatre. But the fact that even an outspoken nativist critic of the Irish Revival gestures toward a transnational version of Irish culture suggests that the divide between nativists and cosmopolitans in early-twentieth-century Ireland was often more rhetorical and symbolic than substantive. In fact, despite Moran's nativist rancor, his indigenous critique of turn-of-the-century anglicized Ireland looks forward to those works of "late" Irish modernism that successfully represented (at least formally and imaginatively) a community Celtic and cosmopolitan, Gaelic and avant-garde: Flann O'Brien's *At Swim-Two-Birds* (1939) and *An Béal Bocht* (1941), Máirtín Ó Cadhain's *Cré na Cille* (1949). O'Brien's works in particular, whether written in English or Irish, offer compelling instances of avant-garde fiction fully engaged with contemporary world literature (consider the student-narrator's complex play of allusions in *At Swim-Two-Birds* to American, French, and Russian modernist fiction), while making novel use of the distinctive stories, genres, and stylistic devices of an "ancient" Irish-language literary tradition. Significantly, O'Brien's fiction (like Ó Cadhain's) does not undertake a simple uncritical return to the "premodern" forms of Irish literature; his work modernizes and transforms "archaic" genres (e.g., the Irish saga, the historical chronicle, the saint's life, the folk tale, and the fairy story) in the course of resuscitating them for modern readers. O'Brien's peculiarly hybridized work, written in both Irish and English, and combining archaic and modern genres, pre-modern and contemporary characters, Gaelic materials with a Joycean range of allusions to world literature, instantiates a conception of Irishness not easily circumscribed by the boundaries of the Free State or the Irish Republic.

To be sure, the nativist arguments of Moran could be used on behalf of chauvinistic definitions of Irishness and policies of cultural protectionism and state censorship. But if a nativist and romanticized view of the Gaeltacht and of an Ireland rejuvenated by the "native" tongue is implicitly criticized by Joyce in "The Dead" (1914) and openly satirized in the "Cyclops" episode of *Ulysses* (1922), it is nonetheless worth reflecting that Moran's philosophy of Irish Ireland offered a roadmap for later Irish writers such as O'Brien and Ó Cadhain who sought to produce a modern cosmopolitan Irish literature via an intensive cultivation of the local, the archaic, and the vernacular. They aimed to create a pronouncedly "minor literature" as Ireland's distinctive contribution to an ever more hybridized world culture.[11] They, like their fellow modernists, Hugh MacDiarmid in Scotland, José María Arguedas in Peru, C. P. Cavafy in Alexandria, and Isaac Bashevis Singer in America, contributed to an international and collaborative, if uncoordinated, project to craft a contemporary "world" literature by emphasizing those very local cultural traditions and "minor" languages (Irish, Scots-Gaelic, Quechua, classical and demotic Greek, Yiddish) that only seemed incompatible with the world-historical forces of globalization.

III

Critics of Irish nativism have tended to view nationalist turns to the past as so many attempts to ground a modern (if imagined) community within sharply delimited sovereign borders.[12] But I suggest that some archaic forms of Irishness paradoxically offered the prospect of traversing national boundaries, breaking down the nation into smaller subnational communities, and of opening a closed "national" collective to the heterogeneous cultural influences of the outside world. The resuscitation of a Gaelic Ireland provides only one such example. A self-conscious turn to an imperial history (adumbrated by Moran's polemics), even a British one, offered another unexpected if controversial means of realizing a national destiny hospitable to a cosmopolitan future. Moran's promotion of the modernizing, enlightened, liberal-democratic, world-wandering, and commercially-intrepid Gael finds an odd counterpart in Griffith's embrace of the "Hungarian" solution to Ireland's political problems in the wake of Parnell's fall and the apparent collapse of the Home Rule movement: "two independent nations, agreeing for their better security and territorial integrity to have a common sovereign and to act in concert in regard to foreign affairs."[13] Griffith's much-criticized plan, modeled on the 1867 Austro-Hungarian constitution, illustrates it was possible to conceive of a popular (if contentious) form of Irish national self-rule that embraced rather than rejected a monarchic and "imperial" regime. Whereas Griffith sought a pragmatic (if limited) form of national autonomy at a time when the prospects for Ireland's political independence seemed bleak (1904), his ingenious (and ultimately explosive) proposal casts a weird retrospective light on the imperial dimensions of Oscar Wilde's *Salomé* (1896), an internationally influential avant-garde drama written in French by an avowed Anglo-Irish nationalist and first produced for the stage in Paris.

Assuming we read the Biblical setting of Wilde's play as a historical transposition of the contemporary political conditions of 1890s Ireland immediately following the fall of Parnell, *Salomé* hints at the temptations facing a decaying Herodian dynasty (the Anglo-Irish Ascendancy to which Wilde belonged), a ruling elite with a questionable claim to legitimacy caught between its dependence on imperial Rome (Britain) and the revolutionary energies of a new local prophet, Iokanaan, a nationalist striving to save his race, a chosen people, from the corrupting influence of a foreign power and its local puppet-rulers. Wilde's symbolist drama would likely not have proved so artistically influential (it was the source for Richard Strauss's seminal modernist opera of the same name, first performed in Dresden in 1905) had it been more obviously propagandistic, more insistently local in its political concerns, and less dramatically complex and tragic. The dramatic appeal of *Salomé* is attributed in part to its refusal to embrace unequivocally the imperial or the native revolutionary cause. Salomé's tragedy emerges out of her profound attraction to and repulsion from Iokanaan and the religiously strict and purified form of community he represents; in like fashion, although the Princess repudiates and denounces the decadent manners, aesthetic sophistication, corrupting power, and cosmopolitan tastes of the Herodian court and its Roman overlords, she cannot help but embody and exult in these very same "imperial" qualities. The consequent perversion of her tastes (manifested by her erotic desire for the severed head of Iokanaan) and her evident betrayal of her own class and sect (figured both literally and symbolically by Wilde's *coup de théatre*, Salomé's proleptic veneration of the first martyr of the Catholic Church – she preserves and kisses a holy relic, the remains of St. John the Baptist) marks her as an outcast even from her own caste and leads to her summary execution at Herod's command.

Salomé's death dramatizes her tragic double bind. On the one hand, she yearns for the wealth, power, glamor, and cosmopolitan sophistication that an imperial culture promises. On the other hand, she pines for an intimate attachment to the people, or at least to a new sort of man who voices their long-repressed yearning for a purified and independent community. In Hegelian terms, Salomé must choose between two incompatible "goods." But her double bind can also be stated in negative terms. If Wilde's tragic heroine is attracted to an imperial and a national identity, she is also repelled by the same two prospects. She finds the Romans to be arrogant, cruel, and tyrannical and the Jews small-minded, quarrelsome, and tiresome. Iokaanan first seems to offer an attractive alternative to disputatious Pharisees and rabbis, but the prophet's political zealotry and moral intolerance makes no allowance for Salomé's erotic desires, aesthetic sensibilities, and cosmopolitan inclinations. The prophet condemns the Princess and casts her out of any future community founded on the new (or newly restored) religion. Salomé's death might be said to resolve the dramatic conflict, but only by an act of pure negation. In her time, the Princess can no more reconcile the cosmopolitan allure of a glamorous imperial existence with a fully integrated and purified life among a chosen people than could Wilde, her creator, in his day.

IV

The fate of Wilde's Salomé, whose death arises from the fatal tension between native and imperial affiliation, adumbrates, if in an obverse manner, that of Murphy, the literary antihero of a later Protestant Anglo-Irish modernist who objected both to what he regarded as the maudlin cultural provincialism of Irish nationalism and to the oppressive materialism and injustice of British imperial culture. Beckett's eponymous protagonist in *Murphy* (1938), lacking a Christian name and bearing only a quintessentially Irish surname, provides a satiric counterpart to Wilde's tragic heroine. A "postcolonial" Irish émigré ostensibly looking for work in the more prosperous capital of imperial England in the 1930s, Murphy famously succumbs to the fleshly temptations and spiritual liberties of London before meeting an ignominious death as a result of a gas explosion, ironically becoming for his Irish friends, teachers, and lovers who seek him out in the land of the Sasanach, the embodiment of "the bays, the bogs, the moors, the glens, the lakes, the rivers, the streams, the brooks, the mists, the – er – fens" of "the dear land" of his birth from which he so eagerly decamped.[14]

A self-reflexive work that advertises its own fictiveness and assiduously parodies and subverts the conventions of the realist novel (e.g., in a bizarre and fantastic scene that slyly alludes to Salomé's dance of the seven veils, a naked Murphy impossibly binds his own hands and feet to a rocking chair with seven scarves), Beckett's fiction responds – albeit satirically – to the same predicament as Wilde's play: the "choice" between a national and an imperial identity. But whereas Salomé is destroyed by her incompatible desires for both (even while she is repelled by the same), Murphy is literally (if accidentally) unmade by his reluctance to embrace either. Neither the Ireland in which he sardonically wishes his earthly remains to be flushed (down the commode at the Abbey Theatre during a performance) nor the England in which he meets his fiery end, neither nation nor empire, constitutes the kind of free community that answers to the trans-mundane desires and disembodied wanderings of Beckett's ever-impractical Irishman. In the ecstatic "third zone" into which he rocks himself, Murphy momentarily experiences a perfect "will-lessness"; he becomes "a mote in its absolute freedom."[15] Alas, much to his distress, while in London, Murphy, the Irish wanderer and no-man, discovers, though he is loath to admit it, that he nevertheless craves "a brotherhood" – he seeks in the Magdalen Mental Mercyseat a "race of people" like himself, perfect isolates bound in a crazy communion. Inevitably, Beckett's antihero learns from his unsuccessful efforts to bond with the psychotic and utterly unresponsive inmate, Mr. Endon, that a transcendent form of absolute freedom is incompatible with human solidarity. The irreconcilable forms of existence Murphy seeks can be satisfied neither by nation-state nor empire, indeed, cannot be embodied in the real world or even in a realist novel.

Murphy's accidental death signals at the level of plot what Beckett works to achieve at the formal and aesthetic level: the dismantling or explosion of the realist novel, its formal self-immolation. In the strange country that Beckett invents for his antihero, characters such as Miss Carridge are not always "subject to the usual conditions of time and space."[16] The unnamed narrator (let's call him Beckett) routinely revises or contradicts his own statements of fact, and key events – such as Murphy's mysterious death – appear to depend on the implied author's intervening into the diegetic universe of the characters and manipulating physical objects without their or the reader's knowledge. By turning on the gas that fuels the fatal explosion, the implied author violates his tacit contract with the reader of the realistic novel who is asked willingly to suspend his disbelief, provided the novelist tells "the truth" (i.e. adheres to the rules and conventions of literary realism). Implicitly rejecting the only kinds of actual political communities – a nation, an empire – readily available to his protagonist, Beckett creates for Murphy a no-place (a-topia) that exists strictly and entirely as a fictive construct, or rather as a deconstructed aesthetic object, a self-consuming artifact. The tensions between the worldliness of empire and the solidarity of nationhood are dissolved formally, if not materially. Whereas Wilde's heroine ultimately discovers that her desires cannot be satisfied because their variety and complexity require an impossible synthesis of incompatible forms of political life, Beckett's antihero finds that political life as such, in all its forms, is inherently oppressive. The dramatic resolution of Salomé's predicament may be formally represented as symbolist tragedy, while the end of Murphy's transcendental quest requires the comprehensive dismantling of mimetic forms and conventions.

V

To be sure, there were influential literary attempts before *Murphy* that addressed on a formal level the competing claims of a national or an imperial imaginary for Ireland. Most notably, Joyce offered an oneiric conflation of vernacular and cosmopolitan identities in the "Circe" episode of *Ulysses*. In the dramatic and surrealistic dream-sequence that makes up the longest episode in the novel, Leopold Bloom appears simultaneously as the successor to Parnell, the founder of the new Bloomusalem in the Nova Hibernia of the future, the national liberator par excellence, and as a Roman Emperor (figured once more as a stand-in for British imperial authority) modeled on

Caligula.[17] If Joyce does not share Bloom's enthusiasm for a British imperial identity, he nonetheless sympathizes with his character's frustrations with the xenophobic conception of nationhood advocated by the Citizen in the "Cyclops" episode, as well as with Bloom's penchant for the exotic, fascination with travel abroad, and yearning for a more worldly existence. But because the synthesis of vernacular and cosmopolitan identities must, within the historical context of Dublin in 1904, remain only "a dream" for Bloom, Joyce seizes on and modifies an internationally available literary-formal representation of the unconscious at work – the Nordic "dream play" derived from August Strindberg, Henrik Ibsen, Johann Wolfgang von Goethe, and Richard Wagner – to dramatize this impossible reconciliation in "Circe." Joyce nativizes and transforms an "exotic" literary genre so that it becomes the wish-fulfillment of an Irish everyman who asserts his rootedness in the country in which he was born (Ireland), claims his birthright as a Jew whose family immigrated from central Europe, and proclaims his universal human rights as a free citizen of the world.

But to appreciate fully the ways in which Irish literary modernists, most particularly, but not exclusively, Irish-Catholic writers such as Joyce (and later Flann O'Brien) negotiated the differences between the vernacular and cosmopolitan, and between local and "global" imaginaries, we must attend to yet another ancient model of the transnational community in which their distinctive fictional worlds were embedded: the Catholic (universal) Church. Like the Enlightenment dream of a universal order of free, rational, autonomous, and equal citizens, the "Gaelic" legacy of a transnational community of nomadic Celtic peoples, or the ideal of self-governing regimes joined in an imperial commonwealth, the promise of a single church uniting all peoples in a catholic faith animates many works of Irish modernism.

Virginia Woolf's characterization of *Ulysses* as "an illiterate, underbred book ... the book of a self-taught working man" bespeaks not only the snobbery and class privilege of Bloomsbury, but also, if only implicitly, a profound underestimation of Joyce's Catholic learning and education. Joyce's "fellow" modernist conspicuously notes in her diaries that reading *Ulysses* made her "ready for the classics again."[18] My purpose here is not to slight Woolf, who elsewhere wrote and spoke more generously of Joyce's literary achievement, but to suggest how easy it was for the author of *Mrs. Dalloway* (1925), whose own formal literary experiments owed much to Joyce's example, to dismiss the Catholic and cosmopolitan erudition of *Ulysses* (a tradition of learning that was rooted in and helped to preserve the classics) because its purported vulgarity violated the aesthetic decorum, moral proprieties, and generic expectations of Bloomsbury. In her early assessments of *Ulysses*, well before she became personally acquainted with its author, Woolf conspicuously fails to recognize or acknowledge the profound Jesuitical and Catholic cultural contributions to Joyce's fiction, whether formal or diegetic, and erroneously identifies the "vulgarity" of his novel – its conspicuous representation of the body and the bodily – as *prima facie* evidence of Joyce's lack of breeding and formal education.

As with Moran's nativist embrace of all things Gaelic, Joyce's life-long immersion in and fascination with the forms of Catholic literary, philosophical, and spiritual life provided him an entrée into a world culture that was anything but provincial or merely national. Although critics long ago ceased discussing Joyce's commitment to a specifically autobiographical form of literary modernism (something he shared with Proust), it is worth pausing to consider that in *A Portrait of the Artist as a Young Man* (1916) Joyce revolutionized two literary subgenres, the *Bildungsroman* and the *Künstlerroman*, that first arose in the context of Goethe's Lutheran Germany. Along with Proust, Joyce transubstantiated two literary subgenres deeply rooted in a Protestant theological and cultural milieu by exploring with great psychological subtlety how a specifically Catholic education and Jesuitical training might form (and also deform) an artist with worldly ambitions. Stephen ultimately refuses to take orders, rejects the Catholic faith, resents his Jesuitical training, and endeavors to fly the nets of religion and nation. It is nonetheless to his Catholic education that Joyce's autobiographical hero owes his mastery of Latin (and Greek), his love of romance languages, his affinity for and knowledge of the classical authors, his admiration for the theology of the church fathers, the aesthetic insights of Aquinas, the philosophy of the Spanish scholastics, the prose style of John Henry Newman, and, finally, his titanic ambition to become a great man in the world republic of letters (an aspiration that at least in *A Portrait* promises to take him from Dublin to Paris).

Catholicism provides Joyce with the crucial diegetic material for a fictional autobiography that explores how the writings, dogma, and spiritual exercises of the Church paradoxically produce a distinctively modernist sensibility and artistic vocation. The literary traditions of the Church also contribute several of the most distinctive formal, generic, and stylistic devices to Joyce's modernist literary arsenal. Woolf famously objected to the grossness, the vulgarity, the rawness of *Ulysses*: "how ... raw, striking, & ultimately nauseating. When one can have cooked flesh, why have the raw? But if you are anaemic, as Tom [Eliot] is, there is glory in blood."[19] Although Woolf makes no explicit mention of their differences in religious upbringing, her comments about Joyce's shocking style (which T. S. Eliot, the future convert to Anglo-Catholicism appreciated) suggestively, if perhaps unknowingly, echo the Protestant critique of the Catholic iconographic tradition and its graphic representation of the wounds of Christ's body and the bloodied flesh of the martyred saints. The shock of the new, which Joyce partially achieved by means of a vivid and realistic portrait of the body and its functions, owes much to French literary naturalism (a forerunner of literary modernism), but it also descends from a Catholic iconographic tradition (one that also energized Spanish, French, Catalan, Polish, and Italian modernists).

Although many might be cited, I consider just two examples of how a cosmopolitan Catholic literary tradition helped germinate Joyce's modernist aesthetic. Father Arnall's sermon on hell, which appears in Part III of *A Portrait*, is modeled on Giovanni Pietro Pinamonti's seventeenth-century theological treatise, *Hell Opened to Christians, to Caution Them from Entering into It* (1688), a text partly derived from Ignatius Loyola's *The Spiritual Exercises* (1548). "Ithaca," the penultimate episode of *Ulysses*, is a generic transformation of the Roman Catholic catechism. It is possible to understand Joyce's principle of formal construction as the conjoining of heterogeneous but inert literary forms (empty containers of content) that make up a larger artificial whole. But that would be to under-appreciate the dialectical relations among the literary modes and genres Joyce combines.

Father Arnall's two sermons are interpolated with passages of free-indirect discourse that reveal how these "treatises on hell" transform Stephen's inner thoughts and thereby become exercises in high modernist fictional autobiography that invite modern psychoanalytic analysis.[20] Arnall's sermons contain the generative language that will ultimately define Stephen's modernist credo: "*non serviam: I will not serve.*"[21] What the young Catholic initially feels in the depths of his soul as a profound punishment – in "hell all laws are overturned: there is no thought of family or country, of ties, of relationships" – is transformed by his psyche into the guiding principles of a young modernist's revolt. Stephen will fly from such ties on behalf of a new aesthetic project, trading one "universal" and idealized community (that of Catholic believers) for another (free-spirited cosmopolitan artists).[22]

Likewise, in Joyce's modernist alembic, the catechism of "Ithaca" becomes a lesson on the character of modern life fully conversant with a range of modern sciences including oceanography, geology, astronomy, chemistry, medicine, and pharmacology. The Roman Catholic cathecism was intended as a statement of the articles of faith valid for all peoples everywhere. But from the perspective of Ireland's Protestant elite and its secular English counterparts, it could be and sometimes was unfairly viewed as only of provincial import (i.e., significant "only" to Irish-Catholic school children). By melding it with the "universally valid" tenets of modern science, Joyce reformulates the catechism as a hybridized modernist subgenre and reinvigorates its claims to universal relevance. Joyce's new modernist credo can once more presume to offer a truly catholic body of knowledge that transcends the limits of nation, sect, ethnicity, and language. In both *A Portrait* and *Ulysses*, Joyce thus accomplishes something more than simply inserting the forms of a Catholic literary tradition into a heterogeneous modernist collage: by placing them in dialectical relation with other (typically newer) literary genres, he reanimates their cosmopolitan potential. He does not so much transform the local or national imaginary into a worldly one (in the manner of the Revivalists and their heirs) as demonstrate that what his critics regarded as a merely sectarian and provincial concern was all along an expression of the worldly and cosmopolitan.

VI

For the sake of conceptual clarity, I have approached the works of modern Irish writers as if they were embedded in only one or two preexisting global networks: Gaelic and Celtic; liberal and commercial; imperial and British; Catholic and theological. But as I suggested in Section I, these networks were never perfectly distinct from one another. They were in fact sedimented, mutable, and intersecting. Nor were they synchronized or necessarily hospitable to one another. In fact, none of these networks was entirely homogeneous or perfectly self-integrated, but instead often evolved out of separate and sometimes antipatheic elements. The Catholic Church and the British Empire, for example, only emerged over centuries as a result of the convergence and conflict of a wide array of often conflicting forces, institutions, and ideological projects. Nor do the examples I analyze exhaust the list of global networks that constituted the matrix out of which Irish modernism emerged. I have, for example, made no mention of international socialism and modern feminism, which arose shortly before and contemporaneously with Irish modernism.

A comprehensive and detailed examination of any single work of Irish literary modernism would reveal its complex and tension-filled web of relationships to several or all of the global networks of affiliation mentioned. For example, Yeats's aesthetically revolutionary drama, *At the Hawk's Well* (1916), staged not at the Abbey, but at the private home of Lady Cunard in London on April 2, 1916 before a small coterie audience, draws on *Cuchulain of Muirthemne* (1902), Lady Gregory's modern English translation of the Ulster cycle of Irish sagas. Yeats's first "dance play" also reworks elements of a Japanese Noh drama by Motokiyo Zeami (c. 1363– c.1443), *Yoro*, contained in the papers of Ernest Fenollosa, to which Ezra Pound had introduced the elder Irish poet. If Yeats's drama draws on "Celtic" sources for its subject matter, then the staging of the play in an aristocratic home in Cavendish Square, London during Easter week in 1916, before guests that included the American poets Eliot and Pound, and which featured "Egyptian" costumes created by the French-born Edmund Dulac, evokes the war-time imperial and international context of its first production. The appearance of Michio Ito, a Japanese dancer trained in the Dalcroze method in Paris, as the Hawk-Woman signals the rising global importance of the Japanese Empire (just as the presence of Pound and Eliot betokens the growing power of the American). The casting of a European-trained Japanese practitioner of modern dance and Noh drama in *At the Hawk's Well* also reflects the liberal networks of international trade and commercial exchange that made possible the simultaneous presence of Yeats, Pound, Eliot, Dulac, and Ito in London. And whereas this, the first of Yeats's Noh-inspired dramas, did not draw explicitly on the Catholic tradition of the passion play – as did his later dance-play, *Calvary* (1921) – it makes use of certain ritual elements (masks, chanted verse accompanied by music, a small chorus, stylized gestures and movement, symbolic vestments and props) borrowed from an aristocratic and premodern Japanese theatrical tradition, that functioned as nonsectarian and translatable substitutes for the ritual elements of Greek theatre and the Catholic Mass.[23]

Whether one finds Moran's nationalist polemics, O'Brien's gaelicized cosmopolitan literary pastiches, Wilde's symbolist drama, Beckett's early self-subverting fiction, Joyce's hybridized novels, or Yeats's dance-plays to be successful fusions of varied, discrete, and conflicting cultural traditions, or merely hubristic attempts to cobble together hopelessly chaotic and ideologically contradictory forms drawn from incompatible cultural sources, is a matter for individual judgment. But our critical assessments must begin with the recognition that the Irish modernists were endlessly resourceful and inventive, idiosyncratic, and unpredictable in the wildly various ways they constantly renegotiated the dialectical relationship between local and global, national and global imaginaries. Irish modernism was a plural and protean thing, a complex of intersecting literary and cultural traditions and transnational imaginaries that were always and already fully embedded in an ancient, dynamic, and evolving world literature.

NOTES

1 For three influential works emphasizing the "vernacular" characteristics of Irish literary modernism, see Declan Kiberd, *Inventing Ireland* (Cambridge, MA: Harvard University Press, 1995); Terry Eagleton, *Heathcliff and the Great Hunger* (London: Verso, 1995); and Seamus Deane, *Strange Country* (Oxford: Oxford University Press, 1997). For an influential account of Irish literary

modernism as illustrative of how a national (and minority) literature becomes part of world literature, see Pascale Casanova, *The World Republic of Letters*, M. B. DeBevoise, trans. (Cambridge, MA: Harvard University Press, 2004), especially 303–23. For a historically deep analysis of world literature, see David Damrosch, *What is World Literature?* (Princeton, NJ: Princeton University Press, 2003).

2 On the history of nationalism and culture, see Benedict Anderson, *Imagined Communities* (London: Verso, 1991); E. J. Hobsbawm, *Nations and Nationalism since 1780: Programme, Myth, Reality* (Cambridge: Cambridge University Press, 1990); and Ernest Gellner, *Nations and Nationalism* (Ithaca, NY: Cornell University Press, 1983). On the dissolution of the nation-state and the rise of global culture, see Michael Valdez Moses, *The Novel and the Globalization of Culture* (Oxford: Oxford University Press, 1995); Tyler Cowen, *Creative Destruction: How Globalization is Changing the World* (Princeton, NJ: Princeton University Press, 2002); Martin Van Creveld, *The Rise and Decline of the State* (Cambridge: Cambridge University Press, 1999); and Jean–Marie Guéhenno, *The End of the Nation-State*, Victoria Elliott, trans. (Minneapolis: University of Minnesota Press, 1995).

3 See D. P. Moran, *The Philosophy of Irish Ireland* (Dublin: University College Dublin Press), 2006; originally published as six articles in 1898–1900 in the *New Irish Review*, 14, 21–2.

4 Moran, *Irish Ireland*, 26, 30–1.

5 Moran, *Irish Ireland*, 67.

6 Moran, *Irish Ireland*, 75.

7 Moran, *Irish Ireland*, 117, 75.

8 Moan, *Irish Ireland*, 77.

9 Moran, *Irish Ireland*, 92.

10 Moran, *Irish Ireland*, 96.

11 I borrow the term "minor literature" from Gilles Deleuze and Félix Guattari, *Kafka: Toward a Minor Literature*, Dana Polan, trans. (Minneapolis: University of Minnesota Press, 1986).

12 See for example, Terence Brown, *Ireland: A Social and Cultural History, 1922 to the Present* (Ithaca, NY: Cornell University Press, 1985); and David Lloyd, *Anomalous States: Irish Writing and the Post-Colonial Moment* (Durham, NC: Duke University Press, 1993).

13 Arthur Griffith, *The Resurrection of Hungary: A Parallel for Ireland* (Dublin: James Duffy, 1904; 2nd edition), 74.

14 Samuel Beckett, *Murphy* (New York: Grove Press, 1957), 272.

15 Beckett, *Murphy*, 113.

16 Beckett, *Murphy*, 68.

17 James Joyce, *Ulysses* (New York: Random House, 1986), 394–5.

18 Virginia Woolf, *The Diary of Virginia Woolf*, 5 vols., Anne Oliver Bell and Andrew McNeillie, eds. (London: Hogarth Press, 1977–1984), 2: 188–9.

19 Woolf, *Diary*, 189.

20 James Joyce, *A Portrait of the Artist as a Young Man* (New York: Penguin, 1992), 120, 123–5.

21 Joyce, *Portrait*, 126 (italics in original).

22 Joyce, *Portrait*, 131.

23 For a discussion of the staging of the first performance of *At the Hawk's Well*, see Richard Allen Cave, "Commentaries and Notes" in W. B. Yeats, *Selected Plays*, (London: Penguin, 1997), 313–22; for Yeats's discussion of Noh, the Catholic Mass, and ritual theater, see "The Theatre," "Ireland and the Arts," and "Certain Noble Plays of Japan," in W. B. Yeats, *Early Essays: The Collected Works*, vol. IV, George Bornstein and Richard J. Finneran, eds. (New York: Scribner, 2007), 122–7, 150–5, 163–173.

FURTHER READING

General Works

Allison, Jonathan, ed. *Yeats's Political Identities: Selected Essays.* Ann Arbor: University of Michigan Press, 1996.

Armstrong, Gordon S. *Samuel Beckett, W. B. Yeats, and Jack Yeats: Images and Words.* London: Associated University Presses, 1990.

Arnold, Bruce. *Jack Yeats.* New Haven, CT: Yale University Press, 1998.

Begam, Richard and Michael Valdez Moses, eds. *Modernism and Colonialism: British and Irish Literature, 1899–1939.* Durham, NC: Duke University Press, 2007.

Bourke, Angela et al., eds. *The Field Day Anthology of Irish Writing: Irish Women's Writings and Traditions,* Vols. 4–5. Cork: Cork University Press, 2001.

Brooker, Joseph. *Flann O'Brien.* Tavistock: Northcote House, 2005.

Brown, Terence. *The Literature of Ireland: Culture and Criticism.* Cambridge: Cambridge University Press, 2010.

  Louis MacNeice, Sceptical Vision. Dublin: Gill & Macmillan, 1975.

Butler Cullingford, Elizabeth. *Gender and History in Yeats's Love Poetry.* Cambridge: Cambridge University Press, 1993.

Castle, Gregory. *Modernism and the Celtic Revival.* Cambridge: Cambridge University Press, 2001.

Cullen, Fintan, ed. *Sources in Irish Art: A Reader.* Cork: Cork University Press, 2000.

Deane, Seamus, gen. ed. *The Field Day Anthology of Irish Writing,* Vols. 1–3. Derry: Field Day Publications, 1991.

  A Short History of Irish Literature. London: Hutchinson, 1986.

  Celtic Revivals: Essays in Modern Irish Literature, 1880–1890. London: Faber and Faber, 1985.

Deleuze, Gilles. *Francis Bacon: The Logic of Sensation,* trans. Daniel W. Smith. London: Continuum. 2003.

Eagleton, Terry. *Heathcliff and the Great Hunger: Studies in Irish Culture.* London: Verso, 1995.

Ellmann, Maud. *Elizabeth Bowen: The Shadow Across the Page.* Edinburgh: Edinburgh University Press, 2003.

Ellmann, Richard. *Oscar Wilde.* London: Hamish Hamilton, 1987.

  James Joyce. Oxford: Oxford University Press, 1959, rev. 1982.

Ficacci, Luigi. *Francis Bacon, 1909–1992.* London: Taschen, 2003.

Foster, R. F. *W. B. Yeats, A Life: The Arch Poet, 1915–1939,* Vol. II. Oxford: Oxford University Press, 2003.

W. B. Yeats, A Life: The Apprentice Mage, 1865–1914, Vol. I. Oxford: Oxford University Press, 1997.

Holroyd, Michael. *George Bernard Shaw*. London: Chatto & Windus, 1998.

Howes, Marjorie. *Yeats's Nations: Gender, Class and Irishness*. Cambridge: Cambridge University Press, 1996.

Innes, Christopher, ed. *The Cambridge Companion to George Bernard Shaw*. Cambridge: Cambridge University Press, 1998.

Kelleher, Margaret and O'Leary, Philip, eds. *The Cambridge History of Irish Literature*. Cambridge: Cambridge University Press, 2006.

Kennedy, S. B. *Irish Art and Modernism, 1880–1950*. Belfast: Institute of Irish Studies, 1991.

Kennedy, Seán, ed. *Beckett and Ireland*. Cambridge: Cambridge University Press, 2010.

Keown, Edwina and Carol Taaffe, eds. *Irish Modernism: Origins, Contexts, Politics*. Oxford: Peter Lang, 2010.

Kiberd, Declan. *Inventing Ireland: The Literature of the Modern Nation*. London: Jonathan Cape, 1995.

Knowlson, James. *Damned to Fame: The Life of Samuel Beckett*. London: Bloomsbury, 1996.

Lloyd, David. *Anomalous States: Irish Writing and the Postcolonial Moment*. Durham, NC: Duke University Press, 1993.

McDonald, Rónán. *Tragedy and Irish Literature: Synge, O'Casey, Beckett*. London: Palgrave Macmillan, 2002.

Miller, Nicholas. *Modernism, Ireland and the Erotics of Memory*. Cambridge: Cambridge University Press, 2002.

Nolan, Emer. *Joyce and Irish Nationalism*. London: Routledge, 1995.

O'Toole, Tina. *The Irish New Woman*. London: Palgrave Macmillan, 2013.

Raby, Peter, ed. *The Cambridge Companion to Oscar Wilde*. Cambridge: Cambridge University Press, 1997.

Wood, Michael. *Yeats and Violence*. Oxford: Oxford University Press, 2010.

Intellectual and Aesthetic Influences

Burt Foster, John. *Heirs to Dionysus: A Nietzschean Current in Literary Modernism*. Princeton, NJ: Princeton University Press, 1981.

Calinescu, Matei. *Five Faces of Modernity: Modernism, Avant-Garde, Decadence, Kitsch, Postmodernism*. Durham, NC: Duke University Press, 1987.

Levenson, Michael H. *A Genealogy of Modernism: A Study of English Literary Doctrine, 1908–22*. Cambridge: Cambridge University Press, 1984.

Marcus, Phillip L. *Yeats and the Beginning of the Irish Renaissance* (2nd edition). Syracuse, NY: Syracuse University Press, 1987.

Rabaté, Jean-Michel. *1913: The Cradle of Modernism*. Oxford: Blackwell, 2007.

Slote, Sam. *Joyce's Nietzschean Ethics*. London: Palgrave Macmillan, 2013.

Wood, Michael. *Yeats and Violence*. Oxford: Oxford University Press, 2010.

European, American and Imperial Conjunctures

Anderson, Perry. *The Origins of Postmodernity*. London: Verso, 1998.

Arrighi, Giovanni. *The Long Twentieth Century: Money, Power, and the Origins of Our Times*. London: Verso, 1994.

Casanova, Pascale. *The World Republic of Letters*, trans. M. B. DeBevoise. Cambridge, MA: Harvard University Press, 2004.

Deane, Seamus. *Strange Country: Modernity and Nationhood in Irish Writing since 1790*. Oxford: Clarendon Press, 1997.

Eagleton, Terry. *Exiles and Émigrés: Studies in Modern Literature*. London: Chatto & Windus, 1970.

Esty, Jed. *A Shrinking Island: Modernism and National Culture in England*. Princeton, NJ: Princeton University Press, 2003.

Miller, Tyrus, *Late Modernism: Politics, Fiction and the Arts between the World Wars*. Berkeley: University of California Press, 1999.

The Irish Revival and Modernism

Boyd, Ernest. *Ireland's Literary Renaissance*. Dublin: Maunsel, 1916

Castle, Gregory. *Modernism and the Celtic Revival*. Cambridge: Cambridge University Press, 2001.

Eglinton, John, et al. *Literary Ideals in Ireland*. London: T. Fisher Unwin, 1899.

Garrigan Mattar, Sinéad. *Primitivism, Science and the Irish Revival*. Oxford: Oxford University Press, 2004.

Kiberd, Declan. *Inventing Ireland: The Literature of the Modern Nation*. London: Jonathan Cape, 1995.

Mathews, P. J. *Revival: The Abbey Theatre, Sinn Féin, the Gaelic League and the Cooperative Movement*. Cork: Field Day/Cork University Press, 2003.

Style and Idiom

Cleary, Joe. *Outrageous Fortune: Capital and Culture in Modern Ireland*. Dublin: Field Day Publications, 2007.

Foster, John Wilson. "Irish Modernism." In *Colonial Consequences: Essays in Irish Literature and Culture*, by John Wilson Foster. Dublin: Lilliput, 1991, 44–59.

Deane, Seamus. "Dumbness and Eloquence: A Note on English as We Write It in Ireland." In Carroll, Clare and Patricia King, eds. *Ireland and Postcolonial Theory*. Notre Dame: University of Notre Dame Press, 2003.

Seán de Fréine. *The Great Silence: The Study of a Relationship between Language and Nationality*. Dublin: Mercier Press, 1978.

Kiberd, Declan. *Synge and the Irish Language*. London: Macmillan, 1993

Karen Lawrence. *The Odyssey of Style in Ulysses*. Princeton, NJ: Princeton University Press, 1981

Ó Ríordáin, Seán. "Teangacha príobháideacha." *Scríobh* 4, 1979, pp. 12–22

W. B. Yeats and Modernist Poetry

Brearton, Fran and Alan Gillis, eds. *The Oxford Handbook of Modern Irish Poetry*. Oxford: Oxford University Press, 2012.

Collins, Lucy, ed. *Poetry by Women in Ireland: A Critical Anthology 1870–1970*. Liverpool: Liverpool University Press, 2012.

Coughlan, Patricia and Alex Davis, eds. *Modernism and Ireland: The Poetry of the 1930s*, Cork: Cork University Press, 1995.

MacNeice, Louis. *The Poetry of W. B. Yeats*. New York: Oxford University Press, 1941.

Quinn, Justin. *The Cambridge Introduction to Modern Irish Poetry, 1800–2000*. Cambridge: Cambridge University Press, 2008.

James Joyce and the Mutations of the Modernist Novel

Cleary, Joe. *Outrageous Fortune: Capital and Culture in Modern Ireland*. Dublin: Field Day, 2007.

Cronin, Michael G. *Impure Thoughts: Sexuality, Catholicism and Literature in Twentieth-Century Ireland*. Manchester: Manchester University Press, 2013.

Deane, Seamus. *A Short History of Irish Literature*. London: Hutchinson, 1986.

Dobbins, Gregory. *Lazy Idle Schemers: Irish Modernism and the Cultural Politics of Laziness*. Dublin: Field Day, 2010.

Eagleton, Terry. *Heathcliff and the Great Hunger: Studies in Irish Culture*. London: Verso, 1995.

Ellmann, Maud. *Elizabeth Bowen: The Shadow Across the Page*. Edinburgh: Edinburgh University Press, 2005.

Esty, Jed. *Unseasonable Youth: Modernism, Colonialism, and the Fiction of Development*. Oxford: Oxford University Press, 2011.

Hand, Derek. *A Short History of the Irish Novel*. Cambridge: Cambridge University Press, 2011.

Modernist Experiments in Irish Theatre

Allen, Nicholas. *Modernism, Ireland and Civil War*. Cambridge: Cambridge University Press, 2009.

Dierkes-Thrun, Petra. *Salomé's Modernity: Oscar Wilde and the Aesthetics of Transgression*. Ann Arbor: Michigan University Press, 2011.

Friedman, Alan W. *Party Pieces: Oral Storytelling and Social Performance in Joyce and Beckett*. Syracuse, NY: Syracuse University Press, 2007.

McAteer, Michael. *Yeats and European Drama*. Cambridge: Cambridge University Press, 2010.

McDonald, Rónán. *Tragedy and Irish Literature: Synge, O'Casey, Beckett*. London: Palgrave Macmillan, 2002.

Pilkington, Lionel. *Theatre and the State in Twentieth-Century Ireland: Cultivating the People*. London: Routledge, 2001.

Reynolds, Paige. *Modernism, Drama and the Audience for Irish Spectacle*. Cambridge: Cambridge University Press, 2007.

Taxidou, Olga. *Modernism and Performance: Jarry to Brecht*. London: Palgrave, 2007.

Visual Modernisms

Barber, Fionna. *Art in Ireland Since 1910*. London: Reaktion, 2013.

Juncosa, Enrique and Christina Kennedy, eds. *The Moderns: The Arts in Ireland from the 1900s to the 1970s*. Dublin: Irish Museum of Modern Art, 2011.

Kennedy, S. B. *Irish Art and Modernism, 1880–1950*. Belfast: Institute of Irish Studies 1991.
Keown, Edwina and Taaffe, Carol, eds. *Irish Modernism: Origins, Contexts, Politics*. Oxford: Peter Lang, 2010.
O'Connor, Éimear, ed. *Irish Women Artists, 1800–2009*. Dublin: Four Courts Press, 2008.
Walker, Dorothy. *Modern Art in Ireland*. Dublin: Lilliput, 1997.

Women and Modernism

Bourke, Angela. *Maeve Brennan: Homesick at the New Yorker*. London: Jonathan Cape, 2004.
Ellmann, Maud. *Elizabeth Bowen: The Shadow Across the Page*. Edinburgh: Edinburgh University Press, 2003.
Keown, Edwina and Carol Taaffe, eds. *Irish Modernism: Origins, Contexts, Politics*. Oxford: Peter Lang, 2010.
Leeny, Cathy. *Irish Women Playwrights 1900–1939: Gender and Violence on Stage*. New York: Peter Lang, 2010.
Meaney, Gerardine. *Gender, Ireland and Cultural Change: Race, Sex and Nation*. London: Routledge, 2010.
Mentxaka, Aintzane Legarreta. *Kate O'Brien and the Fiction of Identity: Sex, Art and Politics in Mary Lavelle and Other Writings*. Jefferson, NC: McFarland, 2011.
Molidor, Jennifer. "Dying for Ireland: Violence, Silence and Sacrifice in Dorothy Macardle's *Earth-Bound: Nine Stories of Ireland* (1924)." *New Hibernia Review* 12 (2008), 43–61.
O'Toole, Tina. *The Irish New Woman*. London: Palgrave Macmillan, 2013
Reynolds, Paige. "'Colleen Modernism': Modernism's Afterlife in Irish Women's Writing." *Éire-Ireland* 44 (2009), 94–117.
Tiernan, Sonja. *Eva Gore-Booth: An Image of Such Politics*. Manchester: Manchester University Press, 2012.
Tova Linett, Maren, ed. *The Cambridge Companion to Modernist Women Writers*. Cambridge: Cambridge University Press, 2010.

Irish Language Modernisms

Kelleher, Margaret and O'Leary, Philip, eds. *The Cambridge History of Irish Literature*. Cambridge: Cambridge University Press, 2006.
O'Brien, Frank. *Filíocht Ghaeilge na Linne Seo*. Dublin: An Clóchomhar, 1968.
Ó Coileáin, Seán. *Seán Ó Ríordáin: Beatha agus Saothar*. Dublin: An Clóchomhar 1982.
O'Leary, Philip. *The Prose Literature of the Gaelic Revival, 1881–1921: Ideology and Innovation*. University Park: Pennsylvania State University Press, 1994.
Ó Tuama, Seán. *Repossessions: Selected Essays on the Irish Literary Heritage*. Cork: Cork University Press, 1995.

Irish American Modernisms

Bruccoli, Matthew F. *Some Sort of Epic Grandeur: The Life of F. Scott Fitzgerald*. New York: Scribners, 1994.

Curtis, L. Perry. *Apes and Angels: The Irishman in Victorian Caricature.* Washington, DC: Smithsonian Institute Press, 1997.

Dowd, Christopher. *The Construction of Irish Identity in American Literature.* New York: Routledge, 2011.

Kenny, Kevin. *The American Irish: A History.* Harlow: Pearson Educational, 2000.

Lee, J. J. and Marion R. Casey, *Making the Irish American: History and Heritage of the Irish in the United States.* New York: New York University Press, 2000.

Miller, Kerby A. *Ireland and Irish America: Culture, Class and Transatlantic Migration.* Dublin: Field Day, 2008.

   Emigrants and Exiles: Ireland and the Irish Exodus to North America. New York: Oxford University Press, 1985.

Moglen, Seth. *Mourning Modernity: Literary Modernism and the Injuries of American Capitalism.* Stanford, CA: Stanford University Press, 2007.

Sheaffer, Louis. *O'Neill: Son and Artist.* Boston, MA: Little Brown, 1973.

   O'Neill: Son and Playwright. Boston, MA: Little Brown, 1968.

Soto, Michael. *The Modernist Nation: Generation, Renaissance, and Twentieth-Century American Literature.* Tuscaloosa: The University of Alabama Press, 2004.

Wood, Ralph C. *Flannery O'Connor and the Christ-Haunted South.* Grand Rapids, MI: Wm. B. Eerdmans Publishing, 2005.

Critical Receptions of Literary Modernism

Boyd, Ernest A. *Ireland's Literary Renaissance.* New York: John Lane, 1916.

Brooker, Joseph. *Joyce's Critics: Transitions in Reading and Culture.* Madison: University of Wisconsin Press, 2004.

Brown, Terence. "Ireland, Modernism and the 1930s." In *The Literature of Ireland: Culture and Criticism,* Terence Brown, 88–103. Cambridge: Cambridge University Press, 2010.

Corkery, Daniel. *The Hidden Ireland: A Study of Gaelic Munster in the Eighteenth Century.* Dublin: Gill and Macmillan, 1967.

Foster, John Wilson. "Irish Modernism." In *Colonial Consequences: Essays in Irish Literature and Culture,* by John Wilson Foster. Dublin: Lilliput, 1991, 44–59

Holderman, David and Ben Levitas, eds. *W. B. Yeats in Context.* Cambridge: Cambridge University Press, 2010.

Keown, Edwina and Carol Taaffe, eds. *Irish Modernism: Origins, Contexts, Publics.* Oxford and New York: Peter Lang, 2009.

Mercier, Vivian. *The Irish Comic Tradition.* Oxford: Oxford University Press, 1962.

Ó Faoláin, Seán. *The Vanishing Hero: Studies in Novelists of the 1920s.* London: Eyre and Spottiswoode, 1956.

Irish Modernist Imaginaries

Casanova, Pascale. *The World Republic of Letters,* trans. M. B. DeBovoise. Cambridge, MA: Harvard University Press, 2004.

Cowen, Tyler. *Creative Destruction: How Globalization Is Changing the World's Cultures.* Princeton, NJ: Princeton University Press, 2002.

Damrosch, David. *What Is World Literature?* Princeton, NJ: Princeton University Press, 2003.

Kiberd, Declan. *Inventing Ireland: The Literature of the Modern Nation.* Cambridge, MA: Harvard University Press, 1995.

Moses, Michael Valdez. *The Novel and the Globalization of Culture.* Oxford: Oxford University Press, 1995.

Tomlinson, John. *Cultural Imperialism.* Baltimore, MD: Johns Hopkins University Press, 1991.

Walkowitz, Rebecca L. *Cosmopolitan Style: Modernism Beyond the Nation.* New York: Columbia University Press, 2006.

INDEX

Abbey Theatre, 7, 24, 44, 52, 54, 55, 81,
    111, 115, 154, 212
Abstract Expressionism, 138
Adorno, Theodor, 59
aestheticism, 2, 40–41, 101, 106, 184, 203
Allgood, Molly, 122
American modernism, 6, 42
    impact of Irish Revival, 6–7
    role in displacing Britain as world power,
        36–39, 43–44 *See also* Irish American
        modernism
An Túr Gloine, 130
Anderson, Perry, 38, 58
Anglo-Irish, 8
    declining Ascendancy, 60, 81, 99, 138
    novelists on, 97–99, 107
    revival, 53, 54, 55–56 *See also* Irish
        Revival; Protestantism
Appel, Karel, 139
Archer, William, 41
architectural modernism, 3, 131–32 *See also*
        Scott, Michael; Sullivan, Louis Henry
Arguedas, José María, 209–10
Armstrong, Tim, 156
Arnold, Bruce
    Jack Yeats, 221
Arnold, Matthew, 1, 177
Artaud, Antonin, 116, 120
Asquith, Herbert, 113
Asturias, Miguel Ángel
    Men of Maize, 96
Auden, W.H., 45–46, 201
    'In Memory of W.B. Yeats', 81–82
Austen, Jane
    Pride and Prejudice, 98

Bacon, Francis, 2, 3, 4, 136, 138
    context of revolution and political
        upheaval, 10

Head I to *Head VI* series, 46, 48
    relocation to Dublin, 16, 141
    Rosc exhibition, 139
    Study after Velázquez's Pope Innocent X,
        48, 138
    surrealism, 136, 138
    trained in London, 4, 7, 45, 138
Bakhtin, Mikhail, 105
Balfour, Prime Minister Arthur, 113
Ballagh, Robert, 140, 140–41
Banim, John, 98
Banim, Michael, 98
Banville, John, 110n35
Barrès, Maurice, 31–32
Barry, James, 38–39
Barry, Sebastian, 125
Bartók, Béla, 6
Baudelaire, Charles, 77
Bax, Arnold, 6
Beardsley, Aubrey, 23, 121
Beckett, Samuel, 1, 10, 13–14, 15–16, 45, 46,
        133–34, 218
    antipathy towards Austin Clarke, 85
    Catastrophe, 124
    'Comment Dire', 77, 87
    criticism of parochialism of Irish
        revivalism, 22, 51
    'Dante … Bruno. Vico .. Joyce', 31,
        203
    Endgame, 1, 4, 107, 108, 122–23, 124
    exilic nature of career, 4, 7
    experimentation in theatre, 111, 122,
        123–24
    Happy Days, 124
    Krapp's Last Tape, 124
    modernism, 107–8, 123–24, 184, 196
    monograph on Proust, 31–32
    Murphy, 107, 212–13
    Not I, 124, 125

Beckett, Samuel (*cont.*)
part of declining establishment elite, 175–76
Plays, 124
Poèmes, 87
predominance of Yeats, Joyce and Beckett in Irish modernism, 1–3, 54, 128, 147
'Recent Irish Poetry', 54, 78, 88
The Unnamable, 1, 107
Trilogy, 96, 107
Waiting for Godot, 4, 87, 107–8, 122–23, 124
What Where, 124
'Whoroscope', 7, 77, 87
Behan, Brendan, 124
Belli, Giuseppe Gioachino, 67
Berger, John, 134
Bergson, Henri, 130
Berman, Marshall, 154
Bjørnson, Bjørnstjerne, 149
Blake, William, 22, 23
Boland, Eavan, 90–91
'Mise Éire', 90–91
Bowen, Elizabeth, 2–3, 4, 7, 14, 44, 45, 46–47, 96, 98, 109n7
A World of Love, 156–57
Eva Trout, 157
'James Joyce', 203–4
modernism, 101, 109n7, 147, 148, 156
The Death of the Heart, 47, 156
The Heat of the Day, 156
The House in Paris, 47
The Last September, 47, 96, 100, 156
Boyd, Ernest, 196, 204
Ireland's Literary Renaissance, 52, 57–58, 199–200
Boydell, Brian, 5, 6, 135
Brancusi, Constantin, 136
Braque, Georges, 129
Brecht, Bertolt, 10, 116
Brennan, Maeve, 147, 148, 156, 158, 174
The Springs of Affection, 158
Brennan, Robert, 174
Breton, André, 32
Brown, Sterling, 81
Bruno, Giordano, 30, 31
Bunting, Basil, 81
Burke, Edmund, 38–39, 49
Butler Cullingford, Elizabeth
Gender and History in Yeats's Love Poetry, 14
Byrne, Barry, 131

Cage, John, 6
Campbell-Bannerman, Henry, 113
Čapek, Karel, 120
Carducci, Giosuè, 31–32
Carleton, William, 39
Carr, Marina, 16, 125
Carson, Ciaran, 90
Casanova, Pascale, 8
The World Republic of Letters, 37
Castle, Gregory
Modernism and the Celtic Revival, 57
Catholicism, 84–85, 86, 178–79, 215–16
Eliot, T.S., 83–84
Irish dominance of American Catholic church, 177, 178–79
novelists, 98–99
Cavafy, C.P., 209–10
Celticism, 1, 12–13, 138–39, 140, 177–78, 182–83 See also Irish Revival; *Rosc* exhibitions
Cézanne, Paul, 129
Chopin, Kate, 43, 49, 174, 175, 178
The Awakening, 42
cinematic modernism, 3 See also visual modernism
Clancy, George, 110n22
Clarke, Austin, 85–86
'Ancient Lights', 85
Clarke, Harry, 130, 132
Clarke, T.J., 60
Cleary, Joe, 1–18, 35–49, 174–90
Cocteau, Jean, 121
Coffey, Brian, 2–3, 45, 77–78, 86, 87–88
Coghill, Rhoda, 88
Coleman, James, 140
Collins, Lucy
Poetry by Women in Ireland 1870–1970, 88–89, 90
Colum, Mary, 196
Colum, Padraic, 54, 196
Common, Thomas
Nietzsche as Critic, Philosopher, Poet and Prophet, 23–24
Connolly, Cyril, 135–36
Connolly, James, 207
Connolly, Thurloe, 135
Conrad, Joseph, 97
Corkery, Daniel, 13, 57–58, 195–96, 197, 200, 204
on Irish Revival, 56
Synge and Anglo-Irish Literature, 200–1
The Hidden Ireland, 200
Corot, Jean-Baptiste-Camille, 128

Coughlan, Patricia, 78–79
  Modernism and Ireland: The Poetry of the
    1930s, 78
Counter-Revival, 13–14 *See also* Irish
  Revival
Cousins, James, 6
Cowell, Henry, 5–6, 174, 175
  The Banshee, 6
  The Tides of Mananaun, 6
  The Trumpet of Angus Og, 6
Craig, Edward Gordon, 116–17
Craig-Martin, Michael, 140
Cuala Press, 44
Cubism, 129–30, 132, 135–36
Cullen, Countee, 12–13
Cullen, L.M., 200
Cunard, Nancy, 7, 14–15, 217
Curran, Constance, 121
Cusack, Michael, 207
Cusack, Ralph, 135–36

Dalí, Salvador, 136
Dante, Alighieri, 31
Darwin, Charles, 52
David Hendriks Gallery, 138
Davis, Alex, 78–79
  Modernism and Ireland: The Poetry of the
    1930s, 78
Davis, Thomas, 1, 197
Davitt, Michael, 1, 9
Dawson Gallery, 138
de Goncourt, Edmond, 65
de hIndeberg, Risteard, 161–62
de Kooning, Willem, 139
de Paor, Louis, 16, 161–71
de Valera, Eamon, 103
de Valois, Ninette, 118
Deane, Seamus, 106
  Celtic Revivals, 14
Deevy, Teresa, 156
Degas, Edgar, 128, 130
Delaunay, Robert, 129
Deleuze, Gilles, 138
Devlin, Denis, 2–3, 45, 77–78, 85–86
  'Lough Derg', 86–87
  translation projects, 86
Dhlomo, Herbert, 83
diaspora
  impact on Irish modernism, 2, 4, 6–7, 8–9,
    16, 39, 77–78 *See also* Great Famine
Dickinson, Emily, 39
Dine, Jim, 139
Döblin, Alfred, 38, 95

Dos Passos, John, 95
  The U.S.A. Trilogy, 96
Dublin, period as literary capital, 49
Dublin Drama League, 120, 132
Duffy, Charles Gavan, 53
Duffy, Enda, 13–14, 16, 195–205
Dufy, Raoul, 129
Dujardin, Edouard, 29
Dulac, Edmund, 218

Eagleton, Terry, 51, 58, 99
Edgeworth, Maria, 39
  Castle Rackrent, 97
Edwards, Hilton, 120, 121, 122, 125
Egerton, George (Mary Chavelita Dunne
    Bright), 2, 40, 41, 42–43
  Discords, 41, 149
  feminism, 147, 148, 149–50
  Keynotes, 41, 149–50
Eglinton, John (William Magee), 28–30, 44,
    55, 195, 198–99
  Dana, 28–29, 198
  Irish Literary Portraits, 198–99
  Literary Ideas in Ireland, 198
  Pebbles from a Brook, 28
Eisenstein, Sergei, 138
Eliot, George, *Middlemarch*, 98, 100
Eliot, T.S., 15, 35, 38, 43–44, 55, 59, 79,
    179, 189, 196, 218
  After Strange Gods, 175
  conversion to Catholicism, 83–84
  'Four Quartets', 86–87
  The Waste Land, 39, 88, 103, 134
Ellis, Havelock, 22, 23
Ellmann, Richard, 51
Éluard, Paul, 86
émigré modernists, impact on Irish
    modernism, 2, 4, 6–7, 8–9, 16,
    39, 77–78
Ermarth, Elizabeth Deeds, 151
Ervine, St. John, 44, 67
Expressionism, 132, 133, 135–36, 141

Farrell, Michael, 140
Faulkner, William, 38, 95
Fauvism, 129, 135–36
Felski, Rita
  The Gender of Modernity, 147–48
feminism *See* women and modernism
Field Day Anthology of Irish Writing, 14
*Field Day Anthology of Women's Writing
    and Traditions*, 88–89
Field Day Theatre Company, 16, 124

Film and modernism, 3, 132–33
   See also visual modernism
Fitzgerald, F. Scott, 6–7, 8, 12–13, 16, 42, 43,
   49, 174, 175, 178
   The Great Gatsby, 179–83, 187, 189
   This Side of Paradise, 179, 182
Flaubert, Gustave, 111–12
Fleischmann, Aloys, 5
Fogarty, Anne, 16, 147–58
Frampton, Kenneth, 140
Frankenthaler, Helen, 140
Friel, Brian, 124

Gaelic Athletic Association, 57
Gaelic League, 53, 64, 69, 153, 197, 208
Gaelic Revival, 53, 55–56, 69
   See also Celticism; Irish language
Garnier, Philippe, 131
Garrigan-Mattar, Sinéad
   *Primitivism, Science and the Irish
   Revival*, 57
Gate Theatre, 111, 120–22, 125
Gauguin, Paul, 57, 129
gender equality *See* women and modernism
George, Stefan, 38
Gershwin, George, 6
Geulincx, Arnold
   Ethics, 32
Giacometti, Alberto, 136
Gibbons, Luke, 2, 16, 128–41
Gleizes, Albert, 129–30
von Goethe, Johann Wolfgang, 5, 29, 214
Gógan, Liam, 165–66, 170–71
Gogarty, Oliver St. John, 21, 195, 196
   *As I Was Going Down Sackville Street: A
   Phantasy in Fact*, 21
Goldsmith, Oliver, 49
Gonne, Maud, 25–26, 30, 32, 114,
   122, 207
Gore-Booth, Eva, 148, 153–54
   The Buried Life of Deirdre, 154
   Unseen Kings, 154
Gramsci, Antonio, 201
Graves, Robert, 80
Gray, Eileen, 130–31
   based in Paris, 7
   contribution to Irish visual modernism,
   3, 4, 43
   The *Eileen Gray, Pioneer of Design*
   exhibition, 131
   Transat chair design, 131
Great Depression, 37, 46
Great Famine, 7, 8, 9, 11, 15, 40, 42

impact on Irish modernism, 8–9, 41–42
Greenberg, Clement, 59
Gregory, Lady Augusta, 6, 7, 14–15, 23, 27,
   28, 44, 53, 55, 57, 68, 114, 116, 148,
   154–55, 207
   Cathleen ni Houlihan, 114
   Grania, 155
   Hyacinth Halvey, 114
   Our Irish Theatre, 154
   Spreading the News, 114
   The Gaol Gate, 154–55
Gregory, Sir William, 154
Griffith, Arthur, 52, 207, 210
Gropius, Walter, 131–32
Guinness, May, 3, 7, 43, 129, 135–36
   contribution to Irish modernism, 3, 7,
   43, 129
   influence of Cubism and Fauvism, 135
   The Infant, 129

Hall, Kenneth, 134–35
Hamilton, Letitia, 130
Hamsun, Knut, 2, 41, 149
Hanlon, Jack, 135
Hardwicke Theatre (Dublin), 114
Harris, Frank, 41
Harrison, Lou, 6
Harte, Bret, 38–39
Hartigan, Marianne, 129
Hauptmann, Gerhard, 27
Hawthorne, Nathaniel, 39
Hayes, Gabriel, 128
Hayford, Gladys Casely, 83
Hayman, David, 70
Heaney, Seamus, 60, 90
   'Station Island', 86–87
Heidegger, Martin, 32
Hemingway, Ernest, 184
Henry, Grace, 130
Henry, Paul, 130, 135
Herder, Johann Gottfried, 1
Hewitt, John, 84
Hiberno-English, 64, 66–67, 70 *See also* Irish
   language and modernism
high modernism, 38, 58–59, 108,
   140
Hobson, Bulmer, 114
Holloway, Joseph, 121
Hone, Evie, 129–30, 135, 138
   contribution to Irish modernism, 45,
   129–30
   Cubism, 129–30
   Four Green Fields, 132

work in medium of stained glass, 130,
    131, 132
Hone, Nathaniel, 128
Howes, Marjorie
    Yeats's Nations, 14
Hugh Lane Gallery, 16, 128, 141
Hurst, Brian Desmond, 132–33
Huysmans, Joris-Karl, 111–12
    À rebours, 40
Hyde, Douglas, 53, 57, 197, 207, 208
Hynes, Garry, 125

Ibsen, Henrik, 2, 27, 41, 52, 149, 214
    A Doll's House, 101
    Peer Gynt, 120–21, 154
impressionism, 4, 40, 128, 129
Irish Academy, 44, 47–48
Irish Academy of Letters, 47–48, 174
Irish Agricultural Organisation Society,
    53, 57
Irish American modernism, 3, 8–9, 14, 49,
    174–90 *See also* American modernism
Irish Exhibition of Living Art, 47–48,
    135, 138
Irish Free State, 38
Irish language
    and modernism, 3, 13, 14, 45, 63–73, 89–
        90, 161–71 *See also* Celticism; Gaelic
        Revival; Hiberno-English
Irish Literary Revival, 98–99, 149
Irish Literary Society, 53
Irish Literary Theatre (ILT), 114
Irish modernism, 13–15, 21–22, 42
    alignment of Irishness with traditionalism,
        78–79, 136–37, 162
    dichotomy of Irish and Paris-based
        modernisms, 78–79
    effect of social and political upheaval, 148,
        176–77, 196
    imaginaries, 206–18
    impact of colonialism, 5, 8–9, 10–11, 195
    importance of émigré modernists, 2, 4,
        6–7, 8–9, 16, 39, 77–78
    intellectual influences, 21–32, 140
    Nietzschean quality, 21–32
    patrons, 7, 14–15
    politics of, 10, 40
    precedence given to cultural nationalism,
        5, 11–12
    sectarian divide in Irish university system,
        critical consequences, 195–96
    significance of Irish contribution to global
        modernism, 1–2, 6–7, 49, 63

successive generations, 40–48
    See also high modernism; Irish
        American modernism; Irish Revival; late
        modernism; modernism; novel; poetry;
        theatre; visual modernism
Irish National Theatre Society, 114, 209
Irish nativism *See* Irish Revival
Irish Revival, 5, 6, 11–13, 27, 42, 44, 57,
    104, 113, 161, 164–66, 195–96, 206
    alignment of Irishness with traditionalism,
        78–79, 197
    impact on American Renaissance, 12
    impact on global modernism, 6–7, 197
    opposition to outside cultural influences,
        161–62
    relationship with modernism, 51–61
    See also Counter-Revival; Gaelic
        Revival; Young Ireland
Irish Women's Movement, 90
Irving, Washington, 38–39

James, Henry, 35, 38–39, 43–44, 179
Jameson, Fredric, 108
Jarry, Alfred, 116
Jellett, Mainie, 45, 129–30, 132,
    135–36, 138
    contribution to Irish modernism, 3, 4, 45
    Cubism, 129–30
    Irish Exhibition of Living Art, 47–48,
        135, 138
    spiritual orientation, 130
Johnson, James Weldon, 81
Johnson, Nevill, 136
Johnston, Denis
    Guests of the Nation, 132–33
    The Old Lady Says "No!", 120–21
Josipovici, Gabriel, 60
Joyce, James, 1, 5, 38, 43, 45
    A Portrait of the Artist as a Young Man,
        28, 44, 55, 69, 70–71, 83–84, 96, 102,
        103, 157, 198, 215–17
    credited with inventing modernist Irish
        novel, 95–96, 105–6, 107
    critical of Moore's fiction, 101–2, 105–6
    critical reception, 195, 196, 198–99,
        202–3, 204–5
    criticism of pastoral visions of revivalism,
        54–55, 104–5, 106
    Dubliners, 44, 69–70, 96, 103, 150, 199
    exilic nature of career, 4, 6–7, 39, 44, 78
    Finnegans Wake, 1, 7, 22, 30, 39, 44,
        70–71, 73, 96, 102, 103
    free indirect style, 69–70

Joyce, James (*cont.*)
  meeting with Proust, 27
  meeting with Yeats, 27–28
  modernism, 51, 54, 108, 218
  predominance of Yeats, Joyce and Beckett
    in Irish modernism, 1–2, 15, 128,
    147, 156
  Ulysses, 1, 4, 7, 9, 13, 27–30, 39, 44, 55,
    69–70, 96, 98–99, 102, 103, 198, 209,
    213–17
  use of 'dialect' writing, 68–69
  views on feminism, 101, 102
Joyce, Stanislaus, 44, 69
Joyce, Trevor, 77–78

Kafka, Franz, 38
Kaiser, Georg, 120, 121
  From Morn to Midnight, 132
Kandinsky, Wassily, 131, 135
Kaun, Axel, 123
Kavanagh, Patrick, 54
  'Lough Derg', 86
  resists Yeatsian idealizations of Irish
    peasant, 84–85
  The Great Hunger, 46, 48, 84–85
Keating, Geoffrey (Seathrún Céitinn), 9
Keating, Seán, 3, 45, 132
  Tip Wagons at Poulaphouca, 135–36
Keegan-Dolan, Michael, 125
Kelly, Oisín, 45
Kenner, Hugh, 51
Kernoff, Harry, 132
Kiberd, Declan, 67
  Inventing Ireland, 57
  Synge and the Irish Language, 67, 73n5,n6
Kickham, Charles
  Knocknagow, 98, 103, 105–6
Kilroy, Tom, 124
King, Cecil, 140–41
Kirkwood, Harriet, 130
Klee, Paul, 135
Klein, Axel, 5
Klopstock, Friedrich, 5
Kokoschka, Oskar, 133
Krauss, Rosalind, 139–40
Krop, Hildo, 118

Laird, Heather, 109n7
Lalor, James Fintan, 1
Lane, Hugh, 7, 14–15, 128–29
  Dublin Corporation slow to accept Lane
    offer to house art collection, 128–29
  See also Hugh Lane Gallery

language *See* Irish language
late modernism, 2–3, 32, 96, 108
Laughton, Freda, 88
Lavery, John, 128
Lawless, Emily
  Grania, 100
Lawrence, D.H., 95
Lawrence, Karen, 69
le Brocquy, Louis, 3, 45, 47–48, 136,
  140–41
  A Family, 137–38
  acknowledgement of Irishness, 136–37
  early establishment as British painter, 136
  Image of Chaos, 135
  Irish Exhibition of Living Art, 47–48
  The Spanish Shawl, 135
Le Fanu, Sheridan, 98
Leeney, Cathy, 154
Leopardi, Giacomo, 31–32
Levitas, Ben, 2, 16, 111–27
Lewis, Wyndham, 26, 45, 47
  Time and Western Man, 45
Lhote, André, 129, 132
Lichtenstein, Roy, 139
Littlewood, Joan, 124
Locke, Alain, 12–13
London
  cultural centre for Irish and American
    expatriates, 35–36, 39, 42, 44–45
  focus of British imperial power, 36, 37, 38
  importance to Irish modernism, 4, 6–7, 8
Lorca, Federico García 38, 116
Louis, Morris, 140
Lugné-Poë, Aurélien, 112
Lukács, Georg, 201

Mac Grianna, Seosamh, 170–71
  Mo Bhealach Féin, 165
Mac Liammóir, Micheál, 120–22, 125
Mac Piarais, Pádraig *See* Pearse, Patrick
Macardle, Dorothy, 148
  Earth-Bound: Nine Stories of Ireland,
    155–56
McCrea, Barry, 15, 63–73
MacDiarmid, Hugh, 81, 209–10
McDonagh, Martin, 108, 125
MacDonagh, Thomas
  Pagans, 114
McDonald, Rónán, 11, 15, 51–61
McGonigal, Maurice, 132
MacGreevy, Thomas, 45, 60, 87, 130,
  133, 134
  Catholicism, 45, 87

contribution to Irish modernism, 2–3,
45, 77–78
McGuckian, Medbh, 90, 91
McGuinness, Frank, 124
McGuinness, Norah, 45, 132, 135–36, 138
contribution to Irish modernism, 132,
135–36
Cubism, 135–36
Irish Exhibition of Living Art, 47–48,
135, 138
McKay, Claude, 12–13
MacLean, Sorley, 45
MacLennan, Alastair, 140–41
MacNamara, Brinsley, 106
MacNeice, Louis, 2–3, 13–14, 45–46, 46,
78–79, 82
segregated from the Catholicism of
Irishness, 84
The Poetry of W.B. Yeats, 82, 203
MacNeill, Eoin, 53
MacPherson, Conor, 108
Macpherson, James, 5
McWilliam, F.E., 136
Magee, William *See* Eglinton, John
Magritte, René, 136
Maguire, Patrick, 85
Mahaffy, John Pentland, 195
Mallarmé, Stéphane, 86, 111–12
Manet, Édouard, 128
Olympia, 137–38
Mangan, James Clarence, 9, 39, 196
Manning, Mary, 120, 132, 156
Youth's the Season…?, 122
Márquez, Gabriel García
One Hundred Years of Solitude, 96
Martyn, Edward, 54, 114
Matisse, Henri, 121, 129
Maturin, Charles, 39
Matz, Jesse, 97
May, Frederick, 5, 6
Mays, J.C.C., 148
Melville, Herman, 39
Mercier, Vivian
Beckett/Beckett, 14
The Irish Comic Tradition, 14, 204
Meyerhold, Vsevolod, 116–17
Mhac an tSaoi, Máire, 72, 88, 89–90, 166–
67, 170–71
*Codladh an Ghaiscígh agus Véarsaí
Eile*, 168
Margadh na Saoire, 168
Middleton, Colin, 135–36
Mill, J.S., 208–9

Miller, Jane, 150
Miller, Kerby, 176
Miller, Tyrus, 46
Millevoye, Lucien, 25
Milligan, Alice, 114, 148, 152–53
A Royal Democrat, 152–53
*The Deliverance of Red Hugh
O'Donnell*, 153
Miró, Joan, 139
Mitchel, John, 1, 9
modernism
aesthetics of, 178
contribution of artists from peripheries of
Europe, 38–44
critical reception, 195–205
and Irish language *See* Irish language and
modernism
relationship with Irish Revival, 51–61
significance of Irish contribution, 1–2,
6–7, 51 *See also* Irish modernism; late
modernism; musical modernism; novel;
theatre; visual modernism; women and
modernism
Molnár, Ferenc, 121
Monet, Claude, 128
Moore, George, 2, 4, 7, 15–16, 21, 40,
42–43, 96, 198
A Drama in Muslin, 96, 99–101
Confessions of a Young Man, 40–41
Esther Waters, 99
Hail and Farewell: Ave, Salve and Vale,
21, 99
Impressions and Opinions, 40–41
Modern Painting, 40–41, 128
modernism, 98–101, 128
The Lake, 99, 100, 101
Moore, Henry, 136
Moore, Marianne, 'Marriage', 89
Moore, Thomas, 38–39, 49
Irish Melodies, 5
Moran, D.P., 55–56, 207–10, 215, 218
The Philosophy of Irish Ireland, 207–10
Moretti, Franco, 38
Morisot, Berthe, 130
Morris, Catherine, 153
Moscow Art Theatre, 116
Muldoon, Paul, 90
Müller, Max, 165
Murphy, Gerard Clery, 174–75, 178
Murphy, Tom, 16, 108, 125
musical modernism, 3, 5–6, 175
Bax, Arnold, 6
Boydell, Brian, 5, 6, 135

musical modernism (*cont.*)
  contrasts with European and American
    musical modernism, 5–7
  Cowell, Henry, 5–6, 174, 175
  Fleischmann, Aloys, 5
  May, Frederick, 5, 6
  precedence given to Irish cultural
    nationalism, 5 *See also* Celticism; Irish
    Revival
Musil, Robert, 196
  The Man Without Qualities, 39

National Literary Society, 53
naturalism, 4, 15, 101, 150
New York, 8–9
  Harlem Renaissance, 12–13
Newman, Barnett, 139
Ní Dhomhnaill, Nuala, 90, 91
Nicholls, Nick, 135–36
Nietzsche, Friedrich, 2, 15, 39
  Beyond Good and Evil, 23–24, 30
  influence on Irish modernism, 21–32, 39,
    41, 52, 149
  influence on Yeats, 22–26
  On the Genealogy of Morals, 23–24
  The Birth of Tragedy, 24, 26
  The Case of Wagner, 23, 24
  The Dawn of Day, 24
  Thoughts out of Season, 24
  Thus Spake Zarathustra, 23, 24
Noh theatre, 117, 217–18
Nolan, Emer, 2, 14, 15–16, 55, 95–108
  James Joyce and Nationalism, 14
Noland, Kenneth, 139
novel
  Catholic writers, 98
  Irish language, 106–7
  Joyce credited with inventing modernist
    Irish novel, 95–96, 105–6, 107
  masculine bias in Irish modernism,
    101, 105
  perceived sentimentality of traditionalist
    'Irish' novel, 105–6
  predominance of Anglo-Irish writers,
    97–98, 99, 107–8
  realist novel, 96–101, 105
  See also Beckett, Samuel; Bowen,
    Elizabeth; Moore, George; Ó Cadhain,
    Máirtín; O'Brien, Flann

Ó Cadhain, Máirtín, 2–3, 10, 45, 46, 161,
  167–68, 170–71, 209–10
  An tSraith ar Lár, 169

An tSraith dhá Tógáil, 169
Cré na Cille, 46, 48, 71–72, 96, 106–7,
  168, 209
  politics, 47, 168
  use of Irish language, 71–72
Ó Conaire, Pádraic, 163–64, 165, 170–71
  Deoraíocht, 164
Ó Conchubhair, Brian, 165, 172n13
Ó Criomhthain, Tomás, 165
  An tOileánach, 168
Ó Direáin, Máirtín, 72, 166, 167, 170–71
  Ár Ré Dhearóil, 168–69
Ó Doibhlinn, Breandán, 169
Ó Faoláin, Seán, 13–14, 54, 197, 200, 201–2
  *The Vanishing Hero: Studies in Novelists
    in the Twenties*, 202
Ó Grianna, Séamus, 72, 165
Ó Laoghaire, An tAthair Peadar,
  Séadna, 162
Ó Nualláin, Brian *See* O'Brien, Flann
Ó Ríordáin, Seán, 2–3, 45, 46, 72–73, 166,
  167, 169, 170–71
  Brosna, 168
  Eireaball Spideoige, 167
Ó Súilleabháin, Diarmuid, 169
Ó Súilleabháin, Muiris, 165
Ó Tuairisc, Eoghan, 169
  An Lomnochtán, 170
  Dé Luain, 170
  L'Attaque, 170
  Lux Aeterna, 170
  Na Mairnéalaigh, 170
Ó Tuama, Seán, 167, 169–71
  Faoileán na Beatha, 170
  Saol fó Thoinn, 170
  An Bás i dTír na nÓg, 170
O'Brien, Edna, 99
O'Brien, Flann (Brian Ó Nualláin), 2–3,
  15–16, 45, 46, 168, 170–71, 209–10,
  214, 218
  An Béal Bocht, 48, 105, 106, 168, 209
  At Swim-Two-Birds, 48, 96, 105, 106,
    168, 209
  The Third Policeman, 48, 105
O'Brien, Frank, 162
O'Brien, Kate, 99, 148, 156, 157
  Mary Lavelle, 157
  The Land of Spices, 157–58
O'Casey, Sean, 2–3, 4, 7, 16, 43, 44–45,
  124, 174
  Juno and the Paycock, 60, 68, 119
  politics, 47, 54
  The Plough and the Stars, 68, 119–20

The Shadow of a Gunman, 119
The Silver Tassie, 44, 119, 120
use of language, 67–68
O'Connell, Daniel, 1
O'Connor, Flannery, 16, 174, 175, 178–79,
   184, 187–90
   Wise Blood, 188–89
O'Connor, Frank, 132
O'Connor, Laura, 2, 15, 77–92
O'Conor, Roderic, 128
O'Curry, Eugene, 52
O'Doherty, Brian
   Inside the White Cube, 139–40
   Rope drawings, 140
O'Donovan, John, 52
O'Duffy, Eimar, 106
   The Phoenix on the Roof, 114
O'Faolain, Nuala, 101
O'Flaherty, Liam, 174
O'Grady, Standish James, 6, 9, 52
O'Hara, John, 174, 175, 181
O'Leary, John, 80, 82
O'Leary, Philip, 161, 163
O'Malley, Ernie, 137
O'Neill, Eugene, 6–7, 8, 16, 42, 43, 49, 120,
   174, 178, 183–87
   Long Day's Journey Into Night,
      185–87, 189
   The Iceman Cometh, 186
O'Neill, Mary Devenport, 88
Orpen, William, 128
Osborne, Walter, 128
Owenson, Sydney, 38–39

Paris
   cultural centre for Irish and American
      expatriates, 35–36, 39, 40, 44
   dichotomy of Irish and Paris-based
      modernism, 78–79
   Europe's cultural capital, 37–38
   importance to Irish modernism, 4, 6–7, 8,
      77–78, 86
Parker, Stewart, 16, 124
Parnell, Charles Stewart, 1, 53, 63
Pater, Walter
   The Renaissance, 24
Peacock Theatre, 120, 132
Pearse, Patrick, 53, 90–91, 114, 161–63,
   165, 170–71, 207
   critic of the Irish Revival, 162–63
   Íosagán agus Scéalta Eile, 161
Picasso, Pablo, 38, 129, 139
   Guernica, 137–38

Pike Theatre (Dublin), 124
Pirandello, Luigi, 120
Pissarro, Camille, 128
poetry
   critical conceptions of canon of Irish
      modernist poetry, 77–78, 80
   Máirtín Ó Cadhain and politics, 47, 168
   masculinist bias in modernist poetry,
      88–91, 168–69
   poet as public bard, 83, 91–92
   and religion, 83–88, 91–92, 167
   Seán Ó Ríordáin and crisis of poetic
      identity, 166–67, 168
   tensions between 'Irish' and 'modernist'
      poetry, 78–79
   and translation, 85–86
   W.B. Yeats, 9–10, 60, 77–92, 90–91, 99
Porta, Carlo, 67
postcolonialism, 57–58, 140, 195, 196,
   200–1, 206
postmodernism, 65, 140
Pound, Ezra, 12–13, 26, 27, 38, 43–44, 51,
   79, 117, 176, 217–18
   on British literature, 35–36
   heralding of Joyce as European
      modernist, 54
   modernist, 59
Poussin, Nicolas, 138
Price, Katherine Arnold, 89
Protestantism, 6, 8
   decay of religious world view, 175–76
   dominance of Anglo-Irish Protestants in
      higher professions due to colonialism, 8
Proust, Marcel, 31–32, 70, 95, 196, 215
   meeting with Joyce, 27
Purser, Sarah, 130

Quinn, John, 6, 7, 14–15, 23, 43, 174,
   175, 178

Rabaté, Jean-Michel, 15, 21–23
Rákóczi, Basil, 134–35
Rauschenberg, Robert, 139
Read, Herbert, 135, 136–37
   Contemporary British Art, 136
realism, 96–97, 129, 151
   realist novel, 96–101, 105 *See also* novel,
      social realism
Reid, Nano, 135
Reinhardt, Max, 112
Renan, Ernest, 1, 177
Renoir, Pierre-Auguste, 128
revivalism *See* Irish Revival

Rice, Elmer, 120
Riding, Laura, 80
Rilke, Rainer Maria, 38
Robinson, Lennox, 120, 174
Rolfe, Nigel, 140–41
Rolleston, T.W., 53
Roper, Esther, 153
Rosc exhibitions, 138–41
    controversy surrounding inclusion of
        "Celtic" artefacts, 139–40
Rouault, Georges, 131
Royal Hibernian Academy, 135
Ruane, Medb, 137
Russell, George (Æ), 6, 7, 44, 55, 130, 174
Ryan, Fred, 28

Salkeld, Blanaid, 77–78, 88, 156
    'Arachne', 90
    Hello Eternity, 79, 90
Saturday Review, 41
Sayers, Peig, 165
Schopenhauer, Arthur, 15, 22, 26, 29, 31–32
    *The World as Will and
        Representation*, 31–32
Scott, Michael, 131–32, 138–39
Scott, Patrick, 3, 135, 136, 139, 140–41
Scott, Walter, 98
Scott, William, 136, 140–41
Scully, Sean, 140–41
    contribution to Irish modernism, 3
Shanahan, Jim, 134
Shaw, George Bernard, 2, 4, 7, 16, 38–39,
    40, 41, 42–43, 111
    Back to Methuselah, 113, 120
    Irish Academy of Letters, 47–48, 174
    John Bull's Other Island, 113, 182–83
    Man and Superman, 113
    Mrs Warren's Profession, 113
    Pygmalion, 113
    The Quintessence of Ibsenism, 113
Sheehy-Skeffington, Francis, 110n22
Sheehy-Skeffington, Hanna, 207
Sheridan, Richard Brinsley, 49
Sickert, Walter, 129
Singer, Isaac Bashevis, 209–10
Smith, Michael, 77–78
Smithers, Leonard, 22
social realism, 135–36
Society of Dublin Painters, 130
Soto, Michael, 12
Spanish Civil War, 37
Spender, Stephen, 45–46
Spengler, Oswald, 39

Stead, William Thomas, 39
Stein, Gertrude, 35, 38, 43–44, 79, 95,
    129
    The Making of Americans, 39
Stephens, James, 44, 106
    The Crock of Gold, 136–37
Sterne, Lawrence, 97
Sternhell, Zeev, 25
Stevens, Wallace, 38
Stirner, Max, 30
Stoker, Bram, 38–39, 98
    Dracula, 97
Strachey, Lytton, 66
Strauss, Richard, 112, 211
Stravinsky, Igor
    Le Sacre de Printemps, 57
Strindberg, August, 41, 120, 149, 214
Stuart, Francis, 10, 45–46
    politics, 46, 47
Sullivan, Louis Henry, 6–7, 42, 43, 49, 174,
    175, 178
surrealism, 135–36
Swanzy, Mary, 4, 7, 129, 135–36
    contribution to Irish modernism, 3, 4,
        7, 129
    Irish Exhibition of Living Art, 135–36
    Society of Dublin Painters, 135
Sweeney, James Johnson, 7, 8, 14–15,
    138–39
    *Plastic Redirections in 20th-Century
        Painting*, 7
Swift, Jonathan, 9, 49, 97, 204
symbolism, 23, 41, 52, 154
Symons, Arthur, 22–23, 40–41
    *The Symbolist Movement in
        Literature*, 22–23
Synge, John Millington, 27, 43, 44, 99, 107,
    119, 125
    combined revivalism and modernism, 55,
        56, 200–1
    Deirdre of the Sorrows, 55
    In the Shadow of the Glen, 115
    Riders to the Sea, 115, 132–33,
        200–1
    The Playboy of the Western World, 55, 61,
        115–16, 182, 183, 200–1
    The Well of the Saints, 115
    use of Irish language, 66–67
    See also Abbey Theatre; Irish language;
        Yeats, William Butler

The Bell, 201
The Crane Bag, 204

The Express, 28
The Klaxon, 130
The Savoy, 22–23
theatre
    experimentation, 111–25
    opportunities for expansion of female
        roles, 122
    place in cultural nationalism, 113–14
    political and revolutionary context,
        118–19
    propagandist Celticism, 114–15
    See also Abbey Theatre; Beckett,
        Samuel; Gate Theatre; Gregory,
        Augusta; Hardwicke Theatre; Peacock
        Theatre; Pike Theatre; O'Casey, Sean;
        Shaw, G.B.; Wilde, Oscar
Théâtre de l'Oeuvre (Paris), 112
Thurston, Katherine Cecil, 148,
    150–52
    Max, 150, 151–52, 153
    The Fly on the Wheel, 150–51
Toller, Ernst, 120
    Hoppla, We're Alive, 132
Toynbee, Arnold, 39
Twain, Mark, 39
Tzara, Tristan, 32

Valdez Moses, Michael, 9, 16–17, 206–18
van Alphen, Ernst, 138
van Dalsum, Albert, 118
Varian, John, 6
Velázquez, Diego, 138
Vico, Giambattisto, 15, 30–31
visual modernism, 3, 128–41
    compatibility of Irishness and modernist
        canon, 134–36, 140
    critical receptions, 135
    Dublin Corporation and Hugh Lane art
        collection, 128–29
    female artists as innovators, 129–30
    important figures *See* Arnold, Bruce;
        Bacon, Francis; Gray, Eileen; Guinness,
        May; Jellett, Mainie; le Brocquy, Louis;
        MacGreevy, Thomas; Moore, George;
        Walker, Dorothy; Yeats, Jack. B.
    influence of George Moore, 128
    initial lack of institutional support,
        135, 139
    patrons *See* Lane, Hugh; Quinn, John
    women's contribution to *See* Gray,
        Eileen; Guinness, May; Hone, Evie;
        Jellett, Mainie; *See also* architectural
        modernism; Cubism; Expressionism;

Film and modernism; Hugh Lane
    Gallery; *Irish Exhibition of Living
    Art*; *Rosc* exhibitions; White Stag
    movement

Waddington Gallery, 137, 138
Wagner, Richard, 41, 154, 214
Walker, Dorothy, 139
    on Irish modernism, 130, 141
    The New Tribalism, 141n11
Walsh, Enda, 125
Weaver, Harriet Shaw, 7, 14–15, 44
Weber, Max, 60
Weygandt, Cornelius, 12
Whistler, James McNeill, 38–39, 43–44, 128
White, James, 129
White Stag movement, 134–36
    See also Connolly, Thurloe; Cusack,
        Ralph; Scott, Patrick
Whitelaw, Billie, 122, 125
Whitman, Walt, 39
    Leaves of Grass, 80
Wilde, Oscar, 2, 6–7, 16, 38–39, 40–41,
        42–43, 77, 111, 149, 156, 218
    A Woman of No Importance, 66
    An Ideal Husband, 111, 153–54
    De Profundis, 113
    Irish language question, 65–66
    Lady Windermere's Fan, 111
    Salomé, 4, 41, 42, 111–13, 121–22, 125,
        182, 183, 210–12
    The Importance of Being Earnest, 66,
        111, 121
    The Picture of Dorian Gray, 41,
        65–66, 152
    trials, 23
Wills, Clair, 107
Wilson, Edmund, 59, 182–83, 184
Wingfield, Sheila, 88, 156
women and modernism, 3, 14, 16, 147–58
    exposing women's oppression through
        fiction, 96, 99–101
    introducing modernism to Irish art,
        129–30
    marginalisation in Irish literary sphere, 79,
        88–91, 101, 147
    opportunities in modernist theatre, 122
Woolf, Virginia, 79, 80, 95, 150, 196, 202,
        214–15
World War I, 9, 36–37, 40
World War II, 14, 36, 37, 46
Wright, Frank Lloyd
    Genius and the Mobocracy, 174

Yeats, Jack B., 2, 3, 43, 60, 133, 135–36
  influenced by Irish revolution and political
    upheaval, 133–34
  national or European modernist,
    133–34, 136
  Tinker's Encampment: the Blood of Abel,
    134, 137
Yeats, John B., 128
Yeats, William Butler, 1, 2, 3, 4, 6, 12, 15, 16,
    38, 43, 45, 207
  A Vision, 1, 22, 26
  Abbey Theatre, 24, 55, 81, 91, 116,
    122, 209
  At the Hawk's Well, 117–18, 217–18
  on British literature, 39–40
  Calvary, 118, 218
  Cathleen ni Houlihan, 114, 115
  Celticism, 27–28, 44, 136–37, 182, 183,
    217–18
  combined international and nationalist
    authority, 79, 81–82
  contributions to *The Savoy*, 23
  dichotomy of public persona and
    dramatist, 116–18, 120
  Four Plays for Dancers, 117
  influence of Nietzsche, 22–26
  influence on postcolonial poetics, 82–83
  Irish Academy of Letters, 47–48, 174
  Last Poems, 26, 108
  meeting with Joyce, 27–28
  On Baile's Strand, 114–15
  part of declining establishment elite,
    175–76

poetry, 9–10, 60, 77–92, 90–91, 99
politics of, 10, 25–26, 39–40, 91–92, 149
predominance of Yeats, Joyce and Beckett
  in Irish modernism, 1–2, 147
Responsibilities, 44
revivalism, 51, 53, 55, 59, 95, 114, 196–98
'Sailing to Byzantium', 65
'September 1913', 128–29
solution to Irish language question, 63,
  64–65, 69
The Celtic Twilight, 80–81
The Countess Cathleen, 114
The Dreaming of the Bones, 118
The Hour-Glass, 116–17
The King's Threshold, 24–25, 114–15
'The Lake Isle of Innisfree', 65
The Only Jealousy of Emer, 118
The Shadowy Waters, 116
'The Statues', 108
The Tower, 1, 44, 81, 82
'The Wanderings of Oisin', 77
The Wild Swans at Coole, 44
The Winding Stair, 44
'To Ireland in the Coming Times', 82–83
'Under Ben Bulben', 81–82, 108
  See also Gaelic Revival; Gregory,
    Augusta; Irish modernism; Irish Revival;
    Abbey Theatre; modernism; Synge, John
    Millington
Young Ireland, 52, 80

Zeami, Motokiyo, 217
Žižek, Slavoj, 103

Cambridge Companions to...

AUTHORS

Edward Albee edited by Stephen J. Bottoms

Margaret Atwood edited by Coral Ann Howells

W. H. Auden edited by Stan Smith

Jane Austen edited by Edward Copeland and Juliet McMaster (second edition)

Beckett edited by John Pilling

Bede edited by Scott DeGregorio

Aphra Behn edited by Derek Hughes and Janet Todd

Walter Benjamin edited by David S. Ferris

William Blake edited by Morris Eaves

Brecht edited by Peter Thomson and Glendyr Sacks (second edition)

The Brontës edited by Heather Glen

Bunyan edited by Anne Dunan-Page

Frances Burney edited by Peter Sabor

Byron edited by Drummond Bone

Albert Camus edited by Edward J. Hughes

Willa Cather edited by Marilee Lindemann

Cervantes edited by Anthony J. Cascardi

Chaucer edited by Piero Boitani and Jill Mann (second edition)

Chekhov edited by Vera Gottlieb and Paul Allain

Kate Chopin edited by Janet Beer

Caryl Churchill edited by Elaine Aston and Elin Diamond

Coleridge edited by Lucy Newlyn

Wilkie Collins edited by Jenny Bourne Taylor

Joseph Conrad edited by J. H. Stape

H. D. edited by Nephie J. Christodoulides and Polina Mackay

Dante edited by Rachel Jacoff (second edition)

Daniel Defoe edited by John Richetti

Don DeLillo edited by John N. Duvall

Charles Dickens edited by John O. Jordan

Emily Dickinson edited by Wendy Martin

John Donne edited by Achsah Guibbory

Dostoevskii edited by W. J. Leatherbarrow

Theodore Dreiser edited by Leonard Cassuto and Claire Virginia Eby

John Dryden edited by Steven N. Zwicker

W. E. B. Du Bois edited by Shamoon Zamir

George Eliot edited by George Levine

T. S. Eliot edited by A. David Moody

Ralph Ellison edited by Ross Posnock

Ralph Waldo Emerson edited by Joel Porte and Saundra Morris

William Faulkner edited by Philip M. Weinstein

Henry Fielding edited by Claude Rawson

F. Scott Fitzgerald edited by Ruth Prigozy

Flaubert edited by Timothy Unwin

E. M. Forster edited by David Bradshaw

Benjamin Franklin edited by Carla Mulford

Brian Friel edited by Anthony Roche

Robert Frost edited by Robert Faggen

Gabriel García Márquez edited by Philip Swanson

Elizabeth Gaskell edited by Jill L. Matus

Goethe edited by Lesley Sharpe

Günter Grass edited by Stuart Taberner

Thomas Hardy edited by Dale Kramer

David Hare edited by Richard Boon

Nathaniel Hawthorne edited by Richard Millington

Seamus Heaney edited by Bernard O'Donoghue

Ernest Hemingway edited by Scott Donaldson

Homer edited by Robert Fowler

Horace edited by Stephen Harrison

Ted Hughes edited by Terry Gifford

Ibsen edited by James McFarlane

Henry James edited by Jonathan Freedman

Samuel Johnson edited by Greg Clingham

Ben Jonson edited by Richard Harp and Stanley Stewart

James Joyce edited by Derek Attridge (second edition)

Kafka edited by Julian Preece

Keats edited by Susan J. Wolfson

Rudyard Kipling edited by Howard J. Booth

Lacan edited by Jean-Michel Rabaté

D. H. Lawrence edited by Anne Fernihough

Primo Levi edited by Robert Gordon

Lucretius edited by Stuart Gillespie and Philip Hardie

Machiavelli edited by John M. Najemy

David Mamet edited by Christopher Bigsby

Thomas Mann edited by Ritchie Robertson

Christopher Marlowe edited by Patrick Cheney

Andrew Marvell edited by Derek Hirst and Steven N. Zwicker

Herman Melville edited by Robert S. Levine

Arthur Miller edited by Christopher Bigsby (second edition)

Milton edited by Dennis Danielson (second edition)

Molière edited by David Bradby and Andrew Calder

Toni Morrison edited by Justine Tally

Nabokov edited by Julian W. Connolly

Eugene O'Neill edited by Michael Manheim

George Orwell edited by John Rodden

Ovid edited by Philip Hardie

Harold Pinter edited by Peter Raby (second edition)

Sylvia Plath edited by Jo Gill

Edgar Allan Poe edited by Kevin J. Hayes

Alexander Pope edited by Pat Rogers

Ezra Pound edited by Ira B. Nadel

Proust edited by Richard Bales

Pushkin edited by Andrew Kahn

Rabelais edited by John O'Brien

Rilke edited by Karen Leeder and Robert Vilain

Philip Roth edited by Timothy Parrish

Salman Rushdie edited by Abdulrazak Gurnah

Shakespeare edited by Margareta de Grazia and Stanley Wells (second edition)

Shakespeare on Film edited by Russell Jackson (second edition)

Shakespeare and Popular Culture edited by Robert Shaughnessy

Shakespeare on Stage edited by Stanley Wells and Sarah Stanton

Shakespearean Comedy edited by Alexander Leggatt

Shakespearean Tragedy edited by Claire McEachern

Shakespeare's History Plays edited by Michael Hattaway

Shakespeare's Last Plays edited by Catherine M. S. Alexander

Shakespeare's Poetry edited by Patrick Cheney

George Bernard Shaw edited by Christopher Innes

Shelley edited by Timothy Morton

Mary Shelley edited by Esther Schor

Sam Shepard edited by Matthew C. Roudané

Spenser edited by Andrew Hadfield

Laurence Sterne edited by Thomas Keymer

Wallace Stevens edited by John N. Serio

Tom Stoppard edited by Katherine E. Kelly

Harriet Beecher Stowe edited by Cindy Weinstein

August Strindberg edited by Michael Robinson

Jonathan Swift edited by Christopher Fox

J. M. Synge edited by P. J. Mathews

Tacitus edited by A. J. Woodman

Henry David Thoreau edited by Joel Myerson

Tolstoy edited by Donna Tussing Orwin

Anthony Trollope edited by Carolyn Dever and Lisa Niles

Mark Twain edited by Forrest G. Robinson

John Updike edited by Stacey Olster

Mario Vargas Llosa edited by Efrain Kristal and John King

Virgil edited by Charles Martindale

Voltaire edited by Nicholas Cronk

Edith Wharton edited by Millicent Bell

Walt Whitman edited by Ezra Greenspan

Oscar Wilde edited by Peter Raby

Tennessee Williams edited by Matthew C. Roudané

August Wilson edited by Christopher Bigsby

Mary Wollstonecraft edited by Claudia L. Johnson

Virginia Woolf edited by Susan Sellers (second edition)

Wordsworth edited by Stephen Gill

W. B. Yeats edited by Marjorie Howes and John Kelly

Zola edited by Brian Nelson

TOPICS

The Actress edited by Maggie B. Gale and John Stokes

The African American Novel edited by Maryemma Graham

The African American Slave Narrative edited by Audrey A. Fisch

Allegory edited by Rita Copeland and Peter Struck

American Crime Fiction edited by Catherine Ross Nickerson

American Modernism edited by Walter Kalaidjian

American Realism and Naturalism edited by Donald Pizer

American Travel Writing edited by Alfred Bendixen and Judith Hamera

American Women Playwrights edited by Brenda Murphy

Ancient Rhetoric edited by Erik Gunderson

Arthurian Legend edited by Elizabeth Archibald and Ad Putter

Australian Literature edited by Elizabeth Webby

British Literature of the French Revolution edited by Pamela Clemit

British Romantic Poetry edited by James Chandler and Maureen N. McLane

British Romanticism edited by Stuart Curran (second edition)

British Theatre, 1730–1830 edited by Jane Moody and Daniel O'Quinn

Canadian Literature edited by Eva-Marie Kröller

Children's Literature edited by M. O. Grenby and Andrea Immel

The Classic Russian Novel edited by Malcolm V. Jones and Robin Feuer Miller

Contemporary Irish Poetry edited by Matthew Campbell

Creative Writing edited by David Morley and Philip Neilsen

Crime Fiction edited by Martin Priestman

Early Modern Women's Writing edited by Laura Lunger Knoppers

The Eighteenth-Century Novel edited by John Richetti

Eighteenth-Century Poetry edited by John Sitter

English Literature, 1500–1600 edited by Arthur F. Kinney

English Literature, 1650–1740 edited by Steven N. Zwicker

English Literature, 1740–1830 edited by Thomas Keymer and Jon Mee

English Literature, 1830–1914 edited by Joanne Shattock

English Novelists edited by Adrian Poole

English Poetry, Donne to Marvell edited by Thomas N. Corns

English Poets edited by Claude Rawson

English Renaissance Drama edited by A. R. Braunmuller and Michael Hattaway (second edition)

English Renaissance Tragedy edited by Emma Smith and Garrett A. Sullivan Jr.

English Restoration Theatre edited by Deborah C. Payne Fisk

The Epic edited by Catherine Bates

European Modernism edited by Pericles Lewis

European Novelists edited by Michael Bell

Fantasy Literature edited by Edward James and Farah Mendlesohn

Feminist Literary Theory edited by Ellen Rooney

Fiction in the Romantic Period edited by Richard Maxwell and Katie Trumpener

The Fin de Siècle edited by Gail Marshall

The French Novel: From 1800 to the Present edited by Timothy Unwin

Gay and Lesbian Writing edited by Hugh Stevens

German Romanticism edited by Nicholas Saul

Gothic Fiction edited by Jerrold E. Hogle

The Greek and Roman Novel edited by Tim Whitmarsh

Greek and Roman Theatre edited by Marianne McDonald and J. Michael Walton

Greek Lyric edited by Felix Budelmann

Greek Mythology edited by Roger D. Woodard

Greek Tragedy edited by P. E. Easterling

The Harlem Renaissance edited by George Hutchinson

The Irish Novel edited by John Wilson Foster

The Italian Novel edited by Peter Bondanella and Andrea Ciccarelli

Jewish American Literature edited by Hana Wirth-Nesher and Michael P. Kramer

The Latin American Novel edited by Efraín Kristal

The Literature of the First World War edited by Vincent Sherry

The Literature of London edited by Lawrence Manley

The Literature of Los Angeles edited by Kevin R. McNamara

The Literature of New York edited by Cyrus Patell and Bryan Waterman

Literature on Screen edited by Deborah Cartmell and Imelda Whelehan

The Literature of World War II edited by Marina MacKay

Medieval English Culture edited by Andrew Galloway

Medieval English Literature edited by Larry Scanlon

Medieval English Mysticism edited by Samuel Fanous and Vincent Gillespie

Medieval English Theatre edited by Richard Beadle and Alan J. Fletcher (second edition)

Medieval French Literature edited by Simon Gaunt and Sarah Kay

Medieval Romance edited by Roberta L. Krueger

Medieval Women's Writing edited by Carolyn Dinshaw and David Wallace

Modern American Culture edited by Christopher Bigsby

Modern British Women Playwrights edited by Elaine Aston and Janelle Reinelt

Modern French Culture edited by Nicholas Hewitt

Modern German Culture edited by Eva Kolinsky and Wilfried van der Will

The Modern German Novel edited by Graham Bartram

Modern Irish Culture edited by Joe Cleary and Claire Connolly

Modern Italian Culture edited by Zygmunt G. Baranski and Rebecca J. West

Modern Latin American Culture edited by John King

Modern Russian Culture edited by Nicholas Rzhevsky

Modern Spanish Culture edited by David T. Gies

Modernism edited by Michael Levenson (second edition)

The Modernist Novel edited by Morag Shiach

Modernist Poetry edited by Alex Davis and Lee M. Jenkins

Modernist Women Writers edited by Maren Tova Linett

Narrative edited by David Herman

Native American Literature edited by Joy Porter and Kenneth M. Roemer

Nineteenth-Century American Women's Writing edited by Dale M. Bauer and Philip Gould

Old English Literature edited by Malcolm Godden and Michael Lapidge

Performance Studies edited by Tracy C. Davis

Popular Fiction edited by David Glover and Scott McCracken

Postcolonial Literary Studies edited by Neil Lazarus

Postmodernism edited by Steven Connor

The Pre-Raphaelites edited by Elizabeth Prettejohn

Renaissance Humanism edited by Jill Kraye

The Roman Historians edited by Andrew Feldherr

Roman Satire edited by Kirk Freudenburg

Science Fiction edited by Edward James and Farah Mendlesohn

Scottish Literature edited by Gerald Carruthers and Liam McIlvanney

The Sonnet edited by A. D. Cousins and Peter Howarth

The Spanish Novel: From 1600 to the Present edited by Harriet Turner and Adelaida López de Martínez

Travel Writing edited by Peter Hulme and Tim Youngs

Twentieth-Century British and Irish Women's Poetry edited by Jane Dowson

The Twentieth-Century English Novel edited by Robert L. Caserio

Twentieth-Century English Poetry edited by Neil Corcoran

Twentieth-Century Irish Drama edited by Shaun Richards

Twentieth-Century Russian Literature edited by Marina Balina and Evgeny Dobrenko

Utopian Literature edited by Gregory Claeys

Victorian and Edwardian Theatre edited by Kerry Powell

The Victorian Novel edited by Deirdre David

Victorian Poetry edited by Joseph Bristow

War Writing edited by Kate McLoughlin

Writing of the English Revolution edited by N. H. Keeble